Quick Start Menu

Find your assignment, and then start with the advice and examples listed here.

✱ indicates content in *LaunchPad Solo for Lunsford Handbooks*. (See the outside back cover flap for details.)

Don't see your project listed here?

- See a complete list of chapters on the inside front cover (Brief Contents).
- See a detailed list of sections on the inside back cover (Detailed Contents).
- Search an alphabetical list of topics and terms on pages 403–34 (Index/Glossary).
- Find more examples of student writing in *LaunchPad Solo for Lunsford Handbooks*.

What Are You Writing?	Get Advice	See Student Models
Abstract	**7c** Summarizing **16b** Following APA manuscript format	**16e** Causal analysis with abstract
Annotated bibliography	**12** Evaluating Sources and Taking Notes (in particular **12g**, Creating an annotated bibliography)	**12h** Annotated bibliography entries ✱ Annotated bibliography (Tony Chan) ✱ Reflective annotated bibliography (Nandita Sriram)
Argument	**8** Arguing Ethically and Persuasively	**8g** Argument essay
Blog	**Checklist:** Participating in Class Blogs, Wikis, and Other Forums (p. 45) **9d** Choosing genres for public writing	✱ Reflective blog post (Thanh Nguyen)
Film analysis	**7d** Analyzing **8e** Making an argument	✱ Film analysis (Amrit Rao)
Job application	**1f** Considering audiences **3b** Appropriate formats **8e** Making an argument	✱ Cover letter (Nastassia Lopez) ✱ Résumés (Megan Lange)
Lab report	**9a** Recognizing expectations of academic disciplines **9c** Adapting genre structures	✱ Lab report in chemistry (Allyson Goldberg)
Literary analysis	**7** Reading and Listening Analytically, Critically, and Respectfully **15** MLA Style	**9e** Excerpts from a close reading of poetry ✱ Close reading of poetry (Bonnie Sillay)

What Are You Writing?	Get Advice	See Student Models
Multimodal project	**3** Making Design Decisions **9** Writing in a Variety of Disciplines and Genres	**9e** Samples in a variety of disciplines and genres [Poster, Fundraising web page, Web comic, Newsletter] * Pitch package (Deborah Jane and Jamie Burke)
Personal reflection	**5c** Reflecting on your own work	**5d** Reflection * Portfolio cover letter (James Kung)
Portfolio	**3** Making Design Decisions **5b** Creating a portfolio	**5d** Reflection * Portfolio cover letter (James Kung)
Poster	**3c** Visuals and media **3d** Ethical use of visuals and media **9d** Choosing genres for public writing	**9e** Samples in a variety of disciplines and genres [Poster]
Presentation	**10** Creating Presentations	**10h** Excerpts from a presentation * Presentation (Shuqiao Song)
Proposal	**8** Arguing Ethically and Persuasively	* Pitch package (Deborah Jane and Jamie Burke) * Research proposal (Tara Gupta)
Research project	**Research** (p. 87) **15** MLA Style (literature or languages) **16** APA Style (social sciences) **17** *Chicago* Style (history or the arts) **18** CSE Style (sciences)	**15f** Research-based argument, MLA style **16e** Causal analysis essay with abstract, APA style **17d** Research-based history essay (excerpts), *Chicago* style **18d** Biology literature review (excerpts), CSE style * Complete papers in history and science
Rhetorical analysis	**7c** Summarizing **7d** Analyzing **8e** Making an argument	**7e** Rhetorical analysis
Social media and websites	**1b** Moving between informal and formal writing **1c** Email and other "in-between" writing **3** Making Design Decisions **9d** Choosing genres for public writing	**1b** Moving between informal and formal writing [Student tweets] **9e** Samples in a variety of disciplines and genres [Fundraising web page, Web comic]
Summary	**7c** Summarizing	* Summary of an assigned reading (Sarah Lum)
Visuals	**3c** Visuals and media **3d** Ethical use of visuals and media	**9e** Samples in a variety of disciplines and genres [Poster, Fundraising web page, Web comic, Newsletter]

SEVENTH EDITION

EasyWriter

with Exercises

Andrea A. Lunsford
STANFORD UNIVERSITY

Coverage for multilingual writers with

Paul Kei Matsuda
ARIZONA STATE UNIVERSITY

Christine M. Tardy
UNIVERSITY OF ARIZONA

Boston | New York

FOR BEDFORD/ST. MARTIN'S

Vice President, Editorial, Macmillan Learning Humanities: Edwin Hill
Executive Program Director for English: Leasa Burton
Executive Program Manager: Stacey Purviance
Marketing Manager: Vivian Garcia
Director of Content Development: Jane Knetzger
Development Manager: Caroline Thompson
Editorial Assistant: Aislyn Fredsall
Senior Content Project Manager: Ryan Sullivan
Senior Workflow Project Manager: Jennifer Wetzel
Production Coordinator: Brianna Lester
Senior Media Project Manager: Allison Hart
Senior Media Editor: Barbara Flanagan
Editorial Services: Lumina Datamatics, Inc.
Composition: Lumina Datamatics, Inc.
Text Permissions Manager: Kalina Ingham
Photo Permissions Editor: Angela Boehler
Permissions Associate: Claire Paschal
Photo Researcher: Candice Cheesman, Lumina Datamatics, Inc.
Director of Design, Content Management: Diana Blume
Text Design: Claire Seng-Niemoeller
Cover Design: William Boardman
Printing and Binding: RR Donnelley and Sons

Printed in China.

1 2 3 4 5 6 23 22 21 20

For information, write: Bedford/St. Martin's, 75 Arlington Street, Boston, MA 02116

ISBN 978-1-319-36145-7

ACKNOWLEDGMENTS

Text acknowledgment and copyright appear below. Art acknowledgments and copyrights appear on the same page as the art selections they cover.

Joy Harjo. Excerpt from "Suspended," *Joy Harjo's Poetic Adventures in the Last World Blog*, Mekko Productions, Inc., September 3, 2006, http://joyharjo.blogspot.com/2006/09/suspended-c-joy-harjo.html. Used by permission of the author.

How This Book Can Help You

Some 2,400 years ago, the Greek philosopher Aristotle argued that citizens needed to understand and use rhetoric wisely for two major reasons: to express ideas clearly and persuasively, and to protect themselves against those who might manipulate, deceive, or harm. This advice seems as pertinent today as it did in the fourth century BCE: while current technologies allow writers everywhere to make their voices heard, they have not been nearly as effective at sorting out sense from nonsense, information from disinformation, news from fake news, and facts from opinions.

Take a moment to ask yourself where you get most of your information these days. If you are like many others, that information comes from social media: Twitter, Facebook, Instagram, Snapchat, and similar platforms. But how trustworthy is such information? Unlike traditional news sources, which carefully check and countercheck information before they publish it, writers can present just about anything on a social media site as true. The onslaught of highly charged, often biased information we see is one reason for the deep divisions in our society, divisions that can only be bridged by ethical communicators willing to take time to listen openly and generously to the perspectives of others, to try to understand those viewpoints, and to engage in respectful conversations with them.

You can become a better writer and communicator by sharpening your critical and analytical abilities and by accepting the ethical responsibility to create and share information that is credible and worthy of trust. This new edition of *EasyWriter with Exercises* aims to help you with these goals, guiding you as you practice expressing yourself clearly, persuasively, and ethically. In this book, you'll find lots of tested and helpful advice about how to be an effective writer, reader, and speaker, all in a small package that we've worked hard to make friendly, engaging, and easy to use. You can count on *EasyWriter with Exercises* to provide the following kinds of help:

- **Attention to *good writing,* not just "correctness."** We show that good writing comes from making wise choices about purpose, audience, and topic—and from developing your own voice and style.

- **Advice on critical thinking, critical reading, and argument** that will help you read and analyze a variety of texts and compose effective essays and arguments.
- **Advice for writing in many contexts, disciplines, and genres** that you will encounter in college and beyond.
- **Unique coverage of language, style, and grammar** that helps you think about language in context, about where others are "coming from" in the choices they make, and about how you can communicate ethically and effectively across cultures and across differences.
- **Attention to the challenges of research** and streamlined, easy-to-understand advice on documenting your sources.

New to This Edition

Readers who are familiar with the previous edition of *EasyWriter with Exercises* will notice the following changes.

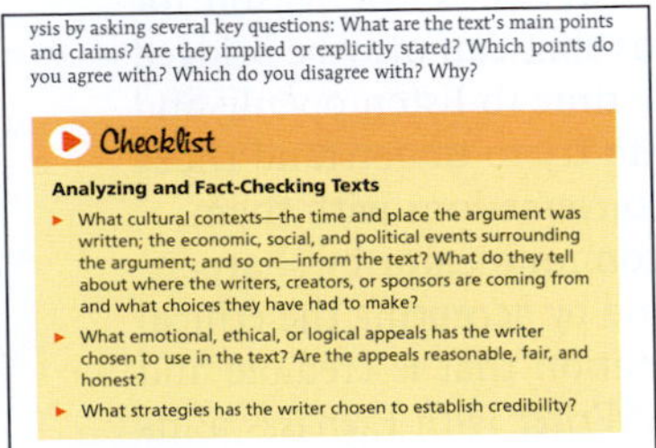
ysis by asking several key questions: What are the text's main points and claims? Are they implied or explicitly stated? Which points do you agree with? Which do you disagree with? Why?

Checklist

Analyzing and Fact-Checking Texts

- What cultural contexts—the time and place the argument was written; the economic, social, and political events surrounding the argument; and so on—inform the text? What do they tell about where the writers, creators, or sponsors are coming from and what choices they have had to make?
- What emotional, ethical, or logical appeals has the writer chosen to use in the text? Are the appeals reasonable, fair, and honest?
- What strategies has the writer chosen to establish credibility?

New Advice for Fact-Checking and Evaluating Sources. New advice for identifying and using credible information appears throughout the book, from a new Checklist, "Analyzing and Fact-Checking Texts" (7d), to new discussions of checking facts (12a) and using sources ethically (13a).

More on Choosing Language That Builds Common Ground. To help you consider differences across communities as you connect with audiences, *EasyWriter with Exercises* includes new advice on considering pronoun preferences, using gender-neutral language, and considering abilities and disabilities (20b, 20d, 34b).

More Help for Writing in a Variety of Disciplines and Genres. A new Chapter 9 offers more advice on recognizing the expectations of academic disciplines as well as expanded coverage of understanding and using genres, with emphasis on how to analyze genres. New student writing examples in this chapter reflect a variety of types of writing, including a poster for a public awareness campaign and excerpts from a chemistry lab report and a close reading of poetry.

More Models of Student Writing. Sixteen student writing examples throughout the book—more than ever before—provide you with models for common assignments. New examples include a student's argument essay, an excerpt from a student presentation, excerpts from annotated bibliographies, and a formal outline for a research project. Complete and additional models are available online in *LaunchPad Solo for Lunsford Handbooks*.

An argument essay **8g** 61

STUDENT WRITING

Mercer-Golden 1

Benjy Mercer-Golden
28 Nov. 2017

Lessons from Tree-Huggers and Corporate Mercenaries:
A New Model of Sustainable Capitalism

Televised images of environmental degradation—seagulls with oil coating their feathers, smokestacks belching gray fumes—often seem designed to shock, but these images also represent very real issues: climate change, dwindling energy resources like coal and oil, a scarcity of clean drinking water. In response, businesspeople around the world are thinking about how they can make their companies greener or more socially beneficial to ensure a brighter future for humanity. But progress in the private sector has been slow and inconsistent. To accelerate the move to sustainability, for-profit businesses need to learn from the hybrid model of social entrepreneurship to ensure that the company is efficient and profitable while still working for social change, and more investors need to support companies with long-term, revolutionary visions for improving the world.

In fact, both for-profit corporations and "social good" businesses could take steps to reshape their strategies. First, for-profit corporations need to operate sustainably and be evaluated for their performance with long-term measurements and incentives. The conventional argument against for-profit companies deeply embedding environmental and social goals into their corporate strategies is that caring about the world does not go hand in hand with lining pockets. This morally toxic case is also problematic from a business standpoint. A 2012 study of 180 high-profile companies by Harvard Business School professors Robert G. Eccles and George Serafeim and London Business School professor Ioannis Ioannou shows that "high sustainability companies," as defined by environmental and social variables, "significantly outperform their

Provocative word choice for title

Emotional appeals through use of vivid imagery

Thesis establishing purpose

Claim related to thesis

Opposing viewpoint to establish writer's credibility

Rebuttal

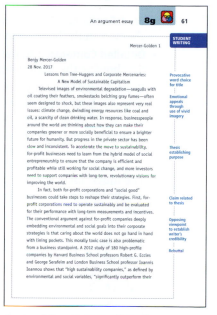

Top Twenty Tips for Editing Your Writing. You'll find this special insert section following Chapter 4, "Reviewing, Revising, and Editing." Based on extensive research into the twenty most common problems teachers are likely to identify in academic writing by first-year students, "Top Twenty Tips for Editing Your Writing" provides examples and brief explanations to guide you toward recognizing, understanding, and editing these common errors.

Updated Guidelines for Documenting Sources. Chapters 15–18 reflect the most current advice for documenting sources in MLA, APA, *Chicago*, and CSE styles. The APA section has been updated in accordance with the *Publication Manual of the American Psychological Association*, 7th edition (2020).

Improved Navigation. We've brought back the detailed table of contents on the inside back cover and added a new Quick Start Menu (see the first book page) to help you find advice and models for specific types of writing projects.

How to Find Help in the Book

EasyWriter with Exercises includes many menus and features to help you find the information you need.

- **Brief Contents.** On the inside front cover is a list of all the chapters in the book, with page numbers.
- **Detailed Contents.** On the inside back cover is a more detailed list showing the section headings within each chapter.
- **Quick Start Menu.** If you're looking for advice and examples to help you with a specific writing project, try the new Quick Start Menu on the first book page.
- **Glossary/Index.** The index is an alphabetical list of every topic or concept that's covered in the book. Simply look up the word or topic you need help with and navigate to the pages listed. The index doubles as a glossary that defines important terms; any **boldface term** you see in the book is defined in the index.
- **Lists of examples for citing your sources.** Each documentation style (MLA, APA, *Chicago*, and CSE) has its own section with color-tabbed pages; look for Lists of Examples within each section to find models for citing your sources. **Source maps** illustrate the process of citing common types of sources.

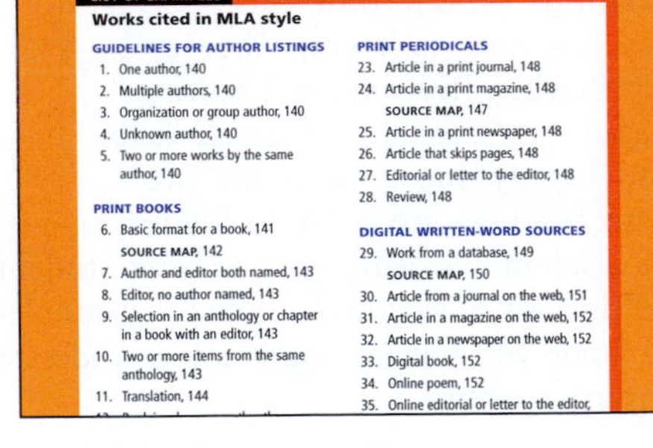
LIST OF EXAMPLES

Works cited in MLA style

GUIDELINES FOR AUTHOR LISTINGS
1. One author, 140
2. Multiple authors, 140
3. Organization or group author, 140
4. Unknown author, 140
5. Two or more works by the same author, 140

PRINT BOOKS
6. Basic format for a book, 141
SOURCE MAP, 142
7. Author and editor both named, 143
8. Editor, no author named, 143
9. Selection in an anthology or chapter in a book with an editor, 143
10. Two or more items from the same anthology, 143
11. Translation, 144

PRINT PERIODICALS
23. Article in a print journal, 148
24. Article in a print magazine, 148
SOURCE MAP, 147
25. Article in a print newspaper, 148
26. Article that skips pages, 148
27. Editorial or letter to the editor, 148
28. Review, 148

DIGITAL WRITTEN-WORD SOURCES
29. Work from a database, 149
SOURCE MAP, 150
30. Article from a journal on the web, 151
31. Article in a magazine on the web, 152
32. Article in a newspaper on the web, 152
33. Digital book, 152
34. Online poem, 152
35. Online editorial or letter to the editor,

- **"Multilingual" icons.** Help for speakers of all kinds of English, and from all educational backgrounds, is identified with a "Multilingual"

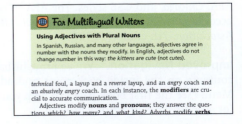

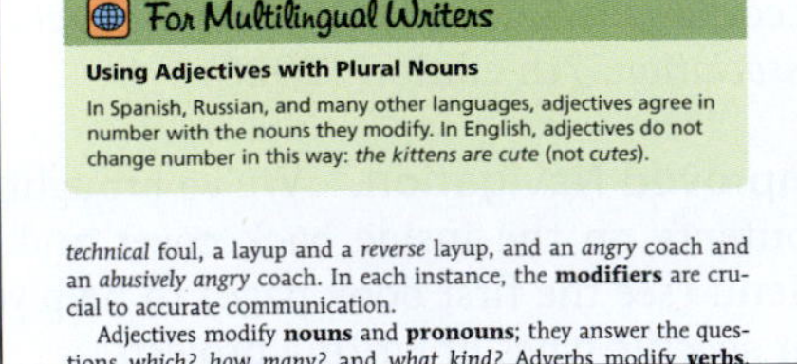
For Multilingual Writers

Using Adjectives with Plural Nouns

In Spanish, Russian, and many other languages, adjectives agree in number with the nouns they modify. In English, adjectives do not change number in this way: *the kittens are cute* (not *cutes*).

technical foul, a layup and a *reverse* layup, and an *angry* coach and an *abusively angry* coach. In each instance, the **modifiers** are crucial to accurate communication.

Adjectives modify **nouns** and **pronouns**; they answer the questions *which? how many?* and *what kind?* Adverbs modify **verbs**, icon, and **For Multilingual Writers** boxes appear throughout the book. A list of all content for multilingual writers appears on p. M-1.

- **Guides at the top of every page.** Headers tell you what chapter or section you're in, the **chapter number** and **section letter**, and the **page number**. **Icons** that indicate the part of the book (building blocks for Grammar, for example) also appear at the top of the page.

- **Cross-references to digital resources.** Cross-references at the bottom of a page point you to *LaunchPad Solo for Lunsford Handbooks* for videos, quizzes, student writing models, LearningCurve, and more. To learn how to get access to these digital resources, see the outside back cover flap.

- **Glossary of Usage.** The alphabetically organized glossary of usage, which begins on page 391, can help you with commonly confused and misused words.

Welcome, then, to *EasyWriter with Exercises*, Seventh Edition. We hope it will be a faithful companion on your journey through college—and beyond.

Ordering Information for Instructors

- To order *EasyWriter with 2020 APA Update,* Seventh Edition, use ISBN 978-1-319-36144-0.
- To order *EasyWriter with Exercises with 2020 APA Update,* Seventh Edition, use ISBN 978-1-319-36145-7.

Do your students need more practice? See the outside back cover flap for more details about the digital resources in *LaunchPad Solo for Lunsford Handbooks*. Contact your Macmillan Learning representative for packaging options.

Writing Processes

1 A Writer's Choices 2

2 Exploring, Planning, and Drafting 10

3 Making Design Decisions 17

4 Reviewing, Revising, and Editing 23

Top 20 Top Twenty Tips for Editing Your Writing 27

5 Sharing and Reflecting on Your Writing 39

1 A Writer's Choices

You text your best friend to confirm weekend plans. Later on, you put together an analysis of cost-cutting possibilities for your boss. And later still, you pull out the notes you took on your biology experiment and write up the lab report that is due tomorrow. In between, you do a lot of other writing as well—notes, lists, blog entries, Facebook status updates, tweets, and so on.

These are the kinds of writing most of us do every day, more or less easily, yet each demands that we make various important choices. In your text message, you probably use a kind of shorthand, not bothering to write complete sentences or even entire words. For your boss, however, you probably choose to be more formal, writing complete sentences and using appropriate punctuation. And for your lab report, you probably choose to follow the format your instructor has demonstrated. In each case, the choices you make are based on your **rhetorical situation**—the entire context in which your writing takes place.

1a Understanding expectations for academic writing

When you write in or out of college, you're in the business of constructing and sharing knowledge, finding out all you can about a subject, sometimes carrying out research of your own, and working with your sources and classmates or friends to share that knowledge with others. To do so, you're going to be making a lot of choices, since there's seldom only one "correct" way to communicate the knowledge you acquire: conventions and styles vary across disciplines and across genres. But in spite of fairly wide variation, most experts on writing agree that several features mark successful academic writing.

Authority. Most instructors expect you to begin to establish your own authority—to become a constructive critic who can analyze and interpret the works of others.

LaunchPad Solo
macmillan learning

Writing Processes: Expectations for College Writing > 2 Video Prompts

Checklist

U.S. Academic Style

- Consider your purpose and audience carefully, making sure that your topic is appropriate to both. (1d–f)
- State your claim or thesis explicitly, and support it with evidence and authorities of various kinds. (2b)
- Carefully document all of your sources, including visual ones. (Chapters 15–18)
- Make explicit links between ideas. (2e)
- Use the appropriate level of formality. (22a)
- Use conventional formats for academic genres. (Chapter 9)
- Use conventional grammar, spelling, punctuation, and mechanics. (Chapters 29–47)
- Use an easy-to-read type size and typeface and conventional margins. For print projects, double-space text. (3b)

To establish authority, assume that your opinions count (as long as they are informed rather than tossed out with little thought) and that your audience expects you to present them in a fair, well-reasoned manner. Show your familiarity with the ideas and works of others, both from the assigned course reading and from good points your instructor and classmates have made.

Directness and clarity. Research for this book confirms that readers depend on writers to organize and present their material—using sections, paragraphs, sentences, arguments, details, and source citations—to aid understanding. Good academic writing offers a clear **thesis**, prepares readers for what is coming next, provides definitions, and includes topic sentences.

To achieve directness in your writing, try the following strategies:

- State your main point early and clearly. Academic writing may call for an explicit **claim** or thesis (2b and 8e).
- Avoid overqualifying your statements. Instead of writing *I think the facts reveal*, come right out and say *The facts reveal*.

- Avoid unnecessary digressions. If you use an anecdote or example from personal experience, be sure it relates directly to the point you are making.
- Use appropriate evidence and authorities of various kinds to support each point you make (2c). Carefully document all of your sources, including visuals and media.
- Make explicit links between ideas (2e). The first sentence of a new paragraph should reach back to the paragraph before and then look forward to what comes next.
- Follow clear, easy-to-follow organizational patterns.

EXERCISE 1.1 Answer the following questions about expectations for college writing.

1. How do you define good college writing? Make a list of the characteristics you come up with. Then make a list of what you think your instructors' expectations are for good college writing, and note how they may differ from yours. Do you need to alter your ideas about good college writing to meet your instructors' expectations? Why, or why not?
2. Research suggests that many students today define good writing as "writing that makes something happen." That is, they see writing as *active and performative,* as *doing something.* Would that match your definition or that of your instructors? What might account for the differences—and the similarities—between students' and instructors' definitions and lists?

1b Moving between informal and formal writing

Of course, a lot of the writing you do will not be academic: in fact, students are doing more writing and reading today than ever before, and much of it is online—on Facebook, Twitter, Tumblr, Snapchat, and other social media sites. Writing on these sites is generally informal and allows almost instant feedback, so anticipating how your readers will respond can make you very savvy about analyzing audiences and about using an appropriate style and tone for the occasion.

Writing on social media sites can help you reach a lot of potential friends, but it can also expose you to trolling as well as to mountains of misinformation and outright lies. As an ethical writer, you want to make sure any information you pass on or retweet is reliable and honest. Be careful not to spread what might be rumor, libel, or lies. Following is an example of two students engaging in purposeful—and ethical—online communication. Student Stephanie Parker tweeted:

> Rain's over, going to Trader Joe's for some healthy stuff to fight this cold . . . suggestions?

Student Erin McLaughlin posted on Facebook:

> Help send one of my Ghanian friends to college. The smallest contribution helps! www.indiegogo.com/teachaman

In these two short messages, Stephanie and Erin show a keen awareness of audience and two common purposes for social writing—to ask for information (healthy food suggestions for Stephanie) and to give information (about a cause Erin supports). Erin is asking her audience to help a friend from Ghana go to college, and since most of her friends are also college students, she assures them they don't need to have tons of money to make a difference. The link goes to a site about a group effort to send a young man, Jey, to the University of Ghana.

Like Stephanie and Erin, you are probably adept at informal writing across a range of genres and media. You may not think much about audience for a tweet or post, or about your purpose for writing in such spaces, but you are probably more skilled than you give yourself credit for when it comes to making appropriate choices for varying kinds of informal writing.

Because social media writing is so common, it's easy to fall into the habit of writing very informally. But remember the importance of a writer's choices: don't forget to adjust style and voice for different occasions and readers.

In the writing you do in college and beyond, you'll need to be able to move easily back and forth between informal and formal situations. So take time to look closely at some of your informal social media writing: What do you know about your audience? your purpose? How do you represent yourself online? What do the photos you post and your "likes" say about you? Do you come across as the person you want others to see you as? How do you establish your credibility? Analyzing the choices you make in an informal writing context will help you develop the ability to make good choices in other contexts as well.

EXERCISE 1.2 Choose a sample of your own informal writing from a social networking site: a blog post, text message, or instant message, for example. Why did you write the post or message? What did you assume about your readers, and why? Why did you choose the words, images, links, or other parts of the text? How do these choices contribute to the way the writing comes across to an audience? Does the writing do what you want it to do? Why, or why not?

1c Email and other "in-between" writing

When writing some academic and professional messages, including emails to instructors, you may find yourself somewhere in the middle of the spectrum between "informal" and "formal" writing. On these occasions, lean toward following the conventions of academic English, and be careful not to irritate your audience. For email especially, this means stating your purpose clearly in the subject line and using a formal greeting (*Dear Professor Banks* rather than *Hey!*).

In addition, keep your messages clear and concise, and sign off with your name. Make sure you have proofread the message and that you've addressed your intended audience. Finally, make sure the username on the account you use for formal messages gives a good impression. If your username is Party2Nite, consider changing it, or use your school account for academic and professional communication. And remember: such messages are permanent and always findable.

1d Considering the assignment and purpose

For writing you do for personal reasons or for work, you may have a clear purpose in mind. But even in those instances, analyzing what you want to accomplish and why can help you communicate more effectively.

An academic assignment may explain why, for whom, and about what you are supposed to write, or it may seem to come out of the blue. In any case, comprehending the assignment is crucial to your success, so make every effort to understand what your instructor expects.

- What is the primary purpose of your writing—to persuade? to explain? to entertain? something else?

Writing Processes: Rhetorical Situations > Storyboards

- What purpose did the instructor want to achieve—to test your understanding? to evaluate your thinking and writing abilities? to encourage you to think outside the box?
- What, exactly, does the assignment ask you to do? Look for words such as *analyze*, *explain*, *prove*, and *survey*. Remember that these words may differ in meaning from discipline to discipline and from job to job.

1e Choosing a topic

Experienced writers say that the best way to choose a topic is to let it choose you. Look to topics that compel, puzzle, or pose a problem for you: these are likely to engage your interests and hence produce your best writing.

- Can you focus the topic enough to write about it effectively in the time and space available?
- What do you know about the topic? What else do you need to learn?
- What seems most important about it?
- What do you expect to conclude about the topic? (Remember, you may change your mind.)

For information on exploring a topic, see 2a.

1f Considering audiences

Every communicator can benefit from thinking carefully about who the audience is, what the audience already knows or thinks, and what the audience needs and expects to find out. As an effective communicator, you'll want to be able to write for a variety of audiences, using language, style, and evidence appropriate to particular readers, listeners, or viewers. Even if your text can theoretically reach people all over the world, focus your analysis on those you most want or need to reach and those likely to take an interest.

- What audience do you most want to reach—people who are already sympathetic to your views? people who disagree with you? members

Writing Processes: Rhetorical Situations > 2 Video Prompts

of a group you belong to? members of a group you don't belong to? If you are writing or speaking to people who disagree with you, make sure that you attend carefully, openly, and respectfully to their views!

- In what ways are the members of your audience different from you? from one another? What do you know about their abilities/disabilities that might have an effect on how they receive and understand your message?
- What assumptions can you legitimately make about the audience? What might they value—brevity, originality, deference, honesty, wit? How can you understand and appeal to their values?
- What sorts of information and evidence will your audience find most compelling—quotations from experts? personal experiences? statistics? images?
- What responses do you want as a result of what you write? How can you make clear what you want to happen? (For more on audience, see 19c.)

EXERCISE 1.3 Write a brief description of a college course for three different audiences: a best friend, your parents, and some high schoolers attending an open house at your college. Then describe how the differences in audience led you to different choices in content, organization, and wording.

1g Considering stance and tone

Knowing your own stance (where you are coming from) can help you connect effectively with your audience. What is your overall attitude toward the topic—approval? disapproval? curiosity? What social, political, religious, or other factors account for your attitude? Be especially aware of any preconceptions about your topic that may affect your stance.

Your purpose, audience, and stance will help to determine the tone your writing should take. Should it be humorous? serious? impassioned? Think about ways to show that you are knowledgeable and trustworthy. Remember, too, that visual and audio elements can influence the tone of your writing as much as the words you choose.

1h Considering time, genre, medium, and format

Many other elements of your context for a particular writing project will shape the final outcome.

- How much time will you have for the project? Do you need to do research or learn unfamiliar technology? Allow time for revision and editing.
- What genre does your text call for—a report? a review? an argument essay? a lab report? a blog post or wiki entry? Study examples to learn the conventions of the genre.
- In what medium will the text appear—on the open Internet? on a password-protected website? in a print essay? in a presentation? Will you use images, video, or audio?
- What kind of organization should you use?
- How will you document your sources? Will your audience expect a particular documentation style (see Chapters 15–18)? Should you embed links?

1i Collaborating

Research for this book shows that student writers are collaborating more and more with other writers, for class assignments as well as for writing online. Since you will need to work well with others not only during college but especially in your work life, pay attention to what makes for successful collaboration. Here are some strategies:

- Make sure every writer has an equal opportunity—and responsibility—to contribute.
- Exchange contact information, and plan face-to-face meetings (if any).
- Pay close attention to each writer's views. Expect disagreement, and remember that the goal is to listen to each view fairly and to argue through all possibilities.

LaunchPad Solo
macmillan learning

Writing Processes: Working with Others > Tutorial; Video Prompt

- If you are preparing a document collaboratively, divide up the drafting duties and set reasonable deadlines. Work together to iron out the final draft, aiming for consistency of tone. Proofread together, and have one person make corrections.
- Take advantage of free software such as Google Drive to share files, edit documents collaboratively, and track changes.
- Give credit where credit is due: acknowledge all members' contributions as well as any help you receive from outsiders.

2 Exploring, Planning, and Drafting

One student we know defines drafting as the time in writing "when the rubber meets the road." As you explore your topic, decide on a thesis, organize materials to support that central idea, and sketch out a plan, you have already begun the drafting process.

2a Exploring a topic

Among the most important parts of the writing process are choosing a topic (1e), exploring what you know about it, and determining what you need to find out. The following strategies can help you choose and explore your topic:

- When you get to choose your topic, look for one that grabs and holds your interest; writing about topics that are of great interest to you usually results in better writing.
- Brainstorm. Jot down key words and phrases about the topic and see what they prompt you to think about further. Then try out these ideas on friends or your instructor.
- Freewrite without stopping for ten minutes or so to see what insights or ideas you come up with. You can also "freespeak" by recording your thoughts on your phone or another device.
- Draw or make word pictures about your topic.

Writing Processes: Prewriting > 4 Video Prompts; Storyboards

- Try clustering—writing your topic on a sheet of paper and then writing related thoughts near the topic idea. Circle each idea or phrase, and draw lines to show how ideas are connected.
- Ask questions about the topic: *How is it defined? What caused it? What is it like or unlike? What larger system is the topic a part of? What do people say about it?* Or choose the journalist's questions: *Who? What? When? Where? Why? How?*
- Browse sources to find out what others say about the topic.

2b Developing a working thesis

Academic and professional writing in the United States often contains an explicit **thesis statement**. You should establish a **working thesis** early on: while your final thesis may eventually be very different, this working thesis focuses your thinking and research and helps keep you on track.

A working thesis should have two parts: a topic, which indicates the subject matter of the writing, and a comment, which makes an important point about the topic.

► **In the graphic novel *Fun Home*, images and words combine to make meanings that are subtler than either words alone or images alone could convey.**

A successful working thesis has three characteristics:

1. It is potentially *interesting* to the intended audience.
2. It is as *specific* as possible.
3. It limits the topic enough to make it *manageable*.

For Multilingual Writers

Stating a Thesis

In some cultures, people consider it rude to state an opinion outright. In the United States, however, academic and business practices expect writers to make key positions explicitly clear.

You can evaluate a working thesis by checking it against each of these characteristics, as in the following examples:

- **Graphic novels combine words and images.**

  INTERESTING? The topic of graphic novels could be interesting, but this draft of a working thesis has no real comment attached to it—instead, it states a bare fact, and the only place to go from here is to more bare facts.

- **In graphic novels, words and images convey interesting meanings.**

  SPECIFIC? This thesis is not specific. What are "interesting meanings," exactly? How are they conveyed?

- **Graphic novels have evolved in recent decades to become an important literary genre.**

  MANAGEABLE? This thesis would not be manageable for a short-term project because it would require research on several decades of history and on hundreds of novels from all over the world.

2c Gathering credible evidence and doing research

Where can you go to locate evidence that is credible and trustworthy, that avoids misinformation and lies, and is instead based on facts and valid interpretation? What kinds of evidence will be most persuasive to your audience and most effective in the field in which you are working—historical precedents? expert testimony? statistical data? experimental results? personal anecdotes? Knowing what kinds of evidence count most in a particular field will help you make appropriate choices.

If the evidence you need calls for research, determine what research you need to do:

- Make a list of what you already know about your topic.
- Keep track of where information comes from so you can return to your sources later.

- Check your source information for accuracy and credibility.
- What else do you need to know, and where are you likely to find other credible sources of information? library resources? authoritative online sources? trusted field research? other?

(For more on research and evaluating sources, see Chapters 11–14.)

2d Planning and drafting

Sketch out a rough plan for organizing your writing, perhaps simply beginning with your thesis. Then review your notes, research materials, and media, and list all the evidence you have to support the thesis. One informal way to organize your ideas is to figure out what belongs in your introduction, body paragraphs, and conclusion. You may also want—or be required—to make an informal outline, which can help you see exactly how the parts of your writing fit together. (For a sample formal outline, see 14e.)

Thesis statement

I. First main idea
   1. First supporting detail or point
   2. Second supporting detail, and so on

II. Second main idea
   1. First supporting detail
   2. Second supporting detail, and so on

III. Third main idea
   1. First supporting detail
   2. Second supporting detail

Storyboarding—working out a narrative or argument in visual form—can also help you come up with an organizational plan. You can create your own storyboard by using note cards or sticky notes, taking advantage of different colors to keep track of threads of argument, subtopics, and so on. Move the cards and notes around, trying out different arrangements, until you find an organization that works well for your writing situation.

LaunchPad Solo macmillan learning

Writing Processes: Planning & Drafting > 3 Video Prompts; Student Writing: Early draft (Emily Lesk)

Checklist

Drafting

- **Set up a computer folder or file for your essay.** Give the file a clear and relevant name, and save to it often. Number your drafts. If you decide to try a new direction, save the file as a new draft—you can always pick up the old one if the new version doesn't work out.
- **Have all your information close at hand and arranged according to your organizational plan.** Stopping to search for a piece of information can break your concentration or distract you.
- **Try to write in stretches of at least thirty minutes.** Writing can provide momentum, and once you get going, the task becomes easier.
- **Don't let small questions bog you down.** Just make a note of them in brackets—or in all caps—or make a tentative decision and move on.
- **Remember that first drafts aren't perfect.** Concentrate on getting your ideas down, and don't worry about anything else.
- **Stop writing at a place where you know exactly what will come next.** Doing so will help you start easily when you return to the draft.

No matter how good your planning, investigating, and organizing have been, chances are you will need to do more work as you draft. The first principle of successful drafting is to be flexible. If you see that your plan is not working, don't hesitate to alter it. If some information now seems irrelevant, or perhaps unreliable, leave it out. You may learn that you need to do more research, reshape your whole thesis, or narrow your topic further. Very often you will continue planning, investigating, and organizing throughout the writing process.

2e Developing paragraphs

Three qualities essential to most academic paragraphs are unity, development, and coherence.

Writing Processes: Developing Paragraphs > LearningCurve

Unity. In most college writing, an effective paragraph focuses on one main idea. You can achieve unity by stating that main idea clearly in one sentence—the **topic sentence**—and relating all other sentences in the paragraph to that idea. Like a thesis (see 2b), the topic sentence includes a topic and a comment on that topic. A topic sentence often begins a paragraph, but it may come at the end—or be implied rather than stated directly.

Development. In addition to being unified, a good paragraph holds readers' interest and explores its topic fully, using whatever details, evidence, and examples are necessary. Without such development, a paragraph may seem lifeless and abstract.

Most good academic writing backs up general ideas with specifics. Shifting between the general and the specific is especially important at the paragraph level. If a paragraph contains nothing but specific details, its meaning may not be clear to readers—but if a paragraph makes only general statements, it may seem boring or unconvincing.

Coherence. A paragraph has coherence—or flows—if its details fit together in a way that readers can easily follow. The following methods can help you achieve paragraph coherence:

- A general-to-specific or specific-to-general *organization* helps readers move from one point to another.
- Repetition of key words or phrases links sentences and suggests that the words or phrases are important.
- Parallel structures help make writing more coherent (see Chapter 27).
- **Transitions** such as *for example* and *however* help readers follow the progression of one idea to the next.

The same methods that you use to create coherent paragraphs can be used to link paragraphs so that a whole piece of writing flows smoothly. You can create links to previous paragraphs by repeating or paraphrasing key words and phrases and by using parallelism and transitions.

The following sample paragraph from David Craig's research project (15f), which identifies a topic and a comment on the topic and then develops the topic with detailed evidence in support of the point, achieves unity by linking each sentence to the main topic, and achieves coherence with a general-to-specific organization, repetition of key content related to digital communication and teenagers, and transitions that relate this paragraph to the preceding one and relate sentences to one another.

Transition from preceding paragraph

Topic sentence — sticks to this main idea throughout

Supporting evidence

Sentence-to-sentence transition

Based on the preceding statistics, parents and educators appear to be right about the decline in youth literacy. And this trend coincides with another phenomenon: digital communication is rising among the young. According to the Pew Internet & American Life Project, 85 percent of those aged twelve to seventeen at least occasionally write text messages, instant messages, or comments on social networking sites (Lenhart et al.). In 2001, the most conservative estimate based on Pew numbers showed that American youths spent, at a minimum, nearly three million hours per day on messaging services (Lenhart and Lewis 20). These numbers are now exploding thanks to texting, which was "the dominant daily mode of communication" for teens in 2012 (Lenhart), and messaging on popular social networking sites such as Facebook and Tumblr.

Checklist

Strong Paragraphs

Most readers of English have certain expectations about how paragraphs work:

- Paragraphs begin and end with information that is important for the reader.
- The opening sentence is often the topic sentence that tells what the paragraph is about.
- The middle of the paragraph develops the idea.
- The end may sum up the paragraph's contents, closing the discussion of an idea and anticipating the paragraph that follows.
- A paragraph makes sense as a whole; the words and sentences are clearly related.
- A paragraph relates to other paragraphs around it.

3 Making Design Decisions

When millions of messages vie for attention, effective design is especially important: the strongest message may not get through to its audience if it is presented and designed in a bland or boring way. You will want to understand and use effective design to make sure you get—and keep—your audience's attention.

3a Design principles

In designer Robin Williams's *Non-Designer's Design Book*, she identifies four simple principles that are a good starting point for making any print or digital text more effective.

Contrast. Begin with a focal point—a dominant visual or text that readers should look at first—and structure the flow of other information from that point. Use color, boldface or large type, white space, and so on to set off the focal point.

Alignment. Horizontal or vertical alignment of words and visuals gives a text a cleaner, more organized look. In general, wherever you begin aligning elements—on the top or bottom, on the right or left, or in the center—stick with it throughout the text.

Repetition. Readers are guided in large part by the repetition of key words or design elements. Use color, type, style, and other visual elements consistently throughout a document.

Proximity. Parts of a text that are related should be physically close together (*proximate* to each other).

3b Appropriate formats

Think about the most appropriate way to format a document to make it inviting and readable for your intended audience.

White space. Empty space, called "white space," guides the reader's eyes to parts of a page or screen. Consider white space at the page level (margins), paragraph level (spacing between paragraphs or sections), and sentence level (space between lines and between sentences). You can also use white space around particular content, such as a graphic or list, to make it stand out.

Color. Choose colors that relate to the purpose(s) of your text and its intended audience.

- Use color to draw attention to elements you want to emphasize—such as headings, bullets, boxes, or visuals—and be consistent in using color throughout your text.
- For academic work, keep the number of colors fairly small to avoid a jumbled or confused look.
- Make sure the colors you choose are readable in the format you're using. A color that looks clear onscreen may be less legible in print or projected on a screen.

Paper. For print documents, choose paper that is an appropriate size and color for your purpose. A printed essay, poster, and brochure will probably call for different sizes and types of paper. For academic papers, put your last name and the page number in the upper-right-hand corner of each page unless your instructor requires a different formatting style.

Type. Choose an easy-to-read type size and typeface, and be consistent in the styles and sizes of type used throughout your project. For most college writing, 11- or 12-point type is standard. And although unusual fonts may seem attractive at first glance, readers may find them distracting and hard to read over long stretches of material.

Spacing. Final drafts of any printed academic writing should be double-spaced, with the first line of paragraphs indented one-half inch. Other documents, such as memos, letters, and web texts, are usually single-spaced, with a blank line between paragraphs and no paragraph indentation. Some kinds of documents, such as newsletters, may call for multiple columns of text.

Headings. Consider organizing your text with headings that will aid comprehension. Some genres have standard headings (such as *Abstract*) that readers expect.

- Distinguish levels of headings using indents along with type. For example, you might center main headings and align lower-level headings at the left margin.

- Look for the most succinct and informative way to word your headings. You can state the topic in a single word (*Toxicity*); in a noun phrase (*Levels of Toxicity*) or gerund phrase (*Measuring Toxicity*); in a question to be answered in the text (*How Can Toxicity Be Measured?*); or in an imperative that tells readers what to do (*Measure the Toxicity*). Structure all headings of the same level consistently.

3c Visuals and media

Choose visuals and media that will help make a point more vividly and succinctly than words alone. Consider carefully what you want visuals, audio, or video to do for your writing. What will your audience want or need you to show? Choose visuals and media that will enhance your credibility, allow you to make your points more emphatically, and clarify your overall text. (See the series of figures on pp. 20–21 for advice on which visuals to use in particular situations.)

Effective media content can come from many sources—your own drawings or recordings you make, as well as audio or video materials created by others. If your document will be on the web, you can insert clips that readers can watch and listen to as they read your text. Such inserts can make powerful appeals: if you are writing about the ongoing migrant crisis in Europe, for example, a link to a video clip of people barely surviving in border "camps" may make the point better than you can do in words. Include such links as you would other visuals, making sure to provide a caption as well as a lead-in to the clip and a commentary after it if appropriate. And remember: if you are using media created by someone else, be sure to give appropriate credit and to get permission before making it available to the public as part of your work.

Position and identification of visuals and media. Position visuals alongside or after the text that refers to them. In academic and other formal writing, number your visuals (number tables separately from other visuals), and provide informative captions, as shown on p. 20. In some instances, you may need to give readers additional data such as source information in the caption.

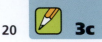

Fig. 1. College Enrollment for Men and Women by Age, 2017 (in millions)

Table 1. Refugee Population by Country or Territory of Origin: 2013–2017, UNHCR, 2018

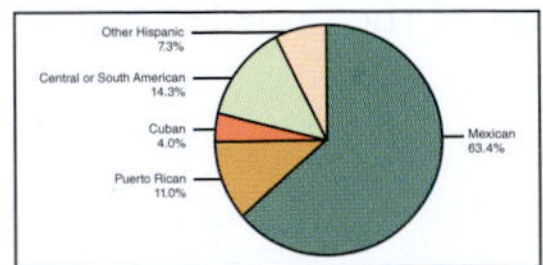

Use *pie charts* to compare parts to the whole.

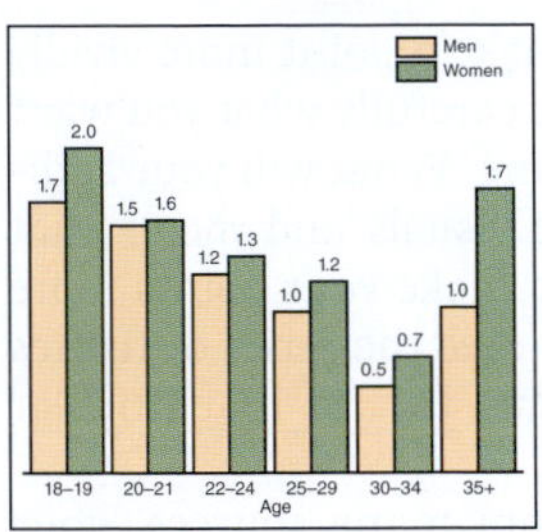

Use *bar graphs* and *line graphs* to compare one element with another, to compare elements over time, or to show correlations and frequency.

Table 10: Commuter Rail Schedule: Reading/ Haverhill Line, Boston

	Train 223	Train 227	Train 231
North Station	3:00 pm	4:36 pm	5:15 pm
Reading	3:38 pm	4:54 pm	5:42 pm
Haverhill	4:04 pm	5:31 pm	6:21 pm

Use *tables* to draw attention to detailed numerical information.

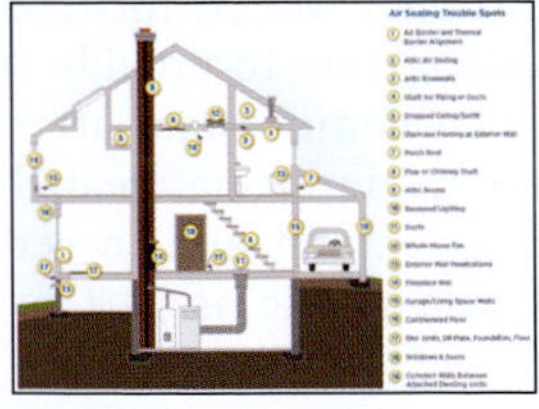

Use *diagrams* to illustrate textual information or to point out details of objects or places described.

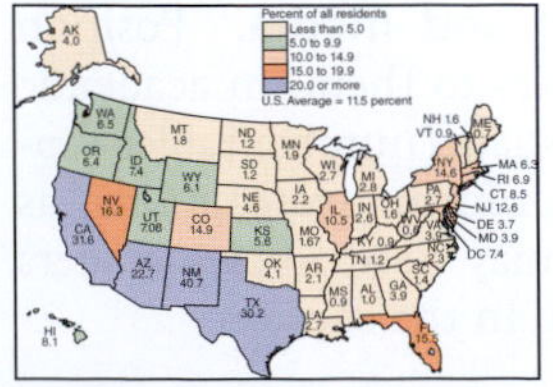

Use *maps* to show geographical locations and to emphasize spatial relationships.

(HOUSE IMAGE) U.S. DEPARTMENT OF ENERGY

Use *cartoons* to illustrate a point dramatically or comically.

Use *photographs* or *illustrations* to show particular people, places, objects, and situations described in the text or to help readers find or understand types of content.

Use *links to audio or video material* to help readers see and hear the point you are making.

(MIDDLE IMAGE) MICHAEL ENRIGHT

3d Ethical use of visuals and media

Technical tools available today make it relatively easy to manipulate or "doctor" images in deceptive ways. As you would with any source material, carefully assess any visuals and video or audio files you find for accuracy as well as effectiveness, appropriateness, and validity.

- Check the context in which the visual appears. Is it part of an official government, school, or library site?
- Does the information you find about the visual or media source seem believable?

Designing & Performing Writing: Communicating in Other Media > 2 Tutorials

 Checklist

Using Visuals and Media Ethically and Effectively

- Use visuals and media files as a part of your text, not just as decoration.
- Tell the audience explicitly what the visual or media file demonstrates, especially if it presents complex information. Do not assume readers will "read" the material the way you do; your commentary on it is important.
- Number and title all of your visuals. Number tables and figures separately.
- Refer to each visual or media file before it actually appears in your text.
- Follow established conventions for documenting sources, and ask permission for use if someone else controls the rights. (13c)
- Get responses to your visuals and media in an early draft. If readers can't follow them or are distracted by them, revise accordingly.
- If you alter a visual or media file, be sure to do so ethically.

- If the visual is a chart, graph, or diagram, are the numbers and labels in it explained? Are the sources of the data given? Will the visual representation help readers make sense of the information, or could it mislead them?
- Is biographical and contact information for the designer, artist, or photographer given?

At times, you may make certain changes to visuals and media that you use, such as cropping an image to show the most important detail, enhancing sound quality, or brightening a dark image. To ensure that your alterations to images are ethical, follow these guidelines:

- Never mislead readers. Show things as accurately as possible.
- Tell your audience what changes you have made.
- Include all relevant information about the original visual or media file, including the source.
- Make sure you have identified the sources of all still and moving images, audio files, and so on.

4 Reviewing, Revising, and Editing

After giving your draft a rest, make time to review it (by yourself and with others), to revise, and to edit. Becoming an astute critic of your own writing will pay off as you get better and better at taking a hard look at your drafts, revising them thoughtfully, and editing them with care.

Checklist

Taking a Writing Inventory

Keeping a writing inventory of all the problems others have identified on your assignments can help you think critically and analytically about how to improve your writing skills.

1. Collect two or three pieces of your writing to which either your instructor or other students have responded.
2. Read through them, adding your own comments about their strengths and weaknesses. How do your comments compare with those of others?
3. Group all the comments into three categories—*broad content* issues (use of evidence and sources, attention to purpose and audience, overall impression), *organization and presentation* (overall and paragraph organization, sentence structure, style, design, formatting), and *surface errors* (spelling, grammar, punctuation, and mechanics).
4. Make an inventory of your own strengths in each of these categories.
5. Study each of your mistakes. Mark every instructor and peer comment that suggests or calls for an improvement, and put all these comments in a list. Consult the relevant part of this book or speak with your instructor if you don't understand a comment.
6. Make a list of the top problem areas you need to work on. How can you make improvements? Then note at least two strengths that you can build on in your writing. Record your findings in a writing log that you can add to as the class proceeds.

4a Reviewing

Reviewing calls for reading your draft with a critical eye and asking others to look over your work. Ask classmates or your instructor to respond to your draft, answering questions like these:

- What do you see as the major point, claim, or thesis?
- How convincing is the evidence? What can I do to support my thesis more fully?
- What points are unclear? How can I clarify them?
- How easy is it to follow my organization? How can I improve?
- What can I do to make my draft more interesting?

4b Revising

Revising means using others' comments along with your own analysis of the draft to make sure it is as complete, clear, and effective as possible. These questions can help you revise:

- How does the draft accomplish its purpose?
- Does the title tell what the draft is about?
- Is the thesis clearly stated, and does it contain a topic and a comment?
- How does the introduction catch readers' attention?
- Are transitions from paragraph to paragraph clear, logical, and smoothly integrated?
- Will the draft interest and appeal to its audience?
- How does the draft indicate your stance on the topic?
- What are the main points that illustrate or support the thesis? Are they clear? Do you need to add material to the points or add new points?
- Are the ideas presented in an order that will make sense to readers?
- Have you documented your research appropriately?
- How are visuals, media, and research sources (if any) integrated into your draft? Have you commented on their significance?
- How does the draft conclude? Is the conclusion memorable?

Writing Processes: Reviewing & Revising > 3 Storyboards; 3 Video Prompts; Practice Peer Review (Emily Lesk)

EXERCISE 4.1 Answer the following questions about your reviewing and revising process.

1. How did you begin reviewing your draft?
2. What kinds of comments on or responses to your draft did you receive? How helpful were they, and why?
3. How long did revising take? How many drafts did you produce?
4. What kinds of changes did you tend to make? For example, did you make changes in organization, paragraphs, sentence structure, wording, or adding or deleting information? Did you revise the use of visuals?
5. What gave you the most trouble as you were revising?
6. What pleased you most? What is your favorite sentence or passage in the draft, and why?
7. What would you most like to change about your process of revising, and how do you plan to go about doing so?

4c Editing and proofreading

Once you are satisfied with your revised draft's big picture, edit your writing to make sure that every detail is as correct as you can make it for the readers you plan to share it with (5a).

- Read your draft aloud to "hear" how smoothly it flows and to find typos.
- Do the opening sentence and paragraph grab your readers' attention?
- Are your sentences varied in length and in pattern or type?
- Have you used active verbs, vivid word images, and effective figurative language?
- Are all sentences complete and correct (unless you are trying for a special effect!)?
- Do any sentences begin with the expletives "it" or "there"? If so, revise to delete these "filler" words.
- Have you used the spell checker—and double-checked its recommendations?
- What tone do you establish and how does it reflect your stance?

Writing Processes: Editing & Proofreading > Student Writing: Final draft (Emily Lesk)

- Have you checked for language that might offend or confuse readers? for the use of gender-neutral pronouns? (Chapter 20)
- Have you chosen an effective design and used fonts, white space, headings, and color appropriately?
- Have you proofread one last time, going word for word?

For more on troubleshooting your writing, see "Top Twenty Tips for Editing Your Writing" on the following pages.

EXERCISE 4.2 Answer each of the following questions about your own editing and proofreading process.

1. What do you look for when editing? What kinds of changes do you tend to make?
2. What decisions are most difficult in editing your work?
3. What patterns of problems, if any, do you tend to notice when you edit your own work? If you have not yet started an editing and proofreading checklist, consider beginning one now.

Top Twenty Tips for Editing Your Writing

As the poet Nikki Giovanni says, "Mistakes are a fact of life." So it is with writing: everyone makes mistakes; some don't make much difference, but others keep people from understanding what you're saying or don't reflect your best work. Even writing teachers don't mark every little mistake and usually concentrate only on ones that are distracting or viewed as particularly serious. On top of that, people differ on what constitutes a "mistake": research for this book shows that some instructors view certain mistakes as serious errors and some view them as stylistic choices and that, in fact, what count as "errors" changes over time.

Such differing opinions and changes don't mean that there is no such thing as correctness in writing—only that *correctness always depends on some context*, on whether the choices you make seem appropriate to your audience, your purpose, and your topic.

All writers want to be considered competent, careful, and compelling. Since instructors often pay attention to how well you control the conventions of grammar, punctuation, and so on—even though such conventions change from time to time—it's helpful to know what mistakes or errors are most likely to appear in college student writing today. To find out, we've analyzed thousands of pieces of first-year student writing from all across the country to identify the twenty most troublesome conventions to students today. Out of this research, we've developed the following Top Twenty Tips for Editing Your Writing. For each one, we provide brief examples, shown with hand corrections and cross-references to other places in this book where you will find more detailed information and examples. And the best news is that, if you learn to use these tips to edit your writing, you'll take care of over 90 percent of the mistakes that can drive teachers crazy!

Checklist

Top Twenty Tips for Editing Your Writing

1	Check for wrong words	*p. 28; Ch. 22, Ch. 35*
2	Use a comma after an introductory element	*p. 29; 38a*
3	Make sure documentation is complete	*p. 30; Chs. 15–18*
4	Check pronoun reference	*p. 30; Ch. 34*
5	Check for spelling (including homonyms)	*p. 31; 22e*
6	Use quotation marks conventionally	*p. 31; 38h, 42b, 46a*
7	Avoid unnecessary commas	*p. 31; 38i*
8	Check for capitalization	*p. 32; Ch. 44*
9	Look for missing words	*p. 32; Ch. 35*
10	Look for confusing sentence structures	*p. 32; Ch. 24, Ch. 27*
11	Use commas with nonrestrictive elements	*p. 33; 38c*
12	Avoid unnecessary shifts in verb tense	*p. 33; 28a*
13	Use a comma between clauses in a compound sentence	*p. 33; 38b*
14	Check apostrophes (including *its/it's*)	*p. 34; Ch. 41*
15	Look for fused (run-on) sentences	*p. 34; Ch. 36*
16	Look for comma splices	*p. 34; Ch. 36*
17	Check for pronoun-antecedent agreement	*p. 35; 20b, Ch. 34*
18	Integrate quotations smoothly	*p. 35; 13b*
19	Check for unnecessary or missing hyphens	*p. 36; Ch. 47*
20	Check for sentence fragments	*p. 36; Ch. 37*

1 Check for wrong words

► Religious texts, for them, take ~~prescience~~ precedence over other kinds of sources.

Prescience means "foresight," and *precedence* means "priority."

- **The child suffered from a severe ~~allegory~~ allergy to peanuts.**

  Allegory is a spell checker's replacement for a misspelling of *allergy*.

- **The panel discussed the ethical implications ~~on~~ of the situation.**

Wrong-word errors can involve using a word with the wrong shade of meaning, using a word with a completely wrong meaning, or using a wrong **preposition** or another wrong word in an idiom. Selecting a word from a thesaurus without knowing its meaning or allowing a spell checker to correct spelling automatically can lead to wrong-word errors, so use these tools with care. If you have trouble with prepositions and idioms, memorize the standard usage. (See Chapter 22 on word choice and Chapter 35 on prepositions and idioms.)

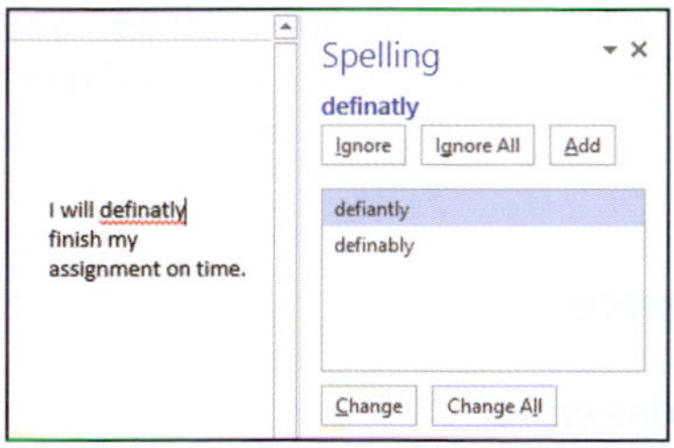

The writer means *definitely,* but the spell checker suggests wrong words.

2 Use a comma after an introductory element

- **Determined to get the job done, we worked all weekend.**

- **Although the research study was flawed, the results may still be useful.**

Readers usually need a small pause—signaled by a comma—between an introductory word, **phrase**, or **clause** and the main part of the **sentence**. Use a comma after every introductory element. When the introductory element is very short, you don't always need a comma, but including it is never wrong. (See 38a.)

3 Make sure documentation is complete

- **Satrapi says, "When we're afraid, we lose all sense of analysis and reflection."** " (263).

  The page number of the print source for this quotation must be included.

- **According to one source, James Joyce wrote two of the five best novels of all time.** ("100 Best").

  The source mentioned should be identified (this online source has no author or page numbers).

Cite each source you refer to in the text, following the guidelines of the documentation style you are using. (The preceding examples follow MLA style—see Chapter 15; for other styles, see Chapters 16–18.) Omitting documentation can result in plagiarism. (See Chapter 13.)

4 Check pronoun reference

POSSIBLE REFERENCE TO MORE THAN ONE WORD

- **Transmitting radio signals by satellite is a way of overcoming the problem of scarce airwaves and limiting how ~~they~~ the airwaves are used.**

  In the original sentence, *they* could refer to the signals or to the airwaves.

REFERENCE IMPLIED BUT NOT STATED

- **The company prohibited smoking, ~~which~~ a policy many employees appreciated.**

  What does *which* refer to? The editing clarifies what employees appreciated.

A **pronoun** should refer clearly to the word or words it replaces (called the *antecedent*) elsewhere in the sentence or in a previous sentence. If more than one word could be the antecedent, or if no specific antecedent is present, edit to make the meaning clear. (See Chapter 34.)

5 Check for spelling (including homonyms)

- Ronald ~~Regan~~ Reagan won the election in a landslide.
- ~~Their~~ They're usually here on time, but not today!
- ~~Every where~~ Everywhere we went, we saw crowds of tourists.

The most common misspellings today are those that spell checkers cannot identify. The categories that spell checkers are most likely to miss include homonyms, compound words incorrectly spelled as separate words, and proper **nouns**, particularly names. After you run the spell checker, proofread carefully for errors such as these—and be sure to run the spell checker to catch other kinds of spelling mistakes. (See 22e.)

6 Use quotation marks conventionally

- **"I grew up the victim of a disconcerting confusion,"/ Rodriguez says (249).**

  The comma should be placed *inside* the quotation marks.

Follow conventions when using quotation marks with commas (38h), colons, and other punctuation. Always use quotation marks in pairs, and follow the guidelines of your documentation style for block quotations. Use quotation marks for titles of short works (42b), but use italics for titles of long works (46a).

7 Avoid unnecessary commas

BEFORE CONJUNCTIONS IN COMPOUND CONSTRUCTIONS THAT ARE NOT COMPOUND SENTENCES

- **This conclusion applies to the United States/ and to the rest of the world.**

  No comma is needed before *and* because it is joining two phrases that modify the same verb, *applies*.

WITH RESTRICTIVE ELEMENTS

- **Many parents/ of gifted children/ do not want them to skip a grade.**

  No comma is needed to set off the restrictive phrase *of gifted children*, which is necessary to indicate which parents the sentence is talking about.

Do not use commas to set off **restrictive elements** that are necessary to the meaning of the words they modify. Do not use a comma before a **coordinating conjunction** (*and*, *but*, *for*, *nor*, *or*, *so*, *yet*) when the conjunction does not join parts of a compound sentence (error 13). Do not use a comma before the first or after the last item in a series, between a **subject** and **verb**, between a verb and its **object** or object/complement, or between a **preposition** and its object. (See 38i.)

8 Check for capitalization

- **Some ~~Traditional~~ [traditional] Chinese ~~Medicines~~ [medicines] containing ~~Ephedra~~ [ephedra] remain legal.**

Capitalize proper nouns and proper adjectives, the first words of sentences, and important words in titles, along with certain words indicating directions and family relationships. Do not capitalize most other words. When in doubt, check a dictionary. (See Chapter 44.)

9 Look for missing words

- **The site foreman discriminated [against] women and promoted men with less experience.**

Proofread carefully for omitted words, including prepositions (35a), parts of two-part verbs (35b), and correlative **conjunctions**. Be particularly careful not to omit words from quotations.

10 Look for confusing sentence structures

- **~~The information which high~~ [High] school athletes are presented with ~~mainly includes~~ information on what credits ~~needed~~ [they need] to graduate,**

> **~~and thinking about the college~~ which ~~athletes are trying~~ colleges to try to play for, and how to apply.**

A sentence that starts with one kind of structure and then changes to another kind can confuse readers. Make sure that each sentence contains a subject and a verb, that subjects and **predicates** make sense together (24b), and that comparisons have clear meanings (24d). When you join elements (such as subjects or verb phrases) with a coordinating conjunction, make sure that the elements have parallel structures (see Chapter 27).

11 Use commas with nonrestrictive elements

- **Marina, who was the president of the club, was first to speak.**

  The clause *who was the president of the club* does not affect the basic meaning of the sentence: Marina was first to speak.

A **nonrestrictive element** gives information not essential to the basic meaning of the sentence. Use commas to set off a nonrestrictive element (38c).

12 Avoid unnecessary shifts in verb tense

- **Priya was watching the great blue heron. Then she ~~slips~~ slipped and ~~falls~~ fell into the swamp.**

Verbs that shift from one **tense** to another with no clear reason can confuse readers (28a).

13 Use a comma between clauses in a compound sentence

- **Meredith waited for Samir, and her sister grew impatient.**

  Without the comma, a reader may think at first that Meredith waited for both Samir and her sister.

A compound sentence consists of two or more parts that could each stand alone as a sentence. When the parts are joined by a coordinating conjunction, use a comma before the conjunction to indicate a pause between the two thoughts (38b).

14 Check apostrophes (including *its/it's*)

- Overambitious parents can be very harmful to a ~~childs~~ ^child's^ well-being.
- The library is having ~~it's~~ ^its^ annual fundraiser. ~~Its~~ ^It's^ for a good cause.

To make a noun **possessive**, add an apostrophe and an *-s* (*Ed's book*) or an apostrophe alone (*the boys' gym*). Do *not* use an apostrophe in the possessive **pronouns** *ours*, *yours*, and *hers*. Use *its* to mean *belonging to it*; use *it's* to mean *it is* or *it has*. (See Chapter 41.)

15 Look for fused (run-on) sentences

- Klee's paintings seem simple, ^but^ they are very sophisticated.
- ~~She~~ ^Although she^ doubted the value of meditation, she decided to try it once.

A **fused sentence** (also called a *run-on*) joins clauses that could each stand alone as a sentence with no punctuation or words to link them. Fused sentences must either be divided into separate sentences or joined by adding words or punctuation. (See Chapter 36.)

16 Look for comma splices

- I was strongly attracted to her, ^for^ she was beautiful and funny.
- We hated the meat loaf/ ^that^ the cafeteria served ~~it~~ every Friday.

A **comma splice** occurs when only a comma separates clauses that could each stand alone as a sentence. To correct a comma splice, you can insert a semicolon or period, connect the clauses with a word such as *and* or *because*, or restructure the sentence. (See Chapter 36.)

17 Check for pronoun-antecedent agreement

- **Each of the puppies thrived in ~~their~~ its new home.**
- **Either Nirupa or Selena will be asked to give ~~their~~ her speech to the graduates.**

Pronouns traditionally agree with their antecedents in gender (male or female) and in number (singular or plural). When antecedents are joined by *or* or *nor*, the pronoun must agree with the closer antecedent. A collective **noun** such as *team* can be either singular or plural, depending on whether the members are seen as a group or as individuals. (See 34b.) Many **indefinite pronouns**, such as *everyone* and *each*, are always singular. When a singular antecedent can refer to a person of any gender (*Every student*), rewriting the sentence in the plural is often a good alternative (*All students must provide their own uniforms*). But note that the use of *they* to refer to a singular antecedent is gaining acceptance (*Every student must provide their own uniform*). (See 20b and 34a.)

18 Integrate quotations smoothly

- **A 1970s study of what makes food appetizing** showed how color affects taste: **"Once it became apparent that the steak was actually blue and the fries were green, some people became ill" (Schlosser 565).**
- According to Lars Eighner, **"Dumpster diving has serious drawbacks as a way of life" (~~Eighner~~ 383). Finding edible food is especially tricky.**

Quotations should all fit smoothly into the surrounding sentence structure. They should be linked clearly to the writing around them (usually with a signal phrase) rather than dropped abruptly into the writing. (See 13b.)

19 Check for unnecessary or missing hyphens

▸ This paper looks at fictional and real-life examples.

A compound adjective modifying a noun that follows it requires a hyphen.

▸ The buyers want to fix up the house and resell it.

A two-word verb should not be hyphenated.

A compound **adjective** that appears before a noun needs a hyphen. However, be careful not to hyphenate two-word verbs or word groups that serve as subject complements. (See Chapter 47.)

20 Check for sentence fragments

NO SUBJECT

▸ Marie Antoinette spent huge sums of money on herself and her favorites. ~~And~~ *Her extravagance* helped bring on the French Revolution.

NO COMPLETE VERB

▸ The old aluminum boat *was* sitting on its trailer.

BEGINNING WITH A SUBORDINATING WORD

▸ We returned to the drugstore~~.~~, ~~Where~~ *where* we waited for our buddies.

A **sentence fragment** is part of a sentence that is written as if it were a complete sentence. Reading your draft out loud, backwards, sentence by sentence, will help you spot sentence fragments. (See Chapter 37.)

EXERCISE Using the Top Twenty Editing Tips

The following sentences are from a student's research-based essay. The student quotes two sources, "Because Partying Is Too Mainstream: Alternative Spring Breaks" by Valeria Delgado (Collegemagazine.com, March 20, 2012) and "We Did Not Give Up Our Spring Break, We Took Advantage of It," a

United Way blog post (Unitedway.org, March 11, 2012). Revise each numbered item, using the twenty most common sentence-level errors written by first-year students to do so. Example:

> **College students are usually eager to spend ~~Spring~~ spring break having as much fun as possible.**

1. After months of stressful schoolwork, students understandably want to spend the week relaxing or blowing off steam with there friends.
2. Popular spring break destinies over the years have included Mexican resorts, Florida beaches, and Caribbean islands.
3. A growing number of students, however, are beginning to recognize that its actually rewarding to spend vacation time in more useful ways.
4. A new trend, known as alternative spring breaks, allows college students to contribute their time to humanitarian causes. Or environmental organizations.
5. Each year, thousands of students decide to skip the wild party scenes, they choose instead to do something meaningful for people or places in need.
6. There are a host of options available to students who want to volunteer over their spring break. "Programs range from working with kids in U.S. cities to building sustainable water systems in Nicaragua" (Delgado).
7. Usually a student will seek out a volunteer opportunity that best suits their talents and interests. Of course, many students still want to go somewhere warm.
8. Students can find the best match for their interests and desired location with the help of large nonprofit organizations such as United Way. They also frequently subsidize the costs of the trips to make them more affordable.
9. Although volunteering opportunities have always been available to students, the concept of alternative spring breaks is fairly recent. United Way began setting alternative spring breaks in 2006.
10. Some students work within their own communities others may travel thousands of miles to volunteer over spring break.
11. Services that students provide include, painting community centers, planting trees in parks, cleaning up the environment, and teaching English as a second language.
12. In Michigan, students who renovated a community recreation center and added a reading corner to encourage children to read after school each day.

13. In New Orleans, Habitat for Humanity brought students together to help build new-houses for people who lost their homes in Hurricane Katrina in 2005.
14. On the Gulf Coast where the 2010 oil spill devastated shorelines students helped clean up beaches and safeguard sea turtle nests.
15. Some students have traveled to Rock Hill, south Carolina, to clean up an old cemetery and repair homes on the Catawba Indian Reservation.
16. All students have their own reasons for embarking on an alternative spring break but many find that they come away with benefits they had not anticipated.
17. According to one source, students may go on an alternative spring break to improve their résumé or to take an affordable trip, but they end up having an important emotional experience and building lifelong memories.
18. Moreover, as noted in a United Way blog entry, "What many students don't realize until they arrive is the impact it will have on their own lives". ("We Did Not Give Up")
19. According to Valeria Delgado, one student reluctantly volunteered at the Boys and Girls Club in Newark, New Jersey, over spring break in 2011 and finds that he enjoyed it much more than he thought he would.
20. Another student Delgado interviewed found that through helping others he was actually helping himself. After volunteering with poor families in south Mississippi he realized how fortunate he was and gained a better sense of his priorities in life (Delgado).

LaunchPad Solo
macmillan learning

The Top Twenty > Top Twenty Editing Quizzes

5 Sharing and Reflecting on Your Writing

Once you have completed a piece of writing, please consider sharing it. You've worked hard on a topic that's important to you, and there's a good chance others will care about it, too. Sharing and talking about a piece of writing that you've finished are also good steps toward reflecting on the entire writing experience and assessing what you learned from it.

5a Sharing with audiences

Chances are, you already share your writing with family, friends, and others via social media (1b). So why not go ahead and share your academic writing with others you think will be interested? And if you invite them, you may well start a conversation that will keep going!

- Can you find interested readers through social media sites like Facebook or Twitter?
- Should you keep a blog to share your writing, using a free site such as Blogger?
- Would your work find audiences on YouTube, Instagram, or other visual platforms?
- Could you submit your writing to student publications or organizations on your campus?

You can also share your ideas by joining conversations started by others. You might contribute to Wikipedia or other wikis; comment on online newspaper or magazine articles, editorials, or videos; write reviews for books and other products on Amazon; post to fan fiction sites; or find other public sites where you can participate in producing content and responding to work others have written. As a writer today, you have nearly limitless possibilities for interaction with other readers and writers.

Writing Processes: Reflecting to Learn > Student Writing: Reflective blog post (Thanh Nguyen)

5b Creating a portfolio

One especially good way to share your writing is by developing a portfolio that showcases your abilities and experience. Most instructors who assign portfolios as a culmination of a course will give you advice about what to include, such as a cover letter, a personal reflection, and several polished pieces of your writing. You may also want to keep a portfolio throughout your college career, adding outstanding examples of your work from year to year.

5c Reflecting on your own work

Thinking back on what you've learned helps make that learning stick. Whether or not your instructor requires you to write a formal reflection on a writing course or piece of writing, make time to think about what you have learned from the experience.

The following questions can help you think critically about your writing and to develop a reflective statement:

- What lessons have you learned from the writing? How will they help you with future writing?
- What about your writing are you most confident of? What needs additional work?
- What confused you during your writing? How did you resolve your questions?
- How has this piece of writing helped you clarify your thinking or extend your understanding?
- Identify a favorite passage of your writing. What pleases you about it? Can you apply what you learn from this analysis to other writing situations?
- How would you describe your development as a writer?
- How might you organize a formal reflection on your writing? Will you begin by describing your writing as it was at the beginning of your course or development of a portfolio and then tracing changes and improvements to your writing? by summing up what you have learned about writing and then "flashing back" to examples of how you learned those lessons? by tracing changes and improvements in a number of pieces of writing?

5d STUDENT WRITING Reflection (excerpt)

Student James Kung wrote a reflective cover letter as part of a portfolio for his first-year writing course. To read the complete letter, go to *LaunchPad Solo for Lunsford Handbooks*.

Dear Professor Ashdown:

"Writing is difficult and takes a long time." You have uttered this simple yet powerful statement so many times in our class that it has essentially become our motto. In just ten weeks, my persuasive writing skills have improved dramatically, thanks to many hours spent writing, revising, polishing, and (when I wasn't writing) thinking about my topic. The various drafts, revisions, and other materials in my course portfolio clearly show this improvement.

Reflects on improvement

I entered this first-quarter Writing and Rhetoric class with both strengths and weaknesses. I was strong in the fundamentals of writing: logic and grammar. I have always written fairly well-organized essays. However, despite this strength, I struggled throughout the term to narrow and define the various aspects of my research-based argument.

Analyzes overall strengths and weaknesses

The first aspect of my essay that I had trouble narrowing and defining was my major claim, or my thesis statement. In my first writing assignment for the class . . .

The rest of the letter analyzes specific pieces of writing.

LaunchPad Solo
macmillan learning

Academic, Professional, & Public Writing: Portfolios > Student Writing: Reflective portfolio cover letter (James Kung)

Contexts for Writing, Reading, and Speaking

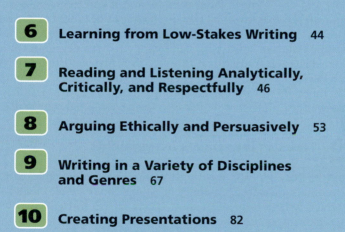

6 Learning from Low-Stakes Writing 44

7 Reading and Listening Analytically, Critically, and Respectfully 46

8 Arguing Ethically and Persuasively 53

9 Writing in a Variety of Disciplines and Genres 67

10 Creating Presentations 82

6 Learning from Low-Stakes Writing

Professor Peter Elbow differentiates between "high-stakes writing"—which you do for formal graded assignments and examinations—and "low-stakes writing"—informal writing that is often ungraded but that helps you think about, learn, and remember course material and stay engaged with your classes. So a very good way to put your writing to work is to use it as a way to learn!

6a The value of low-stakes writing

Sometimes referred to as "writing to learn," low-stakes writing is powerful because it gives you a chance to figure out what you know and don't know about a topic, and it can help you watch your own mind at work—all without having to be judged or graded. Research shows that reflecting on your own thinking, writing, and learning style can contribute significantly to your development as a knowledgeable and critical thinker. Your instructor may assign such low-stakes writing throughout the term; if so, take advantage of it. If not, do some informal writing yourself and see how it helps improve your understanding of course material—and your grades!

6b Types of low-stakes assignments

Quickwrites. A good way to get mental gears going, quickwrites are prompts—usually open-ended questions about a topic of study—to which writers respond in short bursts of two to eight minutes. Instructors often use quickwrites to get class discussion started and focused, but you can use them on your own to get your thinking about a subject down on paper (or screen).

Freewrites. Like quickwrites, freewrites ask you to write about a topic without stopping, usually for ten minutes. Freewrites let you explore your thinking without worrying about correctness, grades, and so on.

Thought pieces. Some instructors assign thought pieces—pieces of writing that sum up background information and your own opinions and analyses of a subject. They can help you see how much you know—and how much more you need to know—about your topic.

Reading responses. These may be the most frequently assigned type of low-stakes writing. In reading responses, you sum up your understanding of an assigned reading and evaluate its effectiveness. Whether or not your instructor assigns such responses, you will profit by setting up a reading log and recording your responses and critical evaluations there.

Class discussion forums. Many instructors set up forums online—on a local course management system, a class blog or wiki, or a class page on Facebook or other social media site—as a space to continue dialogues from the classroom. Active participation in these forums will allow you to get your views out there for others to respond to and help you understand the viewpoints of others.

 Checklist

Participating in Class Blogs, Wikis, and Other Forums

- Take seriously these opportunities to engage with others about the course material and sum up your views in writing; doing so will help you internalize the information.
- Be polite and professional when writing to a class blog, wiki, or other forum.
- Avoid unnecessary criticism of others; the point of these activities is to have productive exchanges about what you are learning. Rather than criticize, simply ask for clarification or offer what you take to be correct information.
- If others criticize you, give them the benefit of the doubt and reply with courtesy and patience.
- For email threads, decide whether to reply off-list to the sender of a message or to the whole group, and be careful to use REPLY or REPLY ALL accordingly to avoid potential confusion.
- Remember that many class forums, blogs, wikis, and email lists are archived, so more people than you think may be reading your messages.

7 Reading and Listening Analytically, Critically, and Respectfully

Reading and listening openly and respectfully to what others have to say is especially important, since what you write is always part of a larger conversation in which you respond to what others have written or said. With so much information bombarding us daily, though, it's tempting to skim. And skimming is certainly an important tool, but high-stakes reading and listening require careful and deep thought, as you ask questions about meaning, about the writer or speaker's purpose, and whether or not the message is trustworthy and convincing.

7a Previewing

Find out all you can about a text before beginning to read or listen to it analytically and critically, considering its context, author, subject, genre, and design.

- Where have you encountered the work? Is it in its original context? What can you infer from the original or current context of the work about its intended audience and purpose?
- What information can you find about the author, creator, or sponsor of the text? What purpose, expertise, and possible agenda might you expect this person to have?
- What do you know about the subject of the text? What opinions do you have about it, and why? What more do you want to learn about it?
- What does the title (or caption or other heading) indicate?
- What role does the medium play in achieving the purpose and connecting to the audience?
- What is the genre of the text? What can it tell you about the intended audience or purpose?
- How is the text presented? What do you notice about its design and general appearance?

Critical Thinking & Argument: Reading Critically > Storyboards; Tutorial; 2 LearningCurve

7b Annotating

As you read or listen to a text for the first time, begin analyzing it by marking it up or taking notes. Make note of the author's main ideas and key terms, considering content, author, intended audience, genre, and design. Jot down questions you'd like to ask the writer, and talk back to the text throughout, noting where you agree and disagree—and why.

- Are you sure you are really hearing what the text is saying rather than rushing to conclusions about it? Are you open to the ideas in the text and respectful of the writer's right to hold them?
- What's confusing or unclear about the text? Where can you look for more information?
- What are the key terms and ideas or patterns? What key images stick in your mind?
- What sources or other works does this text refer to? Are they reliable and trustworthy?
- Which points do you agree with? Which do you disagree with? Why?
- Do the authors or creators present themselves as you anticipated?
- For what audience was this text created? Are you part of its intended audience?
- What underlying assumptions can you identify in the text?
- Are the medium and genre appropriate for the topic, audience, and purpose?
- Is the design appropriate for the subject and genre?
- Does the organization help you see what is more and less important in the text?
- How effectively do words, images, sound, and other media work together?
- How would you describe the style of the text? What contributes to this impression—word choice? references to research or popular culture? formatting? color? something else?

7c Summarizing

A summary *briefly* captures the main ideas of a text—in your own words—and omits information that is less important for the reader. Try to identify the key points in the text, find the essential evidence supporting those points, and then explain the contents concisely and fairly, so that a reader unfamiliar with the original text can make sense of it all. Deciding what to leave out can make summarizing a tricky task. To test your understanding—and to avoid unintentional plagiarism—put the text aside while you write your summary.

7d Analyzing

You can learn many good lessons about how to make appropriate and effective choices in your own writing by studying the choices other writers have made. You may want to begin the process of analysis by asking several key questions: What are the text's main points and claims? Are they implied or explicitly stated? Which points do you agree with? Which do you disagree with? Why?

Analyzing and Fact-Checking Texts

- What cultural contexts—the time and place the argument was written; the economic, social, and political events surrounding the argument; and so on—inform the text? What do they tell about where the writers, creators, or sponsors are coming from and what choices they have had to make?
- What emotional, ethical, or logical appeals has the writer chosen to use in the text? Are the appeals reasonable, fair, and honest?

Critical Thinking & Argument: Reading Critically > Student Writing: Preview notes, annotations, summary
Critical Thinking & Argument: Analyzing Arguments > 2 LearningCurve; 2 Tutorials

- What strategies has the writer chosen to establish credibility?
- What assumptions does the writer make? Are those assumptions valid? Why, or why not?
- Are alternative perspectives included and treated fairly and respectfully? Are some perspectives left out, and if so, how does this exclusion affect the argument?
- What sources does the author use to inform the text? How current, reliable, and trustworthy are they?
- What kinds of examples or evidence does the text offer to support its claims? What other examples or evidence should have been included?
- How solid is the evidence? Have you checked facts, looking for misinformation, incomplete information, falsehoods, or extreme bias? Do other reliable sources corroborate the facts? (See 12a for more about evaluating and fact-checking sources.)
- How has the writer or creator chosen visuals and design to support the main ideas of the text? How well do words and images work together to make a point?
- What surprises, intrigues, puzzles, or irritates you about the text? Why?
- What overall impression does the text create? Are you favorably impressed—or not?
- Do the authors or creators achieve their purpose? Why, or why not?
- What else would you like to know?

EXERCISE 7.1

1. Think about the last film you watched for fun. What did you know about it before you watched it? What did you feel and learn as you watched? What have you told others about the film, both in terms of summarizing the story and of analyzing what the overall experience of viewing the film meant to you?
2. Write a paragraph or create a brief slide show describing how you might use the techniques of previewing, reading, summarizing, and analyzing the next time you are asked to read a written-word text.

7e STUDENT WRITING Rhetorical analysis

For a class assignment, Milena Ateyea was asked to analyze the choices former Harvard president Derek Bok made in a brief text arguing that colleges should seek to persuade rather than censor students who use speech or symbols that offend others. In analyzing "Protecting Freedom of Expression on the Campus," Milena focuses on Bok's choice of particular emotional, ethical, and logical appeals.

LaunchPad Solo
macmillan learning

Critical Thinking & Argument: Reading Critically > Student Writing: 3 analysis samples

STUDENT WRITING

A Curse and a Blessing

When Derek Bok's essay "Protecting Freedom of Expression on the Campus" was first published in the *Boston Globe*, I had just come to America to escape the oppressive Communist regime in Bulgaria. Perhaps my background explains why I support Bok's argument that we should not put arbitrary limits on freedom of expression. Bok wrote the essay in response to a public display of Confederate flags and a swastika at Harvard, a situation that created a heated controversy among the students. As Bok notes, universities have struggled to achieve a balance between maintaining students' right of free speech and avoiding racist attacks. When choices must be made, however, Bok argues for preserving freedom of expression.

In order to support his claim and bridge the controversy, Bok chooses a variety of rhetorical strategies. The author first immerses the reader in the controversy by vividly describing the incident: two Harvard students had hung Confederate flags in public view, thereby "upsetting students who equate the Confederacy with slavery" (69). Another student, protesting the flags, decided to display an even more offensive symbol—the swastika. These actions provoked heated discussions among students. Some students believed that school officials should remove the offensive symbols, whereas others suggested that the symbols "are a form of free speech and should be protected" (69). Bok chooses ways to establish common ground between the factions: he regrets the actions of the offenders but does not believe we should prohibit such actions just because we disagree with them.

The author earns the reader's respect because of his knowledge and through his logical presentation of the issue. In partial support of his position, Bok chooses a U.S. Supreme Court ruling, which reminds us that "the display of swastikas or Confederate flags clearly falls within the protection of the free-speech clause of the First Amendment" (70). The author also emphasizes the danger of

Title suggests mixed response to Bok

Connects article to her own experience to build credibility (ethical appeal)

Brief overview of Bok's argument

Identifies Bok's central claim

Links Bok's claim to strategies he uses to support it

Direct quotations show appeals to emotion through vivid description

Bok establishes common ground between two positions

Emphasizes Bok's credibility (ethical appeal)

STUDENT WRITING

the slippery slope of censorship when he warns the reader, "If we begin to forbid flags, it is only a short step to prohibiting offensive speakers" (70). Overall, however, Bok's choice of appeals lacks the kinds of evidence that statistics, interviews with students, and other representative examples of controversial conduct could provide. Thus, his essay may not be strong enough to persuade all readers to make the leap from this specific situation to his general conclusion.

Links Bok's credibility to use of logical appeals

Comments critically on kinds of evidence Bok's argument lacks

Throughout, Bok chooses to imply his personal feelings rather than state them directly. As a lawyer who was president of Harvard for twenty years, Bok knows how to present his opinions respectfully without offending the feelings of the students. However, qualifying phrases like "I suspect that" and "Under the Supreme Court's rulings, as I read them" could weaken the effectiveness of his position. Furthermore, Bok's attempt to be fair to all seems to dilute the strength of his proposed solution. He suggests that one should either ignore the insensitive deeds in the hope that students might change their behavior, or talk to the offending students to help them comprehend how their behavior is affecting other students.

Reiterates Bok's credibility

Identifies qualifying phrases that may weaken claim

Analyzes weaknesses of Bok's proposed solution

Nevertheless, although Bok's proposed solution to the controversy does not appear at first reading to be very strong, it may ultimately be effective. His rhetorical choices leave enough flexibility to withstand various tests, and Bok's solution is general enough that it can change with the times and adapt to community standards.

Raises possibility that Bok's imperfect solution may work

In writing this essay, Bok faced a challenging task: to write a short response to a specific situation that represents a very broad and controversial issue. Some people may find that freedom of expression is both a curse and a blessing because of the difficulties it creates. As one who has lived under a regime that permitted very limited, censored expression, I am all too aware that I could not have written this response when I lived in Bulgaria. As a result, like Derek Bok, I believe that freedom of expression is a blessing, in spite of any temporary problems associated with it.

Summarizes Bok's task

Ties conclusion back to title

Returns to own experience, which argues for accepting Bok's solution

STUDENT WRITING

Work Cited

Bok, Derek. "Protecting Freedom of Expression on the Campus." *Current Issues and Enduring Questions*, edited by Sylvan Barnet and Hugo Bedau, 10th ed., Bedford/St. Martin's, 2014, pp. 69-71. Originally published in *The Boston Globe*, 25 May 1991.

8 Arguing Ethically and Persuasively

Research conducted for this book shows that argument is the most frequently assigned genre in first- and second-year writing classes. Learning how to respond successfully to such assignments and to compose your own persuasive and ethical arguments will serve you well not just in college but beyond.

8a Listening (and reading) purposefully and openly

The arguments you make are always in response to something others have written or said, so in a very important sense, your own arguments depend on how well you have attended to the conversation surrounding the topic you are addressing. As you do research and reading on your topic, make sure you are doing so carefully, purposefully, and openly: what you take in about your topic from others can help you craft an effective argument, but you need to make sure that you are giving respectful attention to those sources that inform your work.

LaunchPad Solo
macmillan learning
Critical Thinking & Argument: Constructing Arguments > 3 LearningCurve

8b Identifying basic appeals in an argument

Emotional appeals. Emotional appeals stir our feelings and remind us of deeply held values. In analyzing any text, look carefully to see how the writer has chosen to use emotional appeals to rouse the audience's emotions.

Ethical appeals. Ethical appeals support the credibility, moral character, and goodwill of the argument's creator. To identify these appeals, ask how knowledgeable, credible, and trustworthy the author is about the topic. What words, phrases, or examples show that knowledge, credibility, and trustworthiness?

Logical appeals. Recent scientific research demonstrates that most people make decisions based on emotion more than anything else, but logical appeals are still important to Western audiences. As some say, "The facts don't lie" (though as you know, even facts can be manipulated, taken out of context, or presented in unfair ways). In addition to carefully checking the facts of any text, then, look for firsthand evidence drawn from observations, interviews, surveys or questionnaires, experiments, and personal experience, as well as secondhand evidence from authorities, precedents, the testimony of others, statistics, and other research sources. As you evaluate these sources, ask how trustworthy they are and whether all terms are clearly defined.

8c Analyzing the elements of an argument

According to philosopher Stephen Toulmin's framework for analyzing arguments, most arguments contain common features: a **claim** (or claims); reasons for the claim; stated or unstated assumptions that underlie the argument (Toulmin calls these **warrants**); **evidence** such as facts, authoritative opinion, examples, and statistics; and qualifiers that limit the claim in some way.

Suppose you read a brief argument about abolishing the Electoral College, often a hot topic. The diagram that follows shows how you can use the elements of argument for analysis.

Elements of a Toulmin Argument

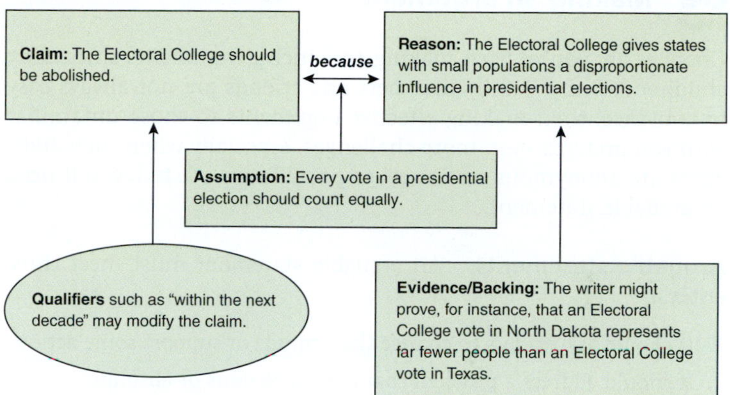
Claim: The Electoral College should be abolished.
because
Reason: The Electoral College gives states with small populations a disproportionate influence in presidential elections.
Assumption: Every vote in a presidential election should count equally.
Qualifiers such as "within the next decade" may modify the claim.
Evidence/Backing: The writer might prove, for instance, that an Electoral College vote in North Dakota represents far fewer people than an Electoral College vote in Texas.

8d Arguing purposefully

Since all language is in some sense argumentative, the purposes of argument vary widely.

Arguing to win. In the most traditional purpose of academic argument, arguing to win, you aim to present a position that prevails over the positions of others.

Arguing to convince. A frequent goal of argument is to convince others to change their minds about an issue. To convince, you must provide reasons so compelling that the audience willingly agrees with your conclusion.

Arguing to understand. Rogerian argument (named for psychologist Carl Rogers) and invitational argument (named by researchers Sonja Foss and Cindy Griffin) both call for understanding as a major goal of arguing. Your purpose in many situations will be to share information and perspectives in order to make informed political, professional, and personal choices.

8e Making an argument

Chances are you've been making convincing arguments since early childhood. But if family members and friends are not always easy to convince, then making effective arguments to those unfamiliar with you presents even more challenges, especially when such audiences are anonymous and in cyberspace. To get started, you'll need an arguable statement.

Arguable statements. An arguable statement must meet three criteria:

1. It should ask readers to change their minds or support some action.
2. It should address a problem that has no obvious or absolute solution or answer.
3. It should present a position that readers can have varying perspectives on.

ARGUABLE STATEMENT	Violent video games lead to violent behavior.
UNARGUABLE STATEMENT	Video games earn millions of dollars every year.

EXERCISE 8.1 Using the three criteria just listed, decide which of the following sentences are arguable and which are not. Example:

One of the best health decisions a person can make is to become a vegetarian. *arguable*

1. Humans were never intended to eat meat, and we would all live longer, healthier lives if we stopped eating it.
2. Health experts agree that vegetarians tend to have lower blood pressure and a lower mortality rate from heart disease than meat eaters do.
3. Killing animals for food is cruel, unethical, and unnecessary.
4. During World War I, the U.S. government encouraged citizens to eat vegetarian diets one day per week—on "Meatless Tuesdays"—to conserve meat for the troops.
5. Nothing is more disgusting than the way animals in slaughterhouses are killed for their meat.

Critical Thinking & Argument: Constructing Arguments > Video Prompt

Argumentative thesis or claim. To make the move from an arguable statement to an argumentative thesis, begin with an arguable statement:

ARGUABLE STATEMENT	Pesticides should be banned.

Attach at least one good reason.

REASON	Pesticides endanger the lives of farmworkers.

You now have a working argumentative thesis.

ARGUMENTATIVE THESIS	Because they endanger the lives of farmworkers, pesticides should be banned.

Develop the underlying assumption that supports your argument.

ASSUMPTION	Farmworkers have a right to a safe working environment.

Identifying this assumption will help you gather evidence in support of your argument. Finally, consider whether you need to qualify your claim in any way.

Ethical appeals. To make any argument effective, you need to establish your credibility. Here are some good ways to do so:

- Demonstrate that you are knowledgeable about the issues and topic.
- Show that you respect the views of your audience and have their best interests at heart.
- Demonstrate that you are fair and evenhanded by showing that you understand alternative or opposing viewpoints and can make a reasonable and fair counterargument.

Visuals can also make ethical appeals. Just as you consider the impression your Facebook profile photo makes on your audience, you should think about what kind of case you're making when you choose images and design elements for your argument.

Logical appeals. Audiences almost always want proof—logical reasons that back up your argument. You can create good logical appeals in the following ways:

- Provide strong examples that are representative and that clearly support your point.
- Introduce precedents—particular examples from the past—that support your point.
- Use narratives or stories in support of your point.
- Cite authorities and their testimony, as long as each authority is timely and is genuinely qualified to speak on the topic.
- Establish that one event is the cause—or the effect—of another.

Visuals that make logical appeals can be useful in arguments, since they present factual information that can be taken in at a glance. Consider how long it would take to explain all the information in the following map by using words alone.

A Visual That Makes a Logical Appeal

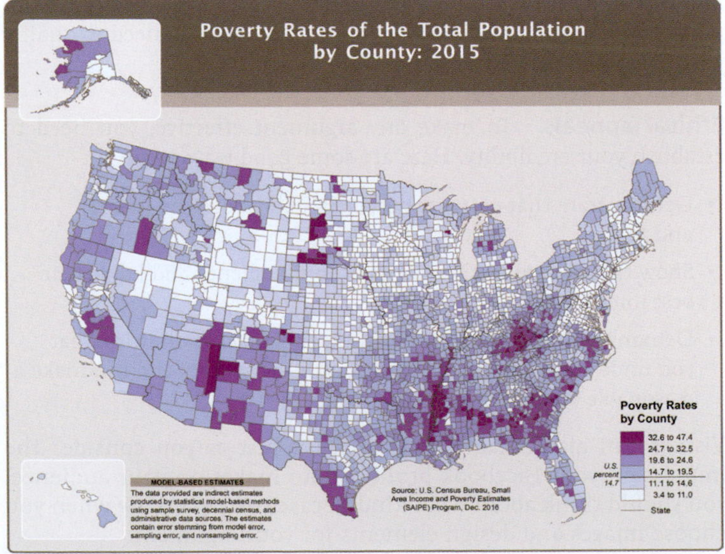

U.S. CENSUS BUREAU

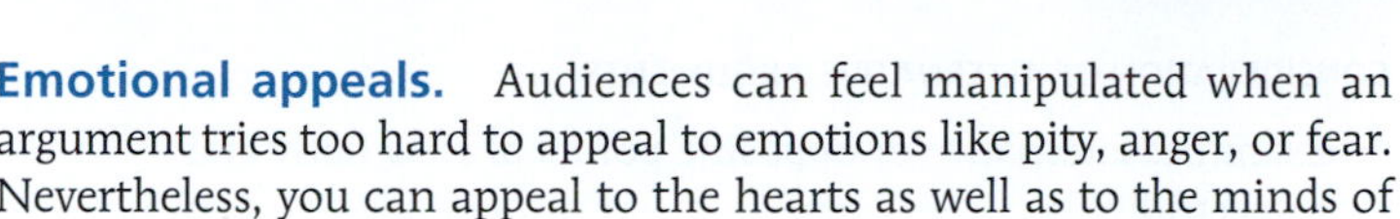

Emotional appeals. Audiences can feel manipulated when an argument tries too hard to appeal to emotions like pity, anger, or fear. Nevertheless, you can appeal to the hearts as well as to the minds of your audience with the ethical use of strong emotional appeals:

- Introduce a powerful and credible quotation or visual that supports your point.
- Use concrete language and details to make your points more vivid.
- Use figurative language—metaphors, similes, analogies, and so on—to make your point both lively and memorable.

Visuals that make emotional appeals can add substance to your argument as long as you test them with potential readers to check whether they interpret the visual the same way you do.

8f Organizing an argument

Although there is no universally "ideal" organizational framework for an argument, the following pattern (often referred to as the classical system) has been used throughout the history of the Western world:

INTRODUCTION

- Gets readers' attention and interest
- Establishes your qualifications to write about your topic
- Establishes common ground with readers
- Demonstrates fairness and trustworthiness
- States or implies your argumentative thesis

BACKGROUND

- Presents any necessary background data or information, including pertinent personal narratives or stories

LINES OF ARGUMENT

- Present good reasons and evidence (including logical and emotional appeals) in support of your thesis, usually in order of importance
- Demonstrate ways your argument is in readers' best interest

CONSIDERATION OF ALTERNATIVE ARGUMENTS

- Examines alternative or opposing points of view fairly and respectfully
- Notes advantages and disadvantages of alternative views
- Explains why one view is more advantageous than other(s)

CONCLUSION

- May summarize the argument briefly
- Elaborates on the implication of your thesis
- Makes clear what you want readers to think and do
- Makes a strong ethical or emotional appeal in a memorable way

8g STUDENT WRITING An argument essay

In this essay, student Benjy Mercer-Golden argues that sustainability and capitalism can and must work together for an effective response to environmental degradation.

STUDENT WRITING

Mercer-Golden 1

Benjy Mercer-Golden
28 Nov. 2017

Lessons from Tree-Huggers and Corporate Mercenaries:
A New Model of Sustainable Capitalism

Provocative word choice for title

Televised images of environmental degradation—seagulls with oil coating their feathers, smokestacks belching gray fumes—often seem designed to shock, but these images also represent very real issues: climate change, dwindling energy resources like coal and oil, a scarcity of clean drinking water. In response, businesspeople around the world are thinking about how they can make their companies greener or more socially beneficial to ensure a brighter future for humanity. But progress in the private sector has been slow and inconsistent. To accelerate the move to sustainability, for-profit businesses need to learn from the hybrid model of social entrepreneurship to ensure that the company is efficient and profitable while still working for social change, and more investors need to support companies with long-term, revolutionary visions for improving the world.

Emotional appeals through use of vivid imagery

Thesis establishing purpose

In fact, both for-profit corporations and "social good" businesses could take steps to reshape their strategies. First, for-profit corporations need to operate sustainably and be evaluated for their performance with long-term measurements and incentives. The conventional argument against for-profit companies deeply embedding environmental and social goals into their corporate strategies is that caring about the world does not go hand in hand with lining pockets. This morally toxic case is also problematic from a business standpoint. A 2012 study of 180 high-profile companies by Harvard Business School professors Robert G. Eccles and George Serafeim and London Business School professor Ioannis Ioannou shows that "high sustainability companies," as defined by environmental and social variables, "significantly outperform their

Claim related to thesis

Opposing viewpoint to establish writer's credibility

Rebuttal

STUDENT WRITING

Mercer-Golden 2

counterparts over the long term, both in terms of stock market and accounting performance." The study argues that the better financial returns of these companies are especially evident in sectors where "companies' products significantly depend upon extracting large amounts of natural resources" (Eccles et al.).

Transition referring to ideas in previous paragraph

Details of claim

Logical appeals using information and evidence in white paper

Ethical appeal to companies

Partial solution proposed

Such empirical financial evidence to support a shift toward using energy from renewable sources to run manufacturing plants argues that executives should think more sustainably, but other underlying incentives need to evolve in order to bring about tangible change. David Blood and Al Gore of Generation Investment Management, an investment firm focused on "sustainable investing for the long term" ("About"), wrote a groundbreaking white paper that outlined the perverse incentives company managers face. For public companies, the default practice is to issue earnings guidances—announcements of projected future earnings—every quarter. This practice encourages executives to manage for the short term instead of adding long-term value to their company and the earth (Gore and Blood). Only the most uncompromisingly green CEOs would still advocate for stricter carbon emissions standards at the company's factories if a few mediocre quarters left investors demanding that they be fired. Gore and Blood make a powerful case against requiring companies to be subjected to this "What have you done for me lately?" philosophy, arguing that quarterly earnings guidances should be abolished in favor of companies releasing information when they consider it appropriate. And to further persuade managers to think sustainably, companies need to change the way the managers get paid. Currently, the CEO of ExxonMobil is rewarded for a highly profitable year but is not held accountable for depleting nonrenewable oil reserves. A new model should incentivize thinking for the long run. Multiyear milestones for performance

STUDENT WRITING

Mercer-Golden 3

evaluation, as Gore and Blood suggest, are essential to pushing executives to manage sustainably.

Claim extended to socially responsible businesses

Logical appeals

But it's not just for-profit companies that need to rethink strategies. Social good–oriented leaders also stand to learn from the people often vilified in environmental circles: corporate CEOs. To survive in today's economy, companies building sustainable products must operate under the same strict business standards as profit-driven companies. Two social enterprises, Nika Water and Belu, provide perfect examples. Both sell bottled water in the developed world with the mission of providing clean water to impoverished communities through their profits. Both have visionary leaders who define the lesson that all environmental and social entrepreneurs need to understand: financial pragmatism will add far more value to the world than idealistic dreams. Nika Water founder Jeff Church explained this in a speech at Stanford University:

> Social entrepreneurs look at their businesses as nine parts cause, one part business. In the beginning, it needs to be nine parts business, one part cause, because if the business doesn't stay around long enough because it can't make it, you can't do anything about the cause.

Additional logical appeals

When U.K.-based Belu lost £600,000 ($940,000) in 2007, it could only give around £30,000 ($47,000) to charity. Karen Lynch took over as CEO, cutting costs, outsourcing significant parts of the company's operations, and redesigning the entire business model; the company now donates four times as much to charity (Hurley). The conventional portrayal of do-gooders is that they tend to be terrible businesspeople, an argument often grounded in reality. It is easy to criticize the Walmarts of the world for caring little about sustainability or social good, but the idealists with big visions who do not follow through on their promises because their businesses

STUDENT WRITING

Mercer-Golden 4

Return to thesis: businesses should learn from one another

cannot survive are no more praiseworthy. Walmart should learn from nonprofits and social enterprises on advancing a positive environmental and social agenda, but idealist entrepreneurs should also learn from corporations about building successful businesses.

Transition to second part of thesis signaled

Problem explained

Reasons in support of claim

The final piece of the sustainable business ecosystem is the investors who help get potentially world-changing companies off the ground. Industries that require a large amount of money to build complex products with expensive materials, such as solar power companies, rely heavily on investors—often venture capitalists based in California's Silicon Valley (Knight). The problem is that venture capitalists are not doing enough to fund truly groundbreaking companies. In an oft-cited blog post titled "Why Facebook Is Killing Silicon Valley," entrepreneur Steve Blank argues that the financial returns on social media companies have been so quick and so outsized that the companies with the *really* big ideas—like providing efficient, cheap, scalable solar power—are not being backed: "In the past, if you were a great [venture capitalist], you could make $100 million on an investment in 5–7 years. Today, social media startups can return hundreds of millions or even billions in less than 3 years." The point Blank makes is that what is earning investors lots of money right now is not what is best for the United States or the world.

Transition signaling reason for optimism

Reason presented

There are, however, signs of hope. PayPal founder Peter Thiel runs his venture capital firm, the Founders Fund, on the philosophy that investors should support "flying cars" instead of new social media ventures (Packer). While the next company with the mission of making photo-sharing cooler or communicating with friends easier might be both profitable and valuable, Thiel and a select few others fund technology that has the potential to solve the huge problems essential to human survival.

STUDENT WRITING

Mercer-Golden 5

The world's need for sustainable companies that can build products from renewable energy or make nonpolluting cars will inevitably create opportunities for smart companies to make money. In fact, significant opportunities already exist for venture capitalists willing to step away from what is easy today and shift their investment strategies toward what will help us continue to live on this planet tomorrow—even if seeing strong returns may take a few more years. Visionaries like Blank and Thiel need more allies (and dollars) in their fight to help produce more pioneering, sustainable companies. And global warming won't abate before investors wise up. It is vital that this shift happen now.

Emotional appeal

When we think about organizations today, we think about nonprofits, which have long-term social missions, and corporations, which we judge by their immediate financial returns like quarterly earnings. That is a treacherous dichotomy. Instead, we need to see the three major players in the business ecosystem—corporations, social enterprises, and investors—moving toward a *single* model of long-term, sustainable capitalism. We need visionary companies that not only set out to solve humankind's biggest problems but also have the business intelligence to accomplish these goals, and we need investors willing to fund these companies. Gore and Blood argue that "the imperative for change has never been greater." We will see this change when the world realizes that sustainable capitalism shares the same goals as creating a sustainable environment. Let us hope that this realization comes soon.

Logical appeal

Thesis revisited

Quotation, restatement of thesis, and emotional appeal close argument

STUDENT WRITING

Mercer-Golden 6

Works Cited

"About Us." *Generation*, 2012, www.generationim.com/about/.

Blank, Steve. "Why Facebook Is Killing Silicon Valley." *Steveblank .com*, 21 May 2012, steveblank.com/2012/05/21/why -facebook-is-killing-silicon-valley/.

Church, Jeff. "The Wave of Social Entrepreneurship." Entrepreneurial Thought Leaders Seminar, NVIDIA Auditorium, Stanford, 11 Apr. 2012. Lecture.

Eccles, Robert G., et al. "The Impact of a Corporate Culture of Sustainability on Organizational Process and Performance." *Working Knowledge*, Harvard Business School, 14 Nov. 2011, hbswk.hbs.edu/item/the-impact-of-corporate-sustainability -on-organizational-process-and-performance.

Gore, Al, and David Blood. "Sustainable Capitalism." *Generation,* 15 Feb. 2012, www.generationim.com/media/pdf-generation -sustainable-capitalism-v1.pdf.

Hurley, James. "Belu Boss Shows Bottle for a Turnaround." *Daily Telegraph,* 28 Feb. 2012, www.telegraph.co.uk/finance/ businessclub/9109449/Belu-boss-shows-bottle-for -a-turnaround.html.

Knight, Eric R. W. "The Economic Geography of Clean Tech Venture Capital." Oxford University Working Paper Series in Employment, Work, and Finance, 13 Apr. 2010. *Social Science Research Network,* doi:10.2139/ssrn.1588806.

Packer, George. "No Death, No Taxes: The Libertarian Futurism of a Silicon Valley Billionaire." *The New Yorker,* 28 Nov. 2011, www .newyorker.com/magazine/2011/11/28/no-death-no -taxes.

9 Writing in a Variety of Disciplines and Genres

One of your goals as a writer will be to learn to enter the conversations going on in different academic disciplines—learning to "talk the talk" and "walk the walk" in each one. You will begin to get a sense of such differences as you prepare assignments for courses in the humanities, social sciences, and natural sciences. You are also likely to write in other, more public contexts with the goal of making a difference in the world, and you will need to make choices about how to reach your intended audience.

9a Recognizing expectations of academic disciplines

It's frustrating to know that there is no one single "correct" style of communication in any discipline. In addition, effective written styles differ from effective oral styles (Chapter 10), and what is considered good writing in one field of study may not be viewed as appropriate in another. Even the variety of English often referred to as "standard" covers a wide range of styles (21a). In each discipline you study, you can learn how to use different sets of conventions, strategies, and resources.

Even though disciplinary expectations differ, you can begin figuring them out by becoming a bit of a sleuth, looking very closely at examples of good writing from any discipline and seeing what makes them tick.

Study disciplinary vocabulary. A good way to enter into the conversation of a field or discipline is to study its vocabulary. Highlight key terms in your reading or notes to help you distinguish any

Academic, Professional, & Public Writing: Academic Work in Any Discipline > Video Prompt

Academic, Professional, & Public Writing: Writing for the Humanities > 2 Student Writing Samples

Academic, Professional, & Public Writing: Writing for the Natural & Applied Sciences > 2 Student Writing Samples specialized terms. Mark any disciplinary jargon that isn't familiar to you and ask for clarification from the instructor or fellow students. And pay careful attention to your textbook's vocabulary: try to master unfamiliar terms quickly by checking to see if the textbook has a glossary, by asking your instructor questions, and by looking up key words or phrases.

Study disciplinary style. Here are some questions that will help you identify a discipline's stylistic features:

- How would you describe the overall tone of the writing? Do writers in the field usually strive for an objective stance? (See 1g.) Are they more aggressive or argumentative?
- Is the level of writing highly formal, highly technical, aimed at a general audience, or informal and conversational?
- Do they use the first person (*I*) or prefer such terms as *one* or *the investigator*? What is the effect of this choice?
- In general, how long are the sentences and paragraphs?
- Are verbs generally active or passive—and why? (See 29g.)
- How many and what kind of examples seem to be featured?
- How does the writing integrate visual elements—graphs, tables, charts, photographs, or maps—or include video or sound?
- How is the writing organized? Does it typically include certain features, such as an abstract, a discussion of methods, headings, or other formatting elements?

Study the use of evidence. As you grow familiar with any area of study, you will develop a sense of what it takes to prove a point in that field. As you read assigned materials, consider the following questions about evidence:

- How do writers in the field use precedent, authority, and evidence?
- What kinds of quantitative data (items that can be counted and measured) and qualitative data (items that can be systematically observed) are used—and why?
- How is logical reasoning used? How are definition, cause and effect, analogy, and example used in this discipline?

- What are the primary materials—the firsthand sources of information—in this field? What are the secondary materials—the sources of information derived from others? (See 11c.)
- How is research (by others, or by the authors) used and integrated into the text?
- What documentation style is typically used in this field? (See Chapters 15–18.)

EVIDENCE IN THE HUMANITIES. Evidence for assignments in the humanities may come from a primary source you are examining closely, such as a poem, a philosophical treatise, an artifact, or a painting. For certain assignments, secondary sources such as journal articles or reference works can also provide useful evidence. Ground your analysis of each source in key questions about the work you are examining that will lead you to a thesis.

EVIDENCE IN THE SOCIAL SCIENCES. You will need to understand both the quantitative and qualitative evidence used in your sources as well as other evidence you may create from research you conduct on your own. Summarizing and synthesizing information drawn from sources will be key to your success.

EVIDENCE IN THE NATURAL AND APPLIED SCIENCES. You will probably draw on two major sources of evidence: research—including studies, experiments, and analyses—conducted by credible scientists, and research you conduct by yourself or with others. Each source should provide a strong piece of evidence for your project.

9b Understanding and using genres

Early on in your writing in any discipline, consider the **genre** or kind of text the instructor expects you to produce: a lab report for biology, for example, or a review of the literature for psychology, or a proposal for political science. If you are not sure what kind of text you are supposed to write, ask for clarification from your instructor, and check to see if your school's writing center has examples of such genres as well. You can ask your instructor to recommend excellent examples of the kind of writing you will do in the course, and you can also take a look at major scholarly journals to find other examples of the genre you are aiming to write. You may also gather multiple examples to get a sense of how different writers approach the same genre. Then ask what genres seem to be most prevalent in your discipline: what is their major purpose?

Consider organization. Genres often use a generally agreed-upon organizational plan. A typical laboratory report, for instance, follows a fairly standard framework (often the "introduction, methods, results, and discussion" format known as IMRAD) and uses these as major headings in the report. Ask:

- How exactly is the text organized in this genre?
- What are its main parts?
- Are the parts labeled with headings?

Consider format. Genres sometimes have an agreed-upon format. Also ask:

- Is a title page called for? If so, what should be on it?
- What size and shape does the genre call for? a trifold layout? or double-columned or double-sided? Does it feature information in boxes or sidebars?
- Does an abstract precede the main text? If so, how long is it?
- What kind of spacing is used? What are typical fonts?
- Does the genre seem to call for the use of color?
- Does the genre call for use of visuals or other illustrations?
- Does the genre seem to have a typical way of beginning or ending?

9c Adapting genre structures

Learning to borrow and adapt transitional devices and pieces of sentence structure from other writing in the genre in which you are working is one way to help you learn the conventions of that discipline. Avoid copying the whole structure, however, or your borrowed sentences may seem plagiarized (Chapter 13). Find sample sentence structures from similar genres but on different topics so that you borrow a typical structure (which does not belong to anyone) rather than the idea or the particular phrasing. Write your own sentences first, and look at other people's sentences just to guide your revision.

ABSTRACT FROM A SOCIAL SCIENCE PAPER

Using the interpersonal communications research of J. K. Brilhart and G. J. Galanes, along with T. Hartman's personality assessment, I observed and analyzed the group dynamics of my project collaborators in a communications course. Based on results of the Hartman personality assessment, I predicted that a single leader would emerge. However, complementary individual strengths and gender differences encouraged a distributed leadership style.

EFFECTIVE BORROWING OF STRUCTURES

Drawing on the research of Deborah Tannen on conversational styles, I analyzed the conversational styles of six first-year students at DePaul University. Based on Tannen's research, I expected that the three men I observed would use features typical of male conversational style and the three women would use features typical of female conversational style. In general, these predictions were accurate; however, some exceptions were also apparent.

EXERCISE 9.1 Consider some of the genres that you have encountered as a student, jotting down answers to the following questions and bringing them to class for discussion.

1. What are some genres that you read but don't usually write?
2. What are some genres that you write for teachers?
3. What are some genres that you write to or with other students?
4. What are some genres that you will likely encounter in your major or in your career?
5. How are some of the genres you listed different from those you encountered in high school?

9d Choosing genres for public writing

At some point during your college years or soon after, you are highly likely to create writing that is not just something you turn in for a grade but writing that is important to you because it tries to make something good happen. Public writing has a very clear purpose, is intended for a specific audience, and addresses that audience directly, usually in straightforward, everyday language. It uses the genre most suited to its purpose and audience (a poster, a newsletter, a brochure, a letter to the editor), and it appears in a medium (print, online, or both) where the intended audience will see it. For example, if you want to convince your neighbors to pool time, effort, and resources to build a local playground, you might decide that a print flyer delivered door-to-door and posted at neighborhood gathering places would work best. If you want to create a flash mob to publicize ineffective security at chemical plants near your city, on the other hand, an easily forwarded message—text, tweet, or email—will probably work best.

 9e STUDENT WRITING Samples in a variety of disciplines and genres

The following pages show examples of some of the many forms academic and public writing can take.

Student writing in academic disciplines

CLOSE READING OF POETRY. The following excerpt is taken from student Bonnie Sillay's close reading of two poems by E. E. Cummings, an assignment for her second-year American Literature seminar. This excerpt includes the introduction to the essay and Bonnie's reading of the first poem, "since feeling is first," in which she uses evidence from the poem to create her own interpretation. Note that she uses MLA style for her documentation (see Chapter 15). For the complete paper, see *LaunchPad Solo for Lunsford Handbooks.*

Academic, Professional, & Public Writing: Writing to Make Something Happen in the World > 5 Student Writing Samples

Academic, Professional, & Public Writing: Writing for Business > Video Prompt; Tutorial; 4 Student Writing Samples

STUDENT WRITING

Sillay 1

Bonnie Sillay
Instructor Angela Mitchell
English 1102
December 4, 2017

"Life's Not a Paragraph"

Throughout his poetry, E. E. Cummings leads readers deep into a thicket of scrambled words, missing punctuation, and unconventional structure. Within Cummings's poetic bramble, ambiguity leads the reader through what seems at first a confusing and winding maze. However, this confusion actually transforms into a path that leads the reader to the center of the thicket where Cummings's message lies: readers should not allow their experience to be limited by reason and rationality. In order to communicate his belief that emotional experience should triumph over reason, Cummings employs odd juxtapositions, outlandish metaphors, and inversions of traditional grammatical structures that reveal the illogic of reason. Indeed, by breaking down such formal boundaries, Cummings's poems "since feeling is first" and "as freedom is a breakfastfood" suggest that emotion, which provides the compositional fabric for our experience of life, should never be defined or controlled.

Present tense used to discuss poetry

Foreshadows discussion of work to come

Introductory paragraph ends with thesis statement

In "since feeling is first," Cummings urges his reader to reject attempts to control emotion, using English grammar as one example of the restrictive conventions present in society. Stating that "since feeling is first / who pays any attention / to the syntax of things" (lines 1-3), Cummings suggests that emotion should not be forced to fit into some preconceived framework or mold. He carries this message throughout the poem by juxtaposing images of the abstract and the concrete—images of emotion and of English grammar. Cummings's word choice enhances his intentionally strange juxtapositions, with the poet using grammatical terms that suggest regulation or confinement. For example, in the line "And death i think is no parenthesis" (16), Cummings uses the idea that parentheses

STUDENT WRITING

Sillay 2

confine the words they surround in order to warn the reader not to let death confine life or emotions.

Transition sentence connects the previous paragraph to this one

The structure of the poem also rejects traditional conventions. Instead of the final stanzas making the main point, Cummings opens his poem with his primary message, that "feeling is first" (1). Again, Cummings shows that emotion rejects order and structure. How can emotion be bottled in sentences and interrupted by commas, colons, and spaces? To Cummings, emotion is a never-ending run-on sentence that should not be diagrammed or dissected.

Quotation introduced effectively

Metaphor captures the spirit of Cummings's point

In the third stanza of "since feeling is first," Cummings states his point outright, noting "my blood approves, / and kisses are a better fate / than wisdom" (7-9). Here, Cummings argues for reveling in the feeling during a fleeting moment such as a kiss. He continues, "the best gesture of my brain is less than / your eyelids' flutter" (11-12). Cummings wants the reader to focus on a pure emotive response (the flutter of an eyelash) — on the emotional, not the logical — on the meanings of words instead of punctuation and grammar.

Cummings's use of words such as *kisses* and *blood* (8, 7) adds to the focus on the emotional. The ideas behind these words are difficult to confine or restrict to a single definition: kisses mean different things to different people, blood flows through the body freely and continually. The words are not expansive or free enough to encompass all that they suggest. Cummings ultimately paints language as more restrictive than the flowing, powerful force of emotion.

Paragraph reiterates Cummings's claim and sums up his argument

The poet's use of two grammatical terms in the last lines, "for life's not a paragraph / And death i think is no parenthesis," warns against attempts to format lives and feelings into conventional and rule-bound segments (15-16). Attempts to control, rather than feel, are rejected throughout "since feeling is first." Emotion should be limitless, free from any restrictions or rules.

STUDENT WRITING

Sillay 3

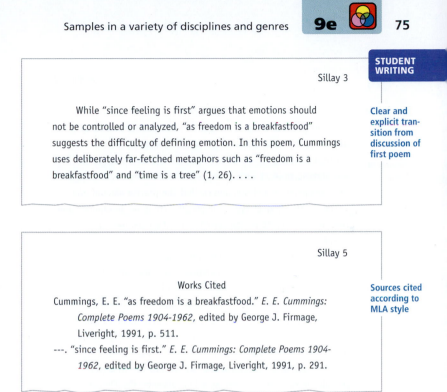

While "since feeling is first" argues that emotions should not be controlled or analyzed, "as freedom is a breakfastfood" suggests the difficulty of defining emotion. In this poem, Cummings uses deliberately far-fetched metaphors such as "freedom is a breakfastfood" and "time is a tree" (1, 26). . . .

Clear and explicit transition from discussion of first poem

Sillay 5

Works Cited

Cummings, E. E. "as freedom is a breakfastfood." *E. E. Cummings: Complete Poems 1904-1962*, edited by George J. Firmage, Liveright, 1991, p. 511.

---. "since feeling is first." *E. E. Cummings: Complete Poems 1904-1962*, edited by George J. Firmage, Liveright, 1991, p. 291.

Sources cited according to MLA style

PSYCHOLOGY LITERATURE REVIEW. For her psychology class, student Tawnya Redding was assigned to write a literature review that follows the conventions of social science writing in this genre. Tawnya chose to analyze published research for evidence of a causal relationship between certain genres of music and depression in adolescents. To read her paper, see 16e.

CHEMISTRY LAB REPORT. Student Allyson Goldberg prepared a lab report on an experiment she was assigned as part of her chemistry class. The excerpt that follows includes the Introduction, Materials and Methods, and Results sections of the report. Not included are the title page, which comes first in such reports, the discussion section, and the conclusion. For the complete report, see *LaunchPad Solo for Lunsford Handbooks.*

STUDENT WRITING

Goldberg 2

Introduction explains purpose of lab and gives overview of results

Introduction

The purpose of this investigation was to experimentally determine the value of the universal gas constant, R. To accomplish this goal, a measured sample of magnesium (Mg) was allowed to react with an excess of hydrochloric acid (HCl) at room temperature and pressure so that the precise amount and volume of the product hydrogen gas (H_2) could be determined and the value of R could be calculated using the ideal gas equation, PV=nRT.

Materials and methods section explains lab setup and procedure

Materials & Methods

Two samples of room temperature water, one about 250mL and the other about 400mL, were measured into a smaller and larger beaker, respectively. 15.0mL of HCl was then transferred into a side arm flask that was connected to the top of a buret (clamped to a ringstand) through a 5/16″ diameter flexible tube. (This "gas buret" was connected to an adjacent "open buret," clamped to the other side of the ringstand and left open to the atmosphere of the laboratory at its wide end, by a 1/4″ diameter flexible tube. These two burets were adjusted on the ringstand so that they were vertically parallel and close together.) The HCl sample was transferred to the flask such that none came in contact with the inner surface of the neck of the flask. The flask was then allowed to rest, in an almost horizontal position, in the smaller beaker.

The open buret was adjusted on the ringstand such that its 20mL mark was horizontally aligned with the 35mL mark on the gas buret. Room temperature water was added to the open buret until the water level of the gas buret was at about 34.00mL.

Passive voice throughout is typical of writing in natural sciences

A piece of magnesium ribbon was obtained, weighed on an analytical balance, and placed in the neck of the horizontal side arm flask. Next, a screw cap was used to cap the flask and form an airtight seal. This setup was then allowed to sit for 5 minutes in order to reach thermal equilibrium.

STUDENT WRITING

Goldberg 3

After 5 minutes, the open buret was adjusted so that the menisci on both burets were level with each other; the side arm flask was then tilted vertically to let the magnesium ribbon react with the HCl. After the brisk reaction, the flask was placed into the larger beaker and allowed to sit for another 5 minutes.

Next, the flask was placed back into the smaller beaker, and the open buret was adjusted on the ringstand such that its meniscus was level with that of the gas buret. After the system sat for an additional 30 minutes, the open buret was again adjusted so that the menisci on both burets were level.

This procedure was repeated two more times, with the exception that HCl was not again added to the side arm flask, as it was already present in enough excess for all reactions from the first trial.

Results and Calculations

Data is organized in a table

Trial #	Lab Temp. (°C)	Lab Pressure (mbar)	Mass of Mg Ribbon Used (g)	Initial Buret Reading (mL)	Final Buret Reading (mL)
1	24.4	1013	0.0147	32.66	19.60
2	24.3	1013	0.0155	33.59	N/A*
3	25.0	1013	0.0153	34.35	19.80

*See note in Discussion section.

Trial #	Volume of H_2 (L)	Moles of H_2 Gas Produced	Lab Temp. (K)	Partial Pressure of H_2 (atm)	Value of R (L atm/ mol K)	Mean Value of R (L atm/ mol K)
1	0.01306	6.05×10^{-4}	298	0.970	0.0704	0.0728
2	N/A	N/A	N/A	N/A	N/A	
3	0.01455	6.30×10^{-4}	298	0.968	0.0751	

Table 1 Experiment results

Student writing in more public contexts

POSTER. Student Hebron Warren won first place in the New York City Police Department's contest for posters encouraging victims to report campus sexual assaults to the police. Hebron's eye-catching design focuses on the action he wants audiences to take: "Speak up!" He uses visual symmetry to emphasize that assaults happen to both men and women, and includes simple statistics to persuade the audience that too few of these crimes are reported. The message is concise and simple enough to be understood quickly by passers-by.

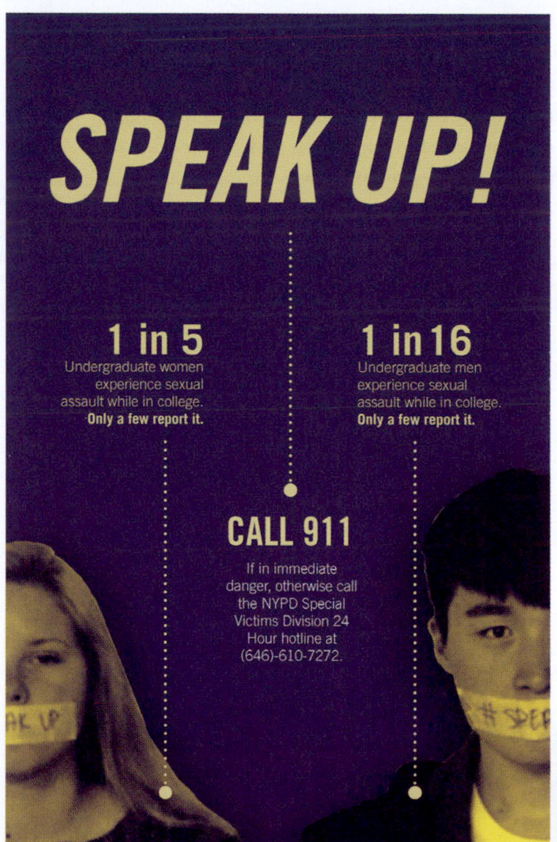

WARREN HEBRON/NYPD

FUNDRAISING WEB PAGE. Student Justin Dart created this fundraising web page with a very clear purpose: to crowd-source the funding to help Jey, a young street vendor in Accra, Ghana, get a college education. Using the Indiegogo template, Justin posted a video spelling out the background and purpose of his fundraiser, a short written description of the project, and a list of perks for donors at various levels. Other tabs offered updates from Justin on his progress, comments from donors, photos, and more. To reach as many people as possible, Justin shared this page with his friends and acquaintances and urged them to share it on social media outlets. Justin ended up raising enough to pay for Jey's university tuition for his college career, as well as housing and incidentals.

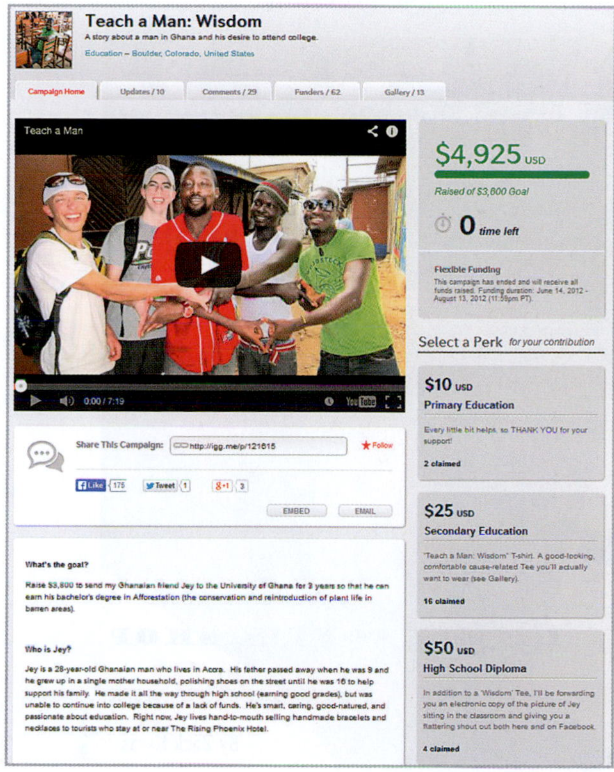

WEB COMIC. Student Zack Karas worked with a team of classmates on an assignment to do field research in a public space. His group chose a local coffee shop, and after conducting observations of the environment and the interactions among people there, they presented a critical analysis of the coffee-drinking scene to the rest of the class.

Zack then used his team's coffee shop experience as the basis for a comic, which he posted on a blog created to host his artwork. The final panels include a twist: Zack's comic avatar fails to recognize that he, like many of the customers, is also a "post-ironic hipster . . . with facial hair, a hoodie, and an iPhone." Turning the report into a comic allowed Zack to reach an audience beyond his classmates—readers who share his interest in humor, online comics, and the critique of the coffee-culture demographic.

ZACK KARAS

NEWSLETTER. As with the creators of the fundraising web page and web comic, yoga teacher Joelle Hann has a clear purpose in mind for her e-newsletter: to provide information to her audience—students and others interested in her yoga classes and developments in the yoga community. Emailing the newsletter to her subscribers allows Joelle to reach an interested audience quickly and to provide links to more of the content she's discussing, and it also means that she can include photos, illustrations, and color to enhance her document's design impact.

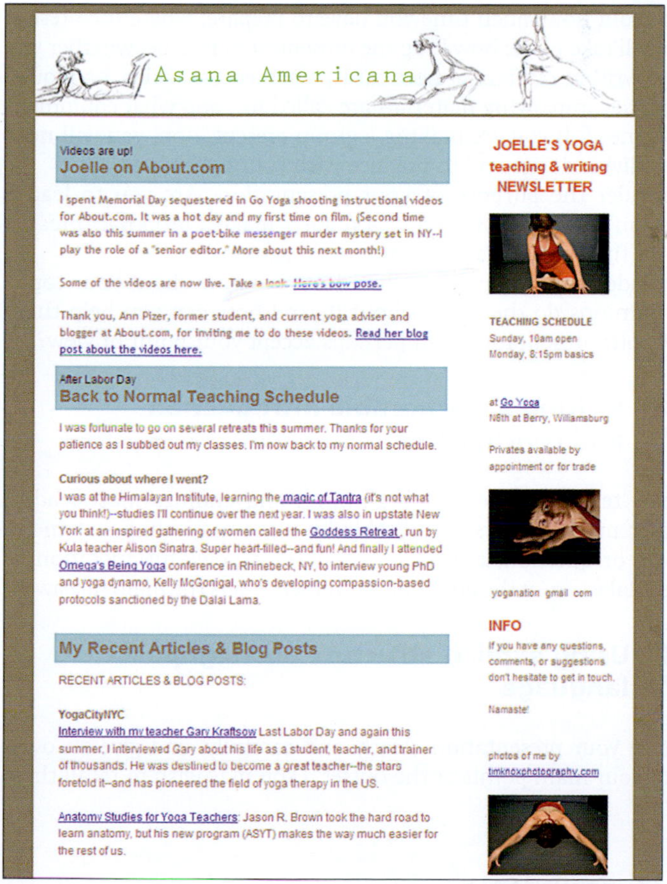

Asana Americana

Videos are up!

Joelle on About.com

I spent Memorial Day sequestered in Go Yoga shooting instructional videos for About.com. It was a hot day and my first time on film. (Second time was also this summer in a poet-bike messenger murder mystery set in NY--I play the role of a "senior editor." More about this next month!)

Some of the videos are now live. Take a look. Here's bow pose.

Thank you, Ann Pizer, former student, and current yoga adviser and blogger at About.com, for inviting me to do these videos. Read her blog post about the videos here.

After Labor Day

Back to Normal Teaching Schedule

I was fortunate to go on several retreats this summer. Thanks for your patience as I subbed out my classes. I'm now back to my normal schedule.

Curious about where I went?

I was at the Himalayan Institute, learning the magic of Tantra (it's not what you think!)--studies I'll continue over the next year. I was also in upstate New York at an inspired gathering of women called the Goddess Retreat, run by Kula teacher Alison Sinatra. Super heart-filled--and fun! And finally I attended Omega's Being Yoga conference in Rhinebeck, NY, to interview young PhD and yoga dynamo, Kelly McGonigal, who's developing compassion-based protocols sanctioned by the Dalai Lama.

My Recent Articles & Blog Posts

RECENT ARTICLES & BLOG POSTS:

YogaCityNYC

Interview with my teacher Gary Kraftsow Last Labor Day and again this summer, I interviewed Gary about his life as a student, teacher, and trainer of thousands. He was destined to become a great teacher--the stars foretold it--and has pioneered the field of yoga therapy in the US.

Anatomy Studies for Yoga Teachers: Jason R. Brown took the hard road to learn anatomy, but his new program (ASYT) makes the way much easier for the rest of us.

JOELLE'S YOGA teaching & writing NEWSLETTER

TEACHING SCHEDULE
Sunday, 10am open
Monday, 8:15pm basics

at Go Yoga
N6th at Berry, Williamsburg

Privates available by appointment or for trade

yoganation gmail com

INFO

If you have any questions, comments, or suggestions don't hesitate to get in touch.

Namaste!

photos of me by
timknoxphotography.com

10 Creating Presentations

It's a good idea to jump at every opportunity you can to make presentations, since this form of creating and sharing knowledge is getting more and more prominent in almost all fields. This chapter will help you put your best foot forward as you do so.

10a Considering task, purpose, and audience

Think about how much time you have to prepare; where the presentation will take place; how long the presentation is to be; whether you will use written-out text or note cards; whether visual aids, handouts, or other accompanying materials are called for; and what equipment you will need. If you are making a group presentation, you will need time to divide duties and to practice with your classmates.

Consider the purpose of your presentation. Are you to lead a discussion? teach a lesson? give a report? make a proposal? present research findings? engage a group in an activity?

Consider your audience. What do they know about your topic, what opinions do they have about it, and how can you help them follow your presentation and perhaps accept your point of view?

10b Writing a memorable introduction and conclusion

Listeners tend to remember beginnings and endings most readily. Consider making yours memorable by using a startling statement, opinion, or question; a vivid anecdote; or a powerful quotation or image. Make sure at the end that the audience gets the main takeaway!

10c Using explicit structure and signpost language

Organize your presentation clearly and carefully, and give an overview of your main points at the outset. (You may wish to recall these

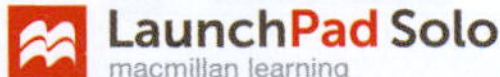

Designing & Performing Writing: Presentations > 4 Video Prompts; Tutorial

points toward the end of the talk.) Then pause between major points, and use signpost language as you move from one idea to the next. Such signposts should be clear and concrete: *The second crisis point in the breakup of the Soviet Union occurred hard on the heels of the first* instead of *Another thing about the Soviet Union's problems. . . .* You can also offer signposts by repeating key words and ideas; avoiding long, complicated sentences; and using as many concrete verbs and nouns as possible. If you are talking about abstract ideas, try to provide concrete examples for each.

10d Preparing a script for ease of presentation

If you decide to speak from a full script of your presentation, use fairly large double- or triple-spaced print that will be easy to read. End each page with the end of a sentence so that you won't have to pause while you turn a page. Whether you speak from a full text, a detailed outline, note cards, or points on flip charts or slides, mark the places where you want to pause, and highlight the words you want to emphasize. (If you are using presentation software, print out a paper version and mark it up.)

10e Planning visuals

Visuals carry a lot of the message the speaker wants to convey, so think of your visuals not as add-ons but as a major means of getting your points across. Many speakers use presentation software (such as PowerPoint or Prezi) to help keep themselves on track and to guide the audience. In addition, posters, flip charts, chalkboards, or interactive whiteboards can also help you make strong visual statements.

When you work with visuals for your own presentation, remember that they must be large enough to be easily seen and read. Be sure the information is simple, clear, and easy to understand. And remember *not* to read from your visuals or turn your back on your audience as you refer to them. Most important, make sure your visuals engage and help your listeners rather than distract them from your message. Try out each visual on classmates or friends: if they do not clearly grasp the meaning and purpose of the visual, scrap it and try again.

Slides. Here are some guidelines for preparing effective slides:

- Don't put too much information on one slide; one simple word or picture may make your point most effectively. Avoid using more than three to five bullet points (or more than forty words) on any slide, and never read them to your audience. Instead, say something to enhance, explain, or emphasize what's on the slide.
- Use light backgrounds in a darkened room, dark backgrounds in a lighted one.
- Make sure that audio or video clips with sound are clearly audible.
- Use only images large and sharp enough to be clearly visible to your audience.

Handouts. You may also want to prepare handouts for your audience: pertinent bibliographies, for example, or text too extensive to be presented otherwise. Unless the handouts include material you want your audience to use while you speak, distribute them at the end of the presentation.

 Checklist

Reviewing Your Presentation

Before your instructor or another audience evaluates your presentation, do a review for yourself:

- Does your presentation have a clear thesis, a compelling introduction and conclusion, and a simple, clear structure?
- Do you use sources to support your points and demonstrate your knowledge? Do you include a works-cited slide at the end of the presentation?
- Is your use of media (posters, slides, video clips, and so on) appropriate for your topic and thesis? If you are using slides, will they appeal to your audience and make your points effectively?
- Do you use clear signpost language and effective repetition?
- Are you satisfied with your delivery—your tone and projection of voice, pacing, and stance?

10f Practicing

Set aside enough time to practice your presentation—including the use of all visuals—at least twice. You might also record your rehearsals, or practice in front of a mirror or with friends who can comment on content and style.

Timing your run-throughs will tell you whether you need to cut (or expand) material to make the presentation an appropriate length.

10g Delivering the presentation

To calm your nerves and get off to a good start, know your material thoroughly and use the following strategies to good advantage before, during, and after your presentation:

- Visualize your presentation with the aim of feeling comfortable during it.
- Do some deep-breathing exercises before the presentation, and concentrate on relaxing; avoid too much caffeine.
- If possible, stand up. Most speakers make a stronger impression standing rather than sitting.
- Face your audience, and make eye contact as much as possible.
- Allow time for questions.
- Thank the audience at the end of your presentation.

 STUDENT WRITING Excerpts from a presentation

Here's the opening of the script Shuqiao Song prepared for her oral/multimedia presentation, "Words, Images, and the Mystical Way They Work Together in Alison Bechdel's *Fun Home*."

> Welcome, everyone. I'm Shuqiao Song and I'm here today to talk about "The Residents of a Dys*FUN*ctional *HOME*." We meet these characters in a graphic memoir called *Fun Home,* which later became a hit Broadway

> musical. [Here Song showed a three-second video clip of author Alison Bechdel saying, "I love words, and I love pictures. But especially, I love them together—in a mystical way I can't even explain."]
>
> That was Alison Bechdel, author of *Fun Home*. In that clip, she conveniently introduces the topics of my presentation today: Words. Pictures. And the mystical way they work together.

Note that this presentation opens with a play on words ("Dys*FUN*ctional *HOME*"), to which Song returns later on, and with a short, vivid video clip that sums up her main topic. Also note the use of short sentences and fragments, special effects that act like drumbeats to get and hold the audience's attention.

Song developed a series of very simple slides to underscore her points and keep her audience focused on them. See her full presentation, with slides, in *LaunchPad Solo for Lunsford Handbooks*.

Research

11 Conducting Research 88

12 Evaluating Sources and Taking Notes 97

13 Integrating Sources and Avoiding Plagiarism 112

14 Writing a Research Project 119

11 Conducting Research

Your employer asks you to recommend the best software for a project. You need to plan a week's stay in Toronto. Your instructor assigns a term project about a groundbreaking musician. Each of these situations calls for research, for examining various kinds of sources—and each calls for you to assess the data you collect, synthesize your findings, and come up with an original recommendation or conclusion. Many tasks that call for research require that your work culminate in a document—whether print or digital—that refers to and lists the sources you used.

11a Understanding challenges to research today

Writers today have more information at their fingertips than any at time in history, so you'd think research would be easier to conduct. But think again: just because there's more information available doesn't mean it is good or credible information; misinformation and even "reports" full of outright lies are now commonplace on social media. So what's a poor researcher to do? First, recognize the challenges that face you and remember not to take sources at face value. That's what two University of Washington science professors are doing with a new course that teaches students to recognize how statistics and visual representation of data (especially "big" data) can be used to misinform and confuse. So get accustomed to digging into source information to find out who is responsible for it and to check facts. (See 12a for concrete steps you can take to do so.) And remember never to rely solely on social media as your main source: instead, stick with fully credible sources you can access through library databases and reliable, ethical websites. (See 11d and 11e.) As a researcher, you want to be able to vouch for your sources, to make sure that they are accurate, credible, and trustworthy.

11b Beginning the research process

Once you have your skeptical/critical hat on and have a topic that's assigned to you or that you chose, move as efficiently as possible to analyze the assignment, articulate a research question to answer, and form a hypothesis. Then, after your preliminary research is complete, you can refine your hypothesis into a working thesis and begin your research in earnest.

Considering context. Ask yourself what the *purpose* of the research project is—perhaps to describe, survey, analyze, persuade, explain, classify, compare, or contrast. Then consider your *audience.* Who will be most interested, and what will they need to know? What assumptions might they hold? What response do you want from them? Also examine your own *stance* or *attitude* toward your topic. Do you feel curious, critical, confused, or some other way about it? What influences have shaped your stance?

Then consider how many and what *kinds of sources* you need to find. What kinds of evidence will help your audience understand or agree with your position? What visuals—charts, photographs, and so on—might you need? Would it help to do field research, such as interviews, surveys, or observations? Finally, consider how long your project will be, how much time it will take, and when it is due.

Formulating a research question and hypothesis. After analyzing your project's context, work from your general topic to a research question and a hypothesis.

TOPIC	Farming
NARROWED TOPIC	Small family farms in the United States
ISSUE	Making a living from a small family farm
RESEARCH QUESTION	How can small family farms in the United States successfully compete with big agriculture?

HYPOTHESIS	Small family farmers can succeed by growing specialty products that consumers want and by participating in farmers' markets and community-supported agriculture programs that forge relationships with customers.

After you have explored sources to test your hypothesis and sharpened it by reading, writing, and talking with others, you can refine it into a working thesis (2b).

WORKING THESIS	Although recent data show that small family farms are more endangered than ever, some enterprising farmers have reversed the trend by growing specialized products and connecting with consumers through farmers' markets and community-supported agriculture programs.

Planning research. Once you have formulated your hypothesis, determine what you already know about it and where you found this information. Think hard about the kinds of sources you expect to consult—articles, print or digital books, specialized reference works, experts on your own campus, and so on—and the number you think you will need, how current they should be, and where you might find them.

11c Choosing among types of sources

Keep in mind some important differences among types of sources.

Primary and secondary sources. **Primary sources** provide you with firsthand knowledge, while **secondary sources** report on or analyze the research of others. Primary sources are basic sources of raw information, including your own field research; films, works of art, or other objects you examine; literary works you read; and eyewitness accounts, photographs, news reports, and historical documents. Secondary sources are descriptions or interpretations of primary sources, such as researchers' reports, reviews, biographies, and encyclopedia articles. What constitutes a primary or secondary source depends on the purpose of your research. A film review, for instance, serves as a secondary source if you are writing about the film but as a primary source if you are studying the critic's writing.

Scholarly and popular sources. Nonacademic sources like magazines can be helpful if they are written by knowledgeable and credible people, but you will usually want to depend more on authorities in a field, whose work has been vetted by others and generally appears in scholarly journals. Here are some tips for distinguishing between scholarly and popular sources:

SCHOLARLY	POPULAR
Title often contains the word *Journal*	*Journal* usually does not appear in title
Source is available mainly through libraries and library databases	Source is generally available outside of libraries (at newsstands or from a home Internet connection)
Few or no commercial advertisements	Many advertisements
Authors are identified with academic credentials	Authors are usually journalists or reporters hired by the publication, not academics or experts
Summary or abstract appears on first page of article; articles are fairly long	No summary or abstract; articles are fairly short
Articles cite sources and provide bibliographies	Articles may include quotations but do not cite sources or provide bibliographies

SCHOLARLY

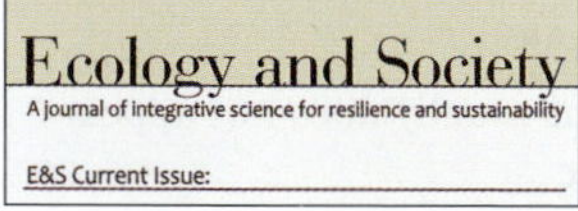

POPULAR

Older and more current sources. Most projects can benefit from both older, historical sources and more current ones. Some older sources are classics; others are simply dated.

11d Using library resources

Almost any research project should begin with a visit to your school's library.

Reference librarians. Your library's staff—especially reference librarians—can be a valuable resource. You can talk with a librarian about your research project and get specific recommendations about databases and other helpful places to begin your research. Many libraries also have online tours and chat rooms where students can ask questions.

Catalogs. Library catalogs show whether a book is housed in the library and, if so, offer a call number that helps you find the

Checklist

Effective Search Techniques

You can access many online catalogs, databases, and websites without actually going to the library. You can search the Internet by using carefully chosen keywords to limit the scope of your search and refine your search depending on what you find.

- Advanced search tools let you focus your search more narrowly—by combining terms with AND or eliminating them with NOT, by specifying dates and media types, and so on—so they may give you more relevant results.
- If you don't see an advanced search option, start with keywords. (Simply entering terms in the search box may bring up an advanced search option.) Check the first page or two of results. If you get many irrelevant options, think about how to refine your keywords to get more targeted results.
- Databases and search engines don't all refine searches the same way—for instance, some use AND, while others use the + symbol. Look for tips on making the most of the search tool you're using.
- Most college libraries classify material using the *Library of Congress Subject Headings*, or LCSH. When you find a library source that seems especially relevant, be sure to use the subject headings for that source as search terms to bring up all the entries under each heading.

book on the shelf. Because books are organized by subject, browsing through books near the one you've found in the catalog can help locate other works related to your topic. Catalogs also indicate where to find a particular periodical, either in print or in an online database, at the library.

Indexes and databases. Remember that most college libraries subscribe to a large number of indexes and databases that students can access online for free, and these sources contain much information that you will not have access to in a general Google search. Some databases include the full text of articles from newspapers, magazines, journals, and other works; some offer only short abstracts (summaries), which give an overview so you can decide whether to spend time finding and reading the whole text. Indexes of reviews provide information about a potential source's critical reception.

Check with a librarian for discipline-specific indexes and databases related to your topic.

Reference works. General reference works, such as encyclopedias, biographical resources, almanacs, digests, and atlases, can help you get an overview of a topic, identify subtopics, find more specialized sources, and identify keywords for searches.

Bibliographies. Bibliographies—lists of sources—in books or articles related to your topic can lead you to other valuable resources. Ask a librarian whether your library has more extensive bibliographies related to your research topic.

Other resources. Your library can help you borrow materials from other libraries (this can take time, so plan ahead). Check with reference librarians, too, about audio, video, multimedia, and art collections; government documents; and other special collections or archives that student researchers may be able to use.

11e Finding credible Internet sources

Many college students prefer to begin their research with general Internet searches. But remember that library databases come from identifiable and professionally edited resources—often with materials that you can get for free only through the library. So take special care to make sure information online is reliable and trustworthy (12a and 12b).

Internet searches. Research using a search tool such as Google usually begins with a keyword search (see the Checklist on p. 93). Many keyword searches bring up thousands of hits; you may find what you need on the first page or two of results, but if not, choose new keywords that lead to more specific sources.

Bookmarking tools. Today's powerful bookmarking tools can help you browse, sort, and track resources online. Social bookmarking sites allow users to tag information and share it with others. Users' tags are visible to all other users. If you find a helpful site, you can check how others have tagged it and browse similar tags for related information. You can also sort and group information with tags. Fellow users whose tags you trust can become part of your network so you can follow their sites of interest.

Web browsers can also help you bookmark online resources. However, unlike bookmarking tools in a browser, which are tied to one machine, you can use social bookmarking tools wherever you have an Internet connection.

Authoritative sources online. Many sources online are authoritative and reliable. You can browse collections in online virtual libraries, for example, or collections housed in government sites such as the Library of Congress, the National Institutes of Health, and the U.S. Census Bureau. For current national news, consult online versions of reputable newspapers such as the *Washington Post* or the *Wall Street Journal*, or sites for news services such as C-SPAN. Google Scholar can help you limit searches to scholarly works.

Some journals (such as those from Berkeley Electronic Press) and general-interest magazines (such as *Salon*) are published only online; many other print publications make at least some of their content available free on the web.

11f Doing field research

For many research projects, you will need to collect field data. Consider *where* you can find relevant information, *how* to gather it, and *who* might be your best providers of information. You may also want to talk with your instructor about any field research you plan to do, to make sure your research will not violate your college's guidelines for doing research that involves people.

Interviews. Some information is best obtained by asking direct questions of other people. If you can talk with an expert—in person, on the telephone, or online—you may get information you cannot obtain through any other kind of research.

- Determine your exact purpose, and be sure it relates to your research question and your hypothesis.
- Set up the interview well in advance. Specify how long it will take, and if you wish to record the session, ask permission to do so.
- Prepare a written list of factual and open-ended questions. If the interview proceeds in a direction that seems fruitful, don't feel that you have to ask all of your prepared questions.
- Record the subject, date, time, and place of the interview.
- Thank those you interview, either in person or in a letter or email.

Observation. Trained observers report that making a faithful record of an observation requires intense concentration and mental agility.

- Determine the purpose of the observation, how it relates to your research question and hypothesis, and what you think you may find.
- Brainstorm about what you are looking for, but don't be rigidly bound to your expectations.
- Develop an appropriate system for recording data. Consider using a split notebook or page: on one side, record your observations directly; on the other, record your thoughts or interpretations.
- Record the date, time, and place of observation.

Opinion surveys. Surveys usually depend on questionnaires. On any questionnaire, the questions should be clear and easy to understand and designed so that you can analyze the answers without difficulty. Questions that ask respondents to say *yes* or *no* or to rank items on a scale are easiest to tabulate.

- Write out your purpose, and determine the kinds of questions to ask.
- Figure out how to reach respondents—either online via email, apps, or social media; over the phone; or in person.
- Draft questions that call for short, specific answers.

- Test the questions on several people, and revise questions that seem unfair, ambiguous, or too hard or time-consuming.
- Draft a cover letter or invitation email. Be sure to state a deadline.
- If you are using a print questionnaire, leave adequate space for answers.
- Proofread the questionnaire carefully.

12 Evaluating Sources and Taking Notes

All research builds on the careful and sometimes inspired use of sources—that is, on research done by others. Since you want the information you glean from sources to be reliable and persuasive, evaluate each potential source carefully.

12a Checking facts

Especially with online sources, practice what media analyst Howard Rheingold calls "crap detection," which means identifying information that is faulty or deceptive. Rheingold recommends finding three separate credible online sources that corroborate the point you want to make. Here are some tips for becoming a good fact-checker:

- Consider the facts carefully. How accurate, complete, and trustworthy is the information in the source? How thorough is the bibliography or list of works cited that accompanies the source?
- Look for other credible sources that corroborate the facts you are checking. If you cannot find another source that verifies the fact, be suspicious!
- Become familiar with nonpartisan fact-checkers that can help you, like PolitiFact, FactCheck.org, and the Sunlight Foundation. Snopes .com is also useful for fact-checking general rumors and Internet memes.

- Be on the lookout for claims that are unsubstantiated, for quotations or statistics that are not attributed to a reliable source, for clickbait headlines or titles—that is, those that say "click me, click me"—and for nonstandard URLs.
- Also be attentive to the tone with which facts are presented or represented: if it is sensationalistic or highly exaggerated, take special care that the facts are not also exaggerated.

12b Evaluating the usefulness and credibility of potential sources

Use these guidelines to assess further the value of a source, and add useful sources to your working bibliography with notes about why you need them.

- **Your purpose.** How does the source add to your research project? Does it help you support a major point? demonstrate that you have researched the topic fully? help establish your credibility?
- **Relevance.** Is the source closely related to your research question? Read beyond the title and opening paragraph to check for relevance.
- **Publisher's credentials.** What do you know about the publisher of the source? For example, is it a major newspaper known for integrity in reporting, or is it a tabloid? Is the publisher a popular source, or is it sponsored by a professional or scholarly organization?
- **Author or sponsor's credentials.** Is the author an expert on the topic? Such credentials may be presented in the article, book, or website, or you can search the Internet for information on the author.
- **Author's purpose.** What claims is the source making? Look for unstated assumptions and biases behind such claims—and question them.

LaunchPad Solo
macmillan learning

Research: Evaluating Sources > 2 LearningCurve

- **Date of publication.** Recent sources are often more useful than older ones, particularly in fields that change rapidly. However, the most authoritative works may be older ones. The publication dates of Internet sites can often be difficult to pin down. And even for sites that include the dates of posting, remember that the material posted may have been composed sometime earlier.
- **Stance of source.** Identify the source's point of view or rhetorical stance, and scrutinize it carefully. Does the source present facts that you can verify? Does it interpret or evaluate them and if so, is this interpretation overly biased? If it presents facts, what is included and what is omitted, and why? If it interprets or evaluates information that is not disputed, the source's stance may be obvious, but at other times you will need to think carefully about the source's goals. What does the author or sponsoring group want—to convince you of an idea? sell you something? call you to action in some way?
- **Cross-referencing.** Is the source cited in other works? If it is cited by others, look at how they cite it and what they say about it to gain additional clues about its credibility.
- **Level of specialization.** General sources can be helpful as you begin your research, but you may then need the authority or currency of more specialized sources. On the other hand, extremely specialized works may be very hard to understand.
- **Audience of source.** Was the source written for the general public? specialists? advocates or opponents? a group with a particular bias or ideology?

For more on evaluating web sources and articles, see the source maps on pp. 100–103.

SOURCE MAP: Evaluating Web Sources

Is the sponsor credible?

1. Who is the **sponsor or publisher** of the source? See what information you can get from the URL. The domain names for government sites may end in *.gov* or *.mil* and for educational sites in *.edu*. The ending *.org* may—but does not always—indicate a nonprofit organization. If you see a tilde (~) or percent sign (%) followed by a name, or if you see a word such as *users* or *members*, the page's creator may be an individual, not an institution. Also check the header and footer, which may identify the sponsor. The web page on p. 101 comes from a site sponsored by the nonprofit Nieman Foundation for Journalism at Harvard University.

2. Look for an ***About page*** or a link to a home page for background information on the sponsor. Is a mission statement included? What are the sponsoring organization's purpose and point of view? Is the mission statement balanced? What is the purpose of the site (to inform, to persuade, to advocate, to advertise, or something else)? Does the information on the site come directly from the sponsor, or is the material reprinted from another source? If it is reprinted, check the original.

Is the author credible?

3. What are the **author's credentials**? Look for information accompanying the material on the page. You can also run a search on the author to find out more. Does the author seem qualified to write about this topic?

Is the information credible and current?

4. When was the information **posted or last updated**? Is it recent enough to be useful?

5. Does the page document sources with **footnotes or links**? If so, do the sources seem credible and current? Does the author include any additional resources for further information? Are the facts accurate? Look for ways to corroborate the information the author provides.

In addition, consider the following questions:

- What is the source's stance or point of view? What are the author's goals? What does the author want you to know or believe?
- How does this source fit in with your other sources? Does any of the information it provides contradict or challenge other sources?

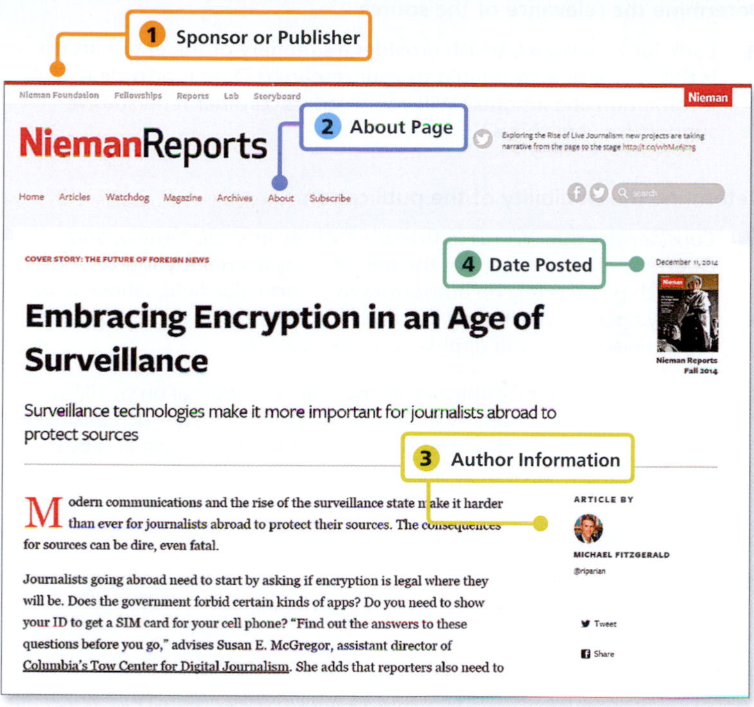
1 Sponsor or Publisher
Nieman Foundation
Fellowships
Reports
Lab
Storyboard
Nieman
NiemanReports
2 About Page
Home
Articles
Watchdog
Magazine
Archives
About
Subscribe
COVER STORY: THE FUTURE OF FOREIGN NEWS
4 Date Posted
December 11, 2014
Nieman Reports
Fall 2014
Embracing Encryption in an Age of Surveillance
Surveillance technologies make it more important for journalists abroad to protect sources
3 Author Information
ARTICLE BY
MICHAEL FITZGERALD
@riparian
Modern communications and the rise of the surveillance state make it harder than ever for journalists abroad to protect their sources. The consequences for sources can be dire, even fatal.
Journalists going abroad need to start by asking if encryption is legal where they will be. Does the government forbid certain kinds of apps? Do you need to show your ID to get a SIM card for your cell phone? "Find out the answers to these questions before you go," advises Susan E. McGregor, assistant director of Columbia's Tow Center for Digital Journalism. She adds that reporters also need to
Tweet
Share

SOURCE MAP: Evaluating Articles

Determine the relevance of the source.

1. Look for an **abstract**, which provides a summary of the entire article. Is this source directly related to your research? Does it provide useful information and insights? Will your readers consider it persuasive support for your thesis?

Determine the credibility of the publication.

2. Consider the **title**. Words in the title such as *Journal, Review*, and *Quarterly* may indicate that the periodical is a scholarly source. Most research projects rely on authorities in a particular field, whose work usually appears in scholarly journals. For more on distinguishing between scholarly and popular sources, see 11c.

3. Try to determine the **publisher or sponsor**. The journal on p. 103 is published by the University of Illinois. Academic presses such as this one generally review articles carefully before publishing them and bear the authority of their academic sponsors.

Determine the credibility of the author.

4. Evaluate the **author's credentials**. In this case, they are given in a note that indicates the author is a college professor.

Determine the currency of the article.

5. Look at the **publication date**, and think about whether your topic and your credibility depend on your use of very current sources.

Determine the accuracy of the article.

6. Look at the **sources cited** by the author of the article. Here, they are listed in a bibliography. Ask yourself whether the works the author has cited seem credible and current. Are any of these works cited in other articles you've considered?

In addition, consider the following questions:

- What is the article's stance or point of view? What are the author's goals? What does the author want you to know or believe?
- How does this source fit in with your other sources? Does any of the information it provides contradict or challenge other sources?

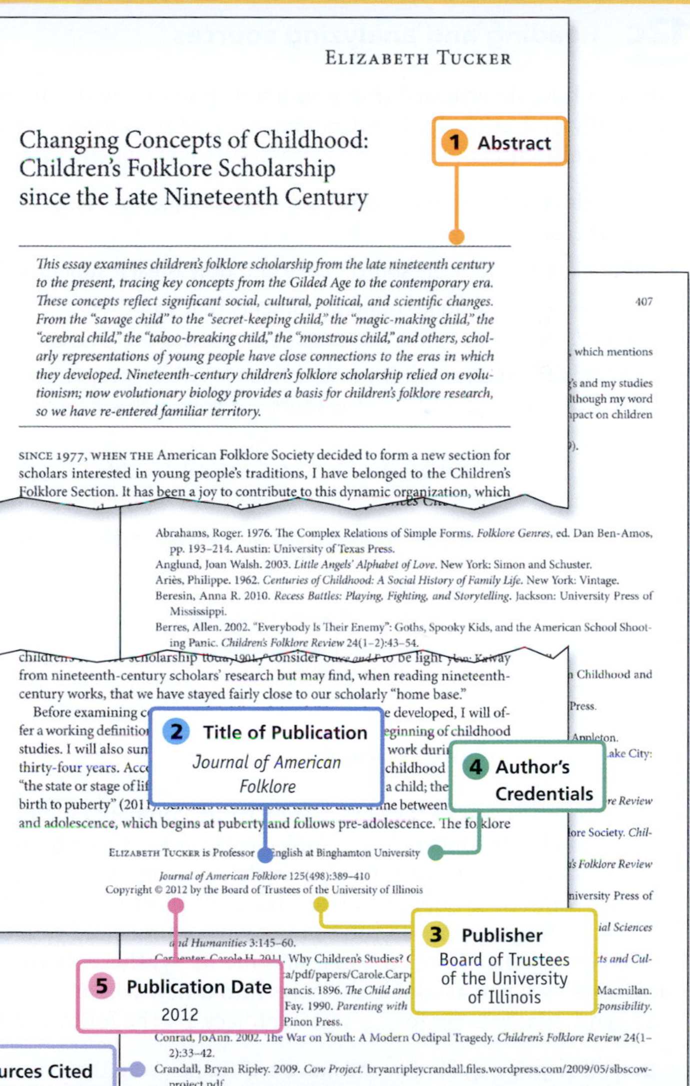

ELIZABETH TUCKER

Changing Concepts of Childhood: Children's Folklore Scholarship since the Late Nineteenth Century

This essay examines children's folklore scholarship from the late nineteenth century to the present, tracing key concepts from the Gilded Age to the contemporary era. These concepts reflect significant social, cultural, political, and scientific changes. From the "savage child" to the "secret-keeping child," the "magic-making child," the "cerebral child," the "taboo-breaking child," the "monstrous child," and others, scholarly representations of young people have close connections to the eras in which they developed. Nineteenth-century children's folklore scholarship relied on evolutionism; now evolutionary biology provides a basis for children's folklore research, so we have re-entered familiar territory.

SINCE 1977, WHEN THE American Folklore Society decided to form a new section for scholars interested in young people's traditions, I have belonged to the Children's Folklore Section. It has been a joy to contribute to this dynamic organization, which

407

which mentions

's and my studies

lthough my word

pact on children

).

Abrahams, Roger. 1976. The Complex Relations of Simple Forms. *Folklore Genres*, ed. Dan Ben-Amos, pp. 193–214. Austin: University of Texas Press.

Anglund, Joan Walsh. 2003. *Little Angels' Alphabet of Love*. New York: Simon and Schuster.

Ariès, Philippe. 1962. *Centuries of Childhood: A Social History of Family Life*. New York: Vintage.

Beresin, Anna R. 2010. *Recess Battles: Playing, Fighting, and Storytelling*. Jackson: University Press of Mississippi.

Berres, Allen. 2002. "Everybody Is Their Enemy": Goths, Spooky Kids, and the American School Shooting Panic. *Children's Folklore Review* 24(1–2):43–54.

from nineteenth-century scholars' research but may find, when reading nineteenth-century works, that we have stayed fairly close to our scholarly "home base."

Before examining c... e developed, I will offer a working definitio... eginning of childhood studies. I will also sun... work duri... thirty-four years. Acc... childhood "the state or stage of lif... a child; the birth to puberty" (2011)... ne between ... and adolescence, which begins at puberty and follows pre-adolescence. The folklore

ELIZABETH TUCKER is Professor of English at Binghamton University

Journal of American Folklore 125(498):389–410

Copyright © 2012 by the Board of Trustees of the University of Illinois

...nd Humanities 3:145–60.

Carpenter, Carole H. 2011. Why Children's Studies? ... a/pdf/papers/Carole.Carp...

...rancis. 1896. *The Child and*... Macmillan.

...Fay. 1990. *Parenting with*... ponsibility. ...Pinon Press.

Conrad, JoAnn. 2002. The War on Youth: A Modern Oedipal Tragedy. *Children's Folklore Review* 24(1–2):33–42.

Crandall, Bryan Ripley. 2009. *Cow Project*. bryanripleycrandall.files.wordpress.com/2009/05/slbscow-project.pdf.

Darwin, Charles. 1859. *On the Origin of Species by Means of Natural Selection, or the Preservation of Favoured Races in the Struggle for Life* (1st edition). London: John Murray.

Dégh, Linda. 2001. *Legend and Belief*. Bloomington: Indiana University Press.

Dorson, Richard M. 1968. *The British Folklorists: A History*. Chicago: University of Chicago Press.

Douglas, Norman. [1916] 1968. *London Street Games*. Detroit: Singing Tree Press.

12c Reading and analyzing sources

After you have determined that a source is potentially useful, read it carefully and critically (see Chapter 7), asking yourself the following questions about how this research fits your writing project:

- How relevant is this material to your research question and hypothesis?
- What claim(s) does the source make and how is each supported?
- Does the source include counterarguments that you should address?
- How credible and persuasive is the evidence? Does it represent alternative views fairly? Will the source be convincing to your audience?
- Will you need to change your thesis to account for this information?
- What quotations or paraphrases from this source might you want to use?

As you read and take notes on your sources, keep in mind that you will need to present data and sources clearly to other readers so that they can understand your point.

12d Synthesizing sources

Analysis requires you to take apart something complex (such as an article in a scholarly journal) and look closely at each part to understand how the parts fit together (or don't!). Academic writing also calls for *synthesis*—grouping similar pieces of information together and looking for patterns—so you can put your sources and your own knowledge together in an original argument. Synthesis is the flip side of analysis: you assemble the parts into a new whole.

To synthesize sources for a research project, try the following tips:

- **Don't just grab a quotation and move on.** Rather, read the material carefully (see Chapter 7). A national study of first-year college

LaunchPad Solo
macmillan learning
Research: Integrating Sources > Storyboards; Student Writing: Synthesis project

writing found that student writers often used sources they hadn't read carefully enough to realize they were not really relevant to their point. Another study showed that some students tended to use quotations *only* from the first one or two pages of a source, suggesting that they may not really know how relevant it is.

- **Understand the purpose of each source.** Make sure the source is relevant and necessary to your argument.
- **Determine the important ideas in each source.** Take notes on each source (12e). Identify and summarize the key ideas.
- **Formulate a position.** Figure out how the pieces fit together. Look for patterns. Consider multiple perspectives on the topic before deciding what you want to say.
- **Gather evidence to support your position.** Consider using paraphrases, summaries, or direct quotations from your sources as evidence (12f), and don't forget your own personal experience or prior knowledge.
- **Consider alternative viewpoints.** Recognize and respect valid perspectives that differ from yours, and try to understand them fully before explaining why you don't accept them.
- **Combine your source materials effectively.** Be careful to avoid simply summarizing all of your research. Try to weave the various sources together rather than discuss each of your sources one by one.

Even after you have fully evaluated a source, take time to look at how well the source works in your specific rhetorical situation. (If you change the focus of your work after you have begun doing research, be especially careful to check whether your sources still fit.)

12e Keeping track of sources

Because sources are so readily available, it's sometimes hard to keep them under control, and you end up with snippets, bits and pieces, and links that you no longer remember or can identify. You will save

Research: Conducting Research > Tutorial

time in the long run, then, if you have a system for keeping careful track of sources you want to use in your research.

- You can annotate copies or printouts of sources you intend to use by writing your thoughts and questions as well as marking interesting quotations and key terms. (Remember that you can use the "save page as PDF" function in your browser.) Try not to rely too heavily on copying or printing out whole pieces, however; you still need to read the material very carefully. And resist the temptation to keep material you have printed out or copied alongside your own notes, an action that could lead to inadvertent plagiarizing. Using a different color for text pasted from a source will help prevent this problem.
- If you take notes on a source, don't forget to copy down the citation information: author, title, place and date of publication, volume and issue, and page number. You will need this information for your bibliography or list of works cited, so getting the information down will save you a lot of time later on. And remember, too, that you can send an article's citation information to your own account using a management tool like EndNote or RefWorks.
- For online resources, make sure you have the accurate URL so you can find the source again easily.
- Set up a special computer file for your sources, and arrange them in a way most convenient to you—alphabetically by author, according to topics or points in your research essay, and so on.

12f Working with quotations, paraphrases, and summaries

Whatever method you use to capture and annotate your sources, you should make sure that for each one you (1) record enough information to help you recall the major points of the source; (2) put the information in the form in which you are most likely to incorporate it into your research project, whether a quotation, paraphrase, or summary; and (3) note all information you will need to cite the source accurately. Keep a working bibliography that includes citation information for each source in an electronic file or another format that you can rearrange and alter as your project takes shape. Doing so will simplify the process of documenting sources for your final project. For every note or entry you make, be sure to include the author's name, the title, and the page number.

Quoting. Quoting involves bringing a source's exact words into your text. Limit your use of quotations to those necessary to your thesis or memorable for your readers. To guard against unintentional plagiarism, photocopy or print out sources and identify the needed quotations right on the page.

- If you need to copy a quotation into your notes, make sure that all punctuation, capitalization, and spelling are exactly as in the original.
- Enclose the quotation in quotation marks (42a).
- Use brackets if you introduce words of your own into the quotation or make changes in it (43b). Use ellipses if you omit words from the quotation (43f). If you later incorporate the quotation into your research project, copy it from the note precisely, including brackets and ellipses.

Quotation-Style Note

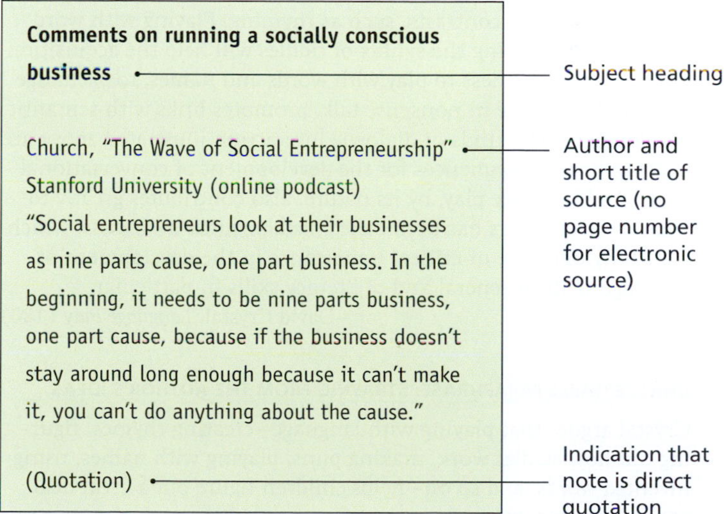

Comments on running a socially conscious business
Subject heading
Church, "The Wave of Social Entrepreneurship"
Stanford University (online podcast)
"Social entrepreneurs look at their businesses as nine parts cause, one part business. In the beginning, it needs to be nine parts business, one part cause, because if the business doesn't stay around long enough because it can't make it, you can't do anything about the cause."
Author and short title of source (no page number for electronic source)
(Quotation)
Indication that note is direct quotation

Paraphrasing. When you paraphrase, you're putting brief material from an author (including major and minor points, usually in the order they are presented) into *your own words and sentence structures.*

- Include all main points and any important details from the original source in the same order in which the author presents them, but in your own words. Put the original source aside to avoid following the wording too closely.
- If you want to include any language from the original, enclose it in quotation marks.
- Save your comments, elaborations, or reactions for another note.
- Recheck to be sure that the words and sentence structures are your own and that they express the author's meaning accurately.
- Finally, identify this note as a paraphrase.

The following examples of paraphrases resemble the original material either too little or too much.

ORIGINAL

Language play, the arguments suggest, will help the development of pronunciation ability through its focus on the properties of sounds and sound contrasts, such as rhyming. Playing with word endings and decoding the syntax of riddles will help the acquisition of grammar. Readiness to play with words and names, to exchange puns and to engage in nonsense talk, promotes links with semantic development. The kinds of dialogue interaction illustrated above are likely to have consequences for the development of conversational skills. And language play, by its nature, also contributes greatly to what in recent years has been called *metalinguistic awareness*, which is turning out to be of critical importance in the development of language skills in general and of literacy skills in particular.

—David Crystal, *Language Play* (180)

UNACCEPTABLE PARAPHRASE: STRAYING FROM THE AUTHOR'S IDEAS

Crystal argues that playing with language—creating rhymes, figuring out how riddles work, making puns, playing with names, using invented words, and so on—helps children figure out a great deal about language, from the basics of pronunciation and grammar to how to carry on a conversation. Increasing their understanding of how language works in turn helps them become more interested in learning new languages and in pursuing education (180).

This paraphrase starts off well enough, but it moves away from paraphrasing the original to inserting the writer's ideas; Crystal says nothing about learning new languages or pursuing education.

UNACCEPTABLE PARAPHRASE: USING THE AUTHOR'S WORDS

Crystal suggests that language play, including rhyme, helps children improve pronunciation ability, that looking at word endings and decoding the syntax of riddles allows them to understand grammar, and that other kinds of dialogue interaction teach conversation. Overall, language play may be of critical importance in the development of language and literacy skills (180).

Because the underlined phrases are either borrowed from the original without quotation marks or changed only superficially, this paraphrase plagiarizes.

UNACCEPTABLE PARAPHRASE: USING THE AUTHOR'S SENTENCE STRUCTURES

Language play, Crystal suggests, will improve pronunciation by zeroing in on sounds such as rhymes. Having fun with word endings and analyzing riddle structure will help a person acquire grammar. Being prepared to play with language, to use puns and talk nonsense, improves the ability to use semantics. These playful methods of communication are likely to influence a person's ability to talk to others. And language play inherently adds enormously to what has recently been known as *metalinguistic awareness*, a concept of great magnitude in developing speech abilities generally and literacy abilities particularly (180).

Here is a paraphrase of the same passage that expresses the author's ideas accurately and acceptably:

ACCEPTABLE PARAPHRASE: IN THE STUDENT WRITER'S OWN WORDS

Crystal argues that playing with language—creating rhymes, figuring out riddles, making puns, playing with names, using invented words, and so on—helps children figure out a great deal, from the basics of pronunciation and grammar to how to carry on a conversation. This kind of play allows children to understand the overall concept of how language works, a concept that is key to learning to use—and read—language effectively (180).

Summarizing. A summary is a significantly shortened version of a passage or even a whole chapter, article, film, or other work that captures main ideas *in your own words.* Unlike a paraphrase, a summary uses just enough information to record the points you wish to emphasize.

- Put the original aside to write your summary. If you later decide to include language from the original, enclose it in quotation marks. Label your work "summary."
- Recheck to be sure you have captured the author's meaning and that the words are entirely your own.

Summary Note

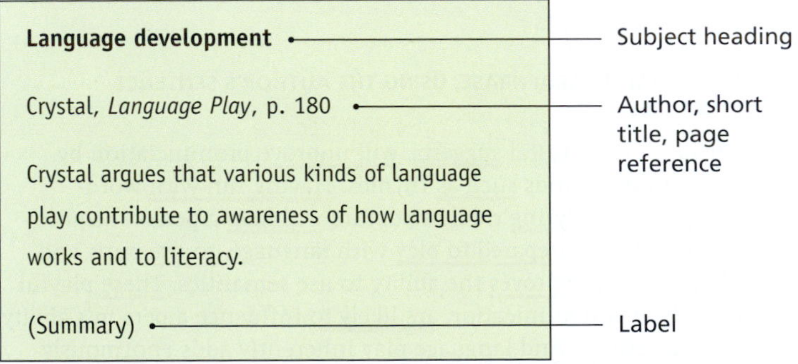

Language development
Subject heading
Crystal, *Language Play*, p. 180
Author, short title, page reference
Crystal argues that various kinds of language play contribute to awareness of how language works and to literacy.
(Summary)
Label

For Multilingual Writers

Identifying Sources

While some language communities and cultures expect audiences to recognize the sources of important documents and texts, thereby eliminating the need to cite them directly, conventions for writing in North America call for careful attribution of any quoted, paraphrased, or summarized material. When in doubt, explicitly identify your sources.

12g Creating an annotated bibliography

You may want to annotate your working bibliography, or your instructor may ask you to submit some annotated bibliography entries as part of your research project. Annotating sources can help you understand and remember what the source says. Here are some tips for doing so:

- Decide whether you will prepare a descriptive or an evaluative annotated entry. A descriptive one sticks to a clear, concise summary of the source's content; an evaluative one adds your assessment of the source's usefulness.
- Decide if the source is worth annotating—that is, whether you will use it in your research project. If not, use one of our students' advice and "detonate" rather than annotate it! If so, however, read the source carefully, being open and fair but also critical. Identify the major points the author makes and what evidence is offered in support. Also check out the author(s) to make sure that they are reliable and credible.
- Write a brief, succinct descriptive summary of the source's content, in your own words. Include major points and claims.
- If you are writing an evaluative entry, add your assessment of the source's usefulness.

12h STUDENT WRITING Annotated bibliography entries

Here are two student annotated bibliography entries, the first descriptive, the second evaluative:

DESCRIPTIVE ANNOTATED BIBLIOGRAPHY ENTRY

Diamond, Edwin, and Stephen Bates. *The Spot: The Rise of Political Advertising on Television*. 3rd ed., MIT Press, 1992.

Diamond and Bates illustrate the impact of television on political strategy and discourse. The two argue that Lyndon Johnson's ad "Daisy Girl" succeeded by exploiting the nascent

Research: Evaluating Sources > 2 Student Writing: Annotated bibliographies

television medium, using violent images and sounds and the words "nuclear bomb" to sway the audience's emotions. Emphasizing Johnson's direct control over the production of the ad, the authors illustrate the role the ad played in portraying Goldwater as a warmonger.

EVALUATIVE ANNOTATED BIBLIOGRAPHY ENTRY

Pearson, Taylor. "Why You Should Fear Your Toaster More Than Nuclear Power." *Everything's an Argument with Readings*, 7th ed., by Andrea A. Lunsford and John J. Ruszkiewicz, Bedford/St. Martin's, 2016, pp. 174-79.

The author argues that since the dangers of nuclear power, such as waste, radiation, and death, are actually less than those of energy sources we rely on today, nuclear plants represent the most practical way to generate the power we need while still reducing greenhouse gases. The journalistic article is well written and provides many interesting facts and examples related to nuclear energy, but it is informally documented and doesn't identify its sources in detail or include a bibliography. As a result, I will need to corroborate the facts with information from other sources.

For complete sample bibliographies, go to *LaunchPad Solo for Lunsford Handbooks*.

13 Integrating Sources and Avoiding Plagiarism

In some ways, there is really nothing new under the sun, in writing and research as well as in life. Whatever writing you do has been influenced by what you have already read and experienced. As you work on your research project, you will need to know how to integrate and acknowledge the work of others. And all writers need to understand current definitions of plagiarism (which have changed over time and differ from culture to culture) as well as the concept of intellectual property—those works protected by copyright and other laws—so that they can give credit where credit is due.

13a Using sources ethically

If you've ever had your words taken out of context or twisted in some way that doesn't represent what you really said, then you know how it feels to have a source (in this case, you!) used unethically. So as you begin to work with your sources, keep these tips in mind:

- Have respect for the author's intentions; don't misrepresent them.
- Don't ignore sources that don't agree with you; rather, take them into consideration.
- Don't take the author's words out of context, and be careful not to lead readers to interpret the source favorably or unfavorably. For example, use neutral language such as "the author states" rather than "the author badgers" or "the author falsely claims."
- Avoid "selective" quoting that chooses only phrases or passages that agree with your point of view while ignoring others that oppose your perspective.
- Finally, never use an author's words or ideas as if they were your own: that's plagiarism (13e).

13b Integrating quotations, paraphrases, and summaries

Integrate source materials into your writing with care to ensure that the integrated materials make grammatical and logical sense and that your readers understand which words and ideas came from your sources.

Quotations. Because your research project is primarily your own work, limit your use of quotations to those necessary to your thesis or especially memorable for your readers. Use an author's exact words when those words are so memorable or express a point so well that you cannot improve or shorten it without weakening it, when the author is an authority whose opinion supports your ideas, or when an author disagrees profoundly with others in the field.

LaunchPad Solo
macmillan learning
Research: Integrating Sources > 2 LearningCurve

Short quotations should run in with your text, enclosed by quotation marks. Longer quotations should be set off from the text (38h). Integrate all quotations into your text so that they flow smoothly and clearly into the surrounding sentences. Be sure that the sentence containing the quotation is grammatically complete, especially if you incorporate a quotation into your own words.

SIGNAL PHRASES. Introduce the quotation with a signal phrase or signal **verb**, such as those underlined in these examples.

- **As Eudora Welty notes, "Learning stamps you with its moments. Childhood's learning," she continues, "is made up of moments. It isn't steady. It's a pulse" (9).**
- **In her essay, Haraway strongly opposes those who condemn technology outright, arguing that we must not indulge in a "demonology of technology" (181).**

Choose a signal verb that is appropriate to the idea you are expressing and that accurately characterizes the author's viewpoint. Other signal verbs include words such as *acknowledges*, *agrees*, *asserts*, *believes*, *claims*, *concludes*, *describes*, *disagrees*, *lists*, *objects*, *offers*, *remarks*, *reports*, *reveals*, *says*, *suggests*, and *writes*.

When you follow Modern Language Association (MLA) style, used in the examples in this chapter, put verbs in signal phrases in the **present tense**. For *Chicago* style, use the present tense (or use the **past tense** to emphasize a point made in the past).

If you are using American Psychological Association (APA) style to describe research results, use the past tense or the **present perfect tense** (*the study showed* or *the study has shown*) in your signal phrase. Use the present tense to explain implications of research (*for future research, these findings suggest*).

When using the Council of Science Editors (CSE) style, in general use the present tense for research reports and the past tense to describe specific methods or observations, or to cite published research.

BRACKETS AND ELLIPSES. In direct quotations, enclose in brackets any words you change or add, and indicate any deletions with ellipsis points.

- **"There is something wrong in the [Three Mile Island] area," one farmer told the Nuclear Regulatory Commission after the plant accident ("Legacy" 33).**

▶ **Economist John Kenneth Galbraith pointed out that "large corporations cannot afford to compete with one another. . . . In a truly competitive market someone loses" (Key 17).**

Be careful that any changes you make in a quotation do not alter its meaning. Use brackets and ellipses sparingly; too many make for difficult reading and might suggest that you have removed some of the context for the quotation.

Paraphrases and summaries. Introduce paraphrases and summaries clearly, usually with a signal phrase that includes the author of the source, as the underlined words in this example indicate.

▶ **Professor of linguistics Deborah Tannen illustrates how communication between women and men breaks down and then suggests that a full awareness of "genderlects" can improve relationships (297).**

EXERCISE 13.1 Read the brief original passage that follows. Then decide which attempts to quote or paraphrase it are acceptable and which are not.

> The strange thing about plagiarism is that it's almost always pointless. The writers who stand accused, from Laurence Sterne to Samuel Taylor Coleridge to Susan Sontag, tend to be more talented than the writers they lift from.
>
> —Malcolm Jones, "Have You Read This Story Somewhere?"

1. According to Malcolm Jones, writers accused of plagiarism are always better writers than those they are supposed to have plagiarized.
2. According to Malcolm Jones, writers accused of plagiarism "tend to be more talented than the writers they lift from."
3. Plagiarism is usually pointless, says writer Malcolm Jones.
4. Those who stand accused of plagiarism, such as Senator Joseph Biden, tend to be better writers than those whose work they use.
5. According to Malcolm Jones, "plagiarism is . . . almost always pointless."

13c Integrating visuals and media

Choose your visuals and media wisely, whether you use video, audio, photographs, illustrations, charts and graphs, or any other kinds of images. Integrate all visuals and media smoothly into your text.

- **Does each visual or media file make a strong contribution to the message?** Purely decorative visuals and media may weaken the power of your writing.
- **Is each fair to your subject?** An obviously biased perspective may seem unfair to your audience.
- **Is each appropriate for your audience?**

While it is considered "fair use" to use such materials in an essay or other project for a college class, once that project is published on the web, you might infringe on copyright protections if you do not ask the copyright holder for permission to use the visual or media file. If you have questions about whether your work might infringe on copyright, ask your instructor for help.

Like quotations, paraphrases, and summaries, visuals and media need to be introduced and commented on in some way.

- Refer to the visual or media element in the text *before* it appears: *As Fig. 3 demonstrates.*
- Explain or comment on the relevance of the visual or media file. This explanation can appear *after* the visual.
- Check the documentation system you are using to make sure you label visual and media elements appropriately; MLA, for instance, asks that you number and title tables and figures (*Table 1: Average Amount of Rainfall by Region*).
- If you are posting your work publicly, make sure you have permission to use any copyrighted visuals.

13d Knowing which sources to acknowledge

As you do your research, remember the distinction between materials that require acknowledgment (in in-text citations, footnotes, or

Research: Acknowledging Sources & Avoiding Plagiarism > Tutorial

endnotes; and in the list of works cited or bibliography) and those that do not.

While you need to prepare accurate and thorough citations in most formal academic assignments, much of the writing you do outside of college will not require formal citations. In writing on social media, for example, or even in highly respected newspapers and magazines like the *New York Times* or the *Atlantic*, providing a link is often the only "citation" the authors need. So learn to be flexible: use formal citations when called for in formal college work, and weave in and acknowledge your sources more informally in most out-of-college writing.

Materials that do not require acknowledgment. You do not usually need to cite a source for the following:

- Common knowledge—facts that most readers are already familiar with
- Facts available in a wide variety of sources, such as encyclopedias, almanacs, or textbooks
- Your own findings from field research. You should, however, acknowledge people you interview as individuals rather than as part of a survey.

Materials that require acknowledgment. You should cite all of your other sources to be certain to avoid plagiarism. Follow the documentation style required (see Chapters 15–18), and list the source in a bibliography or list of works cited. Be especially careful to cite the following:

- Sources for quotations, paraphrases, and summaries that you include
- Facts not widely known or arguable assertions
- All visuals from any source, including your own artwork, photographs you have taken, and graphs or tables you create from data found in a source
- Any help provided by a friend, an instructor, or another person

13e Avoiding plagiarism

Academic integrity enables us to trust those sources we use and to demonstrate that our own work is equally trustworthy. Plagiarism is especially damaging to one's academic integrity, whether it involves inaccurate or incomplete acknowledgment of one's sources in

 For Multilingual Writers

Thinking about Plagiarism as a Cultural Concept

Many cultures do not recognize Western notions of plagiarism, which rest on a belief that writers can own their language and ideas. Indeed, in many cultures and communities, using the words and ideas of others without attribution is considered a sign of deep respect as well as an indication of knowledge. In academic writing in the United States, however, you should credit all materials except those that are common knowledge, that are available in a wide variety of sources, or that are your own creations or your own findings from field research.

citations—sometimes called unintentional plagiarism—or deliberate plagiarism that is intended to pass off one writer's work as another's.

Whether or not it is intentional, plagiarism can have serious consequences. Students who plagiarize may fail the course or be expelled. Others who have plagiarized, even inadvertently, have had degrees revoked or have been stripped of positions or awards.

Unintentional plagiarism. If your paraphrase is too close to the wording or sentence structure of a source (even if you identify the source); if after a quotation you do not identify the source (even if you include the quotation marks); or if you fail to indicate clearly the source of an idea that you did not come up with on your own, you may be accused of plagiarism even if your intent was not to plagiarize. This inaccurate or incomplete acknowledgment of one's sources often results either from carelessness or from not learning how to borrow material properly.

Take responsibility for your research and for acknowledging all sources accurately. To guard against unintentional plagiarism, photocopy or print out sources and identify the needed quotations right on the copy. You can also insert footnotes or endnotes into the text as you write.

Deliberate plagiarism. Deliberate plagiarism—such as handing in an essay written by a friend or purchased or downloaded from an essay-writing company; cutting and pasting passages directly from source materials without marking them with quotation marks and acknowledging their sources; failing to credit the source of an idea or concept in your text—is what most people think of when they hear the word *plagiarism*. This form of plagiarism is particularly troubling because it represents dishonesty and deception: those who intentionally plagiarize present someone else's hard work as their own and claim knowledge they really don't have, thus deceiving their readers.

Deliberate plagiarism is also fairly simple to spot: your instructor will be well acquainted with your writing and likely to notice any sudden shifts in the style or quality of your work. In addition, by typing a few words from a project into a search engine, your instructor can identify "matches" very easily.

14 Writing a Research Project

When you are working on a research project, there comes a time to draw the strands of your research together and articulate your conclusions in writing.

14a Drafting your text, including illustrations

Once you have all the information you think you'll need, try arranging your notes and visuals to identify connections, main ideas, and possible organization. You may also want to develop a working outlinc, a storyboard, or an idea map. And don't forget to figure out where you will place illustrations such as visual images, video clips, and so on.

For almost all research projects, drafting should begin well before the deadline in case you need to gather more information or do more drafting. Begin drafting wherever you feel most confident. If you have an idea for an introduction, begin there.

Working title and introduction. The title and introduction set the stage for what is to come. Ideally, the title announces the subject in an intriguing or memorable way. The introduction should draw readers in and provide any background thcy will need to understand your discussion. Consider opening with a question, a vivid image, or a provocative statement.

Research: Writing a Research Project > Video Prompt

 For Multilingual Writers

Asking Experienced Writers to Review a Thesis

You might find it helpful to ask one or two classmates who have more experience with the particular type of academic writing to look at your explicit thesis statement. Ask if the thesis is as direct and clear as it can be, and revise accordingly.

Conclusion. A good conclusion helps readers know what they have learned. One effective strategy is to begin with a reference to your thesis and then expand to a more general conclusion that reminds readers why your discussion is significant. Try to conclude with something that will have an impact—but avoid sounding preachy.

14b Reviewing and revising a research project

Once you've completed your draft, reread it slowly and carefully. As you do so, reconsider the project's purpose and audience, your stance and thesis, and the evidence you have gathered. Then, ask others to read and respond to your draft. (For more on reviewing and revising, see Chapter 4.)

14c Preparing a list of sources

Once you have a final draft with your source materials in place, you are ready to prepare your list of sources. Create an entry for each source used in your final draft, consulting your notes and working bibliography. Then double-check your draft to make sure that you have listed every source mentioned in the in-text citations or notes and that you have omitted any sources not cited in your project. (For guidelines on documentation styles, see Chapters 15–18.)

14d Editing and proofreading

When you have revised your draft, check grammar, usage, spelling, punctuation, and mechanics. Proofread the final version of your project, and carefully consider the advice of spell checkers and grammar checkers before accepting it. (For more information on editing, see 4c.)

14e STUDENT WRITING Outline of a research project

Student David Craig prepared this outline for his paper about how messaging technologies affect youth literacy. To read his final paper, see pp. 164–73.

Thesis statement: Messaging seems to be a beneficial force in the development of youth literacy because it promotes regular contact with words, the use of a written medium for communication, and the development of an alternative form of literacy.

I. Decline of youth literacy—overview
    A. What many parents, librarians, educators believe
    B. Messaging as possible cause
        1. Definition and example of messaging
        2. Messaging as beneficial to youth literacy

II. Two background issues
    A. Evidence of a decline in youth literacy
    B. Evidence of the prevalence of messaging

III. My field research to verify existence of messaging language
    A. Explanation of how research was done
    B. Results of research
        1. Four types of messaging language
        2. Frequency of messaging language use
        3. Conclusions about vocabulary

IV. What critics of messaging say

V. What linguists and other supporters of messaging say
    A. Traditional literacy not harmed by messaging
    B. Messaging indicative of advanced literacy
        1. Crystal's explanation of metalinguistics and wordplay
        2. Human ability to write in many styles
        3. Messaging helping students shift from language to language

VI. Other possible causes of decline in youth literacy
    A. Lower enrollment in English composition and grammar classes
    B. Messaging exposing literacy problems but not causing them

Documentation

15 **MLA Style** 124

List of examples: In-text citations in MLA style 131

List of examples: Works cited in MLA style 137

16 **APA Style** 174

List of examples: In-text citations in APA style 178

List of examples: References in APA style 183

17 ***Chicago* Style** 210

List of examples: Notes and bibliographic entries in *Chicago* style 214

18 **CSE Style** 234

List of examples: References in CSE style 237

15 MLA Style

Many fields in the humanities ask students to follow Modern Language Association (MLA) style to format manuscripts and to document various kinds of sources. This chapter introduces MLA guidelines. For further reference, consult the *MLA Handbook*, Eighth Edition (2016).

15a Understanding MLA citation style

Why does academic work call for very careful citation practices when writing for the general public may not? The answer is that readers of your academic work expect source citations for several reasons:

- Source citations demonstrate that you've done your homework on your topic and that you are a part of the conversation surrounding it. Careful citation shows your readers what you know, where you stand, and what you think is important.
- Source citations show your readers that you understand the need to give credit when you make use of someone else's intellectual property. Especially in academic writing, when it's better to be safe than sorry, include a citation for any source you think you might need to cite. (See 13d.)
- Source citations give explicit directions to guide readers who want to look for themselves at the works you're using.

The guidelines for MLA style help you with this last purpose, giving you instructions on exactly what information to include in your citation and how to format that information.

15b Considering the context of your sources

New kinds of sources crop up regularly. As the *MLA Handbook* confirms, there are often several "correct" ways to cite a source, so you will need to think carefully about *your own context* for using the source so you can identify the pieces of information that you should emphasize or include and any other information that might be helpful to your readers.

Elements of MLA citations. The first step is to identify elements that are commonly found in most works writers cite.

AUTHOR AND TITLE. The first two elements, both of which are needed for many sources, are the author's name and the title of the work. Each of these elements is followed by a period.

Author. Title.

Even in these elements, your context is important. The author of a novel may be obvious, but who is the "author" of a television episode? The director? The writer? The show's creator? The star? The answer may depend on the focus of your own work. If an actor's performance is central to your discussion, then MLA guidelines ask you to identify the actor as the author. If the plot is your focus, you might name the writer of the episode as the author.

CONTAINER. The next step is to identify elements of what the MLA calls the "container" for the work. The context in which you are discussing the source and the context in which you find the source will help you determine what counts as a container in each case. If you watch a movie in a theater, you won't identify a separate container after the film title. But if you watch the same movie as part of a DVD box set of the director's work, the container title is the name of the box set. If you read an article in a print journal, the first container will be the journal that the article appears in. If you read it online, the journal may also be part of a second, larger container, such as a database. Thinking about a source as nested in larger containers may help you to visualize how a citation works.

The elements you may include in the "container" part of your citation include the following, in this order: the title of the larger container, if it's different from the title of the work; the names of any contributors such as editors or translators; the version or edition; the volume and issue numbers; the publisher or sponsor; the date of publication; and a location such as the page numbers, DOI, permalink, or URL. These elements are separated by commas, and the end of the container is marked with a period.

Author. Title. Container title, contributor names, version or edition, volume and issue numbers, publisher, date, location.

Most sources won't include all these pieces of information, so include only the elements that are available and relevant to create an acceptable citation. If you need a second container—for instance, if you are citing an article from a journal you found in a database—you simply add it after the first one, beginning with the container title and including as many of the same container elements as you can find. The rest of this chapter offers many examples of how elements and containers are combined to create citations.

EXAMPLE FROM STUDENT WRITING. David Craig, whose research writing appears in 15f, found a potentially useful article in Academic Search Premier, a database he accessed through his library website. Many databases are digital collections of articles that originally appeared in print periodicals, and the articles usually have the same written-word content as they did in print form, without changes or updates.

From the screen shown below, David Craig was able to click the link to read the full text of the article. He printed this computer screen in case he needed to cite the article: the image has all the information that he would need to create a complete MLA citation, including the original print publication information for the article, the name of the database, and the location (here, a "digital object identifier," or DOI, which provides the source's permanent location).

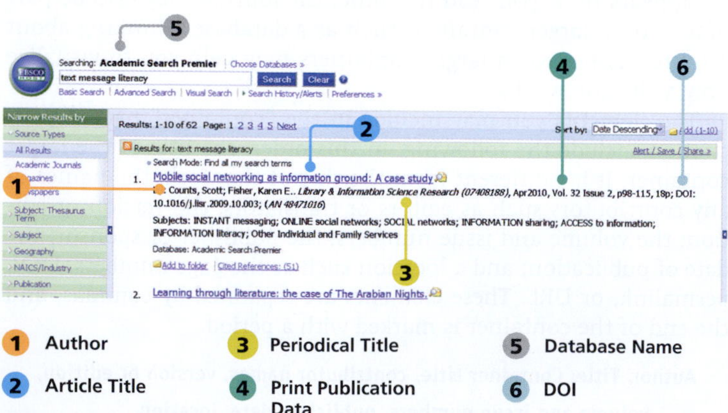

A complete citation for this article would look like this:

Counts, Scott, and Karen E. Fisher. "Mobile Social Networking as Information Ground: A Case Study." *Library and Information Science Research*, vol. 32, no. 2, Apr. 2010, pp. 98-115. *Academic Search Premier*, doi: 10.1016/j.lisr.2009.10.003.

Note that the periodical, *Library and Information Science Research*, is the first container of the article, and the database, *Academic Search Premier*, is the second container. Notice, too, that the first container includes just four relevant elements—the journal title, number (here, that means the volume and issue numbers), date, and page numbers; and the second container includes just two—the database title and location. Publisher information is not readily available for journals and databases, so it is not required.

Types of sources. Refer to the List of Examples: Works Cited in MLA Style on pp. 137–38 to locate guidelines on citing various types of sources, including print books, print periodicals (journals, magazines, and newspapers), digital written-word sources, and other sources (films, artwork) that consist mainly of material other than written words. A digital version of a source may include updates or corrections that the print version of the same work lacks, so MLA guidelines ask you to indicate where you found the source. If you can't find a model exactly like the source you've selected, see the checklist on p. 139.

Parts of citations. MLA citations appear in two parts—a brief in-text citation in parentheses in the body of your written text, and a full citation in the list of works cited, to which the in-text citation directs readers. A basic in-text citation includes the author's name and the page number (for a print source), but many variations on this format are discussed in 15d.

In the text of his research project (see 15f), David Craig quotes material from a print book and from an online report. He cites both parenthetically, pointing readers to entries on his list of works cited, as shown on p. 173. These examples show just two of the many ways to cite sources using in-text citations and a list of works cited. You'll need to make case-by-case decisions based on the types of sources you include.

> for good reason. According to David Crystal, an internationally recognized scholar of linguistics at the University of Wales, as young children develop and learn how words string together to express ideas, they go through many phases of language play. The singsong rhymes and nonsensical chants of preschoolers are vital to learning language, and a healthy appetite for wordplay leads to a better command of language later in life (182).

Craig 10

nd in SAT

Is Yielding

Concern. College

Board, 2002.

Crystal, David. *Language Play*. U of Chicago P, 1998.

Ferguson, Niall. "Texting Makes U Stupid." *Newsweek*, vol. 158, no. 12, 19 Sept. 2011, p. 11. *EBSCOHost*, connection.ebscohost.com/c/articles/65454341/texting-makes-u-stupid.

Leibowitz, Wendy R. "Technology Transforms Writing and the Teaching of Writing." *Chronicle of Higher Education*, 26 Nov. 1999, pp. A67-A68.

Lenhart, Amanda. *Teens, Smartphones, & Texting*. Pew Research Center, 19 Mar. 2012, www.pewinternet.org/files/old-media//Files/Reports/2012/PIP_Teens_Smartphones_and_Texting.pdf.

Lenhart, Amanda, et al. *Writing, Technology & Teens*. Pew Research Center, 24 Apr. 2008, www.pewinternet.org/2008/04/24/writing-technology-and-teens/.

Lenhart, Amanda, and Oliver Lewis. *Teenage Life Online: The Rise of the Instant-Message Generation and the Internet's Impact on Friendships and Family Relationships*. Pew Research Center, 21 June 2001, www.pewinternet.org/2001/06/20/the-rise-of-the-instant-message-generation/.

> is rising among the young. According to the Pew Internet & American Life Project, 85 percent of those aged twelve to seventeen at least occasionally write text messages, instant messages, or comments on social networking sites (Lenhart et al.) In 2001, the most conservative estimate based on

?" *Bedford Bits*, 9 Apr. 2015,

the-english-community/bedford

ma-queen.

ext-Messaging Skills Can Score

1 Mar. 2005, www

sc.html.

"SAT Trends 2011." *Collegeboard.org*, 14 Sept. 2011, research.collegeboard.org/programs/sat/data/archived/cb-seniors-2011/tables.

Explanatory notes. MLA citation style asks you to include explanatory notes for information that doesn't readily fit into your text but is needed for clarification or further explanation. In addition, MLA permits bibliographic notes for information about or evaluation of a source, or to list multiple sources that relate to a single point. Use superscript numbers in the text to refer readers to the notes, which may appear as endnotes (under the heading *Notes* on a separate page immediately before the list of works cited) or as footnotes at the bottom of each page where a superscript number appears.

EXAMPLE OF SUPERSCRIPT NUMBER IN TEXT

Although messaging relies on the written word, many messagers disregard standard writing conventions. For example, here is a snippet from an IM conversation between two teenage girls:[1]

EXAMPLE OF EXPLANATORY NOTE

1. This transcript of an IM conversation was collected on 20 Nov. 2016. The teenagers' names are concealed to protect their privacy.

15c Following MLA manuscript format

The MLA recommends the following format for the manuscript of a research paper. However, check with your instructor before preparing the final draft of a print work.

First page and title. The MLA does not require a title page. Type each of the following items on a separate line on the first page, beginning one inch from the top and flush with the left margin: your name, the instructor's name, the course name and number, and the date. Double-space between each item; then double-space again and center the title. Double-space between the title and the beginning of the text.

Margins and spacing. Leave one-inch margins at the top and bottom and on both sides of each page. Double-space the entire text, including set-off quotations, notes, and the list of works cited. Indent the first line of a paragraph one-half inch. Indent set-off quotations one-half inch.

Page numbers. Include your last name and the page number on each page, one-half inch below the top and flush with the right margin.

Long quotations. When quoting a long passage (more than four typed lines), set the quotation off by starting it on a new line and indenting each line one-half inch from the left margin. Do not enclose the passage in quotation marks (42a).

Headings. MLA style allows, but does not require, headings. However, many students and instructors find them helpful. (See 3b for guidelines on using headings and subheadings.)

Visuals. Visuals (such as photographs, drawings, charts, graphs, and tables) should be placed as near as possible to the relevant text. (See 13c for guidelines on incorporating visuals into your text.) Tables should have a label and number (*Table 1*) and a clear caption. The label and caption should be aligned on the left, on separate lines. Give the source information below the table. All other visuals should be labeled *Figure* (abbreviated *Fig.*), numbered, and captioned. The label and caption should appear on the same line, followed by source information. Remember to refer to each visual before it appears in your text, indicating how it contributes to the point(s) that you are making.

15d Creating MLA in-text citations

MLA style requires a citation in the text of a writing project for every quotation, paraphrase, summary, or other material requiring documentation (see 13d). In-text citations document material from other sources with both signal phrases and parenthetical references. Parenthetical references should include the information your readers need to locate the full reference in the list of works cited at the end of the text. An in-text citation in MLA style gives the reader two kinds of information: (1) it indicates which source on the works-cited page the writer is referring to, and (2) it explains where in the source the material quoted, paraphrased, or summarized can be found, if the source has page numbers or other numbered sections.

The basic MLA in-text citation includes the author's last name either in a signal phrase introducing the source material (see 13b) or in parentheses at the end of the sentence. For sources with stable page numbers, it also includes the page number in parentheses at the end of the sentence.

SAMPLE CITATION USING A SIGNAL PHRASE

In his discussion of Monty Python routines, Crystal notes that the group relished "breaking the normal rules" of language (107).

SAMPLE PARENTHETICAL CITATION

A noted linguist explains that Monty Python humor often relied on "bizarre linguistic interactions" (Crystal 108).

(For digital sources without stable page numbers, see model 2.)

Note in the examples on the following pages where punctuation is placed in relation to the parentheses. We have used underlining in some examples only to draw your attention to important elements. Do not underline anything in your own citations.

LIST OF EXAMPLES

In-text citations in MLA style

1. Basic format for a quotation, 132
2. Digital or nonprint source, 132
3. Two authors, 132
4. Three or more authors, 133
5. Organization as author, 133
6. Unknown author, 133
7. Author of two or more works cited in the same project, 133
8. Two or more authors with the same last name, 133
9. Multivolume work, 133
10. Literary work, 134
11. Work in an anthology or collection, 134
12. Sacred text, 134
13. Encyclopedia or dictionary entry, 134
14. Government source with no author named, 135
15. Entire work, 135
16. Indirect source (author quoting someone else), 135
17. Two or more sources in one citation, 135
18. Visual, 135

1. BASIC FORMAT FOR A QUOTATION. The MLA recommends using the author's name in a signal phrase to introduce the material and citing the page number(s) in parentheses.

> Lee claims that his comic-book creation, Thor, was "the first regularly published superhero to speak in a consistently archaic manner" (199).

When you do not mention the author in a signal phrase, include the author's last name before the page number(s), if any, in the parentheses. Use no punctuation between the author's name and the page number(s).

> The word *Bollywood* is sometimes considered an insult because it implies that Indian movies are merely "a derivative of the American film industry" (Chopra 9).

2. DIGITAL OR NONPRINT SOURCE. Give enough information in a signal phrase or in parentheses for readers to locate the source in your list of works cited. Many works found online or in electronic databases lack stable page numbers; you can omit the page number in such cases. However, if you are citing a work with stable pagination, such as an article in PDF format, include the page number in parentheses.

DIGITAL SOURCE WITHOUT STABLE PAGE NUMBERS

> As a *Slate* analysis explains, "Prominent sports psychologists get praised for their successes and don't get grief for their failures" (Engber).

DIGITAL SOURCE WITH STABLE PAGE NUMBERS

> According to Whitmarsh, the British military had experimented with using balloons for observation as far back as 1879 (328).

If the source includes numbered sections, paragraphs, or screens, include that number preceded by the abbreviation *sec.*, *par.*, or *scr.* in parentheses.

3. TWO AUTHORS. Use both authors' last names in a signal phrase or in parentheses.

> Gilbert and Gubar point out that in the Grimm version of "Snow White," the king "never actually appears in this story at all" (37).

4. THREE OR MORE AUTHORS. Use the first author's name and *et al.* ("and others"), unless your instructor asks you to list every name.

> Similarly, as Belenky et al. assert, examining the lives of women expands our understanding of human development (7).

5. ORGANIZATION AS AUTHOR. Give the group's full name in a signal phrase; in parentheses, abbreviate any common words in the name.

> Any study of social welfare involves a close analysis of "the impacts, the benefits, and the costs" of its policies (Social Research Corp. iii).

6. UNKNOWN AUTHOR. Use the full title, if it is brief, in your text—or a shortened version of the title in parentheses.

> One analysis defines *hype* as "an artificially engendered atmosphere of hysteria" (*Today's* 51).

7. AUTHOR OF TWO OR MORE WORKS CITED IN THE SAME PROJECT. If your list of works cited has more than one work by the same author, include the title of the work you are citing in a signal phrase or a shortened version of the title in parentheses to prevent reader confusion.

> Gardner shows readers their own silliness in his description of a "pointless, ridiculous monster, crouched in the shadows, stinking of dead men, murdered children, and martyred cows" (*Grendel* 2).

8. TWO OR MORE AUTHORS WITH THE SAME LAST NAME. Include the author's first *and* last names in a signal phrase or first initial and last name in a parenthetical reference.

> Children will learn to write if they are allowed to choose their own subjects, James Britton asserts, citing the Schools Council study of the 1960s (37–42).

9. MULTIVOLUME WORK. In a parenthetical reference, note the volume number first and then the page number(s), with a colon and one space between them.

> Modernist writers prized experimentation and gradually even sought to blur the line between poetry and prose, according to Forster (3: 150).

If you name only one volume of the work in your list of works cited, include only the page number in the parentheses.

10. LITERARY WORK. Because literary works are usually available in many different editions, cite the page number(s) from the edition you used followed by a semicolon, and then give other identifying information that will lead readers to the passage in any edition. Indicate the act and/or scene in a play (*37; sc. 1*). For a novel, indicate the part or chapter (*175; ch. 4*).

> In utter despair, Dostoyevsky's character Mitya wonders aloud about the "terrible tragedies realism inflicts on people" (376; bk. 8, ch. 2).

For a poem, cite the part (if there is one) and line(s), separated by a period. If you are citing only line numbers, use the word *line(s)* in the first reference (*lines 33-34*).

> Whitman speculates, "All goes onward and outward, nothing collapses, / And to die is different from what anyone supposed, and luckier" (6.129-30).

For a verse play, give only the act, scene, and line numbers, separated by periods.

> The witches greet Banquo as "lesser than Macbeth, and greater" (1.3.65).

11. WORK IN AN ANTHOLOGY OR COLLECTION. For an essay, short story, or other piece of prose reprinted in an anthology, use the name of the author of the work, not the editor of the anthology, but use the page number(s) from the anthology.

> Narratives of captivity play a major role in early writing by women in the United States, as demonstrated by Silko (219).

12. SACRED TEXT. To cite a sacred text such as the Qur'an or the Bible, give the title of the edition you used, the book, and the chapter and verse (or their equivalent) separated by a period. In your text, spell out the names of books. In parenthetical references, use abbreviations for books with names of five or more letters (*Gen.* for *Genesis*).

> He ignored the admonition "Pride goes before destruction, and a haughty spirit before a fall" (*New Oxford Annotated Bible*, Prov. 16.18).

13. ENCYCLOPEDIA OR DICTIONARY ENTRY. An entry from a reference work—such as an encyclopedia or a dictionary—without an author will appear on the works-cited list under the entry's title. Enclose the entry title in quotation marks, and place it in parentheses. Omit the page number for print reference works that arrange entries alphabetically.

> The term *prion* was coined by Stanley B. Prusiner from the words *proteinaceous* and *infectious* and a suffix meaning *particle* ("Prion").

14. GOVERNMENT SOURCE WITH NO AUTHOR NAMED. Because entries for sources authored by government agencies will appear on your list of works cited under the name of the country (see 15e, item 63), your in-text citation for such a source should include the name of the country as well as the name of the agency responsible for the source.

> To reduce the agricultural runoff into the Chesapeake Bay, the United States Environmental Protection Agency has argued that "[h]igh nutrient loading crops, such as corn and soybean, should be replaced with alternatives in environmentally sensitive areas" (2–26).

15. ENTIRE WORK. Include the reference in the text, without any page numbers.

> Krakauer's *Into the Wild* both criticizes and admires the solitary impulses of its young hero, which end up killing him.

16. INDIRECT SOURCE (AUTHOR QUOTING SOMEONE ELSE). Use the abbreviation *qtd. in* to indicate that you are quoting from someone else's report of a source.

> As Arthur Miller says, "When somebody is destroyed everybody finally contributes to it, but in Willy's case, the end product would be virtually the same" (qtd. in Martin and Meyer 375).

17. TWO OR MORE SOURCES IN ONE CITATION. Separate the information with semicolons.

> Economists recommend that *employment* be redefined to include unpaid domestic labor (Clark 148; Nevins 39).

18. VISUAL. When you include an image in your text, number it and include a parenthetical reference (*see Fig. 2*). Number figures (photos, drawings, cartoons, maps, graphs, and charts) and tables separately. Each visual should include a caption with the figure or table number and information about the source—either a complete citation or enough information to direct readers to the works-cited entry.

> This trend is illustrated in a chart distributed by the College Board as part of its 2011 analysis of aggregate SAT data (see Fig. 1).

Soon after the preceding sentence, readers find the following figure and a caption referring them to the entry in the list of works cited (see 15f):

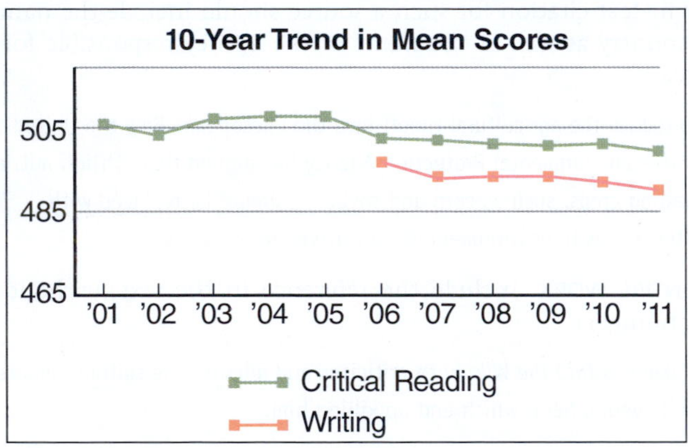

Fig. 1. Ten-year trend in mean SAT reading and writing scores (2001–2011). Data source: "SAT Trends 2011."

An image that you create might appear with a caption like this:

> Fig. 4. Young women reading magazines. Personal photograph by author.

15e Creating an MLA list of works cited

A list of works cited is an alphabetical list of the sources you have referred to in your essay. (If your instructor asks you to list everything you have read as background, call the list *Works Consulted.*)

LaunchPad Solo
macmillan learning
Documentation: MLA Style > 4 Tutorials

LIST OF EXAMPLES

Works cited in MLA style

GUIDELINES FOR AUTHOR LISTINGS

1. One author, 140
2. Multiple authors, 140
3. Organization or group author, 140
4. Unknown author, 140
5. Two or more works by the same author, 140

PRINT BOOKS

6. Basic format for a book, 141
   SOURCE MAP, 142
7. Author and editor both named, 143
8. Editor, no author named, 143
9. Selection in an anthology or chapter in a book with an editor, 143
10. Two or more items from the same anthology, 143
11. Translation, 144
12. Book in a language other than English, 144
13. Graphic narrative or comic, 144
14. Edition other than the first, 144
15. Multivolume work, 145
16. Preface, foreword, introduction, or afterword, 145
17. Entry in a reference book, 145
18. Book that is part of a series, 145
19. Republication (modern edition of an older book), 145
20. More than one publisher's name, 145
21. Book with a title within the title, 145
22. Sacred text, 146

PRINT PERIODICALS

23. Article in a print journal, 148
24. Article in a print magazine, 148
    SOURCE MAP, 147
25. Article in a print newspaper, 148
26. Article that skips pages, 148
27. Editorial or letter to the editor, 148
28. Review, 148

DIGITAL WRITTEN-WORD SOURCES

29. Work from a database, 149
    SOURCE MAP, 150
30. Article from a journal on the web, 151
31. Article in a magazine on the web, 152
32. Article in a newspaper on the web, 152
33. Digital book, 152
34. Online poem, 152
35. Online editorial or letter to the editor, 153
36. Online review, 153
37. Entry in an online reference work or wiki, 153
38. Short work from a website, 153
    SOURCE MAP, 155
39. Entire website, 154
40. Blog, 156
41. Online interview, 156
42. Post or comment on a blog or discussion group, 156
43. Posting on a social networking site, 156
44. Email or message, 157
45. Tweet, 157

LIST OF EXAMPLES

Works cited in MLA style, continued

VISUAL, AUDIO, MULTIMEDIA, AND LIVE SOURCES

46. Film (theatrical, DVD, or other format), 157
47. Online video, 158
48. Television (broadcast or on the web), 158
49. Radio (broadcast or on the web), 158
50. Television or radio interview, 158
51. Personal interview, 158
52. Sound recording, 159
53. Musical composition, 159
54. Video game, 159
55. Lecture or speech, 159
56. Live performance, 160
57. Podcast, 160
58. Work of art or photograph, 160
59. Map or chart, 160
60. Cartoon or comic strip, 161
61. Advertisement, 161

OTHER SOURCES (INCLUDING DIGITAL VERSIONS)

62. Report or pamphlet, 161
63. Government publication, 161
64. Published proceedings of a conference, 162
65. Dissertation, 162
66. Dissertation abstract, 162
67. Letter, 162
68. Manuscript or other unpublished work, 162
69. Legal source, 163

Formatting a list of works cited

- Start your list on a separate page after the text of your document and any notes.
- Center the heading *Works Cited* (not italicized or in quotation marks) one inch from the top of the page.
- Begin each entry flush with the left margin, but indent subsequent lines of each entry one-half inch. Double-space the entire list.
- List sources alphabetically by the first word. Start with the author's name, if available, or the editor's name. If no author or editor is given, start with the title.
- List the author's last name first, followed by a comma and the first name. If a source has two authors, the second author's name appears first name first (see model 2).

- Capitalize every important word in titles and subtitles. Italicize titles of books and long works, but put titles of shorter works in quotation marks.

Guidelines for author listings

The list of works cited is always arranged alphabetically. The in-text citations in your writing point readers toward particular sources on the list.

NAME CITED IN SIGNAL PHRASE IN TEXT

Crystal explains . . .

NAME IN PARENTHETICAL CITATION IN TEXT

. . . (Crystal 107).

BEGINNING OF ENTRY ON LIST OF WORKS CITED

Crystal, David.

 Checklist

Citing Sources That Don't Match Any Model Exactly

What should you do if your source doesn't match any of the models exactly? Suppose, for instance, your source is a translated essay appearing in the fifth edition of an anthology.

- Identify a basic model to follow. For example, if you decide that your source looks most like an essay in an anthology, you would start with a citation that looks like model 9.
- After listing author and title information (if given), enter as many of the elements of the container as you can find (see 15b): title of the larger container, if any; other contributors, such as editor or translator; version or edition; volume; publisher; date; and page numbers or other location information such as a URL or DOI. End the container with a period. If the container is nested in a larger container, collect the information from the second container as well.
- If you aren't sure which model to follow or how to create a combination model with multiple containers, ask your instructor or a consultant in the writing center.

Models 1–5 explain how to arrange author names. The information that follows the name depends on the type of work you are citing. Consult the list of examples on pp. 137–38 and choose the model that most closely resembles the source you are using.

1. ONE AUTHOR. Put the last name first, followed by a comma, the first name (and middle name or initial, if any), and a period.

Crystal, David.

2. MULTIPLE AUTHORS. For two authors, list the first author with the last name first (see model 1). Follow this with a comma, the word *and*, and the name of the second author with the first name first.

Gilbert, Sandra M., and Susan Gubar.

For three or more authors, list the first author followed by a comma and *et al.* ("and others") or list all authors.

Belenky, Mary Field, et al.

Belenky, Mary Field, Blythe McVicker Clinchy, Nancy Rule Goldberger, and Jill Mattuck Tarule.

3. ORGANIZATION OR GROUP AUTHOR. Give the name of the group, government agency, corporation, or other organization listed as the author.

Getty Trust.

United States. Government Accountability Office.

4. UNKNOWN AUTHOR. When the author is not identified, begin the entry with the title, and alphabetize by the first important word. Italicize titles of books and long works, but put titles of articles and other short works in quotation marks.

"California Sues EPA over Emissions."

New Concise World Atlas.

5. TWO OR MORE WORKS BY THE SAME AUTHOR. Arrange the entries alphabetically by title. Include the author's name in the first entry, but in subsequent entries, use three hyphens followed by a period.

Chopra, Anupama. "Bollywood Princess, Hollywood Hopeful." *The New York Times*, 10 Feb. 2008, nyti.ms/1QEtNpF.

---. *King of Bollywood: Shah Rukh Khan and the Seductive World of Indian Cinema*. Warner Books, 2007.

Note: Use three hyphens only when the work is by *exactly* the same author(s) as the previous entry.

Print books

6. BASIC FORMAT FOR A BOOK. Take information from the book's title page and copyright page (on the reverse side of the title page), not from the book's cover or a library catalog. The source map on p. 142 shows where to find information in a typical book.

1. **Author.** List the last name first. End with a period. For variations, see models 2–5.
2. **Title.** Italicize the title and any subtitle; capitalize all major words. End with a period.
3. **Publisher.** Identify the publisher's name as given on the book's title page. If more than one publisher appears on the title page, separate the names with a slash, leaving a space before and after the slash. If no publisher is listed on the title page, check the copyright page. Abbreviate *University* and *Press* as *U* and *P* (*Oxford UP*). Omit terms such as *Company* and *Incorporated*. Follow the publisher's name with a comma.
4. **Year of publication.** If more than one copyright date is given, use the most recent one. End with a period.

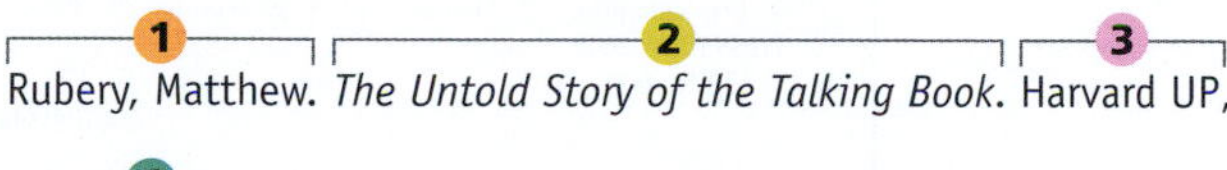

Rubery, Matthew. *The Untold Story of the Talking Book*. Harvard UP, 2016.

MLA SOURCE MAP: Books

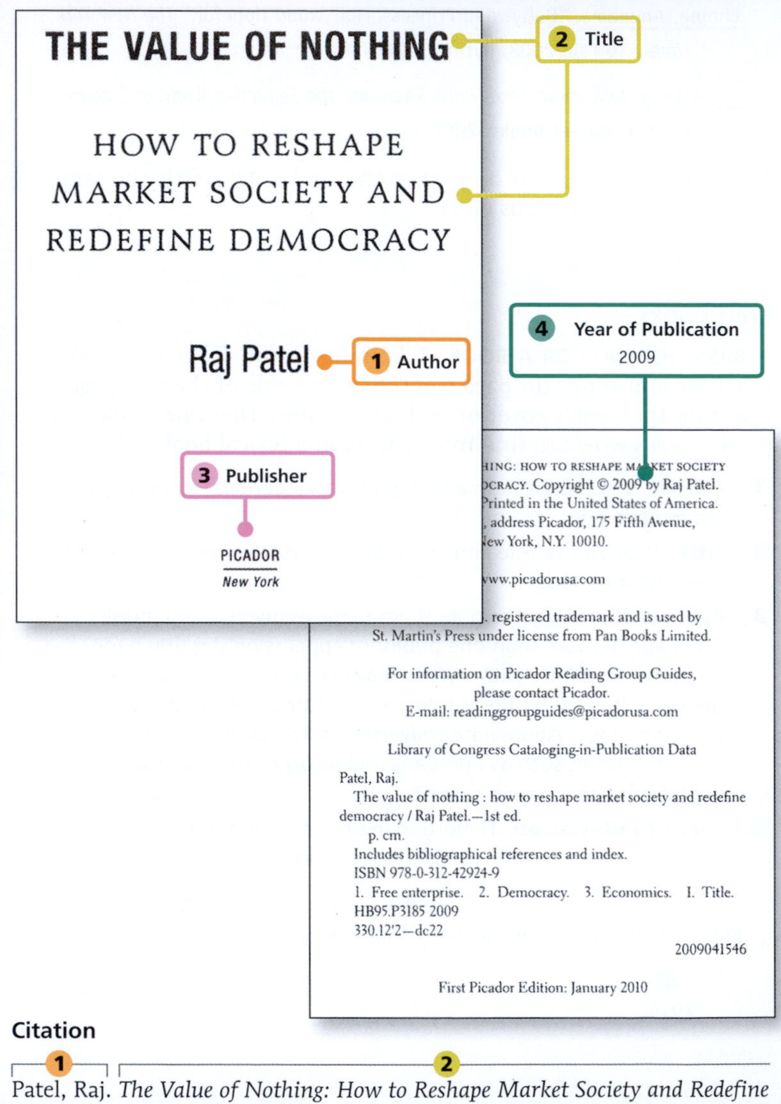

THE VALUE OF NOTHING
HOW TO RESHAPE MARKET SOCIETY AND REDEFINE DEMOCRACY
Raj Patel
PICADOR
New York
2 Title
1 Author
3 Publisher
4 Year of Publication
2009
HING: HOW TO RESHAPE MARKET SOCIETY
CRACY. Copyright © 2009 by Raj Patel.
Printed in the United States of America.
, address Picador, 175 Fifth Avenue,
New York, N.Y. 10010.
www.picadorusa.com
. registered trademark and is used by
St. Martin's Press under license from Pan Books Limited.
For information on Picador Reading Group Guides,
please contact Picador.
E-mail: readinggroupguides@picadorusa.com
Library of Congress Cataloging-in-Publication Data
Patel, Raj.
The value of nothing : how to reshape market society and redefine democracy / Raj Patel.—1st ed.
p. cm.
Includes bibliographical references and index.
ISBN 978-0-312-42924-9
1. Free enterprise. 2. Democracy. 3. Economics. I. Title.
HB95.P3185 2009
330.12'2—dc22
2009041546
First Picador Edition: January 2010

Citation

Patel, Raj. *The Value of Nothing: How to Reshape Market Society and Redefine Democracy*. Picador, 2009.

7. AUTHOR AND EDITOR BOTH NAMED

Bangs, Lester. *Psychotic Reactions and Carburetor Dung.* Edited by Greil Marcus, Alfred A. Knopf, 1988.

Note: To cite the editor's contribution, begin with the editor's name.

Marcus, Greil, editor. *Psychotic Reactions and Carburetor Dung.* By Lester Bangs, Alfred A. Knopf, 1988.

8. EDITOR, NO AUTHOR NAMED

Wall, Cheryl A., editor. *Changing Our Own Words: Essays on Criticism, Theory, and Writing by Black Women.* Rutgers UP, 1989.

9. SELECTION IN AN ANTHOLOGY OR CHAPTER IN A BOOK WITH AN EDITOR. List the author(s) of the selection; the selection title, in quotation marks; the title of the book, italicized; the words *edited by* and the name(s) of the editor(s); the publisher; the year; and the abbreviation *pp.* with the selection's page numbers.

Bird, Gloria. "Autobiography as Spectacle: An Act of Liberation or the Illusion of Liberation?" *Here First: Autobiographical Essays by Native Americans*, edited by Arnold Krupat and Brian Swann, Random House, 2000, pp. 63-74.

Note: To provide original publication information for a reprinted selection, use the original publication information as a second container (see 15b):

Byatt, A. S. "The Thing in the Forest." *The O. Henry Prize Stories 2003*, edited by Laura Furman, Anchor Books, 2003, pp. 3-22. Originally published in *The New Yorker*, 3 June 2002, pp. 80-89.

10. TWO OR MORE ITEMS FROM THE SAME ANTHOLOGY. List the anthology as one entry. Also list each selection separately with a cross-reference to the anthology. In the example below, the first two citations are for the selections used and the third is for the anthology.

Estleman, Loren D. "Big Tim Magoon and the Wild West." Walker, pp. 391-404.

Salzer, Susan K. "Miss Libbie Tells All." Walker, pp. 199-212.

Walker, Dale L., editor. *Westward: A Fictional History of the American West.* Forge Books, 2003.

11. TRANSLATION

Bolaño, Roberto. *2666*. Translated by Natasha Wimmer, Farrar, Straus and Giroux, 2008.

If the book has an editor and a translator, list both names after the title, in the order they appear on the title page.

Kant, Immanuel. *"Toward Perpetual Peace" and Other Writings on Politics, Peace, and History*. Edited by Pauline Kleingeld, translated by David L. Colclasure, Yale UP, 2006.

If different translators have worked on various parts of the book, identify the translator of the part you are citing.

García Lorca, Federico. "The Little Mad Boy." Translated by W. S. Merwin. *The Selected Poems of Federico García Lorca*, edited by Francisco García Lorca and Donald M. Allen, Penguin, 1969, pp. 51-53.

12. BOOK IN A LANGUAGE OTHER THAN ENGLISH. Include a translation of the title in brackets, if necessary.

Benedetti, Mario. *La borra del café [The Coffee Grind]*. Editorial Sudamericana, 2000.

13. GRAPHIC NARRATIVE OR COMIC. If the words and images are created by the same person, cite a graphic narrative just as you would a book (model 6).

Bechdel, Alison. *Are You My Mother? A Comic Drama*. Houghton Mifflin Harcourt, 2012.

If the work is a collaboration, indicate the author or illustrator who is most important to your research before the title of the work. List other contributors after the title, in the order of their appearance on the title page. Label each person's contribution to the work.

Stavans, Ilan, writer. *Latino USA: A Cartoon History*. Illustrated by Lalo Arcaraz, Basic Books, 2000.

14. EDITION OTHER THAN THE FIRST

Walker, John A. *Art in the Age of Mass Media*. 3rd ed., Pluto Press, 2001.

15. MULTIVOLUME WORK. Include the total number of volumes after the publication date. If you cite only one volume, give the number of the volume before the publication information.

Ch'oe, Yong-Ho, et al., editors. *Sources of Korean Tradition.* Columbia UP, 2000. 2 vols.

Ch'oe, Yong-Ho, et al., editors. *Sources of Korean Tradition.* Vol. 2, Columbia UP, 2000. 2 vols.

16. PREFACE, FOREWORD, INTRODUCTION, OR AFTERWORD. After the writer's name, describe the contribution. After the title, indicate the book's author (with *by*) or editor (with *edited by*).

Coates, Ta-Nehisi. Foreword. *The Origin of Others,* by Toni Morrison, Harvard UP, 2017, pp. vii-xvii.

17. ENTRY IN A REFERENCE BOOK. For a well-known encyclopedia, note the edition (if identified) and year of publication. If the entries are alphabetized, omit the page number.

Kettering, Alison McNeil. "Art Nouveau." *World Book Encyclopedia,* 2002 ed.

18. BOOK THAT IS PART OF A SERIES. After the publication information, list the series name (and number, if any) from the title page.

Denham, A. E., editor. *Plato on Art and Beauty.* Palgrave Macmillan, 2012. Philosophers in Depth.

19. REPUBLICATION (MODERN EDITION OF AN OLDER BOOK). Indicate the original publication date after the title.

Austen, Jane. *Sense and Sensibility.* 1813. Dover Publications, 1996.

20. MORE THAN ONE PUBLISHER'S NAME. If the title page gives two publishers' names, separate them with a slash. Include spaces on both sides of the slash.

Hornby, Nick. *About a Boy.* Riverhead / Penguin Putnam, 1998.

21. BOOK WITH A TITLE WITHIN THE TITLE. Do not italicize the title of a book or other long work within an italicized book title. For an article title within a title, italicize as usual and place the article title in quotation marks.

Masur, Louis P. *Runaway Dream:* Born to Run *and Bruce Springsteen's American Vision*. Bloomsbury, 2009.

Lethem, Jonathan. *"Lucky Alan" and Other Stories*. Doubleday, 2015.

22. SACRED TEXT. To cite any individual published editions of sacred books, begin the entry with the title.

Qur'an: The Final Testament (Authorized English Version) with Arabic Text. Translated by Rashad Khalifa, Universal Unity, 2000.

Print periodicals

The source map on p. 147 shows where to find information in a typical periodical.

1. **Author.** List the last name first. End with a period. For variations, see models 2–5.
2. **Article title.** Put the title and any subtitle in quotation marks; capitalize all major words. Place a period inside the closing quotation mark.
3. **Periodical title.** Italicize the title; capitalize all major words. End with a comma.
4. **Volume and issue.** For journals, give the abbreviation *vol.* and the volume number, and the abbreviation *no.* and the issue number, if the journal provides them. Put commas after the volume and issue. (Do not include volume and issue for magazines or newspapers.)
5. **Date of publication.** List day (if given), month (abbreviated except for May, June, and July), and year, or season and year, of publication. Put a comma after the date.
6. **Page numbers.** Give the abbreviation *p.* (for "page") or *pp.* (for "pages") and the inclusive page numbers. If the article skips pages, put the first page number and a plus sign. End with a period.

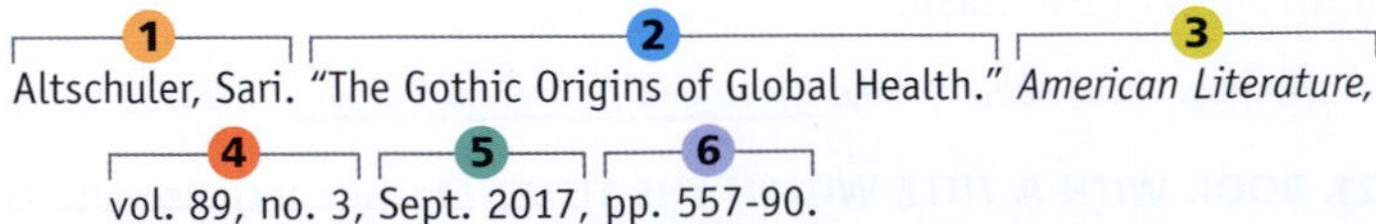

1
2
3
Altschuler, Sari. "The Gothic Origins of Global Health." American Literature,
4
5
6
vol. 89, no. 3, Sept. 2017, pp. 557-90.

MLA SOURCE MAP: Articles in Print Periodicals

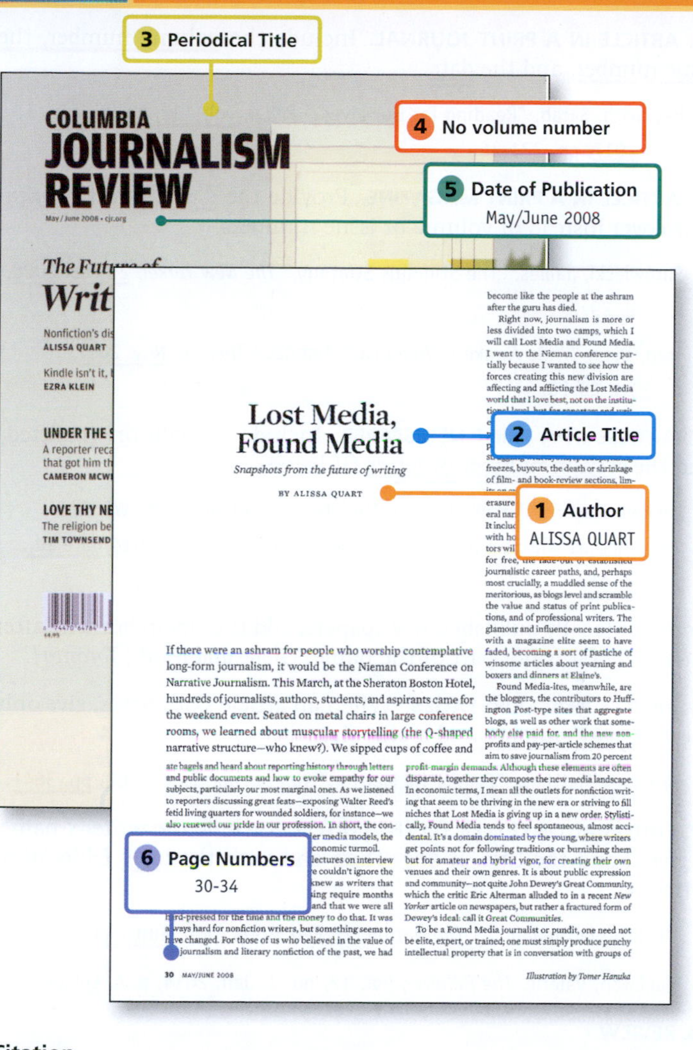

Lost Media, Found Media

Snapshots from the future of writing

BY ALISSA QUART

If there were an ashram for people who worship contemplative long-form journalism, it would be the Nieman Conference on Narrative Journalism. This March, at the Sheraton Boston Hotel, hundreds of journalists, authors, students, and aspirants came for the weekend event. Seated on metal chairs in large conference rooms, we learned about muscular storytelling (the Q-shaped narrative structure—who knew?). We sipped cups of coffee and ate bagels and heard about reporting history through letters and public documents and how to evoke empathy for our subjects, particularly our most marginal ones. As we listened to reporters discussing great feats—exposing Walter Reed's fetid living quarters for wounded soldiers, for instance—we also renewed our pride in our profession. In short, the con- … er media models, the … conomic turmoil. … lectures on interview … e couldn't ignore the … knew as writers that … ing require months … and that we were all hard-pressed for the time and the money to do that. It was always hard for nonfiction writers, but something seems to have changed. For those of us who believed in the value of journalism and literary nonfiction of the past, we had become like the people at the ashram after the guru has died.

Right now, journalism is more or less divided into two camps, which I will call Lost Media and Found Media. I went to the Nieman conference partially because I wanted to see how the forces creating this new division are affecting and afflicting the Lost Media world that I love best, not on the institu- … freezes, buyouts, the death or shrinkage of film- and book-review sections, lim- … erasure … eral nar … It inclu … with ho … tors wil … for free, … journalistic career paths, and, perhaps most crucially, a muddled sense of the meritorious, as blogs level and scramble the value and status of print publications, and of professional writers. The glamour and influence once associated with a magazine elite seem to have faded, becoming a sort of pastiche of winsome articles about yearning and boxers and dinners at Elaine's.

Found Media-ites, meanwhile, are the bloggers, the contributors to Huffington Post-type sites that aggregate blogs, as well as other work that somebody else paid for, and the new nonprofits and pay-per-article schemes that aim to save journalism from 20 percent profit-margin demands. Although these elements are often disparate, together they compose the new media landscape. In economic terms, I mean all the outlets for nonfiction writing that seem to be thriving in the new era or striving to fill niches that Lost Media is giving up in a new order. Stylistically, Found Media tends to feel spontaneous, almost accidental. It's a domain dominated by the young, where writers get points not for following traditions or burnishing them but for amateur and hybrid vigor, for creating their own venues and their own genres. It is about public expression and community—not quite John Dewey's Great Community, which the critic Eric Alterman alluded to in a recent *New Yorker* article on newspapers, but rather a fractured form of Dewey's ideal: call it Great Communities.

To be a Found Media journalist or pundit, one need not be elite, expert, or trained; one must simply produce punchy intellectual property that is in conversation with groups of

30 MAY/JUNE 2008

Illustration by Tomer Hanuka

Citation

Quart, Alissa. "Lost Media, Found Media: Snapshots from the Future of Writing." *Columbia Journalism Review*, May/June 2008, pp. 30-34.

23. ARTICLE IN A PRINT JOURNAL. Include the volume number, the issue number, and the date.

Beckwith, Sarah. "Reading for Our Lives." *PMLA,* vol. 132, no. 2, Mar. 2017, pp. 331-36.

24. ARTICLE IN A PRINT MAGAZINE. Provide the date from the magazine cover instead of volume or issue numbers.

Surowiecki, James. "The Stimulus Strategy." *The New Yorker,* 25 Feb. 2008, p. 29.

Tran, Diep. "Wide Awake in America." *American Theatre,* Nov. 2017, pp. 26-28.

25. ARTICLE IN A PRINT NEWSPAPER. Include the edition (if listed) and the section number or letter (if listed).

Fackler, Martin. "Japan's Foreign Minister Says Apologies to Wartime Victims Will Be Upheld." *The New York Times,* 9 Apr. 2014, late ed., p. A6.

Note: For locally published newspapers, add the city in brackets after the name if it is not part of the name: *Globe and Mail [Toronto]*.

26. ARTICLE THAT SKIPS PAGES. When an article skips pages, give only the first page number and a plus sign.

Tyrnauer, Matthew. "Empire by Martha." *Vanity Fair,* Sept. 2002, pp. 364+.

27. EDITORIAL OR LETTER TO THE EDITOR. Include the writer's name, if given, and the title, if any. Then end with the label *Editorial* or *Letter*.

"California Dreaming." *The Nation,* 25 Feb. 2008, p. 4. Editorial.

MacEwan, Valerie. *The Believer,* vol. 12, no. 1, Jan. 2014, p. 4. Letter.

28. REVIEW

Nussbaum, Emily. "Change Agents: Review of *The Americans* and *Silicon Valley*." *The New Yorker,* 31 Mar. 2014, p. 68.

Schwarz, Benjamin. Review of *The Second World War: A Short History,* by R. A. C. Parker, *The Atlantic Monthly,* May 2002, pp. 110-11.

Digital written-word sources

Digital sources such as websites differ from print sources in the ease with which they can be changed, updated, or eliminated. The most commonly cited electronic sources are documents from websites and databases.

29. WORK FROM A DATABASE. Library subscriptions provide access to huge databases of articles, such as Academic Search Premier, ProQuest, and JSTOR. The source map on p. 150 shows where to find information for a work from a database.

1. **Author.** List the last name first. End with a period. For variations, see models 2–5.
2. **Article title.** Enclose the title and any subtitle in quotation marks. End with a period.
3. **Periodical title.** Italicize it. Follow it with a comma.
4. **Volume and issue.** For journal articles, list the volume and issue number, if any, separated by commas. Use the abbreviations *vol.* and *no.*
5. **Date of publication.** Include the day (if given), month or season, and year, in that order. Add a comma.
6. **Page numbers.** Give the inclusive page numbers from the print version, using the abbreviations *p.* or *pp.* End with a period.
7. **Database name.** Italicize the name of the database. End with a period.
8. **Location.** Give the DOI or other permalink. If neither is available, give the URL for the home page of the database, omitting the protocol *http://*.

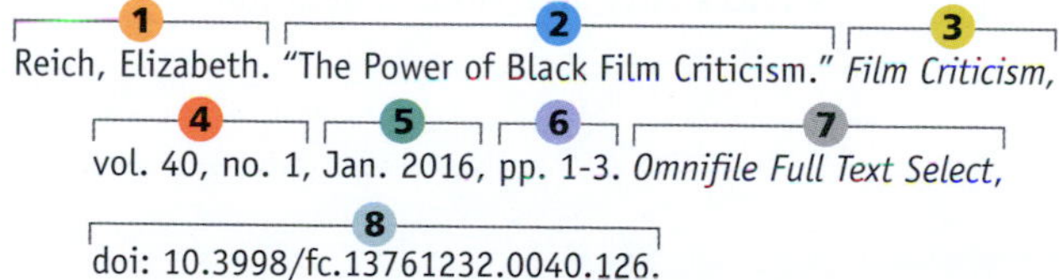

1
2
3
Reich, Elizabeth. "The Power of Black Film Criticism." *Film Criticism*,
4
5
6
7
vol. 40, no. 1, Jan. 2016, pp. 1-3. *Omnifile Full Text Select*,
8
doi: 10.3998/fc.13761232.0040.126.

MLA SOURCE MAP: Articles from Databases

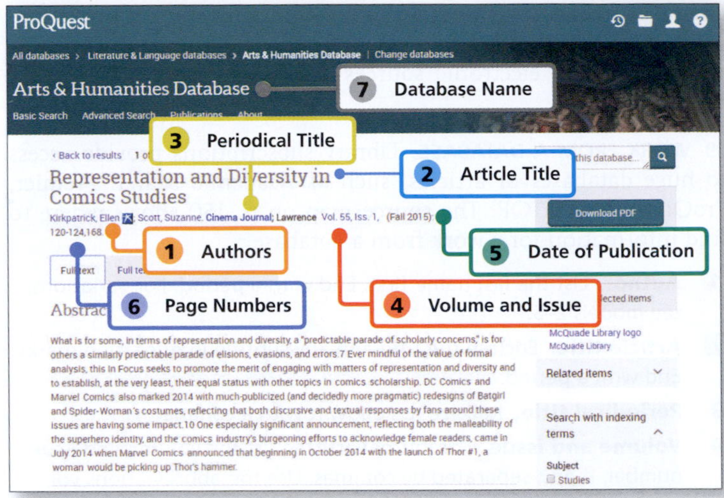

Citation

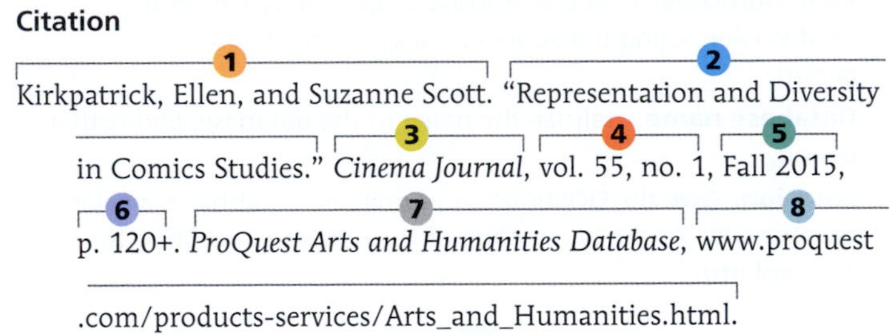

Kirkpatrick, Ellen, and Suzanne Scott. "Representation and Diversity in Comics Studies." *Cinema Journal*, vol. 55, no. 1, Fall 2015, p. 120+. *ProQuest Arts and Humanities Database*, www.proquest.com/products-services/Arts_and_Humanities.html.

30. ARTICLE FROM A JOURNAL ON THE WEB. Begin an entry for an online journal article as you would one for a print journal article (see model 23). End with the online location (permalink, DOI, or URL) and a period.

Clark, Msia Kibona. "Hip Hop as Social Commentary in Accra and Dar es Salaam." *African Studies Quarterly,* vol. 13, no. 3, Summer 2012, asq.africa.ufl.edu/files/Clark-V131s3.pdf.

Checklist

Citing Works from Websites

When citing online sources, give as many of the following elements as you can find:

1. **Author.** Provide the author of the work, if you can find one. End with a period.
2. **Title.** Give the title of the work you are citing, ending with a period. If the work is part of a larger container (such as a video on YouTube), put the title in quotation marks.
3. **Website title.** If the title you identified is not the name of the website itself, list the website title, in italics, followed by a comma.
4. **Publisher or sponsor.** If the site's publisher or sponsor is different from the title of the site, identify the publisher or sponsor, followed by a comma. If the name is very similar to the site title, omit the publisher.
5. **Date of publication.** Give the date of publication or latest update, followed by a comma.
6. **Permalink or URL.** Give a permalink (if you can find one) or URL. End with a period.
7. **Date of access.** If the work does not include any date, add "Accessed" and the day, month (abbreviated, except for May, June, and July), and year you accessed the source. End with a period. If you provided a date before the URL, omit the access date.

31. ARTICLE IN A MAGAZINE ON THE WEB. List the author, article title, and name of the magazine. Then identify the date of publication, and provide a permalink or DOI, if one is available, or a URL.

Landhuis, Esther. "Is Dementia Risk Falling?" *Scientific American*, 25 Jan. 2016, www.scientificamerican.com/article/is-dementia-risk-falling/.

32. ARTICLE IN A NEWSPAPER ON THE WEB. After the name of the newspaper, give the publication date and the permalink (if you can find one) or URL.

Hirsh, Marc. "Pop Perfection: What Makes a Song a Classic?" *Boston Globe*, 10 Nov. 2017, www.bostonglobe.com/arts/music/2017/11/09/pop-perfection-what-makes-song-classic/2SPDGw5PgQty1lPyeTKYRN/story.html.

33. DIGITAL BOOK. Provide information as for a print book (see models 6–22); then give the digital container title and any other relevant information, including the location.

Euripides. *The Trojan Women*. Translated by Gilbert Murray, Oxford UP, 1915. *Internet Sacred Text Archive*, 2011, www.sacred-texts.com/cla/eurip/trok_w.htm.

If you read the book on an e-reader such as a Kindle or Nook, specify the type of reader file you used.

Schaap, Rosie. *Drinking with Men: A Memoir*. Riverhead / Penguin, 2013. Kindle.

34. ONLINE POEM. Include the poet's name, the title of the poem, and the print publication information (if any) for the first container. For the second container, give the title, the date, and the DOI, permalink, or URL.

Geisel, Theodor. "Too Many Daves." *The Sneetches and Other Stories*, Random House, 1961. *Poetry Foundation*, 2015, www.poetryfoundation.org/poem/171612.

35. ONLINE EDITORIAL OR LETTER TO THE EDITOR. Include the author's name (if given) and the title (if any). Follow the appropriate model for the type of source you are using. (Check the list on p. 137.) End with the label *Editorial* or *Letter*.

"Migrant Children Deserve a Voice in Court." *The New York Times,* 8 Mar. 2016, www.nytimes.com/2016/03/08/opinion/migrant-children-deserve-a-voice-in-court.html. Editorial.

Starr, Evva. "Local Reporting Thrives in High Schools." *The Washington Post,* 4 Apr. 2014, wpo.st/7hmJ1. Letter.

36. ONLINE REVIEW. Cite an online review as you would a print review (see model 28). End with the name of the website, the date of publication, and the URL or permalink.

O'Hehir, Andrew. "Aronofsky's Deranged Biblical Action Flick." *Salon,* 27 May 2014, www.salon.com/2014/03/27/noah_aronofskys_deranged_biblical_action_flick/.

37. ENTRY IN AN ONLINE REFERENCE WORK OR WIKI. Begin with the title unless the author is named. (A wiki, which is collectively edited, will not include an author.) Include the title of the entry; the name of the work, italicized; the sponsor or publisher; the date of the latest update; and the location (permalink or URL). Before using a wiki as a source, check with your instructor.

Cartwright, Mark. "Apollo." *Ancient History Encyclopedia,* 18 May 2012, www.ancient.eu/apollo/.

"Gunpowder Plot." *Wikipedia,* 4 Mar. 2016, en.wikipedia.org/wiki/Gunpowder_Plot.

38. SHORT WORK FROM A WEBSITE. To cite a work on a website that is not part of a regularly published journal, magazine, or newspaper, include all of the following elements that are available. You may need to browse other parts of a site to find some of these elements, and some sites may omit elements. Uncover as much information as you can. See the source map on p. 155 for an example.

1. **Author.** List the last name first. End with a period. If no author is given, begin with the title. For variations, see models 2–5.
2. **Title of work.** Enclose the title and any subtitle of the work in quotation marks.
3. **Title of website.** Give the title of the entire website, italicized. Follow it with a comma.
4. **Publisher or sponsor.** Look for the sponsor's name at the bottom of the home page. If the sponsor's name is roughly the same as the site title, omit the sponsor. Follow it with a comma.
5. **Date of publication or latest update.** Give the most recent date, followed by a period.
6. **Location.** Give the permalink, if you can find one, or the site's URL, followed by a period.
7. **Date of access.** If the site is undated, end with *Accessed* and the date you accessed the site.

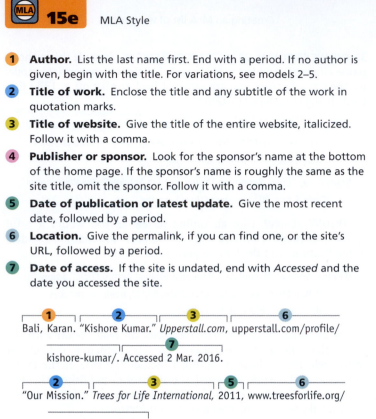

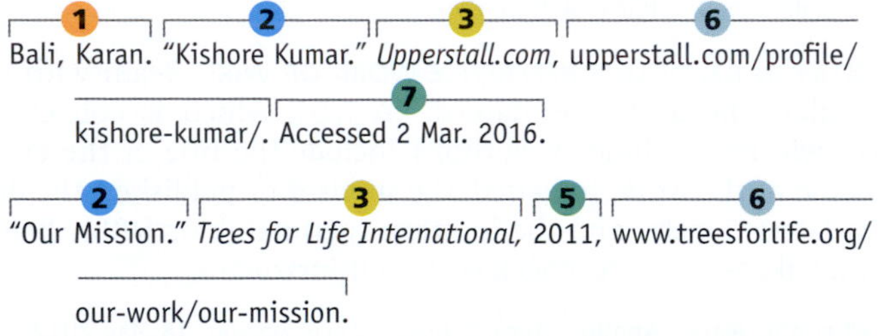

"Our Mission." *Trees for Life International*, 2011, www.treesforlife.org/
our-work/our-mission.

39. ENTIRE WEBSITE. Follow the guidelines for a work from the web, beginning with the name of the author or editor (if any), followed by the title of the website, italicized; the name of the sponsor or publisher (if different from the name of the site); the date of publication or last update; and the location.

Glazier, Loss Pequeño, director. *Electronic Poetry Center*. State U of New York Buffalo, 1994-2016, epc.buffalo.edu/.

Weather.com. Weather Channel Interactive, 1995-2016, weather.com/.

For a personal website, include the name of the person who created the site as you would with a site's author or editor. If the site is undated, end with your date of access.

Bali, Karan. "Kishore Kumar." *Upperstall.com*, upperstall.com/profile/

kishore-kumar/. Accessed 2 Mar. 2016.

Enright, Mike. *Menright.com*. www.menright.com. Accessed 30 Mar. 2016.

MLA SOURCE MAP: Works from Websites

COURTESY OF NOBELPRIZE.ORG

1 Author
Øyvind Tønnesson

2 Title of Work

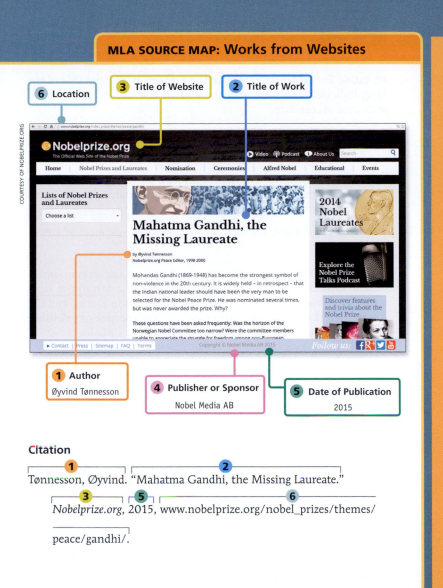

3 Title of Website

4 Publisher or Sponsor
Nobel Media AB

5 Date of Publication
2015

6 Location

Citation

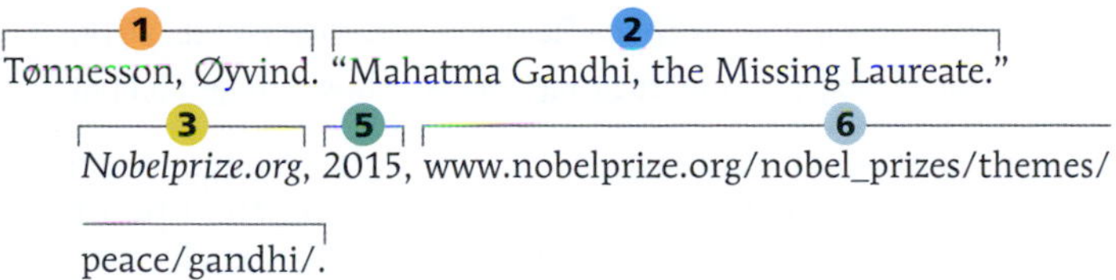

Tønnesson, Øyvind. "Mahatma Gandhi, the Missing Laureate." *Nobelprize.org*, 2015, www.nobelprize.org/nobel_prizes/themes/peace/gandhi/.

40. BLOG. For an entire blog, give the author's name; the title of the blog, italicized; the date; and the URL. If the site is undated, end with your access date.

Levy, Carla Miriam. *Filmi Geek.* 2006-2015, www.filmigeek.com.

Little Green Footballs. littlegreenfootballs.com. Accessed 4 Mar. 2016.

Note: To cite a blogger who writes under a pseudonym, begin with the pseudonym and then put the writer's real name (if you know it) in parentheses.

Atrios (Duncan Black). *Eschaton.* www.eschatonblog.com. Accessed 8 Mar. 2016.

41. ONLINE INTERVIEW. Start with the name of the person interviewed. Give the title, if there is one. If not, give a descriptive label such as *Interview*, neither italicized nor in quotation marks, and the interviewer, if relevant; the title of the site; the sponsor or publisher (if there is one); the date of publication; and the URL.

Ladd, Andrew. "What Ends: An Interview with Andrew Ladd." Interview by Jill. *Looks & Books,* 25 Feb. 2014, www.looksandbooks.com/2014/02/25/what-ends-an-interview-with-andrew-ladd/.

42. POST OR COMMENT ON A BLOG OR DISCUSSION GROUP. Give the author's name; the title of the post, in quotation marks; the title of the site, italicized; the date of the post; and the URL.

Edroso, Roy. "Going Down with the Flagship." *Alicublog,* 24 Feb. 2016, alicublog.blogspot.com/2016/02/going-down-with-flagship.html.

For a comment on an online post, give the writer's name or screen name; a label such as *Comment on*, not italicized; the title of the article commented on; and the label *by* and the article author's name. End with the citation information for the type of article.

JennOfArk. Comment on "Going Down with the Flagship," by Roy Edroso. *Alicublog,* 24 Feb. 2016, alicublog.blogspot.com/2016/02/going-down-with-flagship.html#disqus_thread.

43. POSTING ON A SOCIAL NETWORKING SITE. To cite a posting on Facebook, Instagram, or another social networking site, include the writer's name; up to 140 characters of the posting, in quotation marks (or a description such as *Photograph*, not italicized and not in quotation marks, if there's no text); the name of the site, italicized; the date of the post; and the location of the post (URL).

Cannon, Kevin. "Portrait of Norris Hall in #Savannah, GA—home (for a few months, anyway) of #SCAD's sequential art department." *Instagram,* Mar. 2014, www.instagram.com/p/lgmqk4i6DC/.

44. EMAIL OR MESSAGE. Include the writer's name; the subject line, in quotation marks, if one is provided, or a descriptive message such as *Text message*; *Received by* (not italicized or in quotation marks) followed by the recipient's name; and then the date of the message.

Carbone, Nick. "Screen vs. Print Reading." Received by Karita dos Santos, 17 Apr. 2016.

45. TWEET. Begin with the writer's Twitter handle, and put the real name, if known, in parentheses. Include the entire tweet, in quotation marks. Give the site name in italics (*Twitter*), the date and time of the message, and the tweet's URL.

@LunsfordHandbks (Andrea A. Lunsford). "Technology & social media have changed the way we write. That doesn't mean literacy has declined https://community.macmillan.com/groups/macmillan-news/blog/2016/02/24/the-literacy-revolution... @MacmillanLearn." *Twitter,* 24 Feb. 2016, 10:17 a.m., twitter.com/LunsfordHandbks/status/702512638937460736.

Visual, audio, multimedia, and live sources

46. FILM (THEATRICAL, DVD, OR OTHER FORMAT). If you cite a particular person's work, start with that name. If not, start with the title of the film; then name the director, distributor, and year of release. Other contributors, such as writers or performers, may follow the director. If you cite a feature from a disc, treat the film as the first container and the disc as the second container.

Bale, Christian, performer. *The Big Short.* Directed by Adam McKay, Paramount Pictures, 2015.

Lasseter, John. Introduction. *Spirited Away,* directed by Hayao Miyazaki, 2001. Walt Disney Video, 2003, disc 1.

47. ONLINE VIDEO. Cite an online video as you would a short work from a website (see model 38).

Nayar, Vineet. "Employees First, Customers Second." *YouTube*, 9 June 2015, www.youtube.com/watch?v=cCdu67s_C5E.

48. TELEVISION (BROADCAST OR ON THE WEB). For a show broadcast on television, begin with the title of the program, italicized (for an entire series), or the title of the episode, in quotation marks. Then list important contributors (writer, director, actor); season and episode number (for a specific episode); the network; the local station and city, if the show appeared on a local channel; and the broadcast date(s). For a show accessed on a network website, include the URL after the date of posting.

Breaking Bad. Created by Vince Gilligan, performances by Bryan Cranston, Aaron Paul, and Anna Gunn, AMC, 2008-2013.

"Time Zones." *Mad Men*, written by Matthew Weiner, directed by Scott Hornbacher, season 7, episode 1, AMC, 13 Apr. 2014, www.amc.com/shows/mad-men/season-7/episode-01-time-zones.

49. RADIO (BROADCAST OR ON THE WEB). If you are citing a particular episode or segment, cite a radio broadcast as you would a television episode (see model 48).

"Tarred and Feathered." *This American Life*, narrated by Ira Glass, WNYC, 11 Apr. 2013.

For a show or segment accessed on the web, follow the date of posting with the website title, a comma, the URL, and a period.

50. TELEVISION OR RADIO INTERVIEW. List the person interviewed and then the title, if any. If the interview has no title, use the label *Interview* and the name of the interviewer, if relevant. Then identify the source. End with information about the program and the interview date(s). (For an online interview, see model 41.)

Russell, David O. Interview by Terry Gross. *Fresh Air*, WNYC, 20 Feb. 2014.

51. PERSONAL INTERVIEW. List the person who was interviewed; the label *Telephone interview*, *Personal interview*, or *E-mail interview*; and the date the interview took place.

Freedman, Sasha. Personal interview. 10 Nov. 2015.

52. SOUND RECORDING. List the name of the person or group you wish to emphasize (such as the composer, conductor, or band); the title of the recording or composition; the artist, if appropriate; the manufacturer; and the year of issue. If you are citing a particular song or selection, include its title, in quotation marks.

Bach, Johann Sebastian. *Bach: Violin Concertos.* Performances by Itzhak Perlman and Pinchas Zukerman, English Chamber Orchestra, EMI, 2002.

Rihanna. "Work." *Anti,* Roc Nation, 2016.

Note: If you are citing instrumental music that is identified only by form, number, and key, do not underline, italicize, or enclose it in quotation marks.

Grieg, Edvard. Concerto in A minor, op. 16. Conducted by Eugene Ormandy, Philadelphia Orchestra, RCA, 1989.

53. MUSICAL COMPOSITION. When you are not citing a specific published version, first give the composer's name, followed by the title.

Mozart, Wolfgang Amadeus. *Don Giovanni,* K527.

Mozart, Wolfgang Amadeus. Symphony no. 41 in C major, K551.

Note: Cite a published score as you would a book. If you include the date that the composition was written, do so immediately after the title.

Schoenberg, Arnold. *Chamber Symphony No. 1 for 15 Solo Instruments, Op. 9.* 1906. Dover, 2002.

54. VIDEO GAME. Start with the developer or author (if any). After the title, give the distributor and the date of publication.

Harmonix. *Rock Band Blitz.* MTV Games, 2012.

55. LECTURE OR SPEECH. For a live lecture or speech, list the speaker; the title (if any), in quotation marks; the sponsoring institution or group; the place; and the date. Add the label *Lecture* or *Speech* after the date if readers will not otherwise be able to identify the work.

Eugenides, Jeffrey. Portland Arts and Lectures. Arlene Schnitzer Concert Hall, Portland, OR, 30 Sept. 2003.

For a lecture or speech on the web, cite as you would a short work from a website (see model 38).

Burden, Amanda. "How Public Spaces Make Cities Work." *TED.com,* Mar. 2014, www.ted.com/talks/amanda_burden_how_public_spaces _make_cities_work.

56. LIVE PERFORMANCE. List the title, the appropriate names (such as the writer or performer), the place, and the date.

The Sea Ranch Songs. By Aleksandra Vrebalov, performed by the Kronos Quartet, White Barn, The Sea Ranch, CA, 23 May 2015.

57. PODCAST. Cite a podcast as you would a short work from a website (see model 38).

Fogarty, Mignon. "Begs the Question: Update." *QuickandDirtyTips.com,* Macmillan, 6 Mar. 2014, www.quickanddirtytips.com/education/ grammar/begs-the-question-update.

58. WORK OF ART OR PHOTOGRAPH. List the artist's or photographer's name; the work's title, italicized; and the date of composition. Then cite the name of the museum or other location and the city. To cite a reproduction in a book, add the publication information. To cite online artwork, add the title of the database or website, italicized, and the URL or permalink.

Bronzino, Agnolo. *Lodovico Capponi.* 1550-55, Frick Collection, New York.

General William Palmer in Old Age. 1810, National Army Museum, London. *White Mughals: Love and Betrayal in Eighteenth-Century India,* by William Dalrymple, Penguin Books, 2002, p. 270.

Hura, Sohrab. *Old Man Lighting a Fire.* 2015, *Magnum Photos,* pro .magnumphotos.com/Asset/-2K1HRG6NSSEE.html.

59. MAP OR CHART. Cite a map or chart as you would a short work within a longer work. For an online source, include the location. End with the label *Map* or *Chart* if needed for clarity.

"Australia." *Perry-Castaneda Library Map Collection,* U of Texas, 1999, www.lib.utexas.edu.maps.australia_pol99.jpg.

California. Rand McNally, 2002. Map.

60. CARTOON OR COMIC STRIP. List the artist's name; the title of the cartoon or comic strip, in quotation marks; and the publication information. You may end with a label (*Cartoon* or *Comic strip*) for clarity.

Flake, Emily. *The New Yorker,* 13 Apr. 2015, p. 66. Cartoon.

Munroe, Randall. "Heartbleed Explanation." *xkcd.com,* xkcd.com/1354/. Comic strip.

61. ADVERTISEMENT. Include the label *Advertisement* at the end of the entry.

Ameritrade. *Wired,* Jan. 2014, p. 47. Advertisement.

Lufthansa. *The New York Times,* 16 Apr. 2014, www.nytimes.com. Advertisement.

Other sources (including digital versions)

If an online version is not shown in this section, use the appropriate model for the source and then end with a DOI, permalink, or URL.

62. REPORT OR PAMPHLET. Follow the guidelines for a print book (models 6–22) or a digital book (model 33).

Rainie, Lee, and Maeve Duggan. *Privacy and Information Sharing.* Pew Research Center, 14 Jan. 2016, www.pewinternet.org/files/2016/01/PI_2016.01.14_Privacy-and-Info-Sharing_FINAL.pdf.

63. GOVERNMENT PUBLICATION. Begin with the author, if identified. Otherwise, start with the name of the government, followed by the agency. For congressional documents, cite the number, session, and house of Congress; the type (*Report*, *Resolution*, *Document*); and the number. End with the publication information. For online versions, follow the models for a short work from a website (model 38) or an entire website (model 39).

Gregg, Judd. *Report to Accompany the Genetic Information Act of 2003.* US 108th Congress, 1st session, Senate Report 108-22, Government Printing Office, 2003.

United States, Department of Health and Human Services, National Institutes of Health. *Keep the Beat Recipes: Deliciously Healthy Dinners.* Oct. 2009, healthyeating.nhlbi.nih.gov/pdfs/Dinners_Cookbook_508-compliant.pdf.

64. PUBLISHED PROCEEDINGS OF A CONFERENCE. Cite the proceedings as you would a book.

Cleary, John, and Gary Gurtler, editors. *Proceedings of the Boston Area Colloquium in Ancient Philosophy 2002*. Brill Academic Publishers, 2003.

65. DISSERTATION. Enclose the title in quotation marks. Add the label *Dissertation*, the school, and the year the work was accepted.

Thompson, Brian. "I'm Better Than You and I Can Prove It: Games, Expertise, and the Culture of Competition." Dissertation, Stanford U, 2015.

Note: Cite a published dissertation as a book, adding the identification *Dissertation* and the university after the title.

66. DISSERTATION ABSTRACT. Cite the abstract as you would an unpublished dissertation (model 65), and add the label *Abstract* after the year. For an abstract that uses *Dissertation Abstracts International*, include the volume, year, and page number.

Huang-Tiller, Gillian C. "The Power of the Meta-Genre: Cultural, Sexual, and Racial Politics of the American Modernist Sonnet." Dissertation, U of Notre Dame, 2000. Abstract. *Dissertation Abstracts International*, vol. 61, 2000, p. 1401.

Moore, Courtney L. "Stress and Oppression: Identifying Possible Protective Factors for African American Men." Dissertation, Chicago School of Professional Psychology, 2016. Abstract. *ProQuest Dissertations and Theses*, search.proquest.com/docview/1707351557.

67. LETTER. Cite a published letter as a work in an anthology (see model 9). If the letter is unpublished, follow this form:

Anzaldúa, Gloria. Letter to the author. 10 Sept. 2002.

68. MANUSCRIPT OR OTHER UNPUBLISHED WORK. List the author's name; the title (if any) or a description of the material; any identifying numbers; and the name of the library or research institution housing the material, if applicable.

Woolf, Virginia. "The Searchlight." Papers of Virginia Woolf, 1902-1956, Series III, Box 4, Item 184, Smith College, Northampton.

69. LEGAL SOURCE. To cite a court case, give the names of the first plaintiff and defendant, the case number, the name of the court, and the date of the decision. To cite an act, give the name of the act followed by its Public Law (*Pub. L.*) number, its Statutes at Large (*Stat.*) cataloging number, and the date the act was enacted.

Citizens United vs. FEC. 558 US 310. Supreme Court of the US. 2010. Legal Information Institute, Cornell U Law School, www.law.cornell.edu/supct/pdf/08-205P.ZS.

Museum and Library Services Act of 2003. Pub. L. 108-81. Stat. 117.991. 25 Sept. 2003.

Note: You do not need an entry on the list of works cited when you cite articles of the U.S. Constitution and laws in the U.S. Code.

15f STUDENT WRITING Research-based argument, MLA style

A brief research-based argument by David Craig appears on the following pages. David followed the MLA guidelines described in this chapter.

STUDENT WRITING

Craig 1

Name, instructor, course, and date aligned at left

David Craig
Professor Turkman
English 219
18 December 2017

Title centered

Messaging: The Language of Youth Literacy

Opens with attention-getting statement

Background on the problem of youth literacy

Explicit thesis statement concludes introductory paragraph

The English language is under attack. At least, that is what many people seem to believe. From concerned parents to local librarians, everyone seems to have a negative comment on the state of youth literacy today. They fear that the current generation of grade school students will graduate with an extremely low level of literacy, and they point out that although language education hasn't changed, kids are having more trouble reading and writing than in the past. When asked about the cause of this situation, many adults pin the blame on technologies such as texting and instant messaging, arguing that electronic shortcuts create and compound undesirable reading and writing habits and discourage students from learning conventionally correct ways to use language. But although the arguments against messaging are passionate, evidence suggests that they may not hold up.

Indirect quotation uses "qtd. in" and name of web source on list of works cited

The disagreements about messaging shortcuts are profound, even among academics. John Briggs, an English professor at the University of California, Riverside, says, "Americans have always been informal, but now the informality of precollege culture is so ubiquitous that many students have no practice in using language in any formal setting at all" (qtd. in McCarroll). Such objections are not new; Sven Birkerts of Mount Holyoke College argued in 1999 that "[students] read more casually. They strip-mine what they read" online and consequently produce "quickly generated, casual prose" (qtd. in Leibowitz A67). However, academics are also among the defenders of texting and instant messaging (IM), with

STUDENT WRITING

Craig 2

some suggesting that messaging may be a beneficial force in the development of youth literacy because it promotes regular contact with words and the use of a written medium for communication.

Writer's last name and page number at upper-right corner of every page

Texting and instant messaging allow two individuals who are separated by any distance to engage in real-time, written communication. Although such communication relies on the written word, many messagers disregard standard writing conventions. For example, here is a snippet from an IM conversation between two teenage girls:[1]

Definition and example of messaging

Teen One: sorry im talkinto like 10 ppl at a time
Teen Two: u izzyful person
Teen Two: kwel
Teen One: hey i g2g

As this brief conversation shows, participants must use words to communicate via texting and messaging, but their words do not have to be in standard English.

The issue of youth literacy does demand attention because standardized test scores for language assessments, such as the verbal and writing sections of the College Board's SAT, have declined in recent years. This trend is illustrated in a chart distributed by the College Board as part of its 2011 analysis of aggregate SAT data (see Fig. 1).

Writer considers argument that youth literacy is in decline

Figure explained in text and cited in parenthetical reference

The trend lines illustrate a significant pattern that may lead to the conclusion that youth literacy is on the decline. These lines display the ten-year paths (from 2001 to 2011) of reading and writing scores, respectively. Within this period, the average verbal score dropped a few points — and appears to be headed toward a further decline in the future.

Discussion of Figure 1

1. This transcript of an IM conversation was collected on 20 Nov. 2017. The teenagers' names are concealed to protect privacy.

Explanatory note adds information not found in list of works cited

STUDENT WRITING

Craig 3

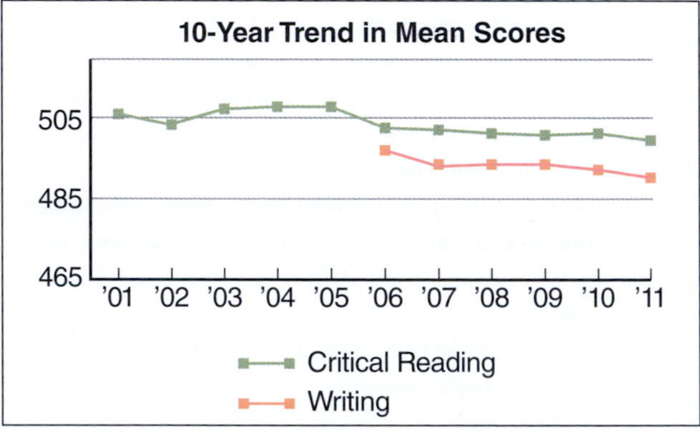

Fig. 1. Ten-year trend in mean SAT reading and writing scores (2001-2011). Data source: "2011 SAT Trends."

Figure labeled, titled, and credited to source; inserted at appropriate point in text

Based on the preceding statistics, parents and educators appear to be right about the decline in youth literacy. And this trend coincides with another phenomenon: digital communication is rising among the young. According to the Pew Internet & American Life Project, 85 percent of those aged twelve to seventeen at least occasionally write text messages, instant messages, or comments on social networking sites (Lenhart et al.). In 2001, the most conservative estimate based on Pew numbers showed that American youths spent, at a minimum, nearly three million hours per day on instant messaging services (Lenhart and Lewis 20). These numbers are now exploding thanks to texting, which was "the dominant daily mode of communication" for teens in 2012 (Lenhart), and messaging on popular social networking sites such as Facebook and Tumblr.

Writer accepts part of critics' argument; transition to next point

For a web source with no page numbers, only author names appear in parentheses

In the interest of establishing the existence of a messaging language, I analyzed 11,341 lines of text from IM conversations

Writer's field research described

Craig 4

between youths in my target demographic: U.S. residents aged twelve to seventeen. Young messagers voluntarily sent me chat logs, but they were unaware of the exact nature of my research. Once all of the logs had been gathered, I went through them, recording the number of times messaging language was used in place of conventional words and phrases. Then I generated graphs to display how often these replacements were used.

During the course of my study, I identified four types of messaging language: phonetic replacements, acronyms, abbreviations, and inanities. An example of phonetic replacement is using *ur* for *you are*. Another popular type of messaging language is the acronym; for a majority of the people in my study, the most common acronym was *lol*, a construction that means *laughing out loud*. Abbreviations are also common in messaging, but I discovered that typical IM abbreviations, such as *etc.*, are not new to the English language. Finally, I found a class of words that I call "inanities." These words include completely new words or expressions, combinations of several slang categories, or simply nonsensical variations of other words. My favorite from this category is *lolz*, an inanity that translates directly to *lol* yet includes a terminating *z* for no obvious reason.

Findings of field research presented

In the chat transcripts that I analyzed, the best display of typical messaging lingo came from the conversations between two thirteen-year-old Texan girls, who are avid IM users. Figure 2 is a graph showing how often they used certain phonetic replacements and abbreviations. On the *y*-axis, frequency of replacement is plotted, a calculation that compares the number of times a word or phrase is used in messaging language with the total number of times that it is communicated in any form. On the *x*-axis, specific messaging words and phrases are listed.

Figure introduced and explained

STUDENT WRITING

Craig 5

Discussion of findings presented in Figure 2

My research shows that the Texan girls use the first ten phonetic replacements or abbreviations at least 50 percent of the time in their normal messaging writing. For example, every time one of them writes *see*, there is a parallel time when *c* is used in its place. In light of this finding, it appears that the popular messaging culture contains at least some elements of its own language. It also seems that much of this language is new: no formal dictionary yet identifies the most common messaging words and phrases. Only in the heyday of the telegraph or on the rolls of a stenographer would you find a similar situation, but these "languages" were never a popular medium of youth communication. Texting and instant messaging, however, are very popular among young people and continue to generate attention and debate in academic circles.

My research shows that messaging is certainly widespread, and it does seem to have its own particular vocabulary, yet these two factors alone do not mean it has a damaging influence on youth literacy. As noted earlier, however, some people claim that

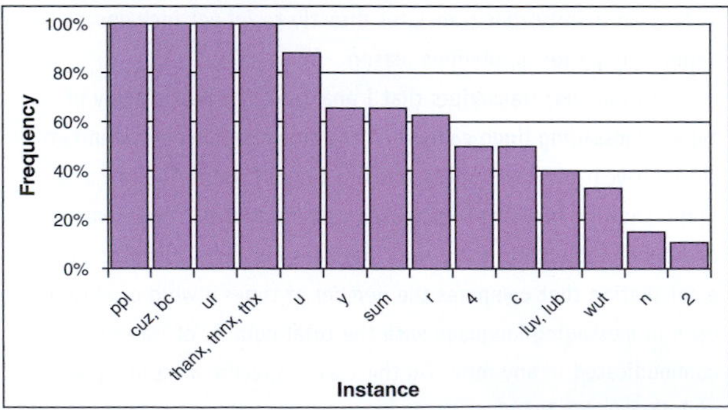

Figure labeled and titled

Fig. 2. Usage of phonetic replacements and abbreviations in messaging.

STUDENT WRITING

Craig 6

the new technology is a threat to the English language. In an article provocatively titled "Texting Makes U Stupid," historian Niall Ferguson argues, "The good news is that today's teenagers are avid readers and prolific writers. The bad news is that what they are reading and writing are text messages." He goes on to accuse texting of causing the United States to "[fall] behind more literate societies."

For author of web source named in signal phrase, no parenthetical citation needed

The critics of messaging are numerous. But if we look to the field of linguistics, a central concept — metalinguistics — challenges these criticisms and leads to a more reasonable conclusion — that messaging has no negative impact on a student's development of or proficiency with traditional literacy.

Transition to support of thesis and refutation of critics

Scholars of metalinguistics offer support for the claim that messaging is not damaging to those who use it. As noted earlier, one of the most prominent components of messaging language is phonetic replacement, in which a word such as *everyone* becomes *every1*. This type of wordplay has a special importance in the development of an advanced literacy, and for good reason. According to David Crystal, an internationally recognized scholar of linguistics at the University of Wales, as young children develop and learn how words string together to express ideas, they go through many phases of language play. The singsong rhymes and nonsensical chants of preschoolers are vital to learning language, and a healthy appetite for wordplay leads to a better command of language later in life (182).

Linguistic authority cited in support of thesis

Author of print source named in signal phrase, so parenthetical citation includes only page number

As justification for his view of the connection between language play and advanced literacy, Crystal presents an argument for metalinguistic awareness. According to Crystal, *metalinguistics* refers to the ability to "step back" and use words to analyze how language works:

STUDENT WRITING

Craig 7

Block format for a quotation of more than four lines

Ellipses and brackets indicate omissions and changes in quotation

> If we are good at stepping back, at thinking in a more abstract way about what we hear and what we say, then we are more likely to be good at acquiring those skills which depend on just such a stepping back in order to be successful—and this means, chiefly, reading and writing. . . . [T]he greater our ability to play with language, . . . the more advanced will be our command of language as a whole. (Crystal 181)

Writer links Crystal's views to thesis

If we accept the findings of linguists such as Crystal that metalinguistic awareness leads to increased literacy, then it seems reasonable to argue that the phonetic language of messaging can also lead to increased metalinguistic awareness and, therefore, increases in overall literacy. As messagers develop proficiency with a variety of phonetic replacements and other types of texting and messaging words, they should increase their subconscious knowledge of metalinguistics.

Another refutation of critics' assumptions

Metalinguistics also involves our ability to write in a variety of distinct styles and tones. Yet in the debate over messaging and literacy, many critics assume that either messaging or academic literacy will eventually win out in a person and that the two modes cannot exist side by side. This assumption is, however, false. Human beings ordinarily develop a large range of language abilities, from the formal to the relaxed and from the mainstream to the subcultural. Mark Twain, for example, had an understanding of local speech that he employed when writing dialogue for *Huckleberry Finn*. Yet few people would argue that Twain's knowledge of this form of English had a negative impact on his ability to write in standard English.

Example from well-known work of literature used as support

However, just as Mark Twain used dialects carefully in dialogue, writers must pay careful attention to the kind of language

Craig 8

they use in any setting. Composition specialist Andrea A. Lunsford backs up this idea in a blog post:

> [W]here English is concerned, there is never one solitary right way to proceed: everything depends on the rhetorical situation and the intended purpose.

Blog post cited in support of claim

The analytical ability that is necessary for writers to choose an appropriate tone and style in their writing is, of course, metalinguistic in nature because it involves the comparison of two or more language systems. Thus, youths who grasp multiple languages will have a greater natural understanding of metalinguistics. More specifically, young people who possess both messaging and traditional skills stand to be better off than their peers who have been trained only in traditional or conventional systems. Far from being hurt by their online pastime, instant messagers can be aided in standard writing by their experience with messaging language.

Writer synthesizes evidence for claim

The fact remains, however, that youth literacy seems to be declining. What, if not messaging, is the main cause of this phenomenon? According to the College Board, which collects data on several questions from its test takers, course work in English composition classes has decreased by 14 percent between 1992 and 2002 (Carnahan and Coletti 11). The possibility of messaging causing a decline in literacy seems inadequate when statistics on English education for US youths provide other evidence of the possible causes. Simply put, students in the United States are not getting as much practice in academic writing as they used to. Rather than blaming texting and messaging language alone for the decline in literacy and test scores, we must also look toward our schools' lack of focus on the teaching of standard English skills.

Transition to final point

Alternative explanation for decline in literacy

STUDENT WRITING

Craig 9

Transition to conclusion

Concluding paragraph sums up argument and reiterates thesis

My findings indicate that the use of messaging poses virtually no threat to the development or maintenance of formal language skills among American youths aged twelve to seventeen. Diverse language skills tend to increase a person's metalinguistic awareness and, thereby, his or her ability to use language effectively to achieve a desired purpose in a particular situation. The current decline in youth literacy is not due to the rise of texting and messaging. Rather, fewer young students seem to be receiving an adequate education in the use of conventional English. Unfortunately, it may always be fashionable to blame new tools for old problems, but in the case of messaging, that blame is not warranted. Although messaging may expose literacy problems, it does not create them.

STUDENT WRITING

Craig 10

Works Cited

Heading centered

Carnahan, Kristin, and Chiara Coletti. *Ten-Year Trend in SAT Scores Indicates Increased Emphasis on Math Is Yielding Results: Reading and Writing Are Causes for Concern*. College Board, 2002.

Crystal, David. *Language Play*. U of Chicago P, 1998.

Ferguson, Niall. "Texting Makes U Stupid." *Newsweek*, vol. 158, no. 12, 19 Sept. 2011, p. 11. *EBSCOHost*, connection .ebscohost.com/c/articles/65454341/texting-makes-u-stupid.

Leibowitz, Wendy R. "Technology Transforms Writing and the Teaching of Writing." *Chronicle of Higher Education*, 26 Nov. 1999, pp. A67-A68.

Lenhart, Amanda. *Teens, Smartphones, & Texting*. Pew Research Center, 19 Mar. 2012, www.pewinternet.org/files/old-media//Files/Reports/2012/PIP_Teens_Smartphones_and_Texting.pdf.

Lenhart, Amanda, et al. *Writing, Technology & Teens*. Pew Research Center, 24 Apr. 2008, www.pewinternet.org/2008/04/24/writing-technology-and-teens/.

Lenhart, Amanda, and Oliver Lewis. *Teenage Life Online: The Rise of the Instant-Message Generation and the Internet's Impact on Friendships and Family Relationships*. Pew Research Center, 21 June 2001, www.pewinternet.org/2001/06/20/the-rise-of-the -instant-message-generation/.

Lunsford, Andrea A. "Are You a 'Comma Queen'?" *Bedford Bits*, 9 Apr. 2015, community.macmillan.com/community/the-english -community/bedford-bits/blog/2015/04/09/are-you-a-comma -queen.

McCarroll, Christina. "Teens Ready to Prove Text-Messaging Skills Can Score SAT Points." *Christian Science Monitor*, 11 Mar. 2005, www.csmonitor.com/2005/0311/p01s02-ussc.html.

"SAT Trends 2011." *Collegeboard.org*, 14 Sept. 2011, research .collegeboard.org/programs/sat/data/archived/cb-seniors -2011/tables.

Report

Print book

Article from database

Print newspaper article

Downloaded file

Online report

Subsequent lines of each entry indented

Blog post

Online newspaper article

Graph source

16 APA Style

Chapter 16 discusses the basic formats prescribed by the American Psychological Association (APA), guidelines that are widely used for research in the social sciences. For further reference, consult the *Publication Manual of the American Psychological Association*, Seventh Edition (2020).

16a Understanding APA citation style

Why does academic work call for very careful citation practices when writing for the general public may not? The answer is that readers of academic work expect source citations for several reasons:

- Source citations demonstrate that you've done your homework on your topic and that you are a part of the conversation surrounding it.
- Source citations show that you understand the need to give credit when you make use of someone else's intellectual property. (See Chapter 13.)
- Source citations give explicit directions to guide readers who want to look for themselves at the works you're using.

The guidelines for APA style tell you exactly what information to include in your citation and how to format that information.

Types of sources. Refer to the List of Examples on p. 183 for guidelines on citing various types of sources—print books (or parts of print books), print periodicals (journals, magazines, and newspapers), and digital written-word sources (an online article or book). A digital version of a source may include updates or corrections that the print version lacks, so it's important to provide the correct information for readers. For sources that consist mainly of material other than written words—such as a film, song, or podcast—consult the "other sources" section of the directory. And if you can't find a model exactly like the source you've selected, see the checklist on p. 185.

ARTICLES FROM WEB AND DATABASE SOURCES. You need a subscription to look through most databases, so individual researchers almost always gain access to articles in databases through a library that pays to subscribe. The easiest way to tell whether a source comes from a database, then, is that its information is *not* generally available for free. Many databases are digital collections of articles that originally appeared in edited print periodicals, ensuring that an authority has vouched for the accuracy of the information. Such sources often have more credibility than free material available on the web.

Parts of citations. APA citations appear in two parts of your text—a brief in-text citation in the body of your written text and a full citation in the list of references, to which the in-text citation directs readers. The most straightforward in-text citations include the author's name, the publication year, and the page number, but many variations on this basic format are discussed in 16c.

In the text of her causal analysis (see 16e), Tawnya Redding includes a paraphrase of material from an online journal that she accessed through the publisher's website. She cites the authors'

9

References

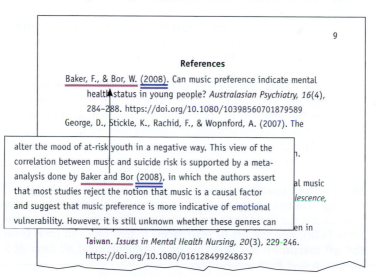

Baker, F., & Bor, W. (2008). Can music preference indicate mental health status in young people? *Australasian Psychiatry, 16*(4), 284–288. https://doi.org/10.1080/10398560701879589

George, D., Stickle, K., Rachid, F., & Wopnford, A. (2007). The

n.

al music

lescence,

en in

Taiwan. *Issues in Mental Health Nursing, 20*(3), 229-246. https://doi.org/10.1080/016128499248637

alter the mood of at-risk youth in a negative way. This view of the correlation between music and suicide risk is supported by a meta-analysis done by Baker and Bor (2008), in which the authors assert that most studies reject the notion that music is a causal factor and suggest that music preference is more indicative of emotional vulnerability. However, it is still unknown whether these genres can names and the year of publication in a parenthetical reference, pointing readers to the entry for "Baker, F., & Bor, W. (2008)" in her references list, shown on p. 209.

Content notes. APA style allows you to use content notes, either at the bottom of the page (footnotes) or on a separate page at the end of the text (endnotes), to expand or supplement your text. Indicate such notes in the text by superscript numerals ([1]), using the footnote function in your word processor. Single-space all footnotes and set them in a 10-point font.

SUPERSCRIPT NUMBER IN TEXT

The age of the children involved in the study was an important factor in the selection of items for the questionnaire.[1]

FOOTNOTE

[1]Marjorie Youngston Forman and William Cole of the Child Study Team provided great assistance in identifying appropriate items for the questionnaire.

16b Following APA manuscript format

The following formatting guidelines for student papers are consistent with APA recommendations. However, check with your instructor before preparing the final draft of a print text.

Title page. Double-space the entire title page. Center the title in boldface type three or four lines from the top margin. Skip one line below the title and list the following information: your name, your school and the department, the course number and name, your instructor's name, and the assignment due date. Insert the page number *1* in the upper right margin.

Margins and spacing. Leave margins of one inch on all sides of the page. Do not justify the right margin. Double-space the entire text (except for footnotes), including any headings, set-off quotations (42a), and the list of references. Indent one-half inch from the left margin for the first line of a paragraph and all lines of a quotation over forty words long.

Page numbers. Place the page number in the upper-right corner of each page, in the same position as on the title page.

Long quotations. For a long, set-off quotation (one having more than forty words), indent it one-half inch from the left margin, and do not use quotation marks. Place the page reference in parentheses one space after the final punctuation.

Abstract. If your instructor asks for an abstract, the abstract should go immediately after the title page, with the word *Abstract* centered in boldface at the top of the page. Double-space the text of the abstract and do not indent the first line. In most cases, a one-paragraph abstract of about one hundred words will be sufficient to introduce readers to your topic and provide a brief summary of your major thesis and supporting points.

Headings. Headings are sometimes used in long or complex APA-style projects. Center first-level headings and put them in boldface type. Left-align any second-level headings and make them boldface. Third-level headings should be left-aligned, boldface, and italicized. Capitalize all major words and any words of four or more letters.

Visuals. All visuals should include a label, number, and title above the visual. Label tables ***Table*** and label any other visuals (such as charts, graphs, photographs, and drawings) ***Figure.*** You may set tables single-spaced, one-and-a-half-spaced, or double-spaced, depending on what is easiest to read. Below the table or figure, include a description and the word *Note* with any source information. Remember to refer to each visual in your text, stating how it contributes to the point(s) you are making. Tables and figures should generally appear near the relevant text.

16c Creating APA in-text citations

An in-text citation in APA style always indicates which source on the references page the writer is referring to, and it explains in what year the material was published; for quoted material, the in-text citation also indicates where in the source the quotation can be found.

Note that APA style generally calls for using the past tense or present perfect tense for signal verbs: *Baker (2018) showed* or *Baker (2018) has shown*. Use the present tense only to discuss results (*the experiment demonstrates*) or widely accepted information (*researchers agree*).

We have used underlining in some examples only to draw your attention to important elements. Do not underline anything in your own citations.

1. BASIC FORMAT FOR A QUOTATION. Generally, use the author's last name in a signal phrase to introduce the cited material, and place the date, in parentheses, immediately after the author's name. The page number, preceded by *p.*, appears in parentheses after the quotation.

> Gitlin (2001) pointed out that "political critics, convinced that the media are rigged against them, are often blind to other substantial reasons why their causes are unpersuasive" (p. 141).

If the author is not named in a signal phrase, place the author's last name, the year, and the page number in parentheses after the

LIST OF EXAMPLES

In-text citations in APA style

1. Basic format for a quotation, 178
2. Basic format for a paraphrase or summary, 179
3. Two authors, 179
4. Three or more authors, 179
5. Corporate or group author, 180
6. Unknown author, 180
7. Two or more authors with the same last name, 180
8. Two or more works by an author in a single year, 180
9. Two or more sources in one parenthetical reference, 180
10. Source reported in another source, 180
11. Personal communication, 181
12. Electronic document, 181
13. Table or figure reproduced in the text, 182

quotation: (Gitlin, 2001, p. 141). For a long, set-off quotation (more than forty words), place the page reference in parentheses one space after the final quotation.

For quotations from works without page numbers, include other information such as a paragraph number, a section heading, or a figure number to help readers find the quoted passage.

> Driver (2007) has noticed "an increasing focus on the role of land" in policy debates over the past decade (para. 1).

2. BASIC FORMAT FOR A PARAPHRASE OR SUMMARY. Include the author's last name and the year as in model 1, but omit the page or paragraph number unless the reader will need it to find the material in a long work.

> Gitlin (2001) has argued that critics sometimes overestimate the influence of the media on modern life.

3. TWO AUTHORS. Use both names in all citations. Use *and* in a signal phrase, but use an ampersand (&) in parentheses.

> Babcock and Laschever (2003) have suggested that many women do not negotiate their salaries and pay raises as vigorously as their male counterparts do.

> A recent study has suggested that many women do not negotiate their salaries and pay raises as vigorously as their male counterparts do (Babcock & Laschever, 2003).

4. THREE OR MORE AUTHORS. List the first author's name followed by "et al." (a Latin abbreviation for "and others").

> Another group of researchers reached somewhat different conclusions by designing a study that was less dependent on subjective judgment than were previous studies (Safer et al., 2017).

> Based on the results, Safer et al. (2017) determined that the apes took significant steps toward self-expression.

5. CORPORATE OR GROUP AUTHOR. If the name of the organization or corporation is long, spell it out the first time you use it, followed by an abbreviation in brackets. In later references, use the abbreviation only.

FIRST CITATION	(Centers for Disease Control and Prevention [CDC], 2018)
LATER CITATIONS	(CDC, 2018)

If a government or corporate source lists multiple nested departments or agencies, use the most specific department or agency as the author.

6. UNKNOWN AUTHOR. Use the title or its first few words in a signal phrase or in parentheses. A book's title is italicized, as in the following example; an article's title is placed in quotation marks.

> The employment profiles for this time period substantiated this trend (*Federal Employment*, 2001).

7. TWO OR MORE AUTHORS WITH THE SAME LAST NAME. Include the authors' initials in each citation.

> S. Bartolomeo (2000) conducted the groundbreaking study on teenage childbearing.

8. TWO OR MORE WORKS BY AN AUTHOR IN A SINGLE YEAR. Assign lowercase letters (*a, b,* and so on) alphabetically by title, and include the letters after the year.

> Gordon (2017b) examined this trend in more detail.

9. TWO OR MORE SOURCES IN ONE PARENTHETICAL REFERENCE. List any sources by different authors in alphabetical order by the authors' last names, separated by semicolons: (Cardone, 2018; Lai, 2014). List works by the same author in chronological order, separated by commas: (Lai, 2014, 2017).

10. SOURCE REPORTED IN ANOTHER SOURCE. Use the phrase *as cited in* to indicate that you are reporting information from a secondary source.

Name the original source in your text, but list the secondary source in your list of references.

> One reviewer commended the author's "sure understanding of the thoughts of young people" (Brailsford, 1990, as cited in Chow, 2019, para. 9).

11. PERSONAL COMMUNICATION. Cite any personal letters, email messages, private electronic postings, telephone conversations, or interviews as shown. Do not include personal communications in the reference list.

> R. Tobin (personal communication, November 4, 2006) supported his claims about music therapy with new evidence.

12. ELECTRONIC DOCUMENT. Cite a web or electronic document as you would a print source, using the author's name and date.

> Link and Phelan (2005) argued for broader interventions in public health that would be accessible to anyone, regardless of individual wealth.

The APA recommends the following for electronic sources without names, dates, or page numbers:

AUTHOR UNKNOWN

Use a shortened form of the title in a signal phrase or in parentheses (see model 6). If an organization is the author, see model 5.

DATE UNKNOWN

Use the abbreviation *n.d.* (for "no date") in place of the year: (*Hopkins*, *n.d.*).

NO PAGE NUMBERS

Many works found online or in electronic databases lack stable page numbers. Use the page numbers for an electronic work in a format, such as PDF, that has stable pagination. If the work does not have page numbers, include other information to help your readers find the cited material. For example, you may include a section heading, a paragraph number, a figure or table number, or a time stamp.

Jacobs and Johnson (2007) have argued that "the South African media is still highly concentrated and not very diverse in terms of race and class" (South African Media after Apartheid).

13. TABLE OR FIGURE REPRODUCED IN THE TEXT. Number figures (graphs, charts, illustrations, and photographs) and tables separately. Place a label (*Table 1*) and an informative heading (*Hartman's Key Personality Traits*) above the table or figure; below, provide information about its source.

Table 1

Hartman's Key Personality Traits

Trait category	Color			
	Red	Blue	White	Yellow
Motive	Power	Intimacy	Peace	Fun
Strengths	Loyal to tasks	Loyal to people	Tolerant	Positive
Limitations	Arrogant	Self-righteous	Timid	Uncommitted

Note. Adapted from *The Hartman Personality Profile*, by N. Hayden. Retrieved February 24, 2016, from http://students.cs.byu.edu/~nhayden/Code/index.php

If you do not cite the source of the table or figure elsewhere in your text, you do not need to include the source on your list of references.

16d Creating an APA list of references

The alphabetical list of the sources cited in your document is called *References*. If your instructor asks that you list everything you have read—not just the sources you cite—call the list *Bibliography*.

LaunchPad Solo
macmillan learning
Documentation: APA Style > 2 Tutorials

LIST OF EXAMPLES

References in APA style

GUIDELINES FOR AUTHOR LISTINGS

1. One author, 185
2. Multiple authors, 185
3. Corporate or group author, 185
4. Unknown author, 186
5. Two or more works by the same author, 186

PRINT BOOKS

6. Basic format for a book, 186
   SOURCE MAP, 187
7. Editor, 188
8. Selection in a book with an editor, 188
9. Translation, 188
10. Edition other than the first, 188
11. Multivolume work with an editor, 188
12. Article in a reference work, 188
13. Republished book, 189
14. Introduction, preface, foreword, or afterword, 189
15. Book with a title within the title, 189

PRINT PERIODICALS

16. Article in a journal, 191
    SOURCE MAP, 190
17. Article in a magazine, 191
18. Article in a newspaper, 191
19. Editorial or letter to the editor, 191
20. Unsigned article, 191
21. Review, 191
22. Published interview, 191

DIGITAL WRITTEN-WORD SOURCES

23. Article from an online periodical, 192
24. Article from a database, 193
    SOURCE MAP, 194
25. Abstract for an online article, 195
26. Comment on an online article, 195
27. Report or long document from a website, 195
    SOURCE MAP, 196
28. Short work from a website, 197
29. Online book, 197
30. Email or private message, 197
31. Posting on public social media, 197
32. Blog post or comment, 197
33. Wiki entry, 198

OTHER SOURCES (INCLUDING ONLINE VERSIONS)

34. Government publication, 198
35. Data set, 198
36. Dissertation, 198
37. Technical or research report, 198
38. Conference proceedings, 199
39. Paper presented at a meeting or symposium, 199
40. Poster session, 199
41. Presentation slides, 199
42. Film, video, DVD, or Blu-ray, 199
43. Online (streaming) audio or video file, 200
44. Television program, single episode, 200
45. Television series, 200
46. Podcast episode, 200
47. Recording, 200

All the entries in this section of the book use hanging indent format, in which the first line aligns on the left and the subsequent lines indent one-half inch. This is the customary APA format.

Guidelines for author listings

List authors' last names first, and use only initials for first and middle names. The in-text citations in your text point readers toward particular sources in your list of references (see 16c).

NAME CITED IN SIGNAL PHRASE IN TEXT

Lapowsky (2017) has noted . . .

NAME IN PARENTHETICAL CITATION IN TEXT

. . . (Lapowsky, 2017).

BEGINNING OF ENTRY IN LIST OF REFERENCES

Lapowsky, I. (2017).

Formatting a List of References

- Start your list on a new page after the text of your document but before appendices or notes. Continue consecutive page numbers.
- Center the heading *References* in boldface one inch from the top of the page.
- Begin each entry flush with the left margin, but indent subsequent lines one-half inch. Double-space the entire list.
- List sources alphabetically by author's last name. If no author is given, alphabetize the source by the first word of the title other than *A*, *An*, or *The*. If the list includes two or more works by the same author, list them in chronological order.
- Italicize titles and subtitles of books and periodicals. Do not italicize titles of articles or websites, and do not enclose them in quotation marks.
- For titles of books and articles, capitalize only the first word of the title and the subtitle and any proper nouns or proper adjectives.
- For titles of periodicals and websites, capitalize all major words.

Checklist

Combining Parts of Models

What should you do if your source doesn't match the model exactly? Suppose, for instance, that your source is a translation of a republished book with an editor.

- Identify a basic model to follow. If you decide that your source looks most like a republished book, for example, start with a citation that looks like model 13.
- Look for models that show additional elements in your source. For this example, you would need elements of model 9 (for the translation) and model 7 (for the editor).
- Add new elements from other models to your basic model in the order that makes the most sense to you.
- If you still aren't sure how to arrange the pieces to create a combination model, ask your instructor.

Models 1–5 below explain how to arrange author names. The information that follows the name of the author depends on the type of work you are citing—a book (models 6–15), a print periodical (models 16–22), a digital written-word source (models 23–33), or another kind of source (models 34–47).

1. ONE AUTHOR. Give the last name, a comma, the initial(s), and the date in parentheses.

Zimbardo, P. G. (2009).

2. MULTIPLE AUTHORS. List up to twenty authors, last name first, with commas separating authors' names and an ampersand (&) before the last author's name.

Walsh, M. E., & Murphy, J. A. (2003).

Note: For a work with more than twenty authors, list the first nineteen, then an ellipsis (. . .), and then the final author's name.

3. CORPORATE OR GROUP AUTHOR

Resources for Rehabilitation. (2016).

4. UNKNOWN AUTHOR. Begin with the work's title. Italicize book titles, but do not italicize article titles or enclose them in quotation marks. Capitalize only the first word of the title and subtitle (if any) and proper nouns and proper adjectives.

Safe youth, safe schools. (2009).

5. TWO OR MORE WORKS BY THE SAME AUTHOR. List works by the same author in chronological order. Repeat the author's name in each entry.

Goodall, J. (2009).

Goodall, J. (2013).

If the works appeared in the same year, list them alphabetically by title, and assign lowercase letters (*a*, *b*, etc.) after the dates.

Shermer, M. (2002a). On estimating the lifetime of civilizations. *Scientific American, 287*(2), 33.

Shermer, M. (2002b). Readers who question evolution. *Scientific American, 287*(1), 37.

Print books

6. BASIC FORMAT FOR A BOOK. The source map on p. 187 shows where to find information in a typical book. Take information from the book's title page and copyright page, not from the book's cover or a library catalog.

1. **Author.** List all authors' last names first, and use only initials for first and middle names. For more about citing authors, see models 1–5.
2. **Publication year.** Enclose the year of publication in parentheses.
3. **Title.** Italicize the title and any subtitle. Capitalize only the first word of the title and the subtitle and any proper nouns or proper adjectives.
4. **Publisher.** List the publisher's name, dropping any corporate abbreviations such as *Inc. or Co.*

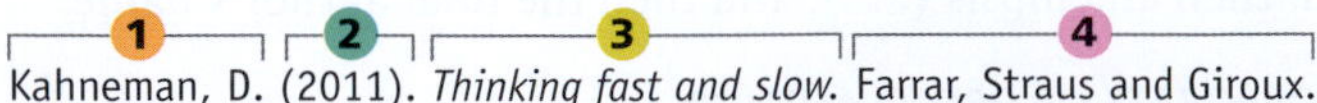

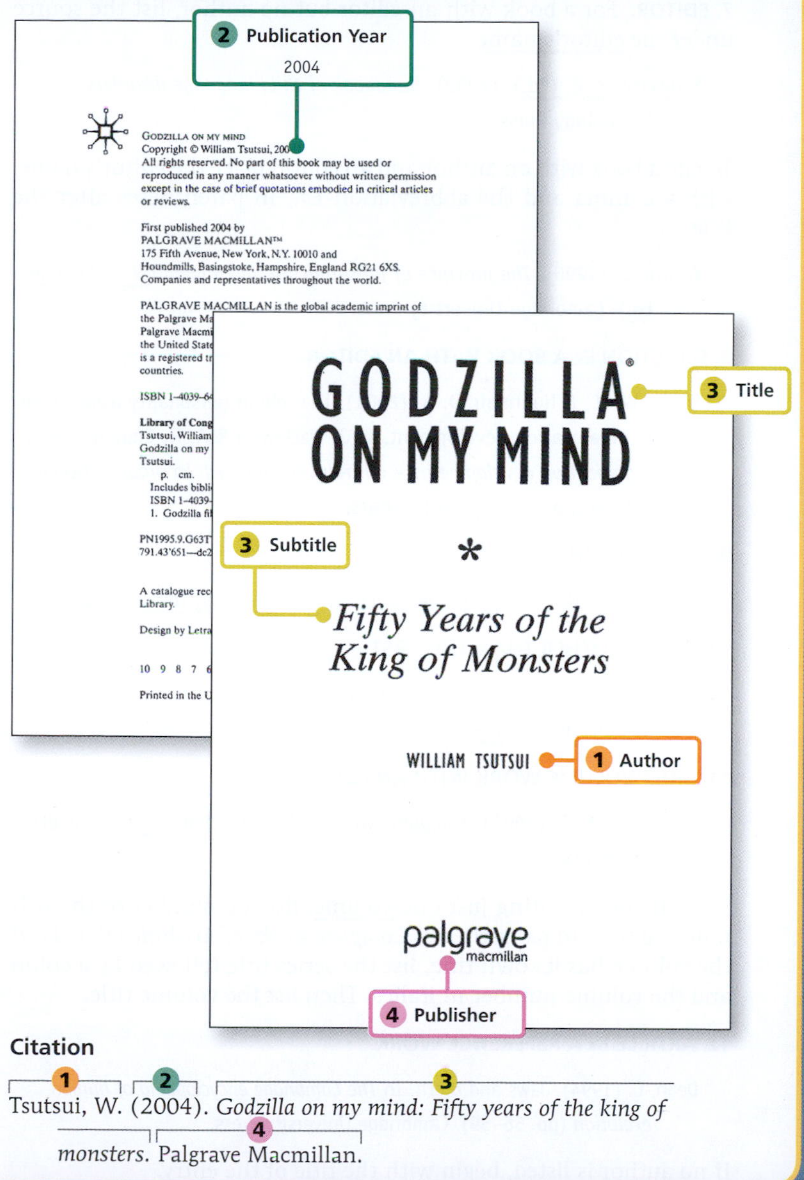
2 Publication Year
2004
GODZILLA ON MY MIND
Copyright © William Tsutsui, 2004
All rights reserved. No part of this book may be used or reproduced in any manner whatsoever without written permission except in the case of brief quotations embodied in critical articles or reviews.
First published 2004 by
PALGRAVE MACMILLAN™
175 Fifth Avenue, New York, N.Y. 10010 and
Houndmills, Basingstoke, Hampshire, England RG21 6XS.
Companies and representatives throughout the world.
PALGRAVE MACMILLAN is the global academic imprint of
GODZILLA
ON MY MIND
3 Title
3 Subtitle
Fifty Years of the King of Monsters
WILLIAM TSUTSUI
1 Author
palgrave macmillan
4 Publisher

Citation

Tsutsui, W. (2004). *Godzilla on my mind: Fifty years of the king of monsters*. Palgrave Macmillan.

7. EDITOR. For a book with an editor but no author, list the source under the editor's name.

Schwartz, R. G. (Ed.). (2009). *Handbook of child language disorders.* Psychology Press.

To cite a book with an author and an editor, place the editor's name, with a comma and the abbreviation *Ed.*, in parentheses after the title.

Austin, J. (1995). *The province of jurisprudence determined* (W. E. Rumble, Ed.). Cambridge University Press.

8. SELECTION IN A BOOK WITH AN EDITOR

Burke, W. W., & Nourmair, D. A. (2001). The role of personality assessment in organization development. In J. Waclawski & A. H. Church (Eds.), *Organization development: A data-driven approach to organizational change* (pp. 55–77). Jossey-Bass.

9. TRANSLATION

Al-Farabi, A. N. (1998). *On the perfect state* (R. Walzer, Trans.). Kazi.

10. EDITION OTHER THAN THE FIRST

Berger, K. S. (2018). *The developing person through childhood and adolescence* (11th ed.). Worth.

11. MULTIVOLUME WORK WITH AN EDITOR

Barnes, J. (Ed.). (1995). *Complete works of Aristotle* (Vols. 1–2). Princeton University Press.

Note: If you are citing just one volume, list the number of the volume you used in parentheses: *Complete works of Aristotle* (Vol. 1). If the volume has its own title, list the series title followed by a colon and the volume number in italics. Then list the volume title.

12. ARTICLE IN A REFERENCE WORK

Dean, C. (1994). Jaws and teeth. In *The Cambridge encyclopedia of human evolution* (pp. 56–59). Cambridge University Press.

If no author is listed, begin with the title of the entry.

13. REPUBLISHED BOOK

Piaget, J. (1952). *The language and thought of the child.* Routledge & Kegan Paul. (Original work published 1932)

14. INTRODUCTION, PREFACE, FOREWORD, OR AFTERWORD

Verghese, A. (2016). Foreword. In P. Kalanithi, *When breath becomes air* (pp. xi–xix). Random House.

15. BOOK WITH A TITLE WITHIN THE TITLE. Do not italicize or enclose in quotation marks a title within a book title.

Klarman, M. J. (2007). Brown v. Board of Education *and the civil rights movement.* Oxford University Press.

Print periodicals

The source map on p. 190 shows where to find information in a sample periodical.

1. **Author.** List all authors' last names first, and use only initials for first and middle names. For more about citing authors, see models 1–5.
2. **Publication date.** Enclose the date in parentheses. For journals, use only the year. For magazines and newspapers, use the year, a comma, the month (spelled out), and the day, if given.
3. **Article title.** Do not italicize or enclose article titles in quotation marks. Capitalize only the first word of the article title and subtitle and any proper nouns or proper adjectives.
4. **Periodical title.** Italicize the periodical title (and subtitle, if any), and capitalize all major words. Follow the periodical title with a comma.
5. **Volume and issue numbers.** Give the volume number (italicized) and, without a space in between, the issue number (if given) in parentheses. Follow with a comma.
6. **Page numbers.** Give the inclusive page numbers of the article. End the citation with a period.

APA SOURCE MAP: Articles from Print Periodicals

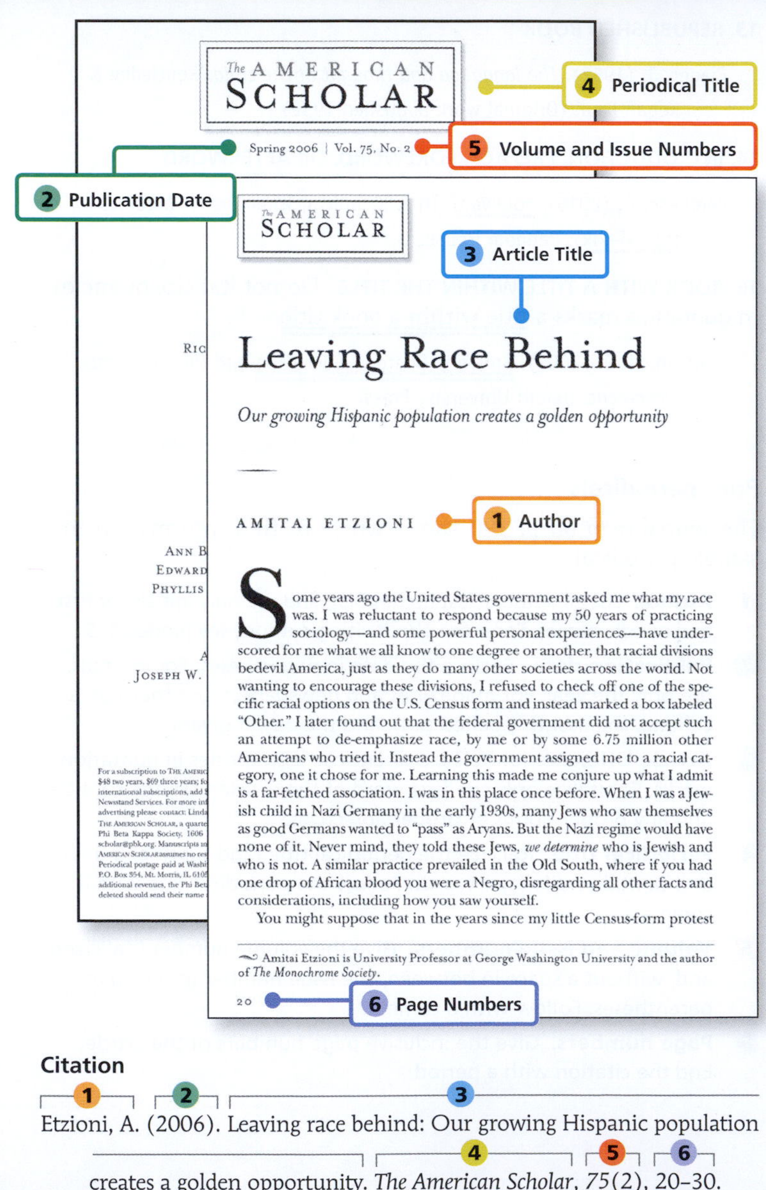

The AMERICAN SCHOLAR

Spring 2006 | Vol. 75, No. 2

The AMERICAN SCHOLAR

Leaving Race Behind

Our growing Hispanic population creates a golden opportunity

AMITAI ETZIONI

Some years ago the United States government asked me what my race was. I was reluctant to respond because my 50 years of practicing sociology—and some powerful personal experiences—have underscored for me what we all know to one degree or another, that racial divisions bedevil America, just as they do many other societies across the world. Not wanting to encourage these divisions, I refused to check off one of the specific racial options on the U.S. Census form and instead marked a box labeled "Other." I later found out that the federal government did not accept such an attempt to de-emphasize race, by me or by some 6.75 million other Americans who tried it. Instead the government assigned me to a racial category, one it chose for me. Learning this made me conjure up what I admit is a far-fetched association. I was in this place once before. When I was a Jewish child in Nazi Germany in the early 1930s, many Jews who saw themselves as good Germans wanted to "pass" as Aryans. But the Nazi regime would have none of it. Never mind, they told these Jews, *we determine* who is Jewish and who is not. A similar practice prevailed in the Old South, where if you had one drop of African blood you were a Negro, disregarding all other facts and considerations, including how you saw yourself.

You might suppose that in the years since my little Census-form protest

Amitai Etzioni is University Professor at George Washington University and the author of *The Monochrome Society*.

20

Citation

Etzioni, A. (2006). Leaving race behind: Our growing Hispanic population creates a golden opportunity. *The American Scholar*, *75*(2), 20–30.

16. ARTICLE IN A JOURNAL Include the issue number (in parentheses and not italicized) after the volume number (italicized).

Hall, R. E. (2000). Marriage as vehicle of racism among women of color. *Psychology: A Journal of Human Behavior, 37*(2), 29–40.

17. ARTICLE IN A MAGAZINE. Include the month (and day, if given).

Vlahos, J. (2019, March). Alexa, I want answers. *Wired*, 58–65.

If the magazine uses volume and issue numbers, include them.

Koch, C. (2019, October). Is death reversible? *Scientific American, 321*(4), 34–37.

18. ARTICLE IN A NEWSPAPER.

Reynolds Lewis, K. (2011, December 22). Why some business owners think now is the time to sell. *The New York Times,* B5.

19. EDITORIAL OR LETTER TO THE EDITOR. Add an identifying label.

Zelneck, B. (2003, July 18). Serving the public at public universities [Letter to the editor]. *The Chronicle Review,* B18.

20. UNSIGNED ARTICLE

Annual meeting announcement. (2003, March). *Cognitive Psychology, 46*(2), 227.

21. REVIEW. Identify the work reviewed.

Hall, W. (2019). [Review of the book *How to change your mind: The new science of psychedelics,* by M. Pollan]. *Addiction, 114*(10), 1892–1893.

22. PUBLISHED INTERVIEW. Follow the model for the source type in which the interview was published (for example, journal, magazine, or newspaper). Typically the interview subject is named in the title, but if not, work the person's name into your text in a signal phrase.

 Checklist

Citing Digital Sources

When citing sources accessed online or from an electronic database, include as many of the following elements as you can find:

- **Author.** Give the author's name, if available.
- **Publication date.** Include the date of electronic publication, if available. When no publication date is available, use *n.d.* ("no date").
- **Title.** If the source is not from a larger work, italicize the title.
- **Print publication information.** For articles from online journals, magazines, or reference databases, give the publication title and other publishing information as you would for a print periodical (see models 16–22).
- **Retrieval information.** If an article from a database has a DOI (digital object identifier), include that number after the publication information, using the format *https://doi.org/* followed by the identifier; do not include the name of the database unless it is the only place where the work is available. For a work found on a website, include the URL. You may shorten lengthy URLs using a site like bitly.com. If the work is intended to be updated frequently, include the retrieval date.

 Checklist

Citing Sources without Models in APA Style

You may need to cite a source for which you cannot find a model in APA style. If so, collect as much information as you can find about the author, title, date, and so on, with the goal of helping readers find the source for themselves. Then look at the models in this section to see which one most closely matches the type of source you are using.

In an academic project, before citing an electronic source for which you have no model, ask your instructor's advice.

Digital written-word sources

23. ARTICLE FROM AN ONLINE PERIODICAL. Give the author, date, title, and publication information as you would for a print document. Include both the volume and issue numbers for all journal articles.

If the article has a digital object identifier (DOI), include it. If there is no DOI, include a stable, direct-link URL, if available. If the URL is lengthy, you can include a shortened form.

Daly, J. (2019, August 2). Duquesne's med school plan part of national trend to train more doctors. *Pittsburgh Post-Gazette*. https://bit.ly/2Vzrm2l

Ganegoda, D. B., & Bordia, P. (2019). I can be happy for you, but not all the time: A contingency model of envy and positive empathy in the workplace. *Journal of Applied Psychology, 104*(6), 776–795. https://doi.org/10.1037/apl0000377

24. ARTICLE FROM A DATABASE. The source map on p. 194 shows where to find information for a typical article from a database.

1. **Author.** Include the author's name as you would for a print source. List all authors' last names first, and use initials for first and middle names. For more about citing authors, see models 1–5.
2. **Publication date.** Enclose the date in parentheses. For journals, use only the year. For magazines and newspapers, use the year, a comma, the month, and the day if given.
3. **Article title.** Capitalize only the first word of the article title and the subtitle and any proper nouns or proper adjectives.
4. **Periodical title.** Italicize the periodical title.
5. **Volume and issue number.** For journals and magazines, give the volume number (italicized) and the issue number (in parentheses).
6. **Page numbers.** Give inclusive page numbers.
7. **Retrieval information.** If the article has a DOI (digital object identifier), include that number after the publication information; do not include the name of the database. If there is no DOI, include a URL only if your readers will have access to the database. Do not add a period after the DOI or URL.

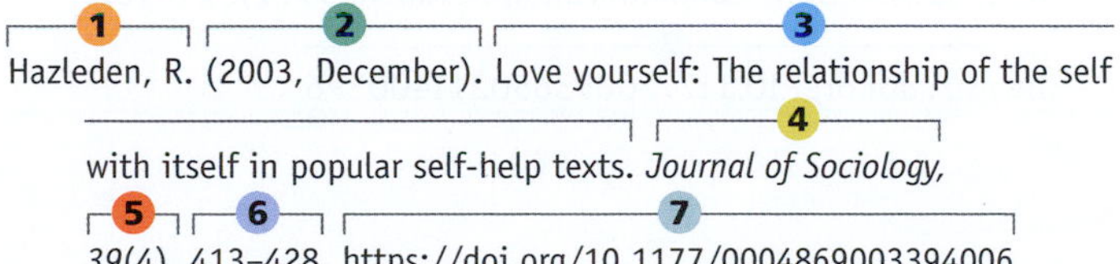

1
2
3
Hazleden, R. (2003, December). Love yourself: The relationship of the self
4
with itself in popular self-help texts. *Journal of Sociology,*
5
6
7
39(4), 413–428. https://doi.org/10.1177/0004869003394006

APA SOURCE MAP: Articles from Databases

3 Article Title

4 Periodical Title

6 Page Numbers

Communication Research
39(1) 79–102
© The Author(s) 2012
Reprints and permission:
sagepub.com/journalsPermissions.nav
DOI: 10.1177/0093650211400596
http://crx.sagepub.com
SAGE

A Losing Battle: Effects of Prolonged Exposure to Thin-Ideal Images on Dieting and Body Satisfaction

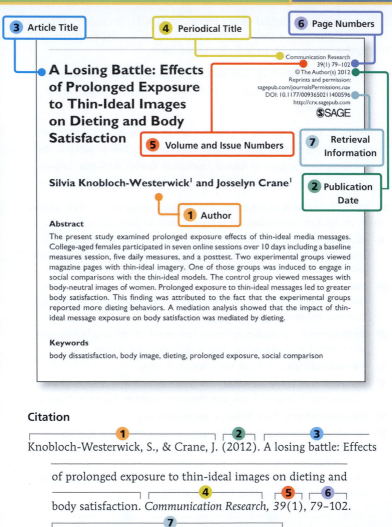

5 Volume and Issue Numbers

7 Retrieval Information

Silvia Knobloch-Westerwick[1] and Josselyn Crane[1]

2 Publication Date

1 Author

Abstract

The present study examined prolonged exposure effects of thin-ideal media messages. College-aged females participated in seven online sessions over 10 days including a baseline measures session, five daily measures, and a posttest. Two experimental groups viewed magazine pages with thin-ideal imagery. One of those groups was induced to engage in social comparisons with the thin-ideal models. The control group viewed messages with body-neutral images of women. Prolonged exposure to thin-ideal messages led to greater body satisfaction. This finding was attributed to the fact that the experimental groups reported more dieting behaviors. A mediation analysis showed that the impact of thin-ideal message exposure on body satisfaction was mediated by dieting.

Keywords

body dissatisfaction, body image, dieting, prolonged exposure, social comparison

Citation

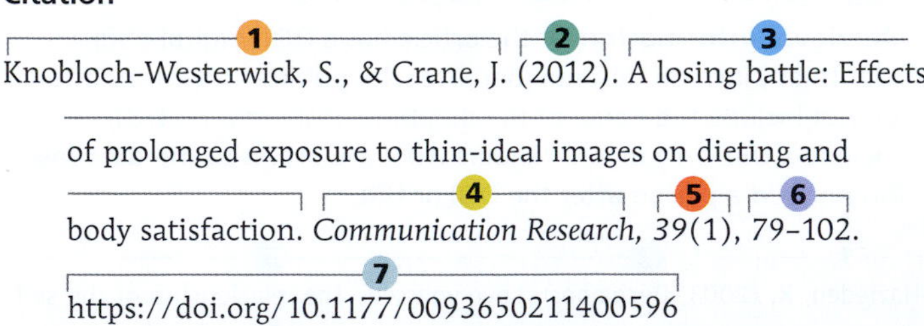

Knobloch-Westerwick, S., & Crane, J. (2012). A losing battle: Effects of prolonged exposure to thin-ideal images on dieting and body satisfaction. *Communication Research, 39*(1), 79–102. https://doi.org/10.1177/0093650211400596

25. ABSTRACT FOR AN ONLINE ARTICLE. Include a label.

Gudjonsson, G. H., & Young, S. (2010). Does confabulation in memory predict suggestibility beyond IQ and memory? [Abstract]. *Personality & Individual Differences, 49*(1), 65–67. https://doi.org/10.1016/j.paid.2010.03.014

26. COMMENT ON AN ONLINE ARTICLE. Give the writer's real name (if known) or screen name. If the comment has no title, use up to the first twenty words as the title. Then, in square brackets, include the words "Comment on the article" and the article title in quotation marks.

lollyl2. (2019, September 25). My husband works in IT in a major city down South. He is a permanent employee now, but for years [Comment on the article "The Google workers who voted to unionize in Pittsburgh are part of tech's huge contractor workforce"]. *Slate*. https://fyre.it/0RT8HmeL.4

27. REPORT OR LONG DOCUMENT FROM A WEBSITE. The source map on p. 196 shows where to find information for a report from a website. Include all of the following information that you can find.

1. **Author.** If one is given, include the author's name (see models 1–5). List last names first, and use only initials for first names. The site's sponsor may be the author. If no author is identified, begin the citation with the title of the document.
2. **Publication date.** Enclose the date of publication in parentheses. Use *n.d.* ("no date") when no publication date is available.
3. **Title of work.** Italicize the title. Capitalize only the first word of the title and subtitle and any proper nouns or proper adjectives.
4. **Retrieval information.** Include the name of the website (with no italics), if different from the author. End with the URL, and do not add a period at the end of the URL.

Ford Foundation International Fellowships Program. (2019). *Leveraging higher education to promote social justice: Evidence from the IFP alumni tracking study*. https://p.widencdn.net/kei61u/IFP-Alumni-Tracking-Study-Report-5

APA SOURCE MAP: Reports and Long Works from Websites

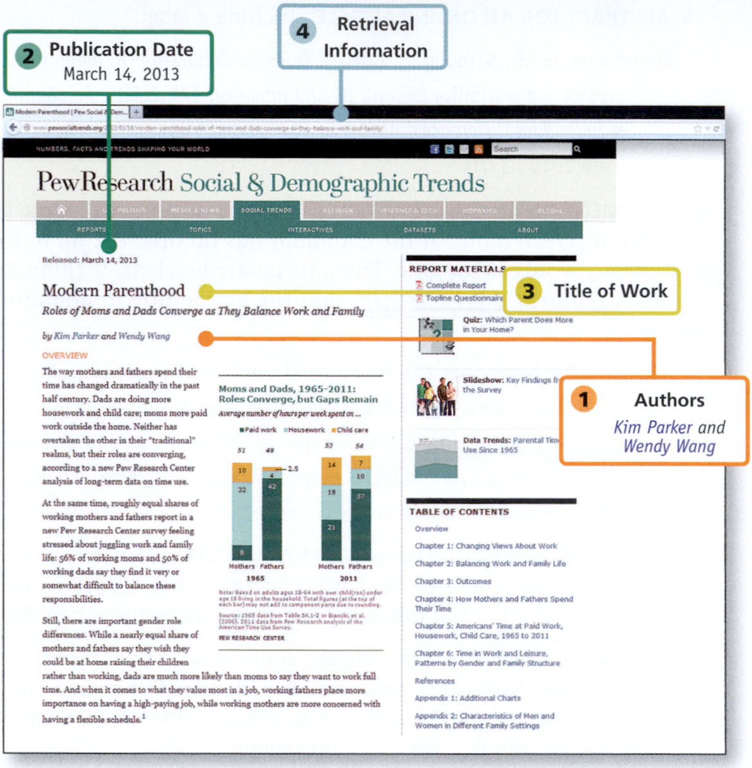

2 Publication Date
March 14, 2013

4 Retrieval Information

Modern Parenthood | Pew Social & Dem...

www.pewsocialtrends.org/2013/03/14/modern-parenthood-roles-of-moms-and-dads-converge-as-they-balance-work-and-family/

NUMBERS, FACTS AND TRENDS SHAPING YOUR WORLD

Search

PewResearch Social & Demographic Trends

U.S. POLITICS | MEDIA & NEWS | SOCIAL TRENDS | RELIGION | INTERNET & TECH | HISPANICS | GLOBAL

REPORTS | TOPICS | INTERACTIVES | DATASETS | ABOUT

Released: March 14, 2013

Modern Parenthood

Roles of Moms and Dads Converge as They Balance Work and Family

by Kim Parker and Wendy Wang

OVERVIEW

The way mothers and fathers spend their time has changed dramatically in the past half century. Dads are doing more housework and child care; moms more paid work outside the home. Neither has overtaken the other in their "traditional" realms, but their roles are converging, according to a new Pew Research Center analysis of long-term data on time use.

At the same time, roughly equal shares of working mothers and fathers report in a new Pew Research Center survey feeling stressed about juggling work and family life: 56% of working moms and 50% of working dads say they find it very or somewhat difficult to balance these responsibilities.

Still, there are important gender role differences. While a nearly equal share of mothers and fathers say they wish they could be at home raising their children rather than working, dads are much more likely than moms to say they want to work full time. And when it comes to what they value most in a job, working fathers place more importance on having a high-paying job, while working mothers are more concerned with having a flexible schedule.[1]

Moms and Dads, 1965-2011: Roles Converge, but Gaps Remain

Average number of hours per week spent on ...

	Mothers 1965	Fathers 1965	Mothers 2011	Fathers 2011
Total	51	49	53	54
Child care	10	2.5	14	7
Housework	32	4	18	10
Paid work	8	42	21	37

Note: Based on adults ages 18-64 with own child(ren) under age 18 living in the household. Total figures (at the top of each bar) may not add to component parts due to rounding.

Source: 1965 data from Table 5A.1-2 in Bianchi, et al. (2006). 2011 data from Pew Research analysis of the American Time Use Survey.

PEW RESEARCH CENTER

REPORT MATERIALS

Complete Report

Topline Questionnaire

3 Title of Work

Quiz: Which Parent Does More in Your Home?

Slideshow: Key Findings from the Survey

Data Trends: Parental Time Use Since 1965

1 Authors
Kim Parker and Wendy Wang

TABLE OF CONTENTS

Overview

Chapter 1: Changing Views About Work

Chapter 2: Balancing Work and Family Life

Chapter 3: Outcomes

Chapter 4: How Mothers and Fathers Spend Their Time

Chapter 5: Americans' Time at Paid Work, Housework, Child Care, 1965 to 2011

Chapter 6: Time in Work and Leisure, Patterns by Gender and Family Structure

References

Appendix 1: Additional Charts

Appendix 2: Characteristics of Men and Women in Different Family Settings

Citation

Parker, K., & Wang, W. (2013, March 14). *Modern parenthood: Roles of moms and dads converge as they balance work and family.* Pew Research Center. http://www.pewsocialtrends.org/2013/03/14/modern-parenthood-roles-of-moms-and-dads-converge-as-they-balance-work-and-family/

4

28. SHORT WORK FROM A WEBSITE. If the work can be cited using a model for another category (e.g., an article from an online periodical), use that model instead.

BBC News. (2019, October 31). *California fires: Goats help save Ronald Reagan Presidential Library*. https://bbc.com/news/world-us-canada-50248549

29. ONLINE BOOK. Give the original print publication date, if different, in parentheses at the end of the entry.

Russell, B. (2008). *The analysis of mind*. Project Gutenberg. https://www.gutenberg.org/files/2529/2529-h/2529-h.htm (Original work published 1921)

30. EMAIL OR PRIVATE MESSAGE. Do not include entries for email messages or any postings that are not retrievable by your readers. Instead, cite these sources in your text as forms of personal communication (see p. 181).

31. POSTING ON PUBLIC SOCIAL MEDIA. Provide the author's name, the date of posting, and the title in italics. If there is no title, include up to the first twenty words of the post or caption, including any emojis, hashtags, or links. Then describe images, recordings, and the type of post in square brackets. Include the name of the social media service and the URL. If the post is not archived, include an access date.

Georgia Aquarium. (2019, June 25). *True love ♥♥ Charlie and Lizzy are a bonded pair of African penguins who have been together for more than* [Image attached] [Status update]. Facebook. https://www.facebook.com/GeorgiaAquarium/photos/a.163898398123/10156900637543124/?type=3&theater

32. BLOG POST OR COMMENT. Treat a blog post like an article in a magazine or newspaper and a comment on a blog post like a comment on an online article (see model 26).

Black, D. (2016, May 14). How to succeed. *Eschaton*. http://www.eschatonblog.com/2016/05/how-to-succeed.html

33. WIKI ENTRY. Use the date of posting, if there is one, or *n.d.* for "no date" if there is none. Include the retrieval date unless you can link to an archived version of the page.

Happiness. (2007, June 14). In *PsychWiki*. Retrieved March 24, 2016, from http://www.psychwiki.com/wiki/Happiness

Other sources (including online versions)

34. GOVERNMENT PUBLICATION

Office of the Federal Register. (2003). *The United States government manual 2003/2004*. U.S. Government Printing Office.

Berchick, E. R., Barnett, J. C., & Upton, R. D. (2019, September 10). *Health insurance coverage in the United States: 2018* (Report No. P60-267). U.S. Census Bureau. https://www.census.gov/library/publications/2019/demo/p60-267.html

35. DATA SET

Reid, L. (2019). *Smarter homes: Experiences of living in low carbon homes 2013–2018* [Data set]. UK Data Service. http://doi.org/10.5255/UKDA-SN-853485

36. DISSERTATION. If you retrieved the dissertation from a database, give the publication number and database name. If you retrieved it from the granting university's website, provide information about that source and the URL.

Bacaksizlar, N. G. (2019). *Understanding social movements through simulations of anger contagion in social media* (Publication No. 13805848) [Doctoral dissertation, University of North Carolina at Charlotte]. ProQuest Dissertations & Theses.

Degli-Esposti, M. (2019). *Child maltreatment and antisocial behaviour in the United Kingdom: Changing risks over time* [Doctoral dissertation, University of Oxford]. Oxford University Research Archive. https://ora.ox.ac.uk/objects/uuid:6d5a8e55-bd19-41a1-8ef5-ef485642af89

37. TECHNICAL OR RESEARCH REPORT. Give the report number, if available, in parentheses after the title.

McCool, R., Fikes, R., & McGuinness, D. (2003). *Semantic web tools for enhanced authoring* (Report No. KSL-03-07). Knowledge Systems Laboratory, Stanford University. www.ksl.stanford.edu/KSL_Abstracts/KSL-03-07.html

38. CONFERENCE PROCEEDINGS

Robertson, S. P., Vatrapu, R. K., & Medina, R. (2009). YouTube and Facebook: Online video "friends" social networking. In *Conference proceedings: YouTube and the 2008 election cycle* (pp. 159–176). University of Massachusetts. http://scholarworks.umass.edu/jitpc2009

39. PAPER PRESENTED AT A MEETING OR SYMPOSIUM, UNPUBLISHED. Include the full dates, name, and location of the meeting.

Vasylets, O. (2019, April 10–13). *Memory accuracy in bilinguals depends on the valence of the emotional event* [Paper presentation]. XIV International Symposium of Psycholinguistics, Tarragona, Spain.

40. POSTER SESSION

Wood, M. (2019, January 3–6). *The effects of an adult development course on students' perceptions of aging* [Poster session]. Forty-First Annual National Institute on the Teaching of Psychology, St. Pete Beach, FL, United States. https://nitop.org/resources/Documents/2019%20Poster%20Session%20II.pdf

41. PRESENTATION SLIDES

Centers for Disease Control and Prevention. (2019, April 16). *Building local response capacity to protect families from emerging health threats* [Presentation slides]. CDC Stacks. https://stacks.cdc.gov/view/cdc/77687

42. FILM, VIDEO, DVD, OR BLU-RAY. Include the director's name and the year of release. You do not need to specify the format unless it is a special version such as *[Extended Blu-ray edition]*. Include the label *[Film]* and the production company (or companies) after the title.

Peele, J. (Director). (2017). *Get out* [Film]. Universal Pictures.

Hitchcock, A. (Director). (1959). *The essentials collection: North by northwest* [Film; five-disc special ed. on DVD]. Metro-Goldwyn-Mayer; Universal Pictures Home Entertainment.

43. ONLINE (STREAMING) AUDIO OR VIDEO FILE List the person or organization that posted the file as the author.

Klusman, P. (2008, February 13). *An engineer's guide to cats* [Video]. http://www.youtube.com/watch?v=mHXBL6bzAR4

BBC. (2018, November 19). *Why do bad managers flourish?* [Audio]. In *Business Matters*. https://www.bbc.co.uk/programmes/p06s8752

44. TELEVISION PROGRAM, SINGLE EPISODE

Waller-Bridge, P. (Writer), & Bradbeer, H. (Director). (2019, March 18). The provocative request (Season 2, Episode 3) [TV series episode]. In P. Waller-Bridge, H. Williams, & J. Williams (Executive Producers), *Fleabag*. Two Brothers Pictures; BBC.

45. TELEVISION SERIES

Waller-Bridge, P., Williams, H., & Williams, J. (Executive Producers). (2016–2019). *Fleabag* [TV series]. Two Brothers Pictures; BBC.

46. PODCAST EPISODE

West, S. (Host). (2018, July 27). Logical positivism (No. 120) [Audio podcast episode]. In *Philosophize this!* https://philosophizethis.org/logical-positivists/

47. RECORDING

Carlile, B. (2018). The mother [Song]. On *By the way, I forgive you*. Low Country Sound; Elektra.

16e STUDENT WRITING Causal analysis essay with abstract, APA style

On the following pages is a paper by Tawnya Redding that conforms to the APA guidelines described in this chapter.

LaunchPad Solo
macmillan learning

Documentation: APA Style > Student Writing: APA-style research project (Martha Bell)

STUDENT WRITING

1

Mood Music: Music Preference and the Risk for Depression and Suicide in Adolescents

Tawnya Redding
Department of Psychology, University of Oregon
PSY 101: Introduction to Psychology
Dr. Juliana Martinez
October 29, 2019

Page number appears flush right on first line of every page

Title centered, boldface, 3-4 lines below top margin, followed by a blank line

Name, department & school, course number & name, instructor's name, and assignment due date, centered

STUDENT WRITING

Abstract included at instructor's request. Heading centered and boldface.

No indentation

Use of passive voice appropriate for social sciences

Clear description of literature under review

Conclusions indicated

2

Abstract

There has long been concern for the effects that certain genres of music (such as heavy metal and country) have on youth. While a correlational link between these genres and increased risk for depression and suicide in adolescents has been established, researchers have been unable to pinpoint what is responsible for this link, and a causal relationship has not been determined. This paper will begin by discussing correlational literature concerning music preference and increased risk for depression and suicide, as well as the possible reasons for this link. Finally, studies concerning the effects of music on mood will be discussed. This examination of the literature on music and increased risk for depression and suicide points out the limitations of previous research and suggests the need for new research establishing a causal relationship for this link as well as research into the specific factors that may contribute to an increased risk for depression and suicide in adolescents.

STUDENT WRITING

3

Mood Music: Music Preference and the Risk for Depression and Suicide in Adolescents

Full title, centered and boldface

Music is a significant part of American culture. Since the explosion of rock and roll in the 1950s there has been a concern for the effects that music may have on listeners, and especially on young people. The genres most likely to come under suspicion in recent decades have included heavy metal, country, and blues. These genres have been suspected of having adverse effects on the mood and behavior of young listeners. But can music really alter the disposition and create self-destructive behaviors in listeners? And if so, which genres and aspects of those genres are responsible? The following review of the literature will establish the correlation between potentially problematic genres of music such as heavy metal and country and depression and suicide risk. First, correlational studies concerning music preference and suicide risk will be discussed, followed by a discussion of the literature concerning the possible reasons for this link. Finally, studies concerning the effects of music on mood will be discussed. Despite the link between genres such as heavy metal and country and suicide risk, previous research has been unable to establish the causal nature of this link.

Paragraphs indented

Background information about topic supplied

Questions focus reader's attention

The Correlation Between Music and Depression and Suicide Risk

Boldface headings help organize review

Studies over the past two decades have set out to answer this question by examining the correlation between youth music preference and risk for depression and suicide. A large portion of these studies have focused on heavy metal and country music as the main genre culprits associated with youth suicidality and depression (Lacourse et al., 2001; Scheel & Westefeld, 1999;

Multiple sources in one parenthetical citation separated by semicolons

STUDENT WRITING

4

In parentheses, two author names joined with &; in text, names joined with *and*

Stack & Gundlach, 1992). Stack and Gundlach (1992) examined the radio airtime devoted to country music in 49 metropolitan areas and found that the higher the percentages of country music airtime, the higher the incidence of suicides among whites. The researchers hypothesized that themes in country music (such as alcohol abuse) promoted audience identification and reinforced a preexisting suicidal mood, and that the themes associated with country music were responsible for elevated suicide rates. Similarly, Scheel and Westefeld (1999) found a correlation between heavy metal music listeners and an increased risk for suicide, as did Lacourse et al. (2001).

Reasons for the Link: Characteristics of Those Who Listen to Problematic Music

Discussion of correlation vs. causation points out limitations of previous studies

Unfortunately, previous studies concerning music preference and suicide risk have been unable to determine a causal relationship and have focused mainly on establishing a correlation between suicide risk and music preference. This leaves the question open as to whether an individual at risk for depression and suicide is attracted to certain genres of music or whether the music helps induce the mood — or both. Some studies have suggested that music preference may simply be a reflection of other underlying problems associated with increased risk for suicide (Lacourse et al., 2001; Scheel & Westefeld, 1999). For example, in research done by Scheel and Westefeld (1999), adolescents who listened to heavy metal were found to have lower scores on the Reason for Living Inventory and several of its subscales, a self-report measure designed to assess potential reasons for not committing suicide. These adolescents were also found to have lower scores on several subscales of the Reason for Living Inventory, including responsibility to family along with survival and coping beliefs. Other risk factors associated with suicide and suicidal behaviors include poor family relationships, depression, alienation, anomie, and drug and alcohol abuse (Lacourse et al., 2001).

Alternative explanations considered

5

Lacourse et al. (2001) examined 275 adolescents in the Montreal region with a preference for heavy metal and found that this preference was not significantly related to suicide risk when other risk factors were controlled for. This was also the conclusion of Scheel and Westefeld (1999), in which music preference for heavy metal was thought to be a red flag for suicide vulnerability, suggesting that the source of the problem may lie more in personal and familial characteristics.

George et al. (2007) further explored the correlation between suicide risk and music preference by attempting to identify the personality characteristics of those with a preference for different genres of music. A sample of 358 individuals was assessed for preference of thirty different styles of music along with a number of personality characteristics, including self-esteem, intelligence, spirituality, social skills, locus of control, openness, conscientiousness, extraversion, agreeableness, emotional stability, hostility, and depression (George et al., 2007). The thirty styles of music were then categorized into eight factors: rebellious (for example, punk and heavy metal), classical, rhythmic and intense (including hip-hop, rap, and pop), easy listening, fringe (for example, techno), contemporary Christian, jazz and blues, and traditional Christian. The results revealed an almost comprehensively negative personality profile for those who preferred to listen to the rebellious and rhythmic and intense categories, while those who preferred classical music tended to have a comprehensively positive profile. Like Scheel and Westefeld (1999) and Lacourse et al. (2001), this study also supports the theory that youth are drawn to certain genres of music based on already existing factors, whether they be related to personality or situational variables.

First author name and *et al.* used for sources with three or more authors.

STUDENT WRITING

6

Reasons for the Link: Characteristics of Problematic Music

Transition links paragraphs

Another possible explanation is that the lyrics and themes of the music have an effect on listeners. In this scenario, music is thought to exacerbate an already depressed mood and hence contribute to an increased risk for suicide. This was the proposed reasoning behind higher suicide rates in whites in Stack and Gundlach's (1992) study linking country music to suicide risk. In this case, the themes associated with country music were thought to promote audience identification and reinforce preexisting self-destructive behaviors (such as excessive alcohol consumption). Stack (2000) also studied individuals with a musical preference for blues to determine whether the genre's themes could increase the level of suicide acceptability. The results demonstrated that blues fans were no more accepting of suicide than nonfans, but that blues listeners were found to have low religiosity levels, an important factor for suicide acceptability (Stack, 2000). Despite this link between possible suicidal behavior and a preference for blues music, the actual suicide behavior of blues fans has not been explored, and thus no concrete associations can be made.

Need for more research indicated

The Effect of Music on Mood

Discussion of previous research

While studies examining the relationship between music genres such as heavy metal, country, and blues have been able to establish a correlation between music preference and suicide risk, it is still unclear from these studies what effect music has on the mood of the listener. Previous research has suggested that some forms of music can both improve and depress mood (Lai, 1999; Siedliecki & Good, 2006; Smith & Noon, 1998). Lai (1999) found that changes in mood were more likely to be found in an experimental group of depressed women versus a control group. It was also found that both the experimental and control groups showed significant increases in the tranquil mood state, but the amount of change was not

7

significant between the groups (Lai, 1999). This study suggests that music can have a positive effect on depressed individuals when they are allowed to choose the music they are listening to. In a similar study, Siedliecki and Good (2006) found that music can increase a listener's sense of power and decrease depression, pain, and disability. Researchers randomly assigned sixty African American and Caucasian participants with chronic nonmalignant pain to a standard music group (offering them a choice of instrumental music types — piano, jazz, orchestra, harp, and synthesizer), a patterning music group (asking them to choose music to ease muscle tension, to facilitate sleep, or to decrease anxiety), or a control group. There were no statistically significant differences between the two music groups. However, the music groups had significantly less pain, depression, and disability than the control group (Siedliecki & Good, 2006). On the other hand, Martin et al. (1993) identified a subgroup of heavy metal fans who reported feeling worse after listening to their music of choice. Although this subgroup did exist, there was also evidence that listening to heavy metal results in more positive affect, and it was hypothesized that those who experience negative effects after listening to their preferred genre of heavy metal may be most at risk for suicidal behaviors (Martin et al., 1993).

Smith and Noon (1998) also determined that music can have a negative effect on mood. Six songs were selected for the particular theme they embodied: (1) vigorous, (2) fatigued, (3) angry, (4) depressed, (5) tense, and (6) all moods. The results indicated that selections 3–6 had significant effects on the mood of participants, with selection 6 (all moods) resulting in the greatest positive change in the mood and selection 5 (tense) resulting in the greatest negative change in mood. Selection 4 (depressed) was found to sap the vigor and increase anger/hostility in participants, while selection 5 (tense) significantly depressed participants and made them more anxious. Although this study did not specifically comment on the effects

STUDENT WRITING

8

of different genres on mood, the results do indicate that certain themes can indeed depress mood. The participants for this study were undergraduate students who were not depressed, and thus it seems that certain types of music can have a negative effect on the mood of healthy individuals.

Is There Evidence for a Causal Relationship?

Conclusion indicates need for further research

Despite the correlation between certain music genres (especially heavy metal) and increased risk for depression and suicidal behaviors in adolescents, it remains unclear whether these types of music can alter the mood of at-risk youth in a negative way. This view of the correlation between music and suicide risk is supported by a meta-analysis done by Baker and Bor (2008), in which the authors assert that most studies reject the notion that music is a causal factor and suggest that music preference is more indicative of emotional vulnerability. However, it is still unknown whether these genres can negatively alter mood at all, and if they can, whether the themes and lyrics associated with the music are responsible. Clearly, more research is needed to further examine this correlation, as a causal link between these genres of music and adolescent suicide risk has yet to be shown. However, even if the theory put forth by Baker and Bor and other researchers is true, it is still important to investigate the effects that music can have on those who may be at risk for suicide and depression. Even if music genres are not the ultimate cause of suicidal behavior, they may act as a catalyst that further pushes adolescents into a state of depression and increased risk for suicidal behavior.

STUDENT WRITING

9

References begin on new page

Print journal article

Journal article from a database with DOI

References

Baker, F., & Bor, W. (2008). Can music preference indicate mental health status in young people? *Australasian Psychiatry, 16*(4), 284–288. https://doi.org/10.1080/10398560701879589

George, D., Stickle, K., Rachid, F., & Wopnford, A. (2007). The association between types of music enjoyed and cognitive, behavioral, and personality factors of those who listen. *Psychomusicology, 19*(2), 32–56.

Lacourse, E., Claes, M., & Villeneuve, M. (2001). Heavy metal music and adolescent suicidal risk. *Journal of Youth and Adolescence, 30*(3), 321–332.

Lai, Y. (1999). Effects of music listening on depressed women in Taiwan. *Issues in Mental Health Nursing, 20*(3), 229–246. https://doi.org/10.1080/016128499248637

Martin, G., Clark, M., & Pearce, C. (1993). Adolescent suicide: Music preference as an indicator of vulnerability. *Journal of the American Academy of Child and Adolescent Psychiatry, 32*(3), 530–535.

Scheel, K., & Westefeld, J. (1999). Heavy metal music and adolescent suicidality: An empirical investigation. *Adolescence, 34*(134), 253–273.

Siedliecki, S., & Good, M. (2006). Effect of music on power, pain, depression and disability. *Journal of Advanced Nursing, 54*(5), 553–562. https://doi.org/10.1111/j.1365-2648.2006.03860.x

Smith, J. L., & Noon, J. (1998). Objective measurement of mood change induced by contemporary music. *Journal of Psychiatric & Mental Health Nursing, 5*(5), 403–408.

Stack, S. (2000). Blues fans and suicide acceptability. *Death Studies, 24*(3), 223–231.

Stack, S., & Gundlach, J. (1992). The effect of country music on suicide. *Social Forces, 71*(1), 211–218. https://doi.org/10.1093/sf/71.1.211

17 Chicago Style

The style guide of the University of Chicago Press has long been used in history as well as in other areas of the arts and humanities. The Seventeenth Edition of *The Chicago Manual of Style* (2017) provides a complete guide to *Chicago* style, including two systems for citing sources. This chapter presents the notes and bibliography system.

17a Understanding *Chicago* citation style

Why does academic work call for very careful citation practices when writing for the general public may not? The answer is that readers of academic work expect source citations for several reasons:

- Source citations demonstrate that you've done your homework on your topic and that you are a part of the conversation surrounding it.
- Source citations show that you understand the need to give credit when you make use of someone else's intellectual property. (See Chapter 13.)
- Source citations give explicit directions to guide readers who want to look for themselves at the works you're using.

Guidelines from *The Chicago Manual of Style* will tell you exactly what information to include in your citation and how to format that information.

Types of sources. Refer to the List of Examples in *Chicago* style on pp. 214–15. You will need to be careful to tell your readers whether you read a print version or a digital version of a source. Digital magazine and newspaper articles may include updates or corrections that the print version lacks; digital books may not number pages or screens the same way the print book does. If you are citing a source with media elements—such as a film, song, or artwork—consult the "other sources" section of the examples. And if you can't find a model exactly like the source you've selected, see the box on p. 215.

ARTICLES FROM WEB AND DATABASE SOURCES. You need a subscription to look through most databases, so individual researchers almost always gain access to articles in databases through a school or public library that pays to subscribe. The easiest way to tell whether a source comes from a database, then, is that its information is *not* generally available free to anyone with an Internet connection. Many databases are digital collections of articles that originally appeared in edited print periodicals, ensuring that an authority has vouched for the accuracy of the information. Such sources may have more credibility than free material available on the web.

Parts of citations. Citations in *Chicago* style will appear in three places in your text—a note number in the text marks the material from the source, a footnote or an endnote includes information to identify the source (or information about supplemental material), and the bibliography provides the full citation.

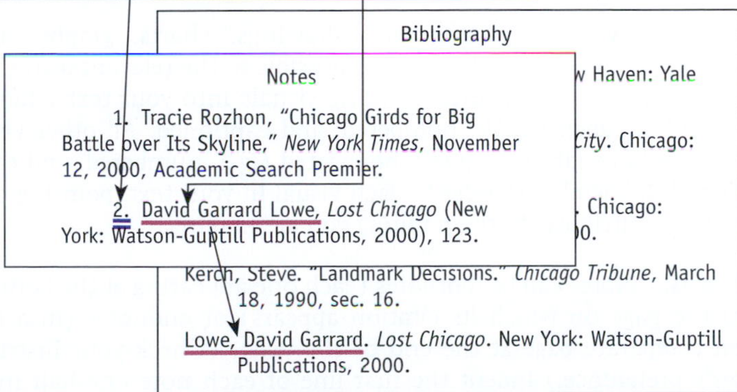

Chicago is a city for the working man. Nowhere is this more evident than in its architecture. David Garrard Lowe, author of *Lost Chicago*, notes that early Chicagoans "sought reality, not fantasy, and the reality of America as seen from the heartland did not include the pavilion of princes or the castles of kings."[2] The inclination toward unadorned, sturdy buildings began in the late nineteenth century.

Notes

1. Tracie Rozhon, "Chicago Girds for Big Battle over Its Skyline," *New York Times*, November 12, 2000, Academic Search Premier.

2. David Garrard Lowe, *Lost Chicago* (New York: Watson-Guptill Publications, 2000), 123.

Bibliography

w Haven: Yale

City. Chicago:

. Chicago:

00.

Kerch, Steve. "Landmark Decisions." *Chicago Tribune*, March 18, 1990, sec. 16.

Lowe, David Garrard. *Lost Chicago*. New York: Watson-Guptill Publications, 2000.

17b Following *Chicago* manuscript format

Title page. About halfway down the title page, center the full title of your project and your name. Unless otherwise instructed, at the bottom of the page also list the course name, the instructor's name, and the date submitted. Do not type a number on this page.

Margins and spacing. Leave one-inch margins at the top, bottom, and sides of your pages. Double-space the entire text, including block quotations and between entries in the notes and bibliography.

Page numbers. Number all pages (except the title page) in the upper right-hand corner. Also use a short title or your name before page numbers. Check to see if your instructor has a preference on whether to count the title page as part of the text (if so, the first text page will be page 2) or as part of the front matter (if so, the first text page will be page 1).

Long quotations. For a long quotation, indent one-half inch (or five spaces) from the left margin and do not use quotation marks. *Chicago* defines a long quotation as one hundred words or eight lines, though you may set off shorter quotes for emphasis (42a).

Headings. *Chicago* style allows, but does not require, headings. Many students and instructors find them helpful.

Visuals. Visuals (photographs, drawings, charts, graphs, and tables) should be placed as near as possible to the relevant text. (See 13c for guidelines on incorporating visuals into your text.) Tables should be labeled *Table,* numbered, and captioned. All other visuals should be labeled *Figure* (abbreviated *Fig.*), numbered, and captioned. Remember to refer to each visual in your text, pointing out how it contributes to the point(s) you are making.

Notes. Notes can be footnotes (each one appearing at the bottom of the page on which its citation appears) or endnotes (in a list on a separate page at the end of the text). (Check your instructor's preference.) Indent the first line of each note one-half inch and begin with a number, a period, and one space before the first word. All remaining lines of the entry are flush with the left margin. Single-space footnotes and endnotes, with a double space between each entry.

Use superscript numbers (^{1}) to mark citations in the text. Place the superscript number for each note just after the relevant quotation, sentence, clause, or phrase. Type the number after any punctuation mark except the dash, and do not leave a space before the superscript. Number citations sequentially throughout the text. When you use signal phrases to introduce source material, note that *Chicago* style requires you to use the present tense (*citing Bebout's studies, Meier argues . . .*).

IN THE TEXT

Thompson points out that African American and Puerto Rican prisoners at Attica were more likely than white prisoners to have their mail censored and family visits restricted.[19]

IN THE FIRST NOTE REFERRING TO THE SOURCE

19. Heather Ann Thompson, *Blood in the Water: The Attica Prison Uprising of 1971 and Its Legacy* (New York: Pantheon Books, 2016), 13.

After giving complete information the first time you cite a work, shorten additional references to that work: list only the author's last name, a shortened version of the title, and the page number. If the second reference to the work immediately follows the first reference, list only the author's name and the page number.

IN FIRST AND SUBSEQUENT NOTES

19. Heather Ann Thompson, *Blood in the Water: The Attica Prison Uprising of 1971 and Its Legacy* (New York: Pantheon Books, 2016), 13.

20. Thompson, 82.

21. Julia Sweig, *Inside the Cuban Revolution* (Cambridge, MA: Harvard University Press, 2002), 21.

22. Thompson, *Blood in the Water,* 304.

Bibliography. Begin the list of sources on a separate page after the main text and any endnotes. Continue numbering the pages consecutively. Center the title *Bibliography* (without underlining, italics, or quotation marks) one inch below the top of the page. Double-space, and then begin each entry at the left margin. Indent the second and subsequent lines of each entry one-half inch, or five spaces.

List sources alphabetically by authors' last names or by the first major word in the title if the author is unknown. See p. 233 for an example of a *Chicago*-style bibliography.

In the bibliographic entry, include the same information as in the first note for that source, but omit the page reference. Give the first author's last name first, followed by a comma and the first name; separate the main elements of the entry with periods rather than commas; and do not enclose the publication information for books in parentheses.

IN THE BIBLIOGRAPHY

Thompson, Heather Ann. *Blood in the Water: The Attica Prison Uprising of 1971 and Its Legacy*. New York: Pantheon Books, 2016.

LIST OF EXAMPLES

Notes and bibliographic entries in *Chicago* style

PRINT AND DIGITAL BOOKS

1. One author, 216
2. Multiple authors, 216
3. Organization as author, 216
4. Unknown author, 217
5. Online book, 217
6. Electronic book (e-book), 217
7. Book with an editor, 217
8. Selection in an anthology or chapter in a book with an editor, 218
9. Introduction, preface, foreword, or afterword, 218
10. Translation, 218
11. Edition other than the first, 218
12. Multivolume work, 219
13. Work with a title within the title, 219
14. Sacred text, 219
15. Source quoted in another source, 219

PRINT AND DIGITAL PERIODICALS

16. Article in a print journal, 220
17. Article in an online journal, 220
18. Journal article from a database, 220

    SOURCE MAP, 222

19. Article in a print magazine, 221
20. Article in an online magazine, 223
21. Magazine article from a database, 223
22. Article in a newspaper, 223
23. Article in an online newspaper, 223
24. Newspaper article from a database, 224
25. Book review, 224

ONLINE SOURCES

26. Work from a website, 224
27. Entire website, 225

    SOURCE MAP, 226 

LIST OF EXAMPLES

Notes and bibliographic entries in *Chicago* style, continued

28. Online reference work, 227
29. Blog post, 227
30. Email, social media messages, and other personal communications, 227
31. Social media post, 227
32. Podcast, 228
33. Online audio or video, 228

OTHER SOURCES

34. Published or broadcast interview, 228
35. DVD or Blu-ray, 229
36. Sound recording, 229
37. Work of art, 229
38. Pamphlet, report, or brochure, 229
39. Government document, 230

17c Creating *Chicago* notes and bibliographic entries

The following examples demonstrate how to format both notes and bibliographic entries according to *Chicago* style. The note, which is numbered, appears first; the bibliographic entry, which is not numbered, appears below the note. We have used underlining in some examples only to draw your attention to important elements. Do not underline anything in your own citations.

 Checklist

Citing Sources without Models in *Chicago* Style

To cite a source for which you cannot find a model, collect as much information as you can find—about the creator, title, date of creation or update, and location of the source—with the goal of helping your readers find the source for themselves, if possible. Then look at the models in this section to see which one most closely matches the type of source you are using.

In an academic writing project, before citing an electronic source for which you have no model, also be sure to ask your instructor's advice.

Print and digital books

The note for a book typically includes five elements: author's name, title and subtitle, city of publication and publisher, year, and page number(s) or electronic locator information for the information in the note. The bibliographic entry usually includes all these elements but the page number (and does include a URL or other locator if the book is digitally published), but it is styled differently: commas separate major elements of a note, but a bibliographic entry uses periods.

1. ONE AUTHOR

1. Nell Irvin Painter, *The History of White People* (New York: W. W. Norton, 2010), 119.

Painter, Nell Irvin. *The History of White People*. New York: W. W. Norton, 2010.

2. MULTIPLE AUTHORS

2. Mark Littman and Fred Espenak, *Totality: The Great American Eclipses of 2017 and 2024* (New York: Oxford University Press, 2017), 35.

Littman, Mark, and Fred Espenak. *Totality: The Great American Eclipses of 2017 and 2024*. New York: Oxford University Press, 2017.

With four or more authors, you may give the first-listed author followed by *et al.* in the note. In the bibliography, list all the authors' names.

2. Stephen J. Blank et al., *Conflict, Culture, and History: Regional Dimensions* (Miami: University Press of the Pacific, 2002), 276.

Blank, Stephen J., Lawrence E. Grinter, Karl P. Magyar, Lewis B. Ware, and Bynum E. Weathers. *Conflict, Culture, and History: Regional Dimensions*. Miami: University Press of the Pacific, 2002.

3. ORGANIZATION AS AUTHOR

3. World Intellectual Property Organization, *Intellectual Property Profile of the Least Developed Countries* (Geneva: World Intellectual Property Organization, 2002), 43.

World Intellectual Property Organization. *Intellectual Property Profile of the Least Developed Countries.* Geneva: World Intellectual Property Organization, 2002.

4. UNKNOWN AUTHOR

4. *Broad Stripes and Bright Stars* (Kansas City, MO: Andrews McMeel, 2002), 10.

Broad Stripes and Bright Stars. Kansas City, MO: Andrews McMeel, 2002.

5. ONLINE BOOK

5. Dorothy Richardson, *Long Day: The Story of a New York Working Girl, as Told by Herself* (New York: Century, 1906; UMDL Texts, 2010), 159, http://quod.lib.umich.edu/cgi/t/text/text-idx?c=moa;idno=AFS7156.0001.001.

Richardson, Dorothy. *Long Day: The Story of a New York Working Girl, as Told by Herself.* New York: Century, 1906. UMDL Texts, 2010. http://quod.lib.umich.edu/cgi/t/text/text-idx?c=moa;idno=AFS7156.0001.001.

6. ELECTRONIC BOOK (E-BOOK)

6. Atul Gawande, *Being Mortal: Medicine and What Matters in the End* (New York: Metropolitan, 2014), chap. 3, Nook.

Gawande, Atul. *Being Mortal: Medicine and What Matters in the End.* New York: Metropolitan, 2014. Nook.

7. BOOK WITH AN EDITOR

7. Leopold von Ranke, *The Theory and Practice of History,* ed. Georg G. Iggers (New York: Routledge, 2010), 135.

von Ranke, Leopold. *The Theory and Practice of History.* Edited by Georg G. Iggers. New York: Routledge, 2010.

If an edited book has no author, put the editor's name first.

7. James H. Fetzer, ed., *The Great Zapruder Film Hoax: Deceit and Deception in the Death of JFK* (Chicago: Open Court, 2003), 56.

Fetzer, James H., ed. *The Great Zapruder Film Hoax: Deceit and Deception in the Death of JFK*. Chicago: Open Court, 2003.

8. SELECTION IN AN ANTHOLOGY OR CHAPTER IN A BOOK WITH AN EDITOR

8. Denise Little, "Born in Blood," in *Alternate Gettysburgs,* ed. Brian Thomsen and Martin H. Greenberg (New York: Berkley Publishing Group, 2002), 245.

Give the inclusive page numbers of the selection or chapter in the bibliographic entry.

Little, Denise. "Born in Blood." In *Alternate Gettysburgs*. Edited by Brian Thomsen and Martin H. Greenberg, 242–55. New York: Berkley Publishing Group, 2002.

9. INTRODUCTION, PREFACE, FOREWORD, OR AFTERWORD

9. Ta-Nehisi Coates, foreword to *The Origin of Others,* by Toni Morrison (Cambridge, MA: Harvard University Press, 2017), xi.

Give the inclusive page number of the section cited in the bibliographic entry.

Coates, Ta-Nehisi. Foreword to *The Origin of Others,* by Toni Morrison, vii–xvii. Cambridge, MA: Harvard University Press, 2017.

10. TRANSLATION

10. Suetonius, *The Twelve Caesars,* trans. Robert Graves (London: Penguin Classics, 1989), 202.

Suetonius. *The Twelve Caesars*. Translated by Robert Graves. London: Penguin Classics, 1989.

11. EDITION OTHER THAN THE FIRST

11. Dee Brown, *Bury My Heart at Wounded Knee: An Indian History of the American West,* 4th ed. (New York: Owl Books, 2007), 12.

Brown, Dee. *Bury My Heart at Wounded Knee: An Indian History of the American West,* 4th ed. New York: Owl Books, 2007.

12. MULTIVOLUME WORK

12. John Watson, *Annals of Philadelphia and Pennsylvania in the Olden Time,* vol. 2 (Washington, DC: Ross & Perry, 2003), 514.

Watson, John. *Annals of Philadelphia and Pennsylvania in the Olden Time.* Vol. 2. Washington, DC: Ross & Perry, 2003.

13. WORK WITH A TITLE WITHIN THE TITLE. Use quotation marks around any title within a book title.

13. John A. Alford, *A Companion to "Piers Plowman"* (Berkeley: University of California Press, 1988), 195.

Alford, John A. *A Companion to "Piers Plowman."* Berkeley: University of California Press, 1988.

14. SACRED TEXT. Do not include sacred texts in the bibliography.

14. Luke 18:24–25 (New International Version).

14. Qur'an 7:40–41.

15. SOURCE QUOTED IN ANOTHER SOURCE. Identify both the original and the secondary source.

15. Frank D. Millet, "The Filipino Leaders," *Harper's Weekly,* March 11, 1899, quoted in Richard Slotkin, *Gunfighter Nation: The Myth of the Frontier in Twentieth-Century America* (New York: HarperCollins, 1992), 110.

Millet, Frank D. "The Filipino Leaders." *Harper's Weekly,* March 11, 1899. Quoted in Richard Slotkin, *Gunfighter Nation: The Myth of the Frontier in Twentieth-Century America* (New York: HarperCollins, 1992), 110.

Print and digital periodicals

The note for an article in a periodical typically includes the author's name, the article title, and the periodical title. The format for other information, including the volume and issue numbers (if any) and the date of publication, as well as the page number(s) to which the note refers, varies according to the type of periodical and whether you consulted it in print, on the web, or in a database. In a bibliographic entry for a journal or magazine article from a database or a print periodical, also give the inclusive page numbers.

16. ARTICLE IN A PRINT JOURNAL

16. Catherine Bishop and Angela Woollacott, "Business and Politics as Women's Work: The Australian Colonies and the Mid-Nineteenth-Century Women's Movement," *Journal of Women's History* 28, no. 1 (2016): 87.

Bishop, Catherine, and Angela Woollacott. "Business and Politics as Women's Work: The Australian Colonies and the Mid-Nineteenth-Century Women's Movement." *Journal of Women's History* 28, no. 1 (2016): 84–106.

17. ARTICLE IN AN ONLINE JOURNAL. Give the DOI, preceded by *https://doi.org/*. If there is no DOI, include the article URL. If page numbers are provided, include them as well.

17. Jeffrey J. Schott, "America, Europe, and the New Trade Order," *Business and Politics* 11, no. 3 (2009), https://doi.org/10.2202/1469-3569.1263.

Schott, Jeffrey J. "America, Europe, and the New Trade Order." *Business and Politics* 11, no. 3 (2009). https://doi.org/10.2202/1469-3569.1263.

18. ARTICLE FROM A DATABASE. The source map on p. 222 shows where to find information for a typical article.

1. **Author.** In a note, list the author(s) first name first. In the bibliographic entry, list the first author last name first, comma, first name; list other authors first name first.
2. **Article title.** Enclose the title and subtitle (if any) in quotation marks, and capitalize major words. In the notes section, put a comma before and after the title. In the bibliography, put a period before and after.
3. **Periodical title.** Italicize the title and subtitle, and capitalize all major words. For a magazine or newspaper, follow with a comma.
4. **Volume and issue numbers (for journals) and date.** For journals, follow the title with the volume number, a comma, the abbreviation *no.*, and the issue number; enclose the publication

year in parentheses and follow with a colon. For other periodicals, give the month and year or month, day, and year, not in parentheses, followed by a colon.

5 **Page numbers.** In a note, give the page where the information is found. In the bibliographic entry, give the page range.

6 **Retrieval information.** Provide the article's DOI, if one is given, the name of the database, or a stable URL for the article. Because you provide stable retrieval information, you do not need to identify the electronic format of the work (i.e., PDF). End with a period.

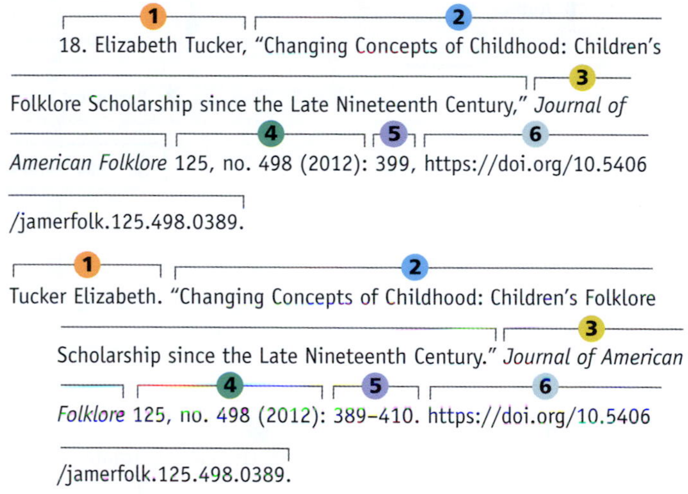

18. Elizabeth Tucker, "Changing Concepts of Childhood: Children's Folklore Scholarship since the Late Nineteenth Century," *Journal of American Folklore* 125, no. 498 (2012): 399, https://doi.org/10.5406/jamerfolk.125.498.0389.

Tucker Elizabeth. "Changing Concepts of Childhood: Children's Folklore Scholarship since the Late Nineteenth Century." *Journal of American Folklore* 125, no. 498 (2012): 389–410. https://doi.org/10.5406/jamerfolk.125.498.0389.

19. ARTICLE IN A PRINT MAGAZINE

19. Terry McDermott, "The Mastermind: Khalid Sheikh Mohammed and the Making of 9/11," *New Yorker*, September 13, 2010, 42.

McDermott, Terry. "The Mastermind: Khalid Sheikh Mohammed and the Making of 9/11." *New Yorker*, September 13, 2010, 38–51.

CHICAGO SOURCE MAP: Articles from Databases

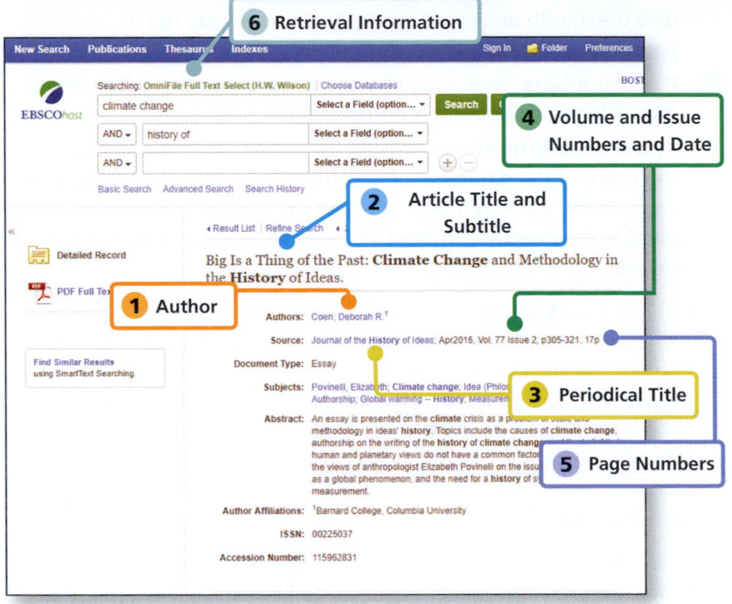

Citation

ENDNOTE

1. Deborah R. Coen, "Big Is a Thing of the Past: Climate Change and Methodology in the History of Ideas," *Journal of the History of Ideas* 77, no. 2, April 2016: 310, OmniFile Full Text Select.

BIBLIOGRAPHIC ENTRY

Coen, Deborah R. "Big Is a Thing of the Past: Climate Change and Methodology in the History of Ideas." *Journal of the History of Ideas* 77, no. 2, April 2016: 305–21. OmniFile Full Text Select.

20. ARTICLE IN AN ONLINE MAGAZINE

20. Tracy Clark-Flory, "Educating Women Saves Kids' Lives," *Salon,* September 17, 2010, http://www.salon.com/life/broadsheet/2010/09/17/education_women/index.html.

Clark-Flory, Tracy. "Educating Women Saves Kids' Lives." *Salon,* September 17, 2010. http://www.salon.com/life/broadsheet/2010/09/17/education_women/index.html.

21. MAGAZINE ARTICLE FROM A DATABASE

21. Sami Yousafzai and Ron Moreau, "Twisting Arms in Afghanistan," *Newsweek,* November 9, 2009, 8, Academic Search Premier.

Yousafzai, Sami, and Ron Moreau. "Twisting Arms in Afghanistan." *Newsweek,* November 9, 2009. 8. Academic Search Premier.

22. ARTICLE IN A NEWSPAPER. Do not include page numbers for a newspaper article, but you may include the section, if any.

22. Caroline E. Mayer, "Wireless Industry to Adopt Voluntary Standards," *Washington Post,* September 9, 2003, sec. E.

Chicago recommends that newspaper articles appear in the notes section only, not in the bibliography. Check your instructor's preference. A bibliography entry would look like this:

Mayer, Caroline E. "Wireless Industry to Adopt Voluntary Standards." *Washington Post,* September 9, 2003, sec. E.

23. ARTICLE IN AN ONLINE NEWSPAPER

23. Somini Sengupta, "How a Seed Bank, Almost Lost in Syria's War, Could Help Feed a Warming Planet," *New York Times,* October 13, 2017, https://www.nytimes.com/2017/10/13/climate/syria-seed-bank.html.

Sengupta, Somini. "How a Seed Bank, Almost Lost in Syria's War, Could Help Feed a Warming Planet." *New York Times,* October 13, 2017. https://www.nytimes.com/2017/10/13/climate/syria-seed-bank.html.

24. NEWSPAPER ARTICLE FROM A DATABASE

24. Demetria Irwin, "A Hatchet, Not a Scalpel, for NYC Budget Cuts," *New York Amsterdam News,* November 13, 2008, Academic Search Premier.

Irwin, Demetria. "A Hatchet, Not a Scalpel, for NYC Budget Cuts." *New York Amsterdam News,* November 13, 2008. Academic Search Premier.

25. BOOK REVIEW. After the information about the book under review, give publication information for the appropriate kind of source (see models 17–24).

25. Roderick MacFarquhar, "China's Astounding Religious Revival," review of *The Souls of China: The Return of Religion After Mao,* by Ian Johnson, *New York Review of Books,* June 8, 2017, http://www.nybooks.com/articles/2017/06/08/chinas-astounding-religious-revival/.

MacFarquhar, Roderick. "China's Astounding Religious Revival." Review of *The Souls of China: The Return of Religion after Mao,* by Ian Johnson. *New York Review of Books,* June 8, 2017. http://www.nybooks.com/articles/2017/06/08/chinas-astounding-religious-revival/.

Online sources

Notes and bibliographic entries for online sources typically include the author; the title of the work; the name of the site; the sponsor of the site, if different from the name of the site or name of the author; the date of publication or most recent update; and a URL. If the online source does not indicate when it was published or last modified, include your date of access.

26. WORK FROM A WEBSITE. See the source map on p. 226.

1. **Author.** In a note, list the author(s) first name first. In a bibliographic entry, list the first author last name first, comma, first name; list additional authors first name first. Note that the host may serve as the author.
2. **Document title.** Enclose the title in quotation marks, and capitalize all major words. In a note, put a comma before and after the title. In the bibliography, put a period before and after the title.

3 **Title of website.** Capitalize all major words. If the site's title is analogous to a book or periodical title, italicize it. In the notes section, put a comma after the title. In the bibliography, put a period after the title.

4 **Sponsor of site.** If the sponsor is the same as the author or site title, you may omit it. End with a comma (in the note) or a period (in the bibliographic entry).

5 **Date of publication or last modification.** If a time stamp is given, include it. If no date is available, include your date of access (with the word *accessed*). End with a comma (in the note) or a period (in the bibliographic entry).

6 **Retrieval information.** Give the URL for the work and end with a period.

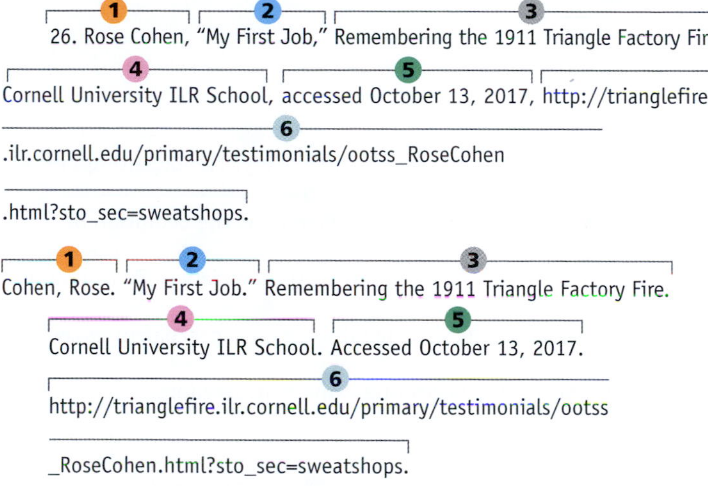

1
2
3
26. Rose Cohen, "My First Job," Remembering the 1911 Triangle Factory Fire,
4
5
Cornell University ILR School, accessed October 13, 2017, http://trianglefire
6
.ilr.cornell.edu/primary/testimonials/ootss_RoseCohen
.html?sto_sec=sweatshops.
1
2
3
Cohen, Rose. "My First Job." Remembering the 1911 Triangle Factory Fire.
4
5
Cornell University ILR School. Accessed October 13, 2017.
6
http://trianglefire.ilr.cornell.edu/primary/testimonials/ootss
_RoseCohen.html?sto_sec=sweatshops.

27. ENTIRE WEBSITE. For clarity, you may add the word *website* in parentheses after the title.

27. Rutgers School of Arts and Sciences, Rutgers Oral History Archive (website), 2017, http://oralhistory.rutgers.edu/.

Rutgers School of Arts and Sciences. Rutgers Oral History Archive (website). 2017. http://oralhistory.rutgers.edu/.

CHICAGO SOURCE MAP: Works from Websites

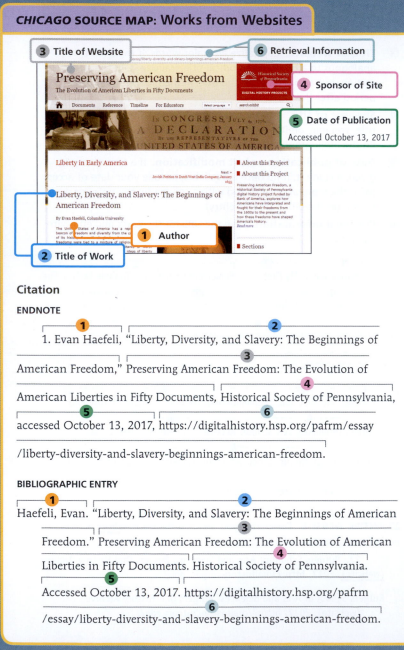

Citation

ENDNOTE

1. Evan Haefeli, "Liberty, Diversity, and Slavery: The Beginnings of American Freedom," Preserving American Freedom: The Evolution of American Liberties in Fifty Documents, Historical Society of Pennsylvania, accessed October 13, 2017, https://digitalhistory.hsp.org/pafrm/essay/liberty-diversity-and-slavery-beginnings-american-freedom.

BIBLIOGRAPHIC ENTRY

Haefeli, Evan. "Liberty, Diversity, and Slavery: The Beginnings of American Freedom." Preserving American Freedom: The Evolution of American Liberties in Fifty Documents. Historical Society of Pennsylvania. Accessed October 13, 2017. https://digitalhistory.hsp.org/pafrm/essay/liberty-diversity-and-slavery-beginnings-american-freedom.

28. ONLINE REFERENCE WORK. In a note, use *s.v.*, the abbreviation for the Latin *sub verbo* ("under the word") to help your reader find the entry. Include the date the entry was posted, last modified, or accessed. Do not list reference works such as encyclopedias or dictionaries in your bibliography.

28. *Encyclopedia Britannica,* s.v. "Monroe Doctrine," accessed October 12, 2017, https://www.britannica.com/event/Monroe-Doctrine.

29. BLOG POST. Treat a blog post as a short work from a website (see model 26).

29. Jai Arjun Singh, "On the Road in the USSR," *Jabberwock* (blog), November 29, 2007, http://jaiarjun.blogspot.com/2007/11/on-road-in-ussr.html.

Chicago recommends that blog posts appear in the notes section only, not in the bibliography. Check your instructor's preference. A bibliography reference would look like this:

Singh, Jai Arjun. "On the Road in the USSR." *Jabberwock* (blog), November 29, 2007. http://jaiarjun.blogspot.com/.

30. EMAIL, SOCIAL MEDIA MESSAGES, AND OTHER PERSONAL COMMUNICATIONS. Cite email messages, social media messages, personal interviews, and other personal communications, such as letters and telephone calls, in the text or in a note only; do not cite them in the bibliography.

30. Kareem Adas, Facebook private message to author, February 11, 2018.

31. SOCIAL MEDIA POST. In place of a title, include the text of the post, up to the first 160 characters.

31. NASA (@nasa), "This galaxy is a whirl of color," Instagram photo, September 23, 2017, https://www.instagram.com/p/BZY8adnnZQJ/.

NASA. "This galaxy is a whirl of color." Instagram photo, September 23, 2017. https://www.instagram.com/p/BZY8adnnZQJ/.

32. PODCAST. Treat a podcast as a short work from a website (see model 26). Include the type of podcast or file format (if downloadable), the time stamp, and the URL.

32. Toyin Falola, "Creativity and Decolonization: Nigerian Cultures and African Epistemologies," Episode 96, November 17, 2015, in *Africa Past and Present,* African Online Digital Library, podcast, MP3 audio, 43:44, http://afripod.aodl.org/2015/11/afripod-96/.

Falola, Toyin. "Creativity and Decolonization: Nigerian Cultures and African Epistemologies." Episode 96, November 17, 2015. *Africa Past and Present*. African Online Digital Library. Podcast, MP3 audio, 43:44. http://afripod.aodl.org/2015/11/afripod-96/.

33. ONLINE AUDIO OR VIDEO. Treat an online audio or video source as a short work from a website (see model 26). If the source is downloadable, give the medium or file format before the URL.

33. Alyssa Katz, "Did the Mortgage Crisis Kill the American Dream?" YouTube video, 4:32, posted by NYCRadio, June 24, 2009, http://www.youtube.com/watch?v=uivtwjwd_Qw.

Katz, Alyssa. "Did the Mortgage Crisis Kill the American Dream?" YouTube video, 4:32. Posted by NYCRadio. June 24, 2009. http://www.youtube.com/watch?v=uivtwjwd_Qw.

Other sources

34. PUBLISHED OR BROADCAST INTERVIEW

34. David O. Russell, interview by Terry Gross, *Fresh Air*, WNYC, February 20, 2014.

Russell, David O. Interview by Terry Gross. *Fresh Air*. WNYC, February 20, 2014.

Interviews you conduct are considered personal communications (see model 30).

35. DVD OR BLU-RAY. Include both the date of the original release and the date of release for the format you are citing.

35. *American History X,* directed by Tony Kaye (1998; Los Angeles: New Line Studios, 2002), DVD.

Kaye, Tony, dir. *American History X.* 1998; Los Angeles: New Line Studios, 2002. DVD.

36. SOUND RECORDING

36. "Work," MP3 audio, track 4 on Rihanna, *Anti*, Roc Nation, 2016.

Rihanna. "Work." *Anti*. Roc Nation, 2016, MP3 audio.

37. WORK OF ART. Works of art usually can be mentioned in the text rather than cited in a note or bibliography entry. Check your instructor's preference.

37. Hope Gangloff, *Vera*, 2015, acrylic on canvas, Kemper Museum of Contemporary Art, Kansas City, MO.

Gangloff, Hope. *Vera*. 2015. Acrylic on canvas. Kemper Museum of Contemporary Art, Kansas City, MO.

If you refer to a reproduction, give the publication information.

37. Mary Cassatt, *The Child's Bath,* 1893, oil on canvas, *Art Access,* The Art Institute of Chicago, accessed October 13, 2017, http://www.artic.edu/aic/collections/exhibitions/Impressionism/Cassatt.

Cassatt, Mary. *The Child's Bath*. 1893. Oil on canvas. *Art Access*. The Art Institute of Chicago. Accessed October 13, 2017. http://www.artic.edu/aic/collections/exhibitions/Impressionism/Cassatt.

38. PAMPHLET, REPORT, OR BROCHURE. Information about the author or publisher may not be readily available, but give enough information to identify your source.

38. International Monetary Fund, *Western Hemisphere: Tale of Two Adjustments,* World Economic and Financial Surveys (Washington, DC: International Monetary Fund, 2017), 29.

International Monetary Fund. *Western Hemisphere: Tale of Two Adjustments.* World Economic and Financial Surveys. Washington, DC: International Monetary Fund, 2017.

39. GOVERNMENT DOCUMENT

39. U.S. House Committee on Ways and Means, *Report on Trade Mission to Sub-Saharan Africa,* 108th Cong., 1st sess. (Washington, DC: Government Printing Office, 2003), 28.

U.S. House Committee on Ways and Means. *Report on Trade Mission to Sub-Saharan Africa.* 108th Cong., 1st sess. Washington, DC: Government Printing Office, 2003.

 17d STUDENT WRITING Excerpts from a research-based history essay, *Chicago* style

On the following pages are excerpts from an essay by Amanda Rinder that conforms to the *Chicago* guidelines described in this chapter. See the complete essay in *LaunchPad Solo for Lunsford Handbooks*.

Rinder 2

Only one city has the "Big Shoulders" described by Carl Sandburg: Chicago (fig. 1). So renowned are its skyscrapers and celebrated building style that an entire school of architecture is named for Chicago. Presently, however, the place that Frank Sinatra called "my kind of town" is beginning to lose sight of exactly what kind of town it is. Many of the buildings that give Chicago its distinctive character are being torn down in order to make room for new growth. Both preserving the classics and encouraging new creation are important; the combination of these elements gives Chicago architecture its unique flavor. Witold Rybczynski, a professor of urbanism, told Tracie Rozhon of the *New York Times,* "Of all the cities we can think of . . . we associate Chicago with new things, with building new. Combining that with preservation is a difficult task, a tricky thing. It's hard to find the middle ground in Chicago."[1] Yet finding a middle ground is essential if the city is to retain the original character that sets it apart from the rest. In order to

Fig. 1. Chicago skyline, circa 1940s. (Postcard courtesy of Minnie Dangburg.)

First page of body text is p. 2

Paper refers to each figure by number

Thesis introduced

Double-spaced text

Source cited using superscript numeral

Figure caption includes number, short title, and source

STUDENT WRITING

Rinder 9

Notes

Newspaper article in database

1. Tracie Rozhon, "Chicago Girds for Big Battle over Its Skyline," *New York Times,* November 12, 2000, Academic Search Premier.

Print book

2. David Garrard Lowe, *Lost Chicago* (New York: Watson-Guptill Publications, 2000), 123.

3. *Columbia Encyclopedia*, 6th ed. (2000), s.v. "Louis Sullivan."

4. Daniel Bluestone, *Constructing Chicago* (New Haven: Yale University Press, 1991), 105.

Indirect source

5. Alan J. Shannon, "When Will It End?" *Chicago Tribune*, September 11, 1987, quoted in Karen J. Dilibert, *From Landmark to Landfill* (Chicago: Chicago Architectural Foundation, 2000), 11.

6. Steve Kerch, "Landmark Decisions," *Chicago Tribune*, March 18, 1990, sec. 16.

7. John W. Stamper, *Chicago's North Michigan Avenue* (Chicago: University of Chicago Press, 1991), 215.

8. Alf Siewers, "Success Spoiling the Magnificent Mile?" *Chicago Sun-Times*, April 9, 1995.

9. Paul Gapp, "McCarthy Building Puts Landmark Law on a Collision Course with Developers," *Chicago Tribune*, April 20, 1986, quoted in Karen J. Dilibert, *From Landmark to Landfill* (Chicago: Chicago Architectural Foundation, 2000), 4.

Reference to previous source

10. Paul Gapp, quoted in Karen J. Dilibert, 4.

Second reference to source

11. Rozhon, "Chicago Girds for Big Battle."

12. Kerch, "Landmark Decisions."

13. Robert Bruegmann, *The Architects and the City* (Chicago: University of Chicago Press, 1997), 443.

STUDENT WRITING

Rinder 10

Bibliography

Bluestone, Daniel. *Constructing Chicago*. New Haven: Yale University Press, 1991.

Bruegmann, Robert. *The Architects and the City*. Chicago: University of Chicago Press, 1997.

Dilibert, Karen J. *From Landmark to Landfill*. Chicago: Chicago Architectural Foundation, 2000.

Kerch, Steve. "Landmark Decisions." *Chicago Tribune*, March 18, 1990, sec. 16.

Lowe, David Garrard. *Lost Chicago*. New York: Watson-Guptill Publications, 2000.

Rozhon, Tracie. "Chicago Girds for Big Battle over Its Skyline." *New York Times*, November 12, 2000. Academic Search Premier.

Siewers, Alf. "Success Spoiling the Magnificent Mile?" *Chicago Sun-Times*, April 9, 1995.

Stamper, John W. *Chicago's North Michigan Avenue*. Chicago: University of Chicago Press, 1991.

Print book

Pamphlet

Newspaper article

Article from database

Bibliography entries use hanging indent and are not numbered

18 CSE Style

Writers in the physical sciences, the life sciences, and mathematics often use the documentation style set forth by the Council of Science Editors (CSE). Guidelines for citing print sources can be found in *Scientific Style and Format: The CSE Manual for Authors, Editors, and Publishers*, Eighth Edition (2014).

18a Following CSE manuscript format

Title page. Center the title of your paper. Beneath it, center your name. Include other relevant information, such as the course name and number, the instructor's name, and the date submitted.

Margins and spacing. Leave standard margins at the top and bottom and on both sides of each page. Double-space the text and the references list.

Page numbers. Type a short version of the paper's title and the page number in the upper right-hand corner of each page. Omit the page number on the title page and number the first page of text as page 2.

Abstract. CSE style frequently calls for a one-paragraph abstract. The abstract should be on a separate page, right after the title page, with the title *Abstract* centered one inch from the top of the page.

Headings. Use headings when possible to help readers quickly find the contents of a section of the paper.

Tables and figures. Tables and figures must be labeled *Table* or *Figure* and numbered separately, one sequence for tables and one for figures. Give each table and figure a short, informative title. Be sure to introduce each table and figure in your text, and comment on its significance.

List of references. Start the list of references on a new page at the end of the paper, and continue to number the pages consecutively. Center the title *References* one inch from the top of the page, and double-space before beginning the first entry.

18b Creating CSE in-text citations

In CSE style, citations within the text follow one of three formats.

- The *citation-sequence format* calls for a superscript number or a number in parentheses after any mention of a source. The sources are numbered in the order they appear. Each number refers to the same source every time it is used. The first source mentioned in the paper is numbered 1, the second source is numbered 2, and so on.
- The *citation-name format* also calls for a superscript number or a number in parentheses after any mention of a source. The numbers are added *after* the list of references is completed and alphabetized, so that the source numbered 1 is alphabetically first in the list of references, 2 is alphabetically second, and so on.
- The *name-year format* calls for the last name of the author and the year of publication in parentheses after any mention of a source. If the last name appears in a signal phrase, the name-year format allows for giving only the year of publication in parentheses.

Before deciding which system to use, ask your instructor's preference.

1. IN-TEXT CITATION USING CITATION-SEQUENCE OR CITATION-NAME FORMAT

> VonBergen[12] provides the most complete discussion of this phenomenon.

For the citation-sequence and citation-name formats, you would use the same superscript ([12]) for each subsequent citation of this work by VonBergen.

2. IN-TEXT CITATION USING NAME-YEAR FORMAT

> VonBergen (2003) provides the most complete discussion of this phenomenon.

> Hussar's two earlier studies of juvenile obesity (1995, 1999) examined only children with diabetes.

> The classic examples of such investigations (Morrow 1968; Bridger et al. 1971; Franklin and Wayson 1972) still shape the assumptions of current studies.

If a work has three more authors, use the first author's name and *et al.* in the in-text citation.

18c Creating a CSE list of references

The citations in the text of a paper correspond to items on a list titled *References*, which starts on a new page at the end of the paper. Continue to number the pages consecutively, center the title *References* one inch from the top of the page, and double-space before beginning the first entry. Start each entry flush left and indent subsequent lines one-quarter inch.

The order of the entries depends on which format you follow:

- **Citation-sequence format:** number and list the references in the order they are first cited in the text.
- **Citation-name format:** list and number the references in alphabetical order.
- **Name-year format:** list the references, unnumbered, in alphabetical order.

In the following examples, you will see that both the citation-sequence and citation-name formats call for listing the date after the publisher's name in references for books and after the periodical name in references for articles. The name-year format calls for listing the date immediately after the author's name in any kind of reference.

CSE style also specifies the treatment and placement of the following basic elements in the list of references:

- **Author.** List all authors last name first, and use only initials for first and middle names. Do not place a comma after the author's last name, and do not place periods after or spaces between the initials. Use a period after the last initial of the last author listed.
- **Title.** Do not italicize titles and subtitles of books and titles of periodicals. Do not enclose titles of articles in quotation marks. For books and articles, capitalize only the first word of the title and any proper nouns or proper adjectives. Abbreviate and capitalize all major words in a periodical title.

As you refer to these examples, pay attention to how publication information (publishers for books, details about periodicals for articles) and other specific elements are styled and punctuated. We have used underlining in some examples only to draw your attention to important elements. Do not underline anything in your own citations.

LIST OF EXAMPLES

References in CSE style

BOOKS

1. One author, 237
2. Two or more authors, 237
3. Organization as author, 238
4. Book prepared by editor(s), 238
5. Section of a book with an editor, 238
6. Chapter of a book, 239
7. Paper or abstract in conference proceedings, 239

PERIODICALS

8. Article in a journal, 239
9. Article in a magazine, 240
10. Article in a newspaper, 240

DIGITAL SOURCES

11. Material from an online database, 241
12. Article in an online journal, 241
13. Article in an online newspaper, 241
14. Online book, 242
15. Website, 242
16. Government website, 242

Books

1. ONE AUTHOR

CITATION-SEQUENCE AND CITATION-NAME

1. Tyson ND. Astrophysics for people in a hurry. New York (NY): Norton; 2017.

NAME-YEAR

Tyson ND. 2017. Astrophysics for people in a hurry. New York (NY): Norton.

2. TWO OR MORE AUTHORS. List all authors up to ten. If there are more than ten authors, follow the tenth with the abbreviation *et al.*

CITATION-SEQUENCE AND CITATION-NAME

2. Wojciechowski BW, Rice NM. Experimental methods in kinetic studies. 2nd ed. St. Louis (MO): Elsevier Science; 2003.

NAME-YEAR

Wojciechowski BW, Rice NM. 2003. Experimental methods in kinetic studies. 2nd ed. St. Louis (MO): Elsevier Science.

3. ORGANIZATION AS AUTHOR

CITATION-SEQUENCE AND CITATION-NAME

3. World Health Organization. The world health report 2002: reducing risks, promoting healthy life. Geneva (Switzerland): The Organization; 2002.

Place the organization's abbreviation at the beginning of the name-year entry, and use the abbreviation in the corresponding in-text citation. Alphabetize the entry by the first word of the full name, not by the abbreviation.

NAME-YEAR

[WHO] World Health Organization. 2002. The world health report 2002: reducing risks, promoting healthy life. Geneva (Switzerland): The Organization.

4. BOOK PREPARED BY EDITOR(S)

CITATION-SEQUENCE AND CITATION-NAME

4. Torrence ME, Isaacson RE, editors. Microbial food safety in animal agriculture: current topics. Ames (IA): Iowa State University Press; 2003.

NAME-YEAR

Torrence ME, Isaacson RE, editors. 2003. Microbial safety in animal agriculture: current topics. Ames (IA): Iowa State University Press.

5. SECTION OF A BOOK WITH AN EDITOR

CITATION-SEQUENCE AND CITATION-NAME

5. Kawamura A. Plankton. In: Perrin MF, Wursig B, Thewissen JGM, editors. Encyclopedia of marine mammals. San Diego (CA): Academic Press; 2002. p. 939–942.

NAME-YEAR

Kawamura A. 2002. Plankton. In: Perrin MF, Wursig B, Thewissen JGM, editors. Encyclopedia of marine mammals. San Diego (CA): Academic Press. p. 939–942.

6. CHAPTER OF A BOOK

CITATION-SEQUENCE AND CITATION-NAME

6. Honigsbaum M. The fever trail: in search of the cure for malaria. New York (NY): Picador; 2003. Chapter 2, The cure; p. 19–38.

NAME-YEAR

Honigsbaum M. 2003. The fever trail: in search of the cure for malaria. New York (NY): Picador. Chapter 2, The cure; p. 19–38.

7. PAPER OR ABSTRACT IN CONFERENCE PROCEEDINGS

CITATION-SEQUENCE AND CITATION-NAME

7. Gutierrez AP. Integrating biological and environmental factors in crop system models [abstract]. In: Integrated Biological Systems Conference; 2003 Apr 14–16; San Antonio, TX. Beaumont (TX): Agroeconomics Research Group; 2003. p. 14–15.

NAME-YEAR

Gutierrez AP. 2003. Integrating biological and environmental factors in crop system models [abstract]. In: Integrated Biological Systems Conference; 2003 Apr 14–16; San Antonio, TX. Beaumont (TX): Agroeconomics Research Group. p. 14–15.

Periodicals

Provide volume and issue numbers for journals. For magazines, include the month and year or the month, day, and year. For newspaper articles, include the section designation and column number, if any, and the date. For all periodicals, give inclusive page numbers. For rules on abbreviating journal titles, consult the CSE manual or ask an instructor.

8. ARTICLE IN A JOURNAL

CITATION-SEQUENCE AND CITATION-NAME

8. Citrin DE. Recent developments in radiotherapy. New Engl J Med. 2017;377(11):1065–1075.

NAME-YEAR

Citrin DE. 2017. Recent developments in radiotherapy. New Engl J Med. 377(11):1065–1075.

9. ARTICLE IN A MAGAZINE

CITATION-SEQUENCE AND CITATION-NAME

9. Livio M. Moving right along: the accelerating universe holds secrets to dark energy, the Big Bang, and the ultimate beauty of nature. Astronomy. 2002 Jul:34–39.

NAME-YEAR

Livio M. 2002 Jul. Moving right along: the accelerating universe holds secrets to dark energy, the Big Bang, and the ultimate beauty of nature. Astronomy. 34–39.

10. ARTICLE IN A NEWSPAPER

CITATION-SEQUENCE AND CITATION-NAME

10. Kolata G. Bone diagnosis gives new data but no answers. New York Times (National Ed.). 2003 Sep 28;Sect. 1:1 (col. 1).

NAME-YEAR

Kolata G. 2003 Sep 28. Bone diagnosis gives new data but no answers. New York Times (National Ed.). Sect. 1:1 (col. 1).

Digital sources

These examples use the citation-sequence or citation-name system. To adapt them to the name-year system, delete the note number and place the update date immediately after the author's name.

The basic entry for most sources accessed through the Internet should include the following elements:

- **Author.** Give the author's name, if available, last name first, followed by the initial(s) and a period.
- **Title.** For book, journal, and article titles, follow the style for print materials. For all other types of electronic material, reproduce the title that appears on the screen.

- **Description.** Identify sources such as images, infographics, podcasts, videos, blogs, and social media posts with descriptive words in brackets: *[infographic]*, *[video]*, *[podcast, episode 12]*.
- **Place of publication.** For online books and websites, include the place of publication as you would for print sources.
- **Publisher.** For material other than journal articles from websites and online databases, include the individual or organization that produces or sponsors the site. If no publisher can be determined, use the words *publisher unknown* in brackets.
- **Dates.** Cite three important dates if possible: the date that the publication was placed on the Internet or the copyright date; the latest date of any update or revision; and the date you accessed the publication.
- **Page, document, volume, and issue numbers.** When citing a portion of a larger work or site, list the inclusive page numbers or document numbers of the specific item being cited. For journals or journal articles, include volume and issue numbers. If exact page numbers are not available, include in brackets the approximate length in computer screens, paragraphs, or bytes: [2 screens], [10 paragraphs], [332K bytes].
- **Address.** Include the URL or other electronic address, followed by a period.

11. MATERIAL FROM AN ONLINE DATABASE

11. Shilts E. Water wanderers. Can Geographic. 2002 [accessed 2010 Jan 27];122(3):72–77. Academic Search Premier. http://www.ebscohost.com/. Document No.: 6626534.

12. ARTICLE IN AN ONLINE JOURNAL

12. Perez P, Calonge TM. Yeast protein kinase C. J Biochem. 2002 Oct [accessed 2008 Nov 3];132(4):513–517. http://edpex104.bcasj.or.jp/jb-pdf/132-4/jb132-4-513.pdf

13. ARTICLE IN AN ONLINE NEWSPAPER

13. Gorman J. Trillions of flies can't all be bad. New York Times. 2017 Nov 13 [accessed 2017 Dec 1]. https://nyti.ms/2hwjhw0

14. ONLINE BOOK

14. Patrick TS, Allison JR, Krakow GA. Protected plants of Georgia. Social Circle (GA): Georgia Department of Natural Resources; c1995 [accessed 2010 Dec 3]. http://www.georgiawildlife.com/content/displaycontent.asp?txtDocument=89&txtPage=9

To cite a portion of an online book, give the name of the part after the publication information: *Chapter 6, Encouraging germination.* See model 6.

15. WEBSITE

15. Geology and public policy. Boulder (CO): Geological Society of America; c2010 [updated 2010 Jun 3; accessed 2010 Sep 19]. http://www.geosociety.org/geopolicy.htm

16. GOVERNMENT WEBSITE

16. Health disparities in cancer: reducing health disparities in cancer. Atlanta (GA): Centers for Disease Control and Prevention (US); 2012 Nov 14 [updated 2014 Jul 21; accessed 2017 Nov 13]. http://www.cdc.gov/cancer/healthdisparities/basic_info/disparities.htm

18d STUDENT WRITING A literature review for biology, CSE style

The following literature review by Joanna Hays for a biology class conforms to the name-year format in the CSE guidelines described in this chapter. To see Hays's complete project, go to *LaunchPad Solo for Lunsford Handbooks*.

STUDENT WRITING

Niemann-Pick Disease 2

Running head has short title, page number

Overview

Niemann-Pick Disease (NP) occurs in patients with deficient acid sphingomyelinase (ASM) activity as well as with the lysosomal accumulation of sphingomyelin. It is an autosomal recessive disorder (Levran et al. 1991). As recently as 1991, researchers had classified two major phenotypes: Type A and Type B (Levran et al. 1991). In more recent studies several more phenotypes have been identified, including Types C and D. Each type of NP has distinct characteristics and effects on the patient. NP is distributed worldwide, but is closely associated with Ashkenazi Jewish descendants. Niemann-Pick Disease is relevant to the molecular world today because of advances being made in the ability to identify mutations, to trace ancestry where the mutation may have originated, and to counsel patients with a high potential of carrying the disease. Genetic counseling primarily consists of confirmation of the particular disease and calculation of the possible future reappearance in the same gene line (Brock 1974). The following discussion will summarize the identification of mutations causing the various forms of NP, the distribution of NP, as well as new genotypes and phenotypes that are correlated with NP.

Mutations Causing NP

Headings organize project

Levran et al. (1991) inform readers of the frequent identification of missense mutations in the gene associated with Ashkenazi Jewish persons afflicted by Type A and Type B NP. This paper identifies the mutations associated with NP and the beginning of many molecular techniques to develop diagnoses. Greer et al. (1998) identify a new mutation that is specifically identified to be the cause of Type D. NP in various forms is closely associated with the founder effect caused by a couple married in the early 1700s in what is now Nova Scotia. Simonaro et al. (2002) discusses the distribution of Type B NP as well as new phenotypes and genotypes. All three of these papers identify

STUDENT WRITING

References

Alphabetical by name

Brock DJH. 1974. Prenatal diagnosis and genetic counseling. J Clin Pathol Suppl. (R Coll Path.) 8:150–155.

Greer WL, Ridell DC, Gillan TL, Girouard GS, Sparrow SM, Byers DM, Dobson MJ, Neumann PE. 1998. The Nova Scotia (type D) form of Niemann-Pick disease is caused by a $G_{3097} \rightarrow T$ transversion in NPC1. Am J Hum Genet 63:52–54.

Levran O, Desnick RJ, Schuchman EH. 1991. Niemann-Pick disease: a frequent missense mutation in the acid sphingomyelinase gene of Ashkenazi Jewish type A and B patients. P Natl Acad Sci USA 88:3748–3752.

Simonaro CM, Desnick RJ, McGovern MM, Wasserstein MP, Schuchman EH. 2002. The demographics and distribution of type B Niemann-Pick disease: novel mutations lead to new genotype/phenotype correlations. Am J Hum Genet 71:1413–1419.

Style: Effective Language

19 Writing across Cultures and Communities 246

20 Language That Builds Common Ground 249

21 Varieties of Language 254

22 Word Choice 258

19 Writing across Cultures and Communities

People today often communicate instantaneously across vast distances and cultures. Businesspeople complete multinational transactions, students take online classes at distant universities, and conversations circle the globe via social media. You may also find yourself writing to (or with) people from other communities, cultures, language groups, and countries. In this era of rapid global communication, you must know how to write effectively across these cultures and communities. As always, remember that people from any community or culture have complex, intersecting identities informed by many factors, including class, ethnicity, race, religion, sexual orientation, gender, ability/disability, age, and others.

19a Thinking about what seems "normal"

More than likely, your judgments about what is "normal" are based on assumptions that you are not aware of. Most of us tend to see our own way as the "normal" or right way to do things. If your ways seem inherently right, then perhaps you assume that other ways are somehow less than right. To communicate effectively with people across cultures and communities, recognize the norms that guide your own behavior and how those norms differ from those of other people.

- Know that most ways of communicating are influenced by cultural contexts and differ from one culture or community to the next.
- Carefully observe the ways that people from cultures or communities other than your own communicate, and be flexible and respectful.
- Respect the differences among individuals within a culture or community. Don't assume that all members of a community behave in the same way or value the same things.

19b Clarifying meaning

All writers face challenges in trying to communicate across space, languages, and cultures. You can address these challenges by working to be sure that you understand what others say—and that they understand you. In such situations, take care to be explicit about the meanings of the words you use. In addition, don't hesitate to ask people to explain a point if you're not absolutely sure you understand, and invite responses by asking whether you're making yourself clear or what you could do to be *more* clear.

19c Meeting audience expectations

When you do your best to meet an audience's expectations about how a text should work, your writing is more likely to have the desired effect. In practice, figuring out what audiences want, need, or expect can be difficult—especially when you are writing in public spaces online and your audiences can be composed of anyone, anywhere. If you know little about your potential audiences, carefully examine your assumptions about your readers.

Expectations about your authority as a writer. Writers communicating across cultures often encounter audiences who have differing attitudes about authority and about the relationship between the writer and the people being addressed. In the United States, students are frequently asked to establish authority in their writing—by drawing on personal experience, by reporting on research, or by taking a position for which they can offer strong evidence and support. But some cultures position student writers as novices, whose job is to learn from others who have greater authority. When you write, think carefully about your audience's expectations and attitudes toward authority.

- What is your relationship to those you are addressing?
- What knowledge are you expected to have? Is it appropriate for you to demonstrate that knowledge—and if so, how?
- What is your goal—to answer a question? to make a point? to agree? something else?
- What tone is appropriate? If in doubt, show respect: politeness is rarely if ever inappropriate.

Expectations about persuasive evidence. You should think carefully about how to use evidence in writing, and pay attention to what counts as evidence to members of groups you are trying to persuade. Are facts, concrete examples, or firsthand experience convincing to the intended audience? Does the testimony of experts count heavily as evidence? What people are considered trustworthy experts, and why? Will the audience value citations from religious or philosophical texts, proverbs, or everyday wisdom? Are there other sources that would be considered strong evidence? If analogies are used as support, which kinds are most powerful?

Once you determine what counts as evidence in your own thinking and writing, consider where you learned to use and value this kind of evidence. You can ask these same questions about how members of other cultures use evidence.

Expectations about organization. The organizational patterns that you find pleasing are likely to be deeply embedded in your own culture. Many U.S. readers expect a well-organized piece of writing to use the following structure: introduction and thesis, necessary background, overview of the parts, systematic presentation of evidence, consideration of other viewpoints, and conclusion.

However, in cultures that value indirection, subtlety, or repetition, writers tend to prefer different organizational patterns. When writing for world audiences, think about how you can organize material to get your message across effectively. Consider where to state your thesis or main point (at the beginning, at the end, somewhere else, or not at all) and whether to use a straightforward organization or to employ digressions to good effect.

Expectations about style. Effective style varies broadly across communities and cultures and depends on the rhetorical situation—your purpose, audience, and so on. Even so, there is one important style question to consider when writing across cultures: what level of formality is most appropriate? In most writing to a general audience in the United States, a fairly informal style is often acceptable, even appreciated. Many cultures, however, tend to value a more formal approach. When in doubt, err on the side of formality in writing to people from other cultures, especially to your elders or to those in authority. Use appropriate titles (*Dr. Moss, Professor Mejía*); avoid slang and informal structures, such as **sentence fragments**; use complete words and sentences (even in email); and use first names only if invited to do so.

20 Language That Builds Common Ground

The supervisor who refers to staff as "team members" (rather than as "my staff" or as "subordinates") has chosen language intended to establish common ground with co-workers. Your own language can work to build common ground if you carefully consider the sensitivities and preferences of others and if you watch for words that betray your assumptions, even though you have not directly stated them.

20a Examining assumptions and avoiding stereotypes

Unstated assumptions that enter into thinking and writing can destroy common ground by ignoring important differences. For example, a student in a religion seminar who uses *we* to refer to Christians and *they* to refer to members of other religions had better be sure that everyone in the class identifies as Christian, or some may rightly feel left out of the discussion.

At the same time, don't overgeneralize about or stereotype a group of people. Because stereotypes are often based on half-truths, misunderstandings, and hand-me-down prejudices, they can lead to intolerance, bias, and bigotry.

Remember that members of your audiences will almost certainly come from many different regions of the United States or from other countries as well as from a wide range of socioeconomic backgrounds and that they will practice a number of different religions. It's also important to recognize and respect the range of sexualities those in your audience may inhabit, including lesbian, gay, bisexual, asexual, and heterosexual orientations. As a writer who seeks to build common ground, you will want to avoid stereotypes about any of these groups. In addition, remember to use labels or references to race, religion, sexual orientation, and so on only if they are relevant or necessary to your discussion.

EXERCISE 20.1 Each of the following sentences stereotypes a person or a group of people. Underline the word or phrase that identifies the stereotyped person or group, and explain why the stereotype may be offensive, demeaning, or unfair. Example:

> **If you have trouble printing, ask a <u>computer geek</u> for help.**
>
> *Assumes that all computer-savvy people are geeky, which is not the case.*

1. For a blue-collar worker, he was extremely well read.
2. All women just adore those flowery romance novels!
3. Did you see a chiropractor or a real doctor for your back problem?
4. Everyone in the South prefers the Confederate flag to that of the United States.
5. How wonderful that you are adopting a child! Were you unable to have children of your own?

20b Examining assumptions about gender and pronoun preferences

Powerful gender-related words can subtly affect our thinking and our behavior. For instance, at one time, speakers commonly referred to hypothetical doctors or engineers as *he* (and then labeled a woman who worked as a doctor *a woman doctor*, as if to say, "She's an exception; doctors are normally men"). Similarly, a label like *male nurse* reflects stereotyped assumptions about proper roles for men. Equally problematic is the traditional use of *man* and *mankind* to refer to all human beings and the use of *he* and *him* to refer generally to any human being. Because such usage ignores huge numbers of people, it hardly helps a writer build common ground.

Eliminating sexist nouns and pronouns. Sexist language, which unnecessarily calls attention to gender, can usually be revised fairly easily by using plural nouns and pronouns or eliminating the need for a pronoun:

▸ ~~A lawyer~~ ^Lawyers^ must pass the bar exam before ~~he~~ ^they^ can practice.

▸ A lawyer must pass the bar exam before ~~he can practice.~~ ^practicing.^

Eliminate common sexist **nouns** from your writing as well.

INSTEAD OF	TRY USING
anchorman, anchorwoman	anchor
businessman	businessperson, business executive
congressman	member of Congress, representative
fireman	firefighter
male nurse	nurse
man, mankind	humans, human beings, humanity, the human race, humankind
policeman, policewoman	police officer
woman engineer	engineer

Considering pronoun preferences. Take special care with personal pronouns and ask for pronoun preferences when possible, since the use of *she* and *he* leaves out many people who do not identify with either of those terms, including some people with transgender or intersex identities. For this reason, some may prefer the use of singular *they/them/theirs*, as in "Fallon asked to borrow my book, so I gave it to *them*." Others prefer alternate **gender-neutral pronouns** such as *ve/ver/vis*, *ze/hir/hirs*, or *ze/zir/zirs*, as in "Ze called me, so I called zir back." Still others are just fine with the traditional *he* or *she*.

EXERCISE 20.2 The following excerpt is taken from a 1961 publication by the U.S. Department of Agriculture's Office of the General Counsel. Read it carefully, noting any language we might today consider sexist. Then try bringing the language up to date by revising the passage, substituting nonsexist language as necessary.

Your Role as a Lawyer in the Department of Agriculture

A stimulating and rewarding career awaits you as a lawyer in the U.S. Department of Agriculture. You will be a member of a 200-man legal staff in the Office of the General Counsel, which performs all the legal work for the Department. You will find an opportunity to practice in the field of your interest. . . .

> An attorney in the Office of the General Counsel has personal contact with the administrative officials who are his clients. He furnishes legal advice directly to these clients through all stages in the development, administration, and enforcement of departmental programs. . . . He has an opportunity to engage in many legal functions that relate to his assigned program area. He gives oral advice, writes opinions and briefs, drafts all kinds of legal documents and regulations, drafts and interprets legislation, and engages in hearings and trial work.

20c Examining assumptions about race and ethnicity

In building common ground, watch for any words that ignore differences not only among individual members of a race or ethnic group but also among subgroups. Be aware, for instance, of the many nations to which American Indians belong and of the diverse places from which Americans of Spanish-speaking ancestry come.

Preferred terms. Identifying preferred terms is sometimes not an easy task, for they can change often and vary widely.

- The word *colored* was once widely used in the United States to refer to Americans of African ancestry. By the 1950s, the preferred term had become *Negro*; in the 1960s, *black* came to be preferred by most, though certainly not all, members of that community. Then, in the late 1980s, some leaders of the community urged that *black* be replaced by *African American*. Today, *African American* and *black* (or *Black*) are both widely used.
- The word *Oriental*, once used to refer to people of East Asian descent, is now considered offensive.
- Once widely preferred, the term *Native American* is challenged by those who argue that the most appropriate way to refer to indigenous peoples is by the specific name such as *Chippewa*, *Tlingit*, or *Hopi*. It has also become common for tribal groups to refer to themselves as *Indians* or *Indian tribes*.
- Among Americans of Spanish-speaking descent, the preferred terms of reference are many: *Chicano/Chicana*, *Hispanic*, *Latin American*, *Latino/Latina*, *Mexican American*, and *Dominican*, to name but a few.

Clearly, then, ethnic terminology changes often enough to challenge even the most careful writers—including writers who belong to the groups they are writing about. The best advice may be to consider your words carefully, to listen for the way members of a group refer to themselves (or ask about preferences), and to check in a current dictionary for any term you're unsure of.

20d Considering abilities and disabilities

According to the most recent U.S. census, one in five Americans has a disability of some kind; millions more will have a disability sometime in their lives. It's likely, then, that you may have a disability—and almost certain that members of your audiences will experience a huge range of abilities and disabilities. Think of everyone you know who wears glasses, hearing aids, or other prosthetic devices, of those who have limited vision or hearing (or none), of those who are color-blind, of those who have cognitive processing differences—we could go on and on. It's a mistake, then, to ignore such differences, since doing so makes it more difficult to reach all audience members and build common ground with them. A few tips may be helpful here:

- When you are using color, remember that everyone won't see it as you may. When putting colors next to one another, then, use those on opposite sides of the color spectrum, such as purple and gold, in order to achieve the highest contrast.
- Make sure all your readers can access the content in a digital text—by providing alternative text for all visuals so they will make sense when read by a screen reader and by providing captions for sound files and longer audio content.
- Check the website for the Americans with Disabilities Act for guidelines on designing accessible web texts (www.ada.gov).
- In peer groups or in class, think about whether members would rather receive printouts in very large type or as audio files. Try to accommodate the needs of all peers.
- In presentations, make sure to face any audience members who are lip reading, or check to see if a sign language interpreter may be needed.

If you have trouble processing letters and sounds in sequence, try "talking pens" that can scan words and read them aloud, or voice-recognition programs that can transcribe dictated text. If you have difficulty taking notes on a computer or in a notebook, try dictating them into a word processor with voice-recognition capability. Or check out other assistive technologies such as reading and writing software that offers help with everything from audio and visual options to mechanics, punctuation, and formatting.

EXERCISE 20.3 Review the following sentences for offensive references or terms. If a sentence contains unacceptable terms, rewrite it. Example:

> Passengers
> **~~Elderly passengers~~ on the cruise ship *Romance Afloat* will enjoy**
> ^
> **swimming, shuffleboard, and nightly movies.**

1. The doctor and the male nurse had different bedside manners when tending to the patients in their care.
2. Barack Obama was the first colored president of the United States.
3. The Oriental girl who works at the bank is always pleasant and efficient.
4. My family recently moved into an area full of rednecks.
5. Our skylight was installed last week by a woman carpenter.

21 Varieties of Language

Comedian Dave Chappelle has said, "Every black American is bilingual. We speak street vernacular, and we speak job interview." As Chappelle understands, English comes in many varieties that differ from one another in pronunciation, vocabulary, usage, and grammar. You probably already adjust the variety of language you use depending on how well—and how formally—you know the audience you are addressing. Language variety can improve your communication with your audience if you think carefully about the effect you want to achieve.

21a Using "standard" English appropriately

One variety of English, usually referred to as "standard" or "academic," is that taught prescriptively in schools, represented in this and most other textbooks, used in the national media, and written and spoken widely by those wielding social and economic power. As the language used in business and most public institutions, "standard" English is a variety with which you will want to be completely familiar. "Standard" English, however, is only one of many effective varieties of English and itself varies according to purpose and audience, from the more formal style used in academic writing to the informal style characteristic of casual conversation. Indeed, the range of what is considered "standard" is broader than ever, as writing for academic and public audiences becomes more conversational and more informal.

21b Using varieties of English

English is a polyglot language, meaning one that has always absorbed words and phrases from other languages, from Latin and French to Scandinavian and African languages. Unlike some countries that have tried to keep their languages "pure," English has been like a sponge, soaking up new terms that enrich our vocabulary. Today, this is especially true of Spanish terms.

So English itself is a huge combination of linguistic influences. And as with any language, English comes in a number of varieties, from international ones such as Canadian, Australian, or British English to national and local varieties, including African American English, Hawaiian Pidgin, what writer Gloria Anzaldua called "Tex-Mex" English, and a number of regional varieties, such as Appalachian, Midwestern, or New England dialects.

All of these varieties and dialects of English are legitimate forms of the language that are recognized and valued: if "variety is the spice of life," then the variety of our languages makes us a particularly spicy culture. Research shows that the ability to communicate in multiple languages and varieties of English is a valuable asset to

Language: Language Variety > Video Prompt

writers, an ability that you can certainly use to your advantage, both in academic and nonacademic writing. In fact, many writers and speakers of English shift easily from one variety to another, using these shifts for special effect and for helping to connect to their audiences, a practice scholars call *code meshing*.

The key to shifting among varieties of English and among languages is appropriateness: you need to consider when such shifts will help your audience appreciate your message and when shifts may do just the opposite. Used appropriately and wisely, *any* variety of English can serve a good purpose.

Using varieties of English to evoke a place or community. Weaving together regional varieties and "standard" or "school" English can be very effective in creating a sense of place in your writing. Here, an anthropologist writing about one Carolina community takes care to let the residents speak their minds—and in their own words:

> For Roadville, schooling is something most folks have not gotten enough of, but everybody believes will do something toward helping an individual "get on." In the words of one oldtime resident, "Folks that ain't got no schooling don't get to be nobody nowadays."
>
> —Shirley Brice Heath, *Ways with Words*

Varieties of language, including slang and colloquial expressions, can also help writers evoke other kinds of communities. (See also 22a.)

For Multilingual Writers

Recognizing Global Varieties of English

Like other world languages, English is used in many countries, so it has many global varieties. For example, British English differs somewhat from U.S. English in certain vocabulary (*bonnet* for *hood* of a car), syntax (*to hospital* rather than *to the hospital*), spelling (*centre* rather than *center*), and pronunciation. If you have learned a non-American variety of English, you will want to recognize, and to appreciate, the ways in which it differs from the variety widely used in U.S. academic settings.

Using varieties of English to build credibility with a community. Whether you are American Indian or trace your ancestry to Europe, Asia, Latin America, Africa, or elsewhere, your heritage lives on in the diversity of the English language. See how one Hawaiian writer uses a local variety of English to paint a picture of young teens hearing a "chicken skin" story from their grandmother.

> "—So, rather dan being rid of da shark, da people were stuck with many little ones, for dere mistake."
>
> Then Grandma Wong wen' pause, for dramatic effect, I guess, and she wen' add, "Dis is one of dose times. . . . Da time of da sharks."
>
> Those words ended another of Grandma's chicken skin stories. The stories she told us had been passed on to her by her grandmother, who had heard them from her grandmother. Always skipping a generation.
>
> —Rodney Morales, "When the Shark Bites"

Notice how the narrator of the story uses different varieties of English—presenting information necessary to the story line mostly in standard English and using a local, ethnic variety to represent spoken language. One important reason for the shift from standard English is to demonstrate that the writer is a member of the community whose language he is representing and thus to build credibility with others in the community. Take care, however, in using the language of communities other than your own. When used inappropriately, such language can have an opposite effect, perhaps destroying credibility and alienating your audience.

EXERCISE 21.1 Read the following excerpt by Amy Tan. See if you can "translate" the passage into academic English. Then, write a brief paragraph (in academic English) discussing (1) the differences you detect between academic English and the example, and (2) the effects achieved by using each variety of English.

> "Why don't you like me the way I am? I'm *not* a genius! I can't play the piano. And even if I could, I wouldn't go on TV if you paid me a million dollars!" I cried.
>
> My mother slapped me. "Who ask you be genius?" she shouted. "Only ask you be your best. For you sake. You think I want you be genius? Hnnh! What for! Who ask you!"
>
> —Amy Tan, *The Joy Luck Club*

22 Word Choice

Deciding which word is the right word can be a challenge. It's not unusual to find many words that have similar but subtly different meanings, and each makes a different impression on your audience. For instance, the "pasta with marinara sauce" presented in a restaurant may look and taste much like the "macaroni and gravy" served at an Italian family dinner, but the choice of one label rather than the other tells us not only about the food but also about the people serving it and the people to whom they expect to serve it.

22a Using appropriate formality

In an email or letter to a friend or close associate, informal language is often appropriate. For most academic and professional writing, however, more formal language is appropriate, since you are addressing people you do not know well.

EMAIL TO SOMEONE YOU KNOW WELL

▸ Myisha is great–hire her if you can!

LETTER OF RECOMMENDATION TO SOMEONE YOU DO NOT KNOW

▸ I am pleased to recommend Myisha Fisher. She will bring good ideas and extraordinary energy to your organization.

Slang and colloquial language. Slang, or extremely informal language, is often confined to a relatively small group and changes very quickly, though some slang gains wide use (*ripoff*, *zine*). Colloquial language, such as *a lot*, *in a bind*, or *snooze*, is less informal, more widely used, and longer lasting than most slang.

Writers who use slang and colloquial language can risk not being understood or not being taken seriously. If you are writing for a general audience about gun-control legislation and you use the term *gat*, some readers may not know what you mean, and others may be irritated by what they see as a frivolous reference to a deadly serious subject.

EXERCISE 22.1 Revise each of the following sentences to use appropriate formality consistently. Example:

Although feel excited as soon as
I can ~~get all enthused~~ about writing, ~~but~~ I sit down to write my
blank.
mind goes ~~right to sleep.~~

1. At the conclusion of Jane Austen's classic novel *Pride and Prejudice*, the two eldest Bennett sisters both get hitched.
2. I agree with many of his environmental policies, but that proposal is totally nuts.
3. The celebrated Shakespearean actor gave the performance of a lifetime, despite the lame supporting cast.
4. Moby Dick's humongous size was matched only by Ahab's obsessive desire to wipe him out.
5. The refugees had suffered great hardships, but now they were able to see the light at the end of the tunnel.

Jargon. Jargon is the special vocabulary of a particular trade or profession, enabling members to speak and write concisely to one another. Reserve jargon for an audience that will understand your terms. The example that follows, from a web page about digital cameras, uses jargon appropriately for an interested and knowledgeable audience.

> The image quality for mirrorless models is extremely similar to that of a dSLR with the same size sensor and an equivalent lens, and the performance of the midrange and higher-end mirrorless models has gotten really competitive, with sophisticated autofocus systems and fast continuous-shooting speeds.
>
> —CNET, Camera Buying Guide

Jargon can be irritating and incomprehensible—or extremely helpful. Before you use technical jargon, remember your readers: if they will not understand the terms, or if you don't know them well enough to judge, then say whatever you need to say in everyday language.

Pompous language, euphemisms, and doublespeak. Stuffy or pompous language is unnecessarily formal for the purpose, audience,

Language: Word Choice > LearningCurve and Exercises
Language: Dictionaries and Vocabulary Building > LearningCurve and Exercises

 For Multilingual Writers

Avoiding Fancy Language

In writing academic English, which is fairly formal, students are often tempted to use many "big words" instead of simple language. Although learning impressive words can be a good way to expand your vocabulary, it is usually best to avoid flowery or fancy language in college writing. Academic writing at U.S. universities tends to value clear, concise prose.

or topic. It often gives writing an insincere or unintentionally humorous tone, making a writer's ideas seem insignificant or even unbelievable.

POMPOUS

- ▸ **Pursuant to the August 9 memorandum regarding the company carbon-footprint-reduction initiative, it is incumbent upon us to endeavor to make maximal utilization of telephonic and digital communication in lieu of personal visitation.**

REVISED

- ▸ **According to the August 9 memo, the company wants us to reduce our use of oil and gas, so we should telephone or email whenever possible rather than make personal visits.**

Euphemisms are words and **phrases** that make unpleasant ideas seem less harsh. *Your position is being eliminated* seeks to soften the blow of being fired or laid off. Although euphemisms can sometimes appeal to an audience by showing that you are considerate of people's feelings, they can also sound insincere or evasive.

Doublespeak is language used to hide or distort the truth. During massive layoffs in the business world, companies may describe a job-cutting policy as *employee repositioning*, *deverticalization*, or *rightsizing*. The public—and particularly those who lose their jobs—recognize such terms as doublespeak.

EXERCISE 22.2 For each of the scenarios that follow, note who the audience would be for the piece of writing. Then indicate the level of formality—formal or informal—that would be appropriate. Be prepared to explain your answer. Example:

An online forum for people who are interested in Harley-Davidson motorcycles
Audience is others who share your passion; informal

1. A text to a childhood friend across the country
2. An email requesting an interview in response to an online job posting
3. A brochure explaining the recycling policies of your community to local residents
4. A letter to the editor of the *Washington Post* explaining that a recent editorial failed to consider all the facts about health insurance
5. A cover letter asking a professor to accept the late paper you are sending after the end of the semester

22b Considering denotation and connotation

The words *enthusiasm*, *passion*, and *obsession* all carry roughly the same denotation, or dictionary meaning. But the connotations, or associations, are quite different: an *enthusiasm* is a pleasurable and absorbing interest; a *passion* has a strong emotional component and may affect someone positively or negatively; an *obsession* is an unhealthy attachment that excludes other interests.

Note the differences in connotation among the following three statements:

- **Students Against Racism (SAR) erected a temporary barrier on the campus oval, saying the structure symbolized "the many barriers to those discriminated against by university policies."**
- **Left-wing agitators threw up an eyesore right on the oval to try to stampede the university into giving in to their demands.**
- **Supporters of human rights for all students challenged the university's investment in racism by erecting a protest barrier on campus.**

The first statement is the most neutral, merely stating facts (and quoting the assertion about university policy to represent it as someone's opinion); the second, by using words with negative connotations (*agitators*, *eyesore*, *stampede*), is strongly critical; the third, by using words with positive connotations (*supporters of human rights*) and presenting opinions as facts gives a favorable slant to the protest.

EXERCISE 22.3 Read each of the following sentences, looking for mistakes in denotation and using your dictionary as needed. Cross out every error that you find. Then examine each error to determine the word intended, and write in the correct word. Example:

> **Some schools are questioning whether selling bottled water on campus is the right ~~incision~~ decision for the environment.**

1. Even if students are customary to recycling on campus, many bottles end up in the trash, adding to landfill waste.
2. Some students abdicate the use of refillable plastic bottles, which they can fill up at home or at water stations on campus.
3. Other students think drinking fountains should suffice to keep the school population hydrogenated.
4. Some students favor the sale of bottled water on campus, and they think it is unfair to sell other items in vending machines while bottled water is exuded.
5. These students ascertain that they should be allowed to purchase water just as they can purchase soda or candy bars.

EXERCISE 22.4 The sentences that follow contain words with strongly judgmental connotative meanings. Underline these words; then revise each sentence to make it more neutral. Example:

> **The current NRA <u>scheme</u> is appealing to patriotism as a <u>smokescreen to obscure the real issue</u> of gun control.**
>
> *The current NRA campaign is appealing to patriotism rather than responding directly to gun-control proposals.*

1. The Democrats are conspiring on a new education bill.
2. CEOs always waltz away with millions in salary, stock options, and pensions while the little people who keep the company running get peanuts.
3. The United States is turning into a nation of fatsos.
4. Tree-huggers ranted about the Explorer's gas mileage outside the Ford dealership.
5. Naive voters often stumble to the polls and blithely pick whatever names they see first.

22c Using general and specific language effectively

Effective writers balance general words (those that name groups or classes) with specific words (those that identify individual and particular things). Abstractions, which are types of general words, refer to things we cannot perceive through our five senses. Specific words are often concrete, naming things we can see, hear, touch, taste, or smell. If your aim is to bring a scene to life in your reader's mind, using specific, concrete words along with action verbs will help you do so.

GENERAL	LESS GENERAL	SPECIFIC	MORE SPECIFIC
book	dictionary	abridged dictionary	the fifth edition of the *American Heritage College Dictionary*
ABSTRACT	**LESS ABSTRACT**	**CONCRETE**	**MORE CONCRETE**
culture	visual art	painting	van Gogh's *Starry Night*

EXERCISE 22.5 Rewrite each of the following sentences to be more specific and more concrete. Example:

The truck entered the roadway.

The red Ford F150 entered Interstate 95.

1. That book was interesting.
2. They couldn't decide what to eat.
3. I pulled over and waited for the tow truck.
4. The castle is very old.
5. Jorge sat at the bus stop.

22d Using figurative language effectively

Figurative language, or figures of speech, paints pictures in readers' minds, allowing readers to "see" a point readily and clearly. Far from being a frill, such language is crucial to understanding.

Metaphors, similes, and analogies. Similes use *like, as, as if,* or *as though* to make explicit the comparison between two seemingly different things. Metaphors are implicit comparisons, omitting the *like, as, as if,* or *as though* of similes, which make explicit comparisons between two seemingly different things. Analogies compare similar features of two dissimilar things; they explain something unfamiliar by relating it to something more familiar.

METAPHOR

▸ **Faces carry history. They're *genetic maps*, but they're *vessels of spiritual memory*, too.**

SIMILE

▸ ***Dunkirk,* set against events that happened over seventy-five years ago, *is like a message from a lost world.***

ANALOGY

▸ ***Dunkirk* is a supreme achievement made from small strokes, a kind of Seurat painting constructed with dark, glittering bits of history.**

—Stephanie Zacharer, *The Miracle of Dunkirk*

Clichés and mixed metaphors. A cliché is an overused figure of speech, such as *busy as a bee.* By definition, we use clichés all the time, especially in speech, and many serve usefully as shorthand for familiar ideas. But if you use clichés to excess in your writing, readers may conclude that what you are saying is not very new or is even insincere.

Mixed metaphors make comparisons that are inconsistent.

▸ **The lectures were like brilliant comets streaking through the night sky, ~~showering~~ ^dazzling^ listeners with ~~a torrential rain~~ ^flashes^ of insight.**

The images of streaking light and heavy precipitation are inconsistent; in the revised sentence, all of the images relate to light.

EXERCISE 22.6 Identify the similes and metaphors in each of the following numbered items, and decide how each contributes to your understanding of the passage or sentence in which it appears. Example:

Her strong arms, her kisses, the clean soap smell of her face, her voice calming me—all of this was gone. She was like a statue in a church.
—Louise Erdrich, "Shamengwa"

like a statue in a church (simile): vividly emphasizes the woman's cold, stone-like persona

1. Smell is a potent wizard that transports us across thousands of miles and all the years we have lived. —Helen Keller, *The World I Live In*
2. He sometimes thinks marriage is like a football game and he's quarterbacking the underdog team. —Stephen King, "Premium Harmony"
3. The senses feed shards of information to the brain like microscopic pieces of a jigsaw puzzle.
—Diane Ackerman, *A Natural History of the Senses*
4. I like cemeteries too because they are huge, densely populated cities.
—Guy de Maupassant, "The Graveyard Sisterhood"
5. The sun was a wide crescent, like a segment of tangerine.
—Annie Dillard, "Total Eclipse"

22e Making spell checkers work for you

Research conducted for this book shows that spelling errors have changed dramatically in the past twenty years, thanks to spell checkers. Although these programs have weeded out many once-common misspellings, they are not foolproof. Look out for these typical errors allowed by spell checkers:

- **Homonyms.** Spell checkers cannot distinguish between words such as *affect* and *effect* that sound alike but are spelled differently.
- **Proper nouns.** A spell checker cannot tell you when you misspell a name.
- **Compound words written as two words.** Spell checkers will not see a problem if you write *nowhere* incorrectly as *no where.*
- **Typos.** The spell checker will not flag *heat* even if you meant to write *heart.*

Spell checkers and wrong words. Wrong-word errors are the most common surface error in college writing today (see p. 28), and spell checkers are partly to blame. Spell checkers may suggest bizarre substitutions for proper names and specialized terms, and if you accept the suggestions automatically, you may introduce wrong-word errors. A student who typed *fantic* instead of *frantic* found that the spell checker had substituted *fanatic*, a replacement that made no sense. Be careful not to take a spell checker's recommendation without paying careful attention to the replacement word.

Adapting spell checkers to your needs. Always proofread carefully, even after running the spell checker. The following tips can help:

- Check a dictionary if a spell checker highlights or suggests a word you are not sure of.
- If you can enter new words in your spell checker's dictionary, include names, non-English terms, or other specialized words that you use regularly. Be careful to enter the correct spelling!
- After you run the spell checker, look again for homonyms that you mix up regularly.
- Remember that spell checkers are not sensitive to capitalization.

EXERCISE 22.7 The following paragraph has already been checked using a word processor's spell checker. Correct any spelling errors that may remain.

Elisha enjoys writing articles four the school news paper. Each week, she has to turn in a column relating to evens on campus. She tries too cover important topics that students have expressed they're concerns about. She has written about security problems inn the dorms, requests for late-night bus service that every one can use, an the need for more meal choices, specially vegetarian options. Elisha doesn't get paid for her stores, and she does not receive college credit for them. She is hopping, thought, that being on the staff oft he paper will help her begin a career in journalism when she gradates form school.

EXERCISE 22.8 Choose the appropriate word in each set of parentheses. Example:

Antifreeze can have a toxic (affect/effect) on pets.

People need antifreeze in (their/there/they're) cars in cold (weather/whether). Unfortunately, antifreeze also tastes (grate/great) to cats and dogs, who drink it from the greenish puddles commonly (scene/seen) on asphalt. Antifreeze made of ethylene glycol causes kidney failure and has (lead/led) to the deaths of many pets. (Its/It's) not (to/too/two) hard to protect (your/you're) animals from antifreeze poisoning, however. First, (buy/by) antifreeze that does not contain ethylene glycol, in spite of (its/it's) higher cost. Second, do not let pets wander out of (cite/sight/site) when they are outdoors. Third, if a pet acts sick, get help even if the animal (seams/seems) to improve—animals with antifreeze poisoning appear to feel better shortly before they (die/dye).

Style: Effective Sentences

23 Varying Sentences 270

24 Consistency and Completeness 272

25 Coordination and Subordination 275

26 Conciseness 279

27 Parallelism 282

28 Shifts 285

23 Varying Sentences

Why should writers pay special attention to style today? Because more than ever before, information is coming at us in fire-hose quantities, so much information that we can't possibly attend to even a fraction of it. In such a time, researchers and media theorists point out, what most attracts and holds our attention is the style in which the information is presented. It's worth spending some time, then, on making sure the sentences you write are stylistically appropriate and powerful. Variety in sentence structures will help you get and keep your readers' attention.

23a Varying sentence length

Is there a "just right" length for a sentence? No. Rather, sentence length depends on your purpose, audience, and topic: a children's story, for instance, may call for mostly short sentences, whereas an article on nuclear disarmament may call for considerably longer ones. While a series of short or long sentences can sometimes be effective, varying sentence length can work well in college writing, as in this example, where the punch of a short sentence after three longer ones is powerful:

> Rachel Maddow is not alone in thinking that Gail Collins is the funniest serious political commentator in the U.S. Previously, Ms. Collins was the first woman at *The Times* to hold the post of editorial page editor. The author of six books, she took time off in 2007—between the editorial page editor job and her column—and returned to write about the 2008 presidential election. She's been at it ever since.
>
> —Susan Lehman, *New York Times*

23b Varying sentence openings

If sentence after sentence begins with a subject, the passage will usually seem "choppy" and monotonous. Take a look at the revisions to the following passage, which help to vary the sentence openings and make the passage more effective and easy to read.

▸ **The way football and basketball are played is as interesting as the players. ~~Football~~ Because football is a game of precision/, ~~Each~~ each play is diagrammed to accomplish a certain goal. Basketball, however, is a game of endurance. ~~A~~ In fact, a basketball game looks like a track meet; the team that drops of exhaustion first, loses. Basketball players are often compared to artists/; ~~The players'~~ their graceful moves and slam dunks are their masterpieces.**

The editing adds variety by using a subordinating word (*Because*) and a prepositional phrase (*In fact*) in linking sentences. Varying sentence openings prevents the passage from seeming to jerk or lurch along.

You can vary your sentence openings by using transitions, phrases, and dependent clauses:

TRANSITIONS

▸ *In contrast*, our approach will save time and money.

▸ *Nevertheless*, the show must go on.

PHRASES

▸ *Before dawn*, the tired commuters drink their first cups of coffee.

▸ *Frustrated by the delays*, the drivers started honking their horns.

DEPENDENT CLAUSES

▸ *What they want* is a place to call home.

▸ *Because the hills were dry*, the fire spread rapidly.

24 Consistency and Completeness

If you listen carefully to the conversations around you, you will hear speakers use different styles to get their points across. The words, tone, and structure they choose have a big impact on your impression of them—their personality and credibility, for example—and their ideas. Often, you will hear inconsistent and incomplete structures. For instance, during an interview with Kelly Ripa and Ryan Seacrest, Oprah Winfrey described a recent trip to New Zealand, part of her "year of adventure":

> It should be on your bucket list. Put it on your bucket list. And look at that water [on the slide] behind me—it is like crystal blue, I mean, no kind of Instagram fixin' up stuff. No filter. Nothing. It just is like . . . because the water's coming off of the glaciers and it enters . . . and it's just like, from the minerals, it's like pure turquoise.

Because Winfrey is talking casually, some of her sentences begin one way but then move in another direction. The mixed structures pose no problem for listeners, but sentences such as these can be confusing in writing. For this reason, using consistent and complete sentence structure will help get and hold your readers' attention, as in the following example from a reaction to the film *Wonder Woman*:

> Wonder Woman hasn't been my thing since the last time Lynda Carter laced up those high-heeled red-and-white boots back in 1979. But the trailer came out for the new movie starring Gal Gadot, and I clicked on it. I agree with most people: she *is* wonder woman. Gadot looks like she could kick my ass without even noticing that she had.
>
> —W. Kamau Bell, "I Need a (Black) Hero"

24a Revising confusing sentence structure

Beginning a sentence with one grammatical pattern and then switching to another one can confuse readers.

MIXED The fact that I get up at 5:00 AM, a wake-up time that explains why I'm always tired in the evening.

Clarity: Consistent and Complete Structures > Exercises

This sentence starts out with a **subject** (*The fact*) followed by a **dependent clause** (*that I get up at 5:00 AM*). The sentence needs a **predicate** to complete the **independent clause**, but instead it moves to another **phrase** followed by a dependent clause (*a wake-up time that explains why I'm always tired in the evening*), and a **fragment** results.

REVISED The fact that I get up at 5:00 AM explains why I'm always tired in the evening.

Deleting *a wake-up time that* changes the rest of the sentence into a predicate.

REVISED I get up at 5:00 AM, a wake-up time that explains why I'm always tired in the evening.

Deleting *The fact that* turns the beginning of the sentence into an independent clause.

24b Matching subjects and predicates

Another kind of mixed structure, called faulty predication, occurs when a subject and predicate do not fit together grammatically or simply do not make sense together.

- A characteristic that I admire is ~~a person who is generous.~~ ^generosity.

  A person is not a characteristic.

- The rules of the corporation ~~expect~~ ^require that employees ~~to~~ be on time.

  Rules cannot expect anything.

Is when, is where, the reason . . . is because. Although you will often hear these expressions in everyday use, such constructions are inappropriate in academic or professional writing.

- A stereotype is ~~when someone characterizes~~ ^an unfair characterization of a group^. ~~unfairly.~~
- Spamming is ~~where companies send~~ ^the practice of sending electronic junk mail.
- ~~The reason~~ I like to play soccer ~~is~~ because it provides aerobic exercise.

24c Using consistent compound structures

Sometimes writers omit certain words in compound structures. If the omitted word does not fit grammatically with other parts of the compound, the omission can be confusing or inappropriate.

▸ **His skills are weak, and his performance ^is^ only average.**

The omitted verb *is* does not match the verb in the other part of the compound (*are*), so the writer needs to include it.

24d Making complete comparisons

When you compare two or more things, make the comparison complete and clear.

▸ **I was often embarrassed because my parents were so different~~.~~ ^from my friends' parents.^**

Adding *from my friends' parents* completes the comparison.

UNCLEAR	Aneil always felt more affection for his brother than his sister.
CLEAR	Aneil always felt more affection for his brother than his sister did.
CLEAR	Aneil always felt more affection for his brother than he did for his sister.

EXERCISE 24.1 Revise this passage so that all sentences are grammatically and logically consistent and complete.

A concentrated animal feeding operation, or CAFO, is when a factory farm raises thousands of animals in a confined space. Vast amounts of factory-farm livestock waste, dumped into giant lagoons, which are an increasingly common sight in rural areas of this country. Are factory-farm operations healthy for neighbors, for people in other parts of the country, and the environment?

One problem with factory farming is the toxic waste that has contaminated groundwater in the Midwest. In addition, air quality produces bad-smelling and sometimes dangerous gases that people nearby have to breathe. When a factory farm's neighbors complain may not be able to close the operation. The reason is because most factory farms have powerful corporate backers.

Not everyone is angry about the CAFO situation; consumers get a short-term benefit from a large supply of pork, beef, and chicken that is cheaper than family farms can raise. However, many people think that these operations damage our air and water more than small family farms.

25 Coordination and Subordination

You may notice a difference between your spoken and your written language. In speech, most people tend to use *and* and *so* as all-purpose connectors.

He enjoys psychology, and he has to study hard.

The meaning of this sentence may be perfectly clear in speech, which provides clues with voice, facial expressions, and gestures. In writing, however, the same sentence could have more than one meaning.

Although he enjoys psychology, he has to study hard.

He enjoys psychology although he has to study hard.

The first sentence links two ideas with a **coordinating conjunction**, *and*; the other two sentences link ideas with a **subordinating conjunction**, *although*. A coordinating conjunction gives the ideas equal emphasis, and a subordinating conjunction emphasizes one idea more than another.

25a Relating equal ideas

When you want to give equal emphasis to different ideas in a sentence, link them with a coordinating conjunction (*and*, *but*, *for*, *nor*, *or*, *so*, *yet*) or a semicolon.

- **They acquired horses, and their ancient nomadic spirit was suddenly free of the ground.**

Style: Coordination and Subordination > LearningCurve and Exercises

- **There is perfect freedom in the mountains, but it belongs to the eagle and the elk, the badger and the bear.**

  —N. Scott Momaday, *The Way to Rainy Mountain*

Coordination can help make explicit the relationship between two separate ideas.

- **My son watches *The Simpsons* religiously. ; ~~Forced~~ forced to choose, he would probably take Homer Simpson over his sister.**

  Connecting these two sentences with a semicolon strengthens the connection between two closely related ideas.

When you connect ideas in a sentence, make sure that the relationship between the ideas is clear.

- **Surfing the Internet is a common way to spend leisure time, ~~and~~ but it should not replace human contact.**

  What does being a common form of leisure have to do with replacing human contact? Changing *and* to *but* better relates the two ideas.

EXERCISE 25.1 Using the principles of coordination to signal equal importance, combine and revise the following ten short sentences into several longer and more effective ones. Add or delete words as necessary.

The beach was deserted. I wondered where all of the surfers were. The waves were calling to me. The sand was burning my feet. I walked toward the ocean. I let the water splash my ankles. Standing at the water's edge, I watched for a very long time. I knew it was getting late. I had to make my way back. I picked up a few seashells to give to my little sister.

25b Distinguishing main ideas

Subordination allows you to distinguish major points from minor points or to bring supporting details into a sentence. If, for instance, you put your main idea in an **independent clause**, you might then put any less significant ideas in **dependent clauses**,

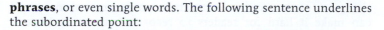

phrases, or even single words. The following sentence underlines the subordinated point:

▸ **Mrs. Viola Cullinan was a plump woman who lived in a three-bedroom house somewhere behind the post office.**

—Maya Angelou, "My Name Is Margaret"

The dependent clause adds some important information about Mrs. Cullinan, but it is subordinate to the independent clause.

Notice that the choice of what to subordinate rests with the writer and depends on the intended meaning. Angelou might have given the same basic information differently:

▸ **Mrs. Viola Cullinan, a plump woman, lived in a three-bedroom house somewhere behind the post office.**

Subordinating the information about Mrs. Cullinan's size to that about her house would suggest a slightly different meaning. As a writer, you must think carefully about what you want to emphasize and subordinate information accordingly.

Subordination also establishes logical relationships among different ideas. These relationships are often specified by subordinating conjunctions.

SOME COMMON SUBORDINATING CONJUNCTIONS

after	in order that	unless
although, even though	once	until
as, as if	since	when
because	than	where
before	that, so that	while
if	though	

The following sentence underlines the subordinate clause and italicizes the subordinating word:

▸ **She usually rested her smile until late afternoon *when* her women friends dropped in and Miss Glory, the cook, served them cold drinks on the closed-in porch.**

—Maya Angelou, "My Name Is Margaret"

Using too many coordinate structures can be monotonous and can make it hard for readers to recognize the most important ideas. Subordinating lesser ideas can help highlight the main ideas.

- Many people check email in the evening, and so they turn on the computer. ~~They~~ ^Though they^ may intend to respond only to urgent messages, a friend sends a link to a blog post, ~~and~~ ^which^ they decide to read ~~it~~ for just a short while/. ~~and~~ ^Eventually,^ they get engrossed in Facebook, and they end up spending the whole evening in front of the screen.

Determining what to subordinate

- ~~Our~~ ^Although our^ new boss can be difficult, ~~although~~ she has revived and maybe even saved the division.

The editing puts the more important information—that the new boss has saved part of the company—in an independent clause and subordinates the rest.

Avoiding too much subordination. When too many subordinate clauses are strung together, readers may not be able to keep track of the main idea in the independent clause.

TOO MUCH SUBORDINATION

- **Philip II sent the Spanish Armada to conquer England, which was ruled by Elizabeth, who had executed Mary because she was plotting to overthrow Elizabeth, who was a Protestant, whereas Mary and Philip were Roman Catholics.**

REVISED

- **Philip II sent the Spanish Armada to conquer England, which was ruled by Elizabeth, a Protestant. She had executed Mary, a Roman Catholic like Philip, because Mary was plotting to overthrow her.**

  Putting the facts about Elizabeth executing Mary into an independent clause makes key information easier to recognize.

EXERCISE 25.2 Revise the following paragraph, using coordination and subordination where appropriate to clarify the relationships among ideas.

Reggae is a style of music. It originated in Jamaica in the late 1960s. Reggae evolved out of earlier types of Jamaican music. Ska was one of reggae's main influences. It has a fast-paced rhythm. It accents the second and fourth beats of each measure. Ska developed in Jamaica in the late 1950s. It combined elements of calypso music and American jazz and rhythm and blues. Reggae emerged in the late 1960s. Reggae songs focus on politics and racial equality. They resonated with the youths of the time. Youths of the time were rising up in protest movements around the world. Musicians Bob Marley and Jimmy Cliff became internationally famous in the 1970s. Reggae gained a permanent place in popular music around the world.

26 Conciseness

If you have a Twitter account, you probably know a lot about being concise—that is, about getting messages across in no more than 280 characters. In 2011, *New York Times* editor Bill Keller tweeted, "Twitter makes you stupid. Discuss." That little comment drew a large number of responses aimed at showing, in 140 characters, that Twitter does *not* make you stupid. In addition, Keller's tweet evoked a concise message from his wife: "I don't know if Twitter makes you stupid, but it's making you late for dinner. Come home."

No matter how you feel about Twitter, you can make any writing more effective by choosing words that convey exactly what you mean to say.

26a Eliminating redundant words

Sometimes writers add words for emphasis, saying that something is large *in size* or red *in color* or that two ingredients should be

Style: Concise Writing > LearningCurve and Exercises

combined *together*. The italicized words are redundant (unnecessary for meaning), as are the deleted words in the following examples.

- ▶ ~~Compulsory a~~Attendance at assemblies is required.
- ▶ The auction featured ~~contemporary~~ "antiques" made recently.
- ▶ Many different forms of hazing occur, such as physical ~~abuse~~ and mental abuse.

26b Eliminating empty words

Words that contribute little or no meaning to a sentence include vague **nouns** like *area*, *kind*, *situation*, and *thing* as well as vague **modifiers** like *definitely*, *major*, *really*, and *very*. Delete such words, or find a more specific way to say what you mean.

- ▶ ~~The h~~Housing ~~situation~~ can strongly influence ~~have a really significant impact on the social aspect of~~ a student's social life.

26c Replacing wordy phrases

Many common **phrases** can be reduced to a word or two with no loss in meaning.

WORDY	CONCISE
at all times	always
at that point in time	then
at the present time	now/today
due to the fact that	because
for the purpose of	for
in order to	to
in the event that	if

EXERCISE 26.1 Make each of the following sentences clear and concise by eliminating unnecessary words and phrases and by making additions or revisions as needed. Example:

> The ~~incredible, unbelievable~~ feats that Houdini performed amazed ~~and astounded all of~~ his audiences ~~who came to see him~~.

1. Harry Houdini, whose real birth name was Ehrich Weiss, made the claim that he had been born in Appleton, Wisconsin, but in actual fact he was born into the world in Budapest, Hungary.
2. Shortly after Houdini's birth, his family moved to Appleton, where his father served as the one and only rabbi in Appleton at that point in time.
3. Houdini gained fame as a really great master escape artist.
4. His many numerous escapes included getting out of a giant sealed envelope without tearing it and walking out of jail cells that were said to be supposedly escape-proof.
5. Before his untimely early death, Houdini told his brother to burn and destroy all papers describing how Houdini's illusions worked.

26d Simplifying sentence structure

Using simple grammatical structures can tighten and strengthen your sentences considerably.

▸ Hurricane Katrina, ~~which was certainly~~ one of the most powerful storms ever to hit the Gulf Coast, caused widespread damage. ~~to a very wide area.~~

Strong verbs. *Be* **verbs** (*is*, *are*, *was*, *were*, *been*) often result in wordiness.

▸ A high-fat, high-cholesterol diet harms ~~is bad for~~ your heart.

Expletives. Sometimes expletive constructions such as *there is*, *there are*, and *it is* introduce a topic effectively; often, however, your writing will be better without them.

- ~~There are m~~[M]any people ~~who~~ fear success because they believe they do not deserve it.

- ~~It is necessary for p~~[P]residential candidates [need] to perform well on television.

Active voice. Some writing situations call for the passive **voice**, but it is always wordier than the active—and often makes for dull or even difficult reading (see 29f).

- ~~In Gower's research, it was~~ [Gower] found that pythons often dwell in trees.

EXERCISE 26.2 Revise the following paragraph so that each sentence is as concise as possible. Combine or divide sentences if necessary.

In this day and age, many people obsess over or dwell on the loss of their youthful appearance when they approach middle age in their thirties and forties. One of the most common professional treatments in the area of skin care is an injection of a substance called or known as Botox. Botox contains small amounts of poisonous toxins that deaden the facial muscles that cause wrinkles in the region of the forehead. Collagen injections are another common and widespread treatment that temporarily fill in wrinkles for a limited time. The injection of collagen can also be utilized for the purpose of making lips appear fuller.

27 Parallelism

If you look and listen, you will see parallel grammatical structures in everyday use. Bumper stickers often use parallelism to make their messages memorable (*Minds are like parachutes; both work best when open*), as do rap lyrics and jump-rope rhymes. In addition to creating pleasing rhythmic effects, parallelism can help clarify meaning.

Clarity: Parallelism > LearningCurve and Exercises

27a Making items in a series or list parallel

All items in a series should be in parallel form—all **nouns**, all **verbs**, all prepositional **phrases**, and so on. Parallelism makes a series both graceful and easy to follow.

► **In the eighteenth century, armed forces could fight in open fields and on the high seas. Today, they can clash on the ground anywhere, on the sea, under the sea, and in the air.**

—Donald Snow and Eugene Brown, *International Relations*

The parallel structure of the phrases, and of the sentences themselves, highlights the contrast between the eighteenth century and today.

► **The children ran down the hill, skipped over the lawn, and ~~were jumping~~** jumped **into the swimming pool.**

► **The duties of the job include baby-sitting, housecleaning, and ~~preparation of~~** preparing **meals.**

Items that are in a list, in a formal outline, and in headings should be parallel.

► **Kitchen rules: (1) Coffee to be made only by library staff.**

(2) Coffee service to be closed at 4:00 am. (3) Doughnuts to be kept in cabinet. (4) ~~No faculty members should handle coffee materials.~~ Coffee materials not to be handled by faculty.

27b Making paired ideas parallel

Parallel structures can help you pair two ideas effectively. The more nearly parallel the two structures are, the stronger the connection between the ideas will be.

► **I type in one place, but I write all over the house.**

—Toni Morrison

► **Writers are often more interesting on the page than they are in ~~person.~~** the flesh.

In these examples, the parallel structures help readers see an important contrast between two ideas or acts.

With conjunctions. When you link ideas with *and*, *but*, *or*, *nor*, *for*, *so*, or *yet*, try to make the ideas parallel in structure. Always use the same structure after both parts of a **correlative conjunction**: *either . . . or*, *both . . . and*, *neither . . . nor*, *not . . . but*, *not only . . . but also*, *just as . . . so*, and *whether . . . or*.

- **Consult a friend** who is **in your class or who is good at math.**
- **The wise politician promises the possible and** ~~**should accept**~~ accepts **the inevitable.**
- **I wanted not only to go away to school but also to** live in **New England.**

EXERCISE 27.1 Complete the following sentences, using parallel words or phrases in each case. Example:

The wise politician *promises the possible*, *encourages the beneficial*, and *accepts the inevitable*.

1. My favorite pastimes include ________, ________, and ________.
2. This summer, I want to ________, ________, and ________.
3. My motto is ________, ________, and ________.
4. In preparation for his wedding day, the groom ________, ________, and ________.
5. ________, ________ and ________ are activities my grandparents enjoy.

27c Using words necessary for clarity

In addition to making parallel elements grammatically similar, be sure to include any words—**prepositions**, articles, verb forms, and so on—that are necessary for clarity.

- **We'll move to a city in the Southwest or** in **Mexico.**

  To a city in Mexico or to Mexico in general? The editing clarifies this.

EXERCISE 27.2 Revise the following paragraph to maintain proper parallelism where it exists and to supply all words necessary for clarity, grammar, and idiom in parallel structures.

Family gatherings for events such as weddings, holidays, and going on vacation are supposed to be happy occasions, but for many people, getting together with family members causes tremendous stress. Everyone hopes to share warm memories and for a picture-perfect family event. Unfortunately, the reality may include an uncle who makes offensive remarks, a critical mother, or anger at a spouse who doesn't lift a finger to help. Neither difficult relatives nor when things go wrong will necessarily ruin a big family gathering, however. The trick is to plan for problems and being able to adapt. People who try to make a family gathering a success will almost always either be able to enjoy the event or laugh about it later.

28 Shifts

A shift is an abrupt change. Sometimes writers or speakers shift deliberately, as Geneva Smitherman does in this passage from *Word from the Mother*:

> There are days when I optimistically predict that Hip Hop will survive—and thrive. . . . In the larger realm of Hip Hop culture, there is cause for optimism as we witness Hip Hop younguns tryna git they political activist game togetha.

Smitherman's shift from formal academic language to vernacular speech calls out for and holds our attention. Although writers make shifts for good rhetorical reasons, unintentional shifts can be confusing to readers.

28a Revising shifts in tense

If **verbs** in a passage refer to actions occurring at different times, they may require different **tenses**. Be careful, however, not to change tenses without a good reason.

► **A few countries produce almost all of the world's illegal drugs, but addiction ~~affected~~ affects many countries.**

Clarity: Shifts > LearningCurve and Exercises

EXERCISE 28.1 Revise the following sentences that include unnecessary shifts in verb tense or in mood. Example:

> **We stood outside the office and ~~ask~~ people not to cross the picket line.** [asked]

1. Many people go into nature when they needed some soul-searching.
2. I waited for almost forty-five minutes on hold, but after a while I give up hope.
3. She is driving to work when she realized what she wanted.
4. As the scandal developed, the executives stop talking to the press.
5. If you made your customers too upset, they decide to shop elsewhere.

28b Revising shifts in voice

Do not shift between the **active voice** (she *sold* it) and the **passive voice** (it *was sold*) without a reason. Sometimes a shift in voice is justified, but often it only confuses readers.

▸ **Two youths approached ~~me,~~ and ~~I was~~ asked [me] for my wallet.**

The original sentence shifts from active to passive voice, so it is unclear who asked for the wallet.

28c Revising shifts in point of view

Unnecessary shifts in point of view between first person (*I* or *we*), second person (*you*), and third person (*he*, *she*, *it*, *one*, or *they*), or between singular and plural subjects, can be very confusing to readers.

▸ **[You] ~~One~~ can do well on this job if you budget your time.**

Is the writer making a general statement or giving advice to someone? Revising the shift eliminates this confusion.

EXERCISE 28.2 Revise each of the following sentences to eliminate an unnecessary shift in voice or point of view. Example:

> **When I remember to take deep breaths and count to ten, [I] ~~you~~ really can control [my] ~~your~~ anger.**

1. If anyone has been pleased with a purchase on our site, would you consider reviewing it?
2. I had planned to walk home after the movie, but you shouldn't be on campus alone after dark.
3. When protests spread from New York to California, fears of possible violence and vandalism were conjured up.
4. Instructors at the studio cooperative offer a wide variety of dance lessons, and art and voice training are also given there.
5. We knew that emails promising free gifts were usually scams, but you couldn't resist clicking on the link just to see.

28d Revising shifts between direct and indirect discourse

When you quote someone's exact words, you are using direct discourse: *She said, "I'm an editor."* When you report what someone says without repeating the exact words, you are using indirect discourse: *She said she was an editor.* Shifting between direct and indirect discourse in the same sentence can cause problems, especially with questions.

▶ **Bob asked what ^he could ~~he~~ do to help~~?~~^.**

The editing eliminates an awkward shift by reporting Bob's question indirectly. It could also be edited to quote Bob directly: *Bob asked, "What can I do to help?"*

EXERCISE 28.3 Eliminate the shifts between direct and indirect discourse in the following sentences by putting the direct discourse into indirect form. Example:

Steven Pinker ~~stated~~ ^states that ~~my~~ ^his book is meant for people who use language and respect it.

1. Richard Rodriguez acknowledges that intimacy was not created by a language; "it is created by intimates."
2. She said that during a semester abroad, "I really missed all my friends."

3. The bewildered neighbor asked him, “What the heck he thought he was doing on the roof?”
4. Loren Eiseley feels an urge to join the birds in their soundless flight, but in the end he knows that he cannot, and “I was, after all, only a man.”
5. The instructor told us, “Please read the next two stories before the next class” and that she might give us a quiz on them.

Grammar

29 Verbs and Verb Phrases 290

30 Nouns and Noun Phrases 305

31 Subject-Verb Agreement 311

32 Adjectives and Adverbs 317

33 Modifier Placement 322

34 Pronouns 326

35 Prepositions and Prepositional Phrases 334

36 Comma Splices and Fused Sentences 338

37 Sentence Fragments 342

29 Verbs and Verb Phrases

One famous restaurant in New Orleans offers to bake, broil, pan-fry, deep-fry, poach, sauté, fricassée, blacken, or scallop any of the fish entrées on its menu. To someone ordering—or cooking—at this restaurant, the important distinctions lie entirely in the **verbs**.

29a Using regular and irregular verb forms

You can create all verb tenses from four verb forms: the **base form**, the past **tense**, the past **participle**, and the present participle. For **regular verbs**, the past tense and past participles are formed by adding *-d* or *-ed*. Present participles are formed by adding *-ing*.

BASE FORM	PAST TENSE	PAST PARTICIPLE	PRESENT PARTICIPLE
love	loved	loved	loving
honor	honored	honored	honoring
obey	obeyed	obeyed	obeying

An **irregular verb** does not follow the *-ed* or *-d* pattern. If you are unsure about whether a verb is regular or irregular, or what the correct form is, consult the following list or a dictionary. Dictionaries list any irregular forms under the entry for the base form.

Some common irregular verbs

BASE FORM	PAST TENSE	PAST PARTICIPLE	PRESENT PARTICIPLE
be	was/were	been	being
become	became	become	becoming
begin	began	begun	beginning
bite	bit	bitten, bit	biting
break	broke	broken	breaking
bring	brought	brought	bringing

LaunchPad Solo
macmillan learning
Grammar: Verbs > 3 LearningCurve

BASE FORM	PAST TENSE	PAST PARTICIPLE	PRESENT PARTICIPLE
catch	caught	caught	catching
choose	chose	chosen	choosing
come	came	come	coming
cost	cost	cost	costing
do	did	done	doing
draw	drew	drawn	drawing
drink	drank	drunk	drinking
eat	ate	eaten	eating
fall	fell	fallen	falling
feel	felt	felt	feeling
find	found	found	finding
fly	flew	flown	flying
get	got	gotten, got	getting
give	gave	given	giving
go	went	gone	going
hang (suspend)[1]	hung	hung	hanging
have	had	had	having
keep	kept	kept	keeping
lead	led	led	leading
leave	left	left	leaving
lie (recline)[2]	lay	lain	lying
make	made	made	making
prove	proved	proved, proven	proving
ring	rang	rung	ringing
run	ran	run	running
speak	spoke	spoken	speaking
spend	spent	spent	spending

[1] *Hang* meaning "execute by hanging" is regular: *hang, hanged, hanged.*

[2] *Lie* meaning "tell a falsehood" is regular: *lie, lied, lied.*

BASE FORM	PAST TENSE	PAST PARTICIPLE	PRESENT PARTICIPLE
swim	swam	swum	swimming
swing	swung	swung	swinging
take	took	taken	taking
teach	taught	taught	teaching
wake	woke, waked	waked, woken	waking
win	won	won	winning
write	wrote	written	writing

EXERCISE 29.1 Underline each verb or verb phrase in the following sentences. Example:

Many cultures celebrate the arrival of spring with a festival of some kind.

1. The spring festival of Holi occurs in northern India every March during the full moon.
2. Holi is known as the festival of colors, not because spring brings colorful flowers but because Holi celebrations always include brightly colored dyes.
3. According to legend, the festival of colors began thousands of years ago when Krishna played pranks on girls in his village and threw water on them.
4. During Holi, people toss fistfuls of powdered dyes or dye-filled water balloons at each other and sing traditional Holi songs.
5. Any person who is walking outside during a Holi celebration will soon be wearing colored powders or colored water.

EXERCISE 29.2 Complete each of the following sentences by filling in each blank with the past tense or past participle of the verb listed in parentheses. Example:

Frida Kahlo *became* (become) one of Mexico's foremost painters.

1. Frida Kahlo ________ (grow) up in Mexico City, where she ________ (spend) most of her life.
2. She ________ (be) born in 1907, but she often ________ (say) that her birth year ________ (be) 1910.

3. In 1925 a bus accident ________ (leave) Kahlo horribly injured.
4. The accident ________ (break) her spinal column and many other bones, so Kahlo ________ (lie) in bed in a body cast for months.
5. She had always ________ (be) a spirited young woman, and she ________ (take) up painting to avoid boredom while convalescing.

29b Building verb phrases

Verb phrases can be built up out of a main **verb** and one or more **helping** (auxiliary) **verbs**.

- Immigration figures are rising every year.
- Immigration figures have risen every year.

Verb phrases have strict rules of order. If you try to rearrange the words in either of these sentences, you will find that most alternatives are impossible. You cannot say *Immigration figures rising are every year.*

Putting auxiliary verbs in order. In the sentence *Immigration figures may have been rising,* the main verb *rising* follows three auxiliaries: *may, have,* and *been.* Together these auxiliaries and the main verb make up a verb phrase.

- *May* is a modal that indicates possibility; it is followed by the base form of a verb.
- *Have* is an auxiliary verb that in this case indicates the perfect tense; it must be followed by a past participle (*been*).

Checklist

Editing the Verbs in Your Writing

- Check verb endings that cause you trouble. (29a)
- Double-check forms of *lie* and *lay*, *sit* and *set*, *rise* and *raise*. (29d)
- Refer to action in a literary work in the present tense. (29e)
- Check that verb tenses in your writing express meaning accurately. (29e)
- Use passive voice appropriately. (29f)

- Any form of *be,* when it is followed by a present participle ending in *-ing* (such as *rising*), indicates the progressive tense.
- *Be* followed by a past participle, as in *New immigration policies have <u>been passed</u> in recent years,* indicates the passive voice (29f).

As the following chart shows, when two or more auxiliaries appear in a verb phrase, they follow a particular order based on the type of auxiliary: (1) modal, (2) a form of *have* that indicates a perfect tense, (3) a form of *be* that indicates a progressive tense, and (4) a form of *be* that indicates the passive voice. (Few sentences include all four kinds of auxiliaries.)

	Modal	**Perfect *Have***	**Progressive *Be***	**Passive *Be***	**Main Verb**	
Sonia	—	has	—	been	invited	to visit a family in Prague.
She	should	—	—	be	finished	with school soon.
The invitation	must	have	—	been	sent	in the spring.
She	—	has	been	—	studying	Czech.
She	may	—	be	—	feeling	nervous.
She	might	have	been	—	expecting	to travel elsewhere.
The trip	will	have	been	being	planned	for a month by the time she leaves.

Only one modal is permitted in a verb phrase.

▶ **She will ~~can~~ *be able to* speak Czech much better soon.**

Forming auxiliary verbs. Whenever you use an auxiliary, check the form of the word that follows.

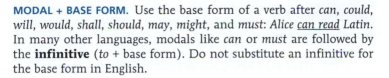

MODAL + BASE FORM. Use the base form of a verb after *can, could, will, would, shall, should, may, might,* and *must*: *Alice can read Latin.* In many other languages, modals like *can* or *must* are followed by the **infinitive** (*to* + base form). Do not substitute an infinitive for the base form in English.

▸ **Alice can ~~to~~ read Latin.**

PERFECT *HAVE, HAS,* OR *HAD* + PAST PARTICIPLE. To form the perfect tenses, use *have, has,* or *had* with a past participle: *Everyone has gone home. They have been working all day.*

PROGRESSIVE *BE* + PRESENT PARTICIPLE. A progressive form of the verb is signaled by two elements, a form of the auxiliary *be* (*am, is, are, was, were, be,* or *been*) and the *-ing* form of the next word: *The children are studying.* Be sure to include both elements.

▸ **The children** ^are **studying science.**

▸ **The children are ~~study~~** ^studying **science.**

Some verbs are rarely used in progressive forms. These are verbs that express unchanging conditions or mental states rather than deliberate actions: *believe, belong, hate, know, like, love, need, own, resemble, understand.*

PASSIVE *BE* + PAST PARTICIPLE. Use *am, is, are, was, were, being, be,* or *been* with a past participle to form the passive voice.

▸ **Tagalog is spoken in the Philippines.**

Notice that the word following the progressive *be* (the present participle) ends in *-ing*, but the word following the passive *be* (the past participle) never ends in *-ing*.

PROGRESSIVE	JaVale is studying music.
PASSIVE	Natasha was taught by a famous violinist.

If the first auxiliary in a verb phrase is a form of *be* or *have,* it must show either present or past tense and must agree with the subject: *JaVale has played in an orchestra.*

EXERCISE 29.3 Rewrite the following passage by adding appropriate forms of *have* and main-verb endings or forms for the verbs in parentheses. Example:

> I ___like___ (like) to try new foods, so I ___have eaten___ (eat) in many different kinds of restaurants in my life.

Several times, I ________ (hear) people musing about the bravery of the first person who ever ________ (eat) a lobster. It ________ (be) an interesting question: what do you ________ (think) ________ (make) anyone do such a thing? But personally, I ________ (wonder) all my life about how ancient people ________ (discover) the art of baking bread. After all, preparing a lobster ________ (be) pretty simple in comparison to baking. Bread ________ (feed) vast numbers of people for centuries, so it certainly ________ (be) a more important food source than lobster, too. Those of us who ________ (love) either lobster or bread (or both) ________ (be) grateful to those who ________ (give) us such a wonderful culinary legacy.

29c Using infinitives and gerunds 

Knowing whether to use an **infinitive** (*to read*) or a **gerund** (*reading*) in a sentence may be a challenge.

INFINITIVE

▸ My adviser urged me to apply to several colleges.

GERUND

▸ Applying took a great deal of time.

In general, infinitives tend to represent intentions, desires, or expectations, while gerunds tend to represent facts. The infinitive in the first sentence tells us that applying is desired but not yet accomplished, while the gerund in the second sentence tells us that the application process was actually carried out.

The association of intention with infinitives and facts with gerunds can often help you decide which one to use when another verb immediately precedes it.

INFINITIVES

- Kumar expected to get a good job after graduation.
- Last year, Jorge decided to become a math major.
- The strikers have agreed to go back to work.

GERUNDS

- Jerzy enjoys going to the theater.
- We resumed working after our coffee break.
- Alycia appreciated getting candy from Sean.

A few verbs can be followed by either an infinitive or a gerund. With some, such as *begin* and *continue,* the choice makes little difference in meaning. With others, however, the difference in meaning is striking.

- **Carlos was working as a medical technician, but he stopped to study English.**

  The infinitive indicates that Carlos left his job because he intended to study English.

- **Carlos stopped studying English when he left the United States.**

  The gerund indicates that Carlos actually studied English but then stopped.

For Multilingual Writers

Checking Usage with Search Engines

Search engines such as Google can help you check sentence structure and word usage. For example, if you are not sure whether you should use an **infinitive** form (*to* verb) or a **gerund** (*-ing*) for the verb *confirm* after the main verb *expect*, you can search for both *"expected confirming"* and *"expected to confirm"* to see which search term yields more results. A search for *"expected to confirm"* yields many more hits than a search for *"expected confirming."* These results indicate that *expected to confirm* is the more commonly used expression. Be sure to click through a few pages of the search engine's results to make sure that most results come from ordinary sentences rather than from headlines or phrases that may be constructed differently from standard English.

The distinction between fact and intention is a tendency, not a rule, and other rules may override it. Always use a gerund—not an infinitive—directly following a **preposition**.

▸ This fruit is safe for ~~to eat.~~ eating.

You can also remove the preposition and keep the infinitive.

▸ This fruit is safe ~~for~~ to eat.

29d Using *lie* and *lay*, *sit* and *set*, *rise* and *raise*

These pairs of verbs cause confusion because both verbs in each pair have similar-sounding forms and somewhat related meanings. In each pair, one verb is transitive, meaning that it is followed by a direct **object** (*I lay the package on the counter*). The other is intransitive, meaning that it does not have an object (*He lies on the floor, unable to move*). The best way to avoid confusing these verbs is to memorize their forms and meanings.

BASE FORM	PAST TENSE	PAST PARTICIPLE	PRESENT PARTICIPLE	-*S* FORM
lie (recline)	lay	lain	lying	lies
lay (put)	laid	laid	laying	lays
sit (be seated)	sat	sat	sitting	sits
set (put)	set	set	setting	sets
rise (get up)	rose	risen	rising	rises
raise (lift)	raised	raised	raising	raises

▸ The doctor asked the patient to ~~lay~~ lie on his side.

▸ Tamika ~~sat~~ set the vase on the table.

▸ Jaime ~~rose~~ raised himself to a sitting position.

EXERCISE 29.4 Choose the appropriate verb form in each of the following sentences. Example:

The boys laid/lay on the couch, hoping for something good on TV.

1. That politician believes people should rise/raise themselves up by their bootstraps.
2. The little girl laid/lay her head on her mother's shoulder and went to sleep.
3. The students sat/set their backpacks down beside their desks and stared grimly at the new teacher.
4. Sit/Set down and stay awhile.
5. Don't just lie/lay there; do something!

29e Using verb tenses

Tenses show when the verb's action takes place. The three **simple tenses** are the **present tense**, the **past tense**, and the **future tense**.

PRESENT TENSE	I ask, write
PAST TENSE	I asked, wrote
FUTURE TENSE	I will ask, will write

More complex aspects of time are expressed through **progressive**, **perfect**, and **perfect progressive** forms of the simple tenses.

PRESENT PROGRESSIVE	she is asking, is writing
PAST PROGRESSIVE	she was asking, was writing
FUTURE PROGRESSIVE	she will be asking, will be writing
PRESENT PERFECT	she has asked, has written
PAST PERFECT	she had asked, had written
FUTURE PERFECT	she will have asked, will have written
PRESENT PERFECT PROGRESSIVE	she has been asking, has been writing
PAST PERFECT PROGRESSIVE	she had been asking, had been writing
FUTURE PERFECT PROGRESSIVE	she will have been asking, will have been writing

The simple tenses locate an action only within the three basic time frames of present, past, and future. Progressive forms express continuing actions; perfect forms express completed actions; perfect progressive forms express actions that continue up to some point in the present, past, or future.

EXERCISE 29.5 From the following list, identify the form of each verb or verb phrase in each of the numbered sentences.

simple present	past perfect
simple past	present progressive
present perfect	past progressive

Example:

Judge Cohen considered the two arguments. Simple past

1. Paul is painting the bedroom, and it looks great so far.
2. She was walking to work when the first plane struck the Twin Towers.
3. By the late 1980s, R.E.M. had become a very popular band.
4. She has admired you for years.
5. Just as we took our seats, the movie began.

Special purposes of the present tense. When writing about action in literary works, use the present tense.

▸ **Ishmael slowly ~~realized~~ realizes all that ~~was~~ is at stake in the search for the white whale.**

General truths or scientific facts should also be in the present tense, even when the **predicate** in the main **clause** is in the past tense.

▸ **Pasteur demonstrated that his boiling process ~~made~~ makes milk safe to drink.**

In general, when you are quoting, summarizing, or paraphrasing a work, use the present tense.

▸ **Adam Banks ~~wrote~~ writes that we should "fly on, reaching for the stars we cannot yet map, see, or scan."**

But when using APA (American Psychological Association) style, report the results of your experiments or another researcher's work in the past tense (*wrote*, *noted*) or the present perfect (*has discovered*). (For more on APA style, see Chapter 16.)

▶ **Comer (1995) ~~notes~~ noted that protesters who deprive themselves of food are seen not as dysfunctional but rather as "caring, sacrificing, even heroic" (p. 5).**

EXERCISE 29.6 Complete each of the following sentences by filling in the blank with an appropriate form of the verb given in parentheses. Because more than one form will sometimes be possible, choose one form and then be prepared to explain the reasons for your choice. Example:

> **People** have been practicing/have practiced **(practice) the art of yoga for thousands of years.**

1. The word *yoga* ________ (come) from Sanskrit.
2. Although many people today ________ (begin) a yoga practice purely for physical exercise, it is actually a path to spirituality that ________ (date) back thousands and thousands of years.
3. Yoga's popularity in America ________ (explode) over the last decade.
4. As a result of this surge in popularity, many yoga studios ________ (open) throughout the city.
5. When you ________ (begin) a yoga practice, it is important to find a reputable teacher who ________ (receive) proper certification.

Sequencing verb tenses. When you use the appropriate tense for each action, readers can follow time changes easily.

▶ **By the time he lent her the money, she** had **declared bankruptcy.**

The revision makes clear that the bankruptcy occurred before the loan.

29f Using active and passive voice

Voice tells whether a **subject** is acting (*He questions us*) or being acted upon (*He is questioned*). When the subject is acting, the verb is in the **active voice**; when the subject is being acted upon, however, the verb is in the **passive voice**. Most contemporary writers use the active voice as much as possible because it makes their prose stronger and livelier. To shift a sentence from passive to active voice, make the performer of the action the subject of the sentence.

My sister took the

▸ **~~The~~ prizewinning photograph. ~~was taken by my sister.~~**

Use the passive voice when you want to emphasize the recipient of an action rather than the performer of the action.

▸ **Colonel Muammar el-Qaddafi was killed during an uprising in his hometown of Surt.**

In scientific and technical writing, use the passive voice to focus attention on what is being studied.

▸ **The volunteers' food intake was closely monitored.**

EXERCISE 29.7 Convert each sentence from active to passive voice or from passive to active, and note the differences in emphasis these changes make. Example:

The largest fish was caught by me.

I caught the largest fish.

1. The car dealerships were overrun by customers during the sale.
2. Campus security mistreated the protesting students.
3. The defenseless settlers at Sand Creek were brutally attacked by U.S. soldiers in 1864.
4. My favorite dinner was cooked by my mother on my birthday.
5. The lead part in the school play was gotten by Ivan.

29g Using mood appropriately

The **mood** of a verb indicates the writer's attitude toward what he or she is saying. The indicative mood states facts or opinions and asks questions: *I did the right thing. Did I do the right thing?* The imperative mood gives commands and instructions: *Do the right thing.* The subjunctive mood (used primarily in **dependent clauses** beginning with *that* or *if*) expresses wishes and conditions that are contrary to fact: *If I were doing the right thing, I'd know it.*

The present subjunctive uses the base form of the verb with all subjects.

- ▸ **It is important that children be ready for a new sibling.**

The past subjunctive is the same as the simple past except for the verb *be*, which uses *were* for all subjects.

- ▸ **He spent money as if he had infinite credit.**
- ▸ **If the store were better located, it would attract more customers.**

Because the subjunctive creates a rather formal tone, many people today substitute the indicative mood in informal conversation.

INFORMAL

- ▸ **If the store was better located, it would attract more customers.**

For academic or professional writing, use the subjunctive in the following contexts:

CLAUSES EXPRESSING A WISH

- ▸ **He wished that his brother ~~was~~ were still living nearby.**

THAT CLAUSES EXPRESSING A REQUEST OR DEMAND

- ▸ **The plant inspector insists that a supervisor ~~is~~ be on site at all times.**

IF CLAUSES EXPRESSING A CONDITION THAT DOES NOT EXIST

- ▸ **If public transportation ~~was~~ were widely available, fewer Americans would commute by car.**

One common error is to use *would* in both clauses. Use the subjunctive in the *if* clause and *would* in the other clause.

- ▸ **If I ~~would have~~ had played harder, I would have won.**

EXERCISE 29.8 Revise the following sentences that do not use the appropriate subjunctive verb forms required in formal or academic writing. Example:

> **If money ~~was~~ were no object, I would have one house in the mountains, one on the beach, and one in the city.**

1. The only requirement is that all applicants are over eighteen years of age.
2. Malcolm is acting as if he was the only one who worked on the project.
3. Even if the rain was to stop, it is much too late now to begin the game.
4. If she would have gone to the doctor sooner, the symptoms would not be so severe.
5. I wish I was five inches taller.

29h Using conditional sentences appropriately

English distinguishes among many different types of conditional sentences: sentences that focus on questions and that are introduced by *if* or its equivalent. Each of the following examples makes different assumptions about the likelihood that what is stated in the *if* **clause** is true.

- **If you *practice* (or *have practiced*) writing often, you *learn* (or *have learned*) what your main problems are.**

  This sentence assumes that what is stated in the *if* clause may be true; any verb tense that is appropriate in a simple sentence may be used in both the *if* clause and the main clause.

- **If you *practice* writing for the rest of this term, you *will* (or *may*) *understand* the process better.**

  This sentence makes a prediction and again assumes that what is stated may turn out to be true. Only the main clause uses the future tense (*will understand*) or a modal that can indicate future time (*may understand*). The *if* clause must use the present tense.

- **If you *practiced* (or *were to practice*) writing every day, it *would* eventually *seem* easier.**

  This sentence indicates doubt that what is stated will happen. In the *if* clause, the verb is either past—actually, past subjunctive (29g)—or *were to* + the base form, though it refers to future time. The main clause contains *would* + the base form of the main verb.

- **If you *practiced* writing on Mars, *you would find* no one to read your work.**

  This sentence imagines an impossible situation. Again, the past subjunctive is used in the *if* clause, although here past time is not being referred to, and *would* + the base form is used in the main clause.

- **If you *had practiced* writing in ancient Egypt, you *would have used* hieroglyphics.**

  This sentence shifts the impossibility back to the past; obviously you won't find yourself in ancient Egypt. But a past impossibility demands a form that is "more past": the past perfect in the *if* clause and *would* + the present perfect form of the main verb in the main clause.

EXERCISE 29.9 Revise each of the following sentences so that both the *if* clause and the main, or independent, clause contain appropriate verb forms. If any sentence does not contain an error, write *Correct*. Example:

> **If you want to work as a computer programmer, you ~~would~~ probably ~~be~~** *are* **having a hard time finding a high-paying U.S. job these days.**

1. Until recently, many people thought that U.S. computer jobs will go unfilled unless college-educated foreign workers will be allowed to work in this country.
2. If the dot-com boom had continued, that prediction might come true.
3. Instead, many highly skilled U.S. technology workers will have few options if they became unemployed tomorrow.
4. If any computer job is announced these days, hundreds of qualified people applied for it.
5. Today, if a company uses many programmers or other computer experts, it may hire workers in India to fill the positions.

30 Nouns and Noun Phrases

Everyday life is filled with **nouns**: orange *juice, hip-hop,* the morning *news*, a *bus* to *work*, *meetings*, *pizza*, *tweets*, *Diet Coke*, *errands*, *dinner* with *friends*, a *chapter* in a good *book*. Every language includes nouns. In English, articles (*a* book, *an* email, *the* news) often accompany nouns.

30a Understanding count and noncount nouns

Nouns in English can be either **count nouns** or **noncount nouns**. Count nouns refer to distinct individuals or things that can be directly counted: *a doctor, an egg, a child; doctors, eggs, children*. Noncount nouns refer to masses, collections, or ideas without distinct parts: *milk, rice, courage*. You cannot count noncount nouns except with a preceding **phrase**: *a glass of milk, three grains of rice, a little courage.*

Count nouns usually have singular and plural forms: *tree, trees*. Noncount nouns usually have only a singular form: *grass*.

COUNT	NONCOUNT
people (plural of *person*)	humanity
tables, chairs, beds	furniture
letters	mail
pebbles	gravel
suggestions	advice

Some nouns can be either count or noncount, depending on their meaning.

COUNT	Before video games, children played with marbles.
NONCOUNT	The palace floor was made of marble.

When you learn a noun in English, you will therefore need to learn whether it is count, noncount, or both. Many dictionaries provide this information.

EXERCISE 30.1 Identify each of the common nouns in the following short paragraph as either a count or a noncount noun. The first one has been done for you.

In his book (count) *Hiroshima*, John Hersey tells the story of six people who survived the destruction of Hiroshima on August 6, 1945. The bomb detonated at 8:15 in the morning. When the explosion occurred, Mrs. Hatsuyo Nakamura was looking out her window and watching a neighbor at work on his house. The force of the explosion lifted her into the air and carried her into the next room, where she was buried by roofing tiles and other debris. When she crawled out, she heard her daughter, Myeko, calling out; she was buried up to her waist and could not move.

30b Using determiners

Determiners are words that identify or quantify a noun, such as *this study*, *all people*, *his suggestions*.

COMMON DETERMINERS

- the articles *a*, *an*, *the*
- *this*, *these*, *that*, *those*
- *my*, *our*, *your*, *his*, *her*, *its*, *their*
- possessive nouns and noun phrases (*Sheila's paper*, *my friend's book*)
- *whose*, *which*, *what*
- *all*, *both*, *each*, *every*, *some*, *any*, *either*, *no*, *neither*, *many*, *much*, (*a*) *few*, (*a*) *little*, *several*, *enough*
- the numerals *one*, *two*, etc.

These determiners . . .	. . . can precede these noun types	Examples
a, an, each, every	singular count nouns	a book an American each word every Buddhist
this, that	singular count nouns noncount nouns	this book that milk
(a) *little, much*	noncount nouns	a little milk much affection
some, enough	noncount nouns plural count nouns	some milk enough trouble some books enough problems
the	singular count nouns plural count nouns noncount nouns	the doctor the doctors the information

These determiners . . .	. . . can precede these noun types	Examples
these, those, (a) few, many, both, several	plural count nouns	these books those plans a few ideas many students both hands several trees

Determiners with singular count nouns. Every singular count noun must be preceded by a determiner. Place any adjectives between the determiner and the noun.

- ▶ ^my sister
- ▶ ^the growing population
- ▶ ^that old neighborhood

Determiners with plural nouns or noncount nouns. Noncount and plural nouns sometimes have determiners and sometimes do not. For example, *This research is important* and *Research is important* are both acceptable but have different meanings.

EXERCISE 30.2 Each of the following sentences contains an error with a noun phrase. Revise each sentence. Example:

Many people use ^a small sponge to clean their kitchen counters.

1. Bacteria are invisible organisms that can sometimes make the people sick.
2. Dangerous germs such as salmonella are commonly found in a some foods.
3. When a cook prepares chicken on cutting board, salmonella germs may be left on the board.
4. Much people regularly clean their kitchen counters and cutting boards to remove bacteria.
5. Unfortunately, a warm, wet kitchen sponge is a ideal home for bacteria.

30c Using articles

Articles (*a, an,* and *the*) are a type of determiner. In English, choosing which article to use—or whether to use an article at all—can be challenging. Although there are exceptions, the following general guidelines can help.

Using *a* or *an*. Use indefinite articles *a* and *an* with singular count nouns. Use *a* before a consonant sound (*a car*) and *an* before a vowel sound (*an uncle*). Consider sound rather than spelling: *a house, an hour.*

A or *an* tells readers they do not have enough information to identify specifically what the noun refers to. Compare the following sentences:

- **I need a new coat for the winter.**
- **I saw a coat that I liked at Dayton's, but it wasn't heavy enough.**

The coat in the first sentence is hypothetical rather than actual. Since it is indefinite to the writer and the reader, it is used with *a,* not *the.* The second sentence refers to an actual coat, but since the writer cannot expect the reader to know which one, it is used with *a* rather than *the.*

If you want to speak of an indefinite quantity rather than just one indefinite thing, use *some* or *any* with a noncount noun or a plural count noun. Use *any* in either negative sentences or questions.

- **This stew needs some more salt.**
- **I saw some plates that I liked at Gump's.**
- **This stew doesn't need any more salt.**

Using *the*. Use the definite article *the* with both count and noncount nouns whose identity is known or is about to be made known to readers. The necessary information for identification can come from the noun phrase itself, from elsewhere in the text, from context, from general knowledge, or from a **superlative**.

- **Let's meet at ^the fountain in front of Dwinelle Hall.**

  The phrase *in front of Dwinelle Hall* identifies the specific fountain.

Grammar: Nouns and Noun Phrases > LearningCurve and Exercises

▸ **Last Saturday, a fire that started in a restaurant spread to a nearby clothing store. ~~Store~~ The store was saved, although it suffered water damage.**

The word *store* is preceded by *the,* which directs our attention to the information in the previous sentence, where the store is first identified.

▸ **She asked him to shut the door when he left her office.**

The context shows that she is referring to her office door.

▸ **~~Pope~~ The pope is expected to visit Mexico City in February.**

There is only one living pope.

▸ **She is now one of the best hip-hop artists in the neighborhood.**

The superlative *best* identifies the noun *hip-hop artists.*

No article. Noncount and plural count nouns can be used without an article to make generalizations:

▸ **In this world nothing is certain but death and taxes.**

—Benjamin Franklin

Franklin refers not to a particular death or specific taxes but to death and taxes in general, so no article is used with *death* or with *taxes*.

English differs from many other languages that use the definite article to make generalizations. In English, a sentence like *The ants live in colonies* can refer only to particular, identifiable ants, not to ants in general.

EXERCISE 30.3 Insert articles as necessary in the following passage. If no article is needed, leave the space blank. Example:

> **One of __the__ things that makes ______ English unique is __the__ number of ______ English words.**

______ English language has ______ very large vocabulary. About ______ 200,000 words are in ______ everyday use, and if ______ less common words are included, ________ total reaches more than ________ million. This makes ________ English ________ rich language, but also ________ difficult one to learn well. In addition, ________ rules of English grammar are sometimes confusing. They were modeled on ________ Latin rules, even though ________ two languages are very different. Finally, ________ fact that ________ English has ________ large number of ________ words imported from ________ other languages makes ________ English spelling very hard to master.

31 Subject-Verb Agreement

The everyday word *agreement* refers to an accord of some sort: you reach an agreement with your boss; friends agree to go to a movie. This meaning covers grammatical **agreement** as well. Verbs must agree with their subjects in number (singular or plural) and in **person** (first, second, or third).

To make a verb in the **present tense** agree with a third-person singular subject, add *-s* or *-es* to the **base form**.

- ▶ A vegetarian diet lowers the risk of heart disease.

To make a verb in the present tense agree with any other subject, use the base form of the verb.

- ▶ I miss my family.
- ▶ They live in another state.

Have and *be* do not follow the *-s* or *-es* pattern with third-person singular subjects. *Have* changes to *has*; *be* has irregular forms in both the present tense and the **past tense**.

- ▶ War is hell.
- ▶ The soldier was brave beyond the call of duty.

LaunchPad Solo
macmillan learning
Grammar: Subject-Verb Agreement > LearningCurve and Exercises

31a Checking for words between subject and verb

Make sure the verb agrees with the simple **subject** and not with another **noun** that falls between them.

▸ **Many books on the best-seller list ~~has~~ ^have^ little literary value.**

The simple subject is *books*, not *list*.

Be careful when you use *as well as*, *along with*, *in addition to*, *together with*, and similar phrases. They do not make a singular subject plural.

▸ **A passenger, as well as the driver, ~~were~~ ^was^ injured in the accident.**

Though this sentence has a grammatically singular subject, it would be clearer with a compound subject: *The driver and a passenger were injured in the accident.*

31b Checking agreement with compound subjects

Compound subjects joined by *and* are generally plural.

▸ **A backpack, a canteen, and a rifle ~~was~~ ^were^ issued to each recruit.**

When subjects joined by *and* are considered a single unit or refer to the same person or thing, they take a singular verb form.

▸ **The lead singer and chief songwriter *wants* to make the new songs available online.**

The singer and songwriter are the same person.

▸ **Drinking and driving ~~remain~~ ^remains^ a major cause of highway accidents and fatalities.**

In this sentence, *drinking and driving* is considered a single activity, and a singular verb is used.

With subjects joined by *or* or *nor*, the verb agrees with the part closer to the verb.

▸ **Neither my roommate nor my neighbors *like* my loud music.**

▸ **Either the witnesses or the defendant *is* lying.**

If you find this sentence awkward, put the plural noun closer to the verb: *Either the defendant or the witnesses are lying.*

EXERCISE 31.1 Underline the appropriate verb form in each of the following sentences. Example:

Bankers, politicians, and philanthropists alike is/are becoming increasingly interested in microfinance.

1. Many microlending institutions, such as the Grameen Bank, has/have been in existence for decades.
2. In microlending, credit or small loans is/are provided to poor entrepreneurs in developing nations.
3. These borrowers and their families usually do/does not possess the collateral required for more traditional loans.
4. A man or woman running a small business or farm is/are often the primary recipient of a loan.
5. A list of the benefits of microlending includes/include economic mobility and support for entrepreneurs.

31c Making verbs agree with collective nouns

Collective nouns—such as *family, team, audience, group, jury, crowd, band, class,* and *committee*—and fractions can take either singular or plural verbs, depending on whether they refer to the group as a single unit or to the multiple members of the group. The meaning of a sentence as a whole is your guide.

Checklist

Editing for Subject-Verb Agreement

- Identify the subject that goes with each verb to check for agreement problems. (31a)
- Check compound subjects joined by *and, or,* and *nor.* (31b)
- Check any collective-noun subjects to determine whether they refer to a group as a single unit or as multiple members. (31c)
- Check indefinite-pronoun subjects. Most take a plural verb. (31d)

- **After deliberating, the jury *reports* its verdict.**

  The jury acts as a single unit.

- **The jury still *disagree* on a number of counts.**

  The members of the jury act as multiple individuals.

- **Two-thirds of the park ~~have~~ has burned.**

  Two-thirds refers to the single portion of the park that burned.

- **One-third of the student body ~~was~~ were commuters.**

  One-third here refers to the students who commuted as individuals.

Treat phrases starting with *the number of* as singular and with *a number of* as plural.

SINGULAR	The number of applicants for the internship *was* unbelievable.
PLURAL	A number of applicants *were* put on the waiting list.

31d Making verbs agree with indefinite pronouns

Indefinite pronouns do not refer to specific persons or things. Most take singular verb forms.

SOME COMMON INDEFINITE PRONOUNS

another	each	much	one
any	either	neither	other
anybody	everybody	nobody	somebody
anyone	everyone	no one	someone
anything	everything	nothing	something

- **Of the two jobs, neither holds much appeal.**

- **Each of the plays ~~depict~~ depicts a hero undone by a tragic flaw.**

Both, *few*, *many*, *others*, and *several* are plural.

- **Though many apply, few are chosen.**

All, any, enough, more, most, none, and *some* can be singular or plural, depending on the noun they refer to.

- **All of the cake *was* eaten.**
- **All of the candidates *promise* to improve the schools.**

31e Making verbs agree with *who, which,* and *that*

When the relative **pronouns** *who, which,* and *that* are used as subjects, the verb agrees with the **antecedent** of the pronoun (34b).

- **Fear is an ingredient that goes into creating stereotypes.**
- **Guilt and fear are ingredients that go into creating stereotypes.**

Problems often occur with the words *one of the.* In general, *one of the* takes a plural verb, while *the only one of the* takes a singular verb.

- **Carla is one of the employees who always ~~works~~ work overtime.**

  Some employees always work overtime. Carla is among them. Thus *who* refers to *employees,* and the verb is plural.

- **Ming is the only one of the employees who always ~~work~~ works overtime.**

  Only one employee, Ming, always works overtime. Thus *one* is the antecedent of *who,* and the verb form must be singular.

31f Making linking verbs agree with subjects

A **linking verb** should agree with its subject, which usually precedes the verb, not with the subject complement, which follows it.

- **These three key treaties ~~is~~ are the topic of my talk.**

  The subject is *treaties,* not *topic.*

- **Nero Wolfe's passion ~~were~~ was orchids.**

  The subject is *passion,* not *orchids.*

31g Making verbs agree with subjects that end in *-s*

Some words that end in *-s* seem to be plural but are singular in meaning and thus take singular verb forms.

▸ **Measles still ~~strike~~ strikes many Americans.**

Some nouns of this kind (such as *statistics* and *politics*) may be either singular or plural, depending on context.

SINGULAR	Statistics *is* a course I really dread.
PLURAL	The statistics in that study *are* questionable.

31h Checking for subjects that follow the verb

In English, verbs usually follow subjects. When this order is reversed, make the verb agree with the subject, not with a noun that happens to precede it.

▸ **Beside the barn ~~stands~~ stand silos filled with grain.**

The subject, *silos*, is plural, so the verb must be *stand*.

In sentences beginning with *there is* or *there are* (or *there was* or *there were*), *there* is just an introductory word; the subject follows the verb.

▸ **There are five basic positions in classical ballet.**

31i Making verbs agree with titles and words used as words

Titles and words used as words always take singular verb forms, even if their own forms are plural.

▸ ***One Writer's Beginnings* ~~describe~~ describes Eudora Welty's childhood.**

▸ ***Steroids* ~~are~~ is a little word that packs a big punch in the world of sports.**

EXERCISE 31.2 Revise each of the following sentences as necessary to establish subject-verb agreement. Example:

A museum displaying O. Winston Link's photographs ~~have~~ has opened in Roanoke, Virginia.

1. Anyone interested in steam locomotives have probably already heard of the photographer O. Winston Link.
2. Imagine that it are the 1950s, and Link is creating his famous photographs.
3. The steam locomotives—the "iron horses" of the nineteenth century—has begun to give way to diesel engines.
4. Only the Norfolk & Western rail line's Appalachian route still use steam engines.
5. Link and his assistant Thomas Garver sets up nighttime shots of steam locomotives.

31j Considering forms of *be* in varieties of English

Conventions for subject-verb agreement with *be* in spoken or vernacular varieties of English may differ from those of academic English. For instance, an Appalachian speaker might say "I been down" rather than "I have been down"; a speaker of African American vernacular might say "He be at work" rather than "He is at work," indicating that the person in question is habitually at work. These usages are legitimate and often very effective forms, and you may want to use such phrases in your writing, especially to create special effects or to connect with your audience. For much formal academic and professional writing, it's still safest to follow the conventions of academic English. (For information on using varieties of English appropriately, see Chapter 21.)

32 Adjectives and Adverbs

Adjectives and **adverbs** can add indispensable differences in meaning to the words they describe or modify. In basketball, for example, there is an important difference between a *flagrant* foul and a

For Multilingual Writers

Using Adjectives with Plural Nouns

In Spanish, Russian, and many other languages, adjectives agree in number with the nouns they modify. In English, adjectives do not change number in this way: *the kittens are cute* (not *cutes*).

technical foul, a layup and a *reverse* layup, and an *angry* coach and an *abusively angry* coach. In each instance, the **modifiers** are crucial to accurate communication.

Adjectives modify **nouns** and **pronouns**; they answer the questions *which? how many?* and *what kind?* Adverbs modify **verbs**, adjectives, and other adverbs; they answer the questions *how? when? where?* and *to what extent?* Many adverbs are formed by adding *-ly* to adjectives (*slight, slightly*), but some are formed in other ways (*outdoors*) or have forms of their own (*very*).

EXERCISE 32.1 Identify the adjectives and adverbs in each of the following sentences, underlining the adjectives once and the adverbs twice. Remember that articles and some pronouns can function as adjectives. Example:

The grand piano waited silently and patiently on the stage.

1. Meerkats are exceptionally social creatures.
2. After spending nearly twenty years in prison, the wrongfully accused man was released.
3. We could not resist choosing the smallest and quietest puppy in the litter.
4. Moreover, some talk-show hosts intentionally bait the audience with misleading information.
5. My only requirement for a new apartment is a walk-in closet.

Grammar: Parts of Speech > LearningCurve
Grammar: Adjectives and Adverbs > LearningCurve and Exercises

32a Using adjectives after linking verbs

When adjectives come after **linking verbs** (such as *is*), they usually describe the **subject**: *I am patient*. Note that in specific sentences, certain verbs may or may not be linking verbs—*appear*, *become*, *feel*, *grow*, *look*, *make*, *prove*, *seem*, *smell*, *sound*, and *taste*, for instance. When a word following one of these verbs modifies the subject, use an adjective; when it modifies the verb, use an adverb.

ADJECTIVE Fluffy looked angry.

ADVERB Fluffy looked angrily at the poodle.

Linking verbs suggest a state of being, not an action. In the preceding examples, *looked angry* suggests the state of being angry; *looked angrily* suggests an angry action.

In everyday conversation, you will often hear (and perhaps use) adjectives in place of adverbs. For example, people often say *go quick* instead of *go quickly*. When you write in academic and professional English, however, use adverbs to modify verbs, adjectives, and other adverbs.

- **You can feel the song's meter if you listen ~~careful.~~** carefully.
- **The audience was ~~real~~** really **disappointed by the show.**

***Good, well, bad,* and *badly*.** The modifiers *good*, *well*, *bad*, and *badly* cause problems for many writers because the distinctions between *good* and *well* and between *bad* and *badly* are often not observed in conversation. Problems also arise because *well* can function as either an adjective or an adverb.

- **I look ~~well~~** good **in blue.**
- **Now that the fever has broken, I feel ~~good~~** well **again.**
- **I play the trumpet ~~good.~~** well.
- **I feel ~~badly~~** bad **for the Toronto fans.**
- **Their team played ~~bad.~~** badly.

EXERCISE 32.2 Expand each of the following sentences by adding appropriate adjectives and adverbs. Delete *the* if need be. Example:

> Three thoroughly nervous
> ~~The~~ veterinarians ^ examined ^ the ^ patient.

1. Our assignment is due Wednesday.
2. Most of us enjoy movies.
3. Each of her superiors praised her work for the Environmental Protection Agency.
4. A corporation can fire workers.
5. The heroine marries the prince.

EXERCISE 32.3 Revise each of the following sentences to maintain correct adverb and adjective use. Then, for each adjective and adverb you've revised, point out the word that it modifies. Example:

> commonly
> **Almost every language ~~common~~ ^ uses nonverbal cues that people can interpret.**

1. Most people understand easy that raised eyebrows indicate surprise.
2. You are sure familiar with the idea that bodily motions are a kind of language, but is the same thing true of nonverbal sounds?
3. If you feel sadly, your friends may express sympathy by saying, "Awww."
4. When food tastes well, diners express their satisfaction by murmuring, "Mmmm!"
5. These nonverbal signals are called "paralanguage," and they are quick becoming an important field of linguistic study.

32b Using comparatives and superlatives

Most adjectives and adverbs have three forms: positive, **comparative**, and **superlative**. You usually form the comparative and superlative of one- or two-syllable adjectives by adding *-er* and *-est*: *short, shorter, shortest*. With some two-syllable adjectives, longer adjectives, and most adverbs, use *more* and *most* (or *less* and *least*): *scientific, more scientific, most scientific; elegantly, more elegantly, most elegantly*. Some short adjectives and adverbs have irregular comparative and superlative forms: *good, better, best; badly, worse, worst*.

Comparatives versus superlatives. In academic writing, use the comparative to compare two things; use the superlative to compare three or more things.

▶ **Rome is a much *older* city than New York.**

▶ **Damascus is one of the ~~older~~ oldest cities in the world.**

Double comparatives and superlatives. Double comparatives and superlatives are those that unnecessarily use both the *-er* or *-est* ending and *more* or *most.* Occasionally, these forms can add a special emphasis, as in the title of Spike Lee's movie *Mo' Better Blues.* In academic and professional writing, however, it's safest not to use *more* or *most* before adjectives or adverbs ending in *-er* or *-est.*

▶ **Paris is the ~~most~~ loveliest city in the world.**

Absolute concepts. Some readers consider modifiers such as *perfect* and *unique* to be absolute concepts; according to this view, a thing is either unique or it isn't, so modified forms of the concept don't make sense. However, many seemingly absolute words have multiple meanings, all of which are widely accepted as correct. For example, *unique* may mean *one of a kind* or *unequaled,* but it can also simply mean *distinctive* or *unusual.*

If you think your readers will object to a construction such as *more perfect* (which appears in the U.S. Constitution), then avoid such uses.

EXERCISE 32.4 Revise the following sentences to use modifiers correctly, clearly, and effectively. A variety of acceptable answers is possible for each sentence. Example:

> **When Macbeth and Lady Macbeth plot to kill the king, she shows herself to be the ~~most~~ more ambitious of the two.**

1. Some critics consider *Hamlet* to be Shakespeare's most finest tragedy.
2. Romeo and Juliet are probably the famousest lovers in all of literature.
3. Did you like the movie *Titus* or the play *Titus Andronicus* best?
4. One of my earlier memories is of seeing my mother onstage.
5. Shakespeare supposedly knew little Latin, but most people today know even littler.

33 Modifier Placement

To be effective, **modifiers** should clearly refer to the words they modify and should be positioned close to those words. Consider this command:

DO NOT USE THE ELEVATORS IN CASE OF FIRE.

Should we avoid the elevators altogether, or only in case there is a fire? Repositioning the modifier *in case of fire* eliminates such confusion—and makes clear that we are to avoid the elevators only if there is a fire: IN CASE OF FIRE, DO NOT USE THE ELEVATORS.

33a Revising misplaced modifiers

Modifiers can cause confusion or ambiguity if they are not close enough to the words they modify or if they seem to modify more than one word in the sentence.

- **She teaches a seminar** on voodoo **this term ~~on voodoo~~ at Skyline College.**

  The voodoo is not at the college; the seminar is.

- **~~Billowing from the window, he~~** He **saw clouds of smoke** billowing from the window.

  People cannot billow from windows.

- After he lost the 1962 race, **Nixon told reporters that he planned to get out of politics. ~~after he lost the 1962 race.~~**

  Nixon did not predict that he would lose the race.

Limiting modifiers. Be especially careful with the placement of limiting modifiers such as *almost*, *even*, *just*, *merely*, and *only*. In general, these modifiers should be placed right before or after the words they modify. Putting them in other positions may produce not just ambiguity but a completely different meaning.

AMBIGUOUS	The court *only* hears civil cases on Tuesdays.
CLEAR	The court hears only civil cases on Tuesdays.
CLEAR	The court hears civil cases on Tuesdays only.

Clarity: Modifier Placement > LearningCurve and Exercises

Squinting modifiers. If a modifier can refer either to the word before it or to the word after it, it is a squinting modifier. Put the modifier where it clearly relates to only a single word.

SQUINTING	Students who practice writing *often* will benefit.
REVISED	Students who often practice writing will benefit.
REVISED	Students who practice writing will often benefit.

EXERCISE 33.1 Revise each of the following sentences by moving any misplaced modifiers so that they clearly modify the words they are intended to. You may have to change grammatical structures for some sentences. Example:

Elderly people and students live in the neighborhood
full of identical tract houses
surrounding the university/. ~~which is full of identical tract houses.~~

1. Doctors recommend a new test for cancer, which is painless.
2. The tenor captivated the entire audience singing with verve.
3. I went through the process of taxiing and taking off in my mind.
4. The city approximately spent twelve million dollars on the new stadium.
5. Am I the only person who cares about modifiers in sentences that are misplaced?

33b Revising disruptive modifiers

Disruptive modifiers interrupt connections between parts of a sentence, making it hard for readers to follow the progress of a thought.

If they are cooked too long, vegetables will
▶ **~~Vegetables will, if they are cooked too long,~~ lose most of their nutritional value.**

Split infinitives. In general, do not place a modifier between the *to* and the **verb** of an **infinitive** (*to often complain*). Doing so makes it hard for readers to recognize that the two go together.

surrender
▶ **Hitler expected the British to fairly quickly. ~~surrender.~~**

In certain sentences, however, a modifier sounds awkward if it does not split the infinitive. Most language experts consider split infinitives acceptable in such cases. Another option is to reword the sentence to eliminate the infinitive altogether.

SPLIT	I hope *to* almost *equal* my last year's income.
REVISED	I hope that I will earn almost as much as I did last year.

EXERCISE 33.2 Revise each of the following sentences by moving disruptive modifiers and split infinitives as well as by repositioning any squinting modifier so that it unambiguously modifies either the word(s) before it or the word(s) after it. Example:

The course we hoped would engross us completely bored us.

The course we hoped would completely engross us bored us.

or

The course we hoped would engross us bored us completely.

1. He remembered vividly enjoying the sound of Mrs. McIntosh's singing.
2. Bookstores sold, in the first week after publication, fifty thousand copies.
3. The mayor promised after her reelection she would not raise taxes.
4. The collector who owned the painting originally planned to leave it to a museum.
5. Doctors can now restore limbs that have been severed partially to a functioning condition.

33c Revising dangling modifiers

Dangling modifiers are words or **phrases** that modify nothing in the rest of a sentence. They often *seem* to modify something that is implied but not actually present in the sentence. Dangling modifiers frequently appear at the beginnings or ends of sentences, as in the following example.

DANGLING	Exploding in rapid bursts of red, white, and blue, the picnickers cheered for the Fourth of July celebration.

REVISED With fireworks exploding in rapid bursts of red, white, and blue, the picnickers cheered for the Fourth of July celebration.

To revise a dangling modifier, often you need to add a **subject** that the modifier clearly refers to; sometimes you have to turn the modifier into a phrase or a **clause**.

our family gave

- **Reluctantly, ^ the hound ~~was given~~ to a neighbor.**

In the original sentence, was the dog reluctant, or was someone else who is not mentioned reluctant?

When he was

- **~~As~~ ^ a young boy, his grandmother told stories of her years as a migrant worker.**

His grandmother was never a young boy.

My

- **~~Thumbing through the magazine, my~~ ^ eyes automatically noticed the perfume ads ^.** *as I was thumbing through the magazine.*

Eyes cannot thumb through a magazine.

EXERCISE 33.3 Revise each of the following sentences to correct the dangling modifiers. Example:

a viewer gets

Watching television news, ^ an impression ~~is given~~ of constant disaster.

1. High ratings are pursued by emphasizing fires and murders.
2. Interviewing grieving relatives, little consideration is shown for their privacy.
3. To provide comic relief, heat waves and blizzards are attributed to the weather forecaster.
4. Chosen for their looks, the newscasters' journalistic credentials are often weak.
5. As a visual medium, complex issues are hard to present in a televised format.

34 Pronouns

As words that stand in for **nouns**, **pronouns** carry a lot of weight in our everyday discourse. The following directions show why it's important for a pronoun to refer clearly to a specific noun or pronoun **antecedent**:

- **When you see a dirt road on the left side of Winston Lane, follow it for two more miles.**

  The word *it* could mean either the dirt road or Winston Lane.

34a Considering a pronoun's role in the sentence

Most speakers of English usually know intuitively when to use *I*, *me*, and *my*. The choices reflect differences in **case**, the form a pronoun takes to indicate its function in a sentence. Pronouns functioning as **subjects** or subject complements are in the subjective case (*I*); those functioning as **objects** are in the objective case (*me*); those functioning as possessives are in the possessive case (*my*).

SUBJECTIVE	OBJECTIVE	POSSESSIVE
I	me	my/mine
we	us	our/ours
you	you	your/yours
he/she/it	him/her/it	his/her/hers/its
they	them	their/theirs
who/whoever	whom/whomever	whose

Problems tend to occur in the following situations.

In subject complements. Americans routinely use the objective case for subject complements in conversation: *Who's there? It's me.* If the subjective case for a subject complement sounds stilted or awkward (*It's I*), try rewriting the sentence using the pronoun as the subject (*I'm here*).

▸ I was the ~~The~~ first person to see Kishore after the awards. ~~was I.~~

Before gerunds. Pronouns before a **gerund** should be in the possessive case.

▸ The doctor argued for ~~them~~ their writing a living will.

With *who, whoever, whom,* and *whomever*. Today's speakers tend not to use *whom* and *whomever*, which can create a very formal tone. But for academic and professional writing in which formality is appropriate, remember that problems distinguishing between *who* and *whom* occur most often in two situations: when they begin a question, and when they introduce a **dependent clause** (37c). You can determine whether to use *who* or *whom* at the beginning of a question by answering the question using a personal pronoun. If the answer is in the subjective case, use *who*; if it is in the objective case, use *whom*.

▸ Whom ~~Who~~ did you visit?

I visited *them*. *Them* is objective, so *whom* is correct.

▸ Who ~~Whom~~ do you think wrote the story?

I think *she* wrote the story. *She* is subjective, so *who* is correct.

If the pronoun acts as a subject or subject complement in the clause, use *who* or *whoever*. If the pronoun acts as an object in the clause, use *whom* or *whomever*.

▸ Anyone can hypnotize a person ~~whom~~ who wants to be hypnotized.

The verb of the clause is *wants*, and its subject is *who*.

▶ ~~Whoever~~ Whomever the party suspected of disloyalty was executed.

Whomever is the object of *suspected* in the clause *whomever the party suspected of disloyalty.*

In compound structures. When a pronoun is part of a compound subject, complement, or object, put it in the same case you would use if the pronoun were alone.

▶ **When ~~him~~ he and Zelda were first married, they lived in New York.**

▶ **This morning saw yet another conflict between my sister and ~~I.~~ me.**

In elliptical constructions. Elliptical constructions are sentences in which some words are understood but left out. When an elliptical construction ends in a pronoun, put the pronoun in the case it would be in if the construction were complete.

▶ **His sister has always been more athletic than *he* [is].**

In some elliptical constructions, the case of the pronoun depends on the meaning intended.

▶ **Nolan likes Lily more than *she* [likes Lily].**

She is the subject of the omitted verb *likes.*

▶ **Nolan likes Lily more than [he likes] *her*.**

Her is the object of the omitted verb *likes.*

With *we* and *us* before a noun. If you are unsure about whether to use *we* or *us* before a noun, use whichever pronoun would be correct if the noun were omitted.

▶ **~~Us~~ We fans never give up hope.**

Without *fans, we* would be the subject.

▶ **The Broncos depend on ~~we~~ us fans.**

Without *fans, us* would be the object of the preposition *on.*

Checklist

Editing Pronouns

- Make sure all pronouns in subject complements are in the subjective case. (34a)
- Check for correct use of *who*, *whom*, *whoever*, and *whomever*. (34a)
- In compound structures, check that pronouns are in the same case they would be in if used alone. (34a)
- When a pronoun follows *than* or *as*, complete the sentence mentally to determine whether the pronoun should be in the subjective or objective case. (34a)
- Check that pronouns agree with indefinite-pronoun antecedents, and revise sexist pronouns. (34b)
- Be sensitive to pronoun preferences; do not assume that all identify with either *he* or *she*. (34b)
- Identify the antecedent that a pronoun refers to. Supply one if none appears in the sentence. If more than one possible antecedent is present, revise the sentence. (34c)

EXERCISE 34.1 Some of the following sentences contain underlined pronouns used incorrectly. Revise each of the incorrect sentences so that they contain correct pronouns. Example:

> **Eventually, the headwaiter told Kim, Stanley, and ~~I~~ *me* that we could be seated.**

1. Who do you think is the better tennis player, Mac or he?
2. The two children wondered which presents under the tree were for themselves.
3. When we asked, the seller promised we that the software would work on our computer.
4. Though even the idea of hang gliding made Gretchen and she nervous, they gave it a try.
5. The teacher said they had asked thoughtful questions.

EXERCISE 34.2 Insert a possessive pronoun in the blank in each sentence. Example:

My date bought flowers for me on Valentine's Day.

1. All day long, people in the office asked admiringly, "_________ flowers are those?"
2. I told them the bouquet was _________.
3. The arrangement was perfectly complemented by _________ vase, which my date had chosen.
4. _________ selection for me was red roses.
5. Every flower has _________ own meaning, according to a Victorian tradition.

EXERCISE 34.3 Insert *who*, *whoever*, *whom*, or *whomever* appropriately in the blank in each of the following sentences. Example:

Marisa is someone who will go far.

1. Professor Quinones asked _________ we wanted to collaborate with.
2. I would appreciate it if _________ made the mess in the kitchen could clean it up.
3. _________ shall I say is calling?
4. Soap operas appeal to _________ is interested in intrigue, suspense, joy, pain, grief, romance, fidelity, sex, and violence.
5. I have no sympathy for _________ was caught driving while intoxicated after the party Friday night.

EXERCISE 34.4 Choose the correct pronoun from the pair in parentheses in each of the following sentences. Example:

Of the group, only (she/her) and I finished the race.

1. All the other job applicants were far more experienced than (I/me).
2. Only (he/him) and the two dressmakers knew what his top-secret fall line would be like.
3. When Jessica and (she/her) first met, they despised each other.
4. I know that I will never again love anybody as much as (he/him).
5. To (we/us) New Englanders, hurricanes are a far bigger worry than tornadoes.

34b Making pronouns agree with antecedents

The **antecedent** of a pronoun is the word the pronoun refers to. Pronouns and antecedents are said to agree when they match up in **person**, number, and gender.

SINGULAR	The choirmaster raised his baton.
PLURAL	The boys picked up their music.

The use of the plural pronoun *they* to refer to singular antecedents is gaining acceptance, especially in speech and informal writing. (See p. 332.)

Compound antecedents. Whenever a compound antecedent is joined by *or* or *nor*, the pronoun agrees with the nearer or nearest antecedent. If the parts of the antecedent are of different genders, however, this kind of sentence can be awkward and may need to be revised.

AWKWARD	Neither Annie nor Lu Ming got *his* work done.
REVISED	Annie didn't get *her* work done, and neither did Lu Ming.

When a compound antecedent contains both singular and plural parts, the sentence may sound awkward unless the plural part comes last.

▸ **Neither the blog nor the newspapers would reveal their sources.**

Collective-noun antecedents. A collective noun such as *herd*, *team*, or *audience* may refer to a group as a single unit. If so, use a singular pronoun.

▸ **The *committee* presented *its* findings to the board.**

When a collective noun refers to the members of the group as individuals, however, use a plural pronoun.

▸ **The *herd* stamped *their* hooves and snorted nervously.**

Indefinite-pronoun antecedents. **Indefinite pronouns** do not refer to specific persons or things. Most indefinite pronouns are always singular; a few are always plural. Some can be singular or plural depending on the context.

▸ **One of the ballerinas lost her balance.**

▸ **Many in the audience jumped to their feet.**

SINGULAR *Some* of the furniture was showing *its* age.

PLURAL *Some* of the farmers abandoned *their* land.

Sexist pronouns. Remember that pronouns often refer to antecedents of unknown gender. Many writers use *he or she, his or her*, and so on to refer to such antecedents: *Every citizen should know his or her legal rights*, for example. However, such wording ignores or even excludes people who do not identify as male or female or who prefer not to use *he* or *she* pronouns (see 20b). Recasting the sentence in the plural is often a more inclusive alternative: *All citizens should know their legal rights*. Also note that the "singular *they*" is gaining acceptance (*Every citizen should know their legal rights*), providing another alternative. But some readers may still consider singular *they* incorrect in formal writing. When in doubt, choose to rewrite in the plural or to eliminate pronouns: *Every citizen should have some knowledge of basic legal rights.*

EXERCISE 34.5 Revise the following sentences as needed to create pronoun-antecedent agreement and to eliminate any sexist or awkward pronoun references. Some sentences can be revised in more than one way. For the sentence that is correct as written, write *Correct*. Example:

Almost everyone will encounter some type of allergy in his lifetime.
Most people will encounter some type of allergy in their lifetime.

1. In general, neither dust mites nor pollen can cause life-threatening reactions, but it is among the most common allergens known.
2. A family that is prone to allergies may have a higher than usual percentage of allergic diseases, but their specific allergies are not necessarily the same for all family members.
3. If a person suspects that he might have an allergy, he can go to the doctor for a skin test or blood test.

4. Because of the severity and frequency of nut allergies in small children, a typical day-care center has rules specifying that they cannot allow any nut products.
5. Every meal and treat that is brought into a center must be screened to make sure their contents are nut-free.

34c Making pronouns refer to clear antecedents

If a pronoun does not refer clearly to a specific antecedent, readers will have trouble making the connection between the two.

Ambiguous antecedents. In cases where a pronoun could refer to more than one antecedent, revise the sentence to make the meaning clear.

the bridge
▸ **The car went over the bridge just before ~~it~~ ^ fell into the water.**

What fell into the water—the car or the bridge? The revision makes the meaning clear.

"I
▸ **Kerry told Ellen, ^ ~~that she~~ should be ready soon.^"**

Reporting Kerry's words directly, in quotation marks, eliminates the ambiguity.

Vague use of *it, this, that,* and *which*. The words *it*, *this*, *that*, and *which* often function as a shortcut for referring to something mentioned earlier. Like other pronouns, each must refer to a specific antecedent.

▸ **When the senators realized the bill would be defeated, they tried**
The entire effort
to postpone the vote but failed. ~~It~~ ^ was a fiasco.

and her sudden wealth
▸ **Jasmine just found out that she won the lottery, ~~which~~ ^ explains her resignation.**

Indefinite use of *you, it,* and *they*. In conversation, we often use *you*, *it*, and *they* in an indefinite sense in such expressions as *you never know* and *on television, they said*. In academic and professional writing, however, use *you* only to mean "you, the reader," and *they* or *it* only to refer to a clear antecedent.

▸ Commercials try to make ~~you~~ people buy without thinking.

▸ ~~On the~~ The Weather Channel ~~it~~ reported a powerful earthquake in China.

▸ ~~In France, they~~ Many restaurants in France allow dogs. ~~in many restaurants.~~

Implied antecedents. A pronoun may suggest a noun antecedent that is implied but not present in the sentence.

▸ Detention centers routinely blocked efforts by ~~detainees'~~ families and lawyers to locate ~~them.~~ detainees.

EXERCISE 34.6 Revise each of the following sentences to clarify pronoun reference. All the items can be revised in more than one way. If a pronoun refers ambiguously to more than one possible antecedent, revise the sentence to reflect each possible meaning. Example:

> **After Jane left, Miranda found her keys.**
> Miranda found Jane's keys after Jane left.
> **or**
> Miranda found her own keys after Jane left.

1. Quint trusted Smith because she had worked for her before.
2. Not long after the company set up the subsidiary, it went bankrupt.
3. When Deyon was reunited with his father, he wept.
4. Bill smilingly announced to Ed his promotion.
5. On the weather forecast, it said to expect snow in the overnight hours.

35 Prepositions and Prepositional Phrases

Words such as *to* and *from,* which show the relations between other words, are **prepositions**. They are one of the more challenging elements of English writing.

35a Choosing the right preposition

Even if you usually know where to use prepositions, you may have difficulty knowing which preposition to use. Each of the most common prepositions has a wide range of different applications, and this range never coincides exactly from one language to another. See, for example, how *in* and *on* are used in English.

- **The peaches are in the refrigerator.**
- **The peaches are on the table.**
- **Is that a diamond ring on your finger?**

The Spanish translations of these sentences all use the same preposition (*en*), a fact that might lead you astray in English.

There is no easy solution to the challenge of using English prepositions idiomatically, but a few strategies can make it less troublesome.

Know typical examples. The **object** of the preposition *in* is often a container that encloses something; the object of the preposition *on* is often a horizontal surface that supports something touching it.

IN	The peaches are *in* the refrigerator.
	There are still some pickles *in* the jar.
ON	The peaches are *on* the table.

Learn related examples. Prepositions that are not used in typical ways may still show some similarities to typical examples.

IN You shouldn't drive *in* a snowstorm.

Like a container, the falling snow surrounds the driver. The preposition *in* is used for many weather-related expressions.

ON Is that a diamond ring *on* your finger?

The preposition *on* is used to describe things you wear.

Grammar: Prepositions and Prepositional Phrases > LearningCurve and Exercises

Use your imagination. Mental images can help you remember figurative uses of prepositions.

IN Michael is *in* love.

Imagine a warm bath—or a raging torrent—in which Michael is immersed.

ON I've just read a book *on* social media.

Imagine the book sitting on a shelf labeled "Social Media."

Learn prepositions as part of a system. In identifying the location of a place or an event, the three prepositions *in, on,* and *at* can be used. *At* specifies the exact point in space or time; *in* is required for expanses of space or time within which a place is located or an event takes place; and *on* must be used with the names of streets (but not exact addresses) and with days of the week or month.

AT There will be a meeting tomorrow *at* 9:30 AM *at* 160 Main Street.

IN I arrived *in* the United States *in* January.

ON The airline's office is *on* Fifth Avenue.
I'll be moving to my new apartment *on* September 30.

EXERCISE 35.1 Insert one or more appropriate prepositions in each of the following sentences. Example:

We will have the answer __by__ four o'clock this afternoon.

1. Shall we eat ________ the restaurant or just take food ________?
2. I hate driving ________ the city ________ rush hour.
3. Have you ever fallen ________ love at first sight?
4. Adults who read to children can provide good examples ________ them.
5. Students should get to school precisely ________ time.

35b Using two-word verbs idiomatically

Some words that look like prepositions do not always function as prepositions. Consider the following sentences:

- **The balloon rose *off* the ground.**
- **The plane took *off* without difficulty.**

In the first sentence, *off* is a preposition that introduces the prepositional phrase *off the ground.* In the second sentence, *off* neither functions as a preposition nor introduces a prepositional phrase. Instead, it combines with *took* to form a two-word **verb** with its own meaning. Such a verb is called a phrasal verb, and the word *off,* when used in this way, is called an adverbial particle. Many prepositions can function as particles to form phrasal verbs.

The verb + particle combination that makes up a phrasal verb is a single entity that cannot usually be torn apart.

off
- **The plane took ^ without difficulty^. ~~off.~~**

Exceptions include some phrasal verbs that are transitive, meaning that they take a direct **object**. Some of these verbs have particles that may be separated from the verb by the object.

- **I *picked up my baggage* at the terminal.**
- **I *picked my baggage up* at the terminal.**

If a personal **pronoun** is used as the direct object, it *must* separate the verb from its particle.

it
- **I picked ^ up ~~it~~ at the terminal.**

In idiomatic two-word verbs where the second word is a preposition, the preposition can never be separated from the verb.

- **We *ran into* our neighbor on the train. [not *ran our neighbor into*]**

  The combination *run* + *into* has a special meaning (find by chance). Therefore, *run into* is a two-word verb.

EXERCISE 35.2 Identify each italicized expression as either a two-word verb or a verb + preposition. Example:

***Look up* John Brown the next time you're in town.** two-word verb

1. George was still *looking for* the keys when we left.
2. I always *turn down* the thermostat when I go to bed or leave the house.
3. Marion *gave back* the engagement ring.

4. Jimmy *takes after* his father, poor thing.
5. The car *turned into* the driveway.

36 Comma Splices and Fused Sentences

A **comma splice** results from placing only a comma between **independent clauses**—groups of words that can stand alone as a sentence. We often see comma splices used effectively to give slogans a catchy rhythm.

▸ **Dogs have owners, cats have staff.** —Bumper Sticker

A related construction is a **fused sentence**, or run-on, which results from joining two independent clauses with no punctuation or connecting word between them. The bumper sticker as a fused sentence would be "Dogs have owners cats have staff."

In academic and professional English, using comma splices or fused sentences will almost always be identified as an error, so be careful if you are using them for special effect.

36a Separating the clauses into two sentences

The simplest way to revise comma splices or fused sentences is to separate them into two sentences.

COMMA SPLICE My mother spends long hours every spring tilling the soil and moving manure/. ~~t~~ This part of gardening is nauseating.

If the clauses are very short, making them two sentences may sound abrupt and terse, so another method of revision may be preferable.

36b Linking the clauses with a comma and a coordinating conjunction

If the two clauses are closely related and equally important, join them with a comma and a **coordinating conjunction** (*and*, *but*, *or*, *nor*, *for*, *so*, or *yet*).

FUSED SENTENCE Interest rates fell, so people began borrowing more money.

36c Linking the clauses with a semicolon

If the ideas in the two clauses are closely related and you want to give them equal emphasis, link them with a semicolon.

COMMA SPLICE This photograph is not at all realistic~~,~~; it uses dreamlike images to convey its message.

Be careful when you link clauses with a **conjunctive adverb** like *however* or *therefore* or with a **transition** like *in fact*. In such sentences, the two clauses must be separated by a semicolon or by a comma and a coordinating conjunction.

COMMA SPLICE Many developing countries have high birthrates~~,~~; therefore, most of their citizens are young.

For Multilingual Writers

Judging Sentence Length

In U.S. academic contexts, readers sometimes find a series of short sentences "choppy" and undesirable. If you want to connect two independent clauses into one sentence, join them using one of the methods discussed in this chapter to avoid creating a comma splice or fused sentence. Another useful tip for writing in American English is to avoid writing several very long sentences in a row. If you find this pattern in your writing, try breaking it up by including a shorter sentence occasionally.

36d Rewriting the two clauses as one independent clause

Sometimes you can reduce two spliced or fused independent clauses to a single independent clause.

FUSED SENTENCE Most ~~A large part~~ of my mail is advertisements and ~~most of the rest is~~ bills.

36e Rewriting one independent clause as a dependent clause

When one independent clause is more important than the other, try converting the less important one to a **dependent clause** by adding an appropriate **subordinating conjunction**.

COMMA SPLICE Although Zora Neale Hurston is now regarded as one of America's major novelists, she died in obscurity.

In the revision, the writer emphasizes the second clause and makes the first one into a dependent clause by adding the subordinating conjunction *although*.

FUSED SENTENCE The arts and crafts movement, which reacted against mass production, called for handmade objects. ~~it reacted against mass production.~~

In the revision, the writer chooses to emphasize the first clause (the one describing what the movement advocated) and make the second clause into a dependent clause.

36f Linking the two clauses with a dash

In informal writing, you can use a dash to join the two clauses, especially when the second clause elaborates on the first clause.

COMMA SPLICE Exercise trends come and go~~,~~—this year yoga is hot.

EXERCISE 36.1 Revise each of the following comma splices or fused sentences by using the method suggested in brackets after the sentence. Example:

> **Americans think of slavery as a problem of the past, it still exists in some parts of the world.** [handwritten insertion: "but" before "it"]
>
> [Join with a comma and a coordinating conjunction.]

1. We tend to think of slavery only in U.S. terms in fact, it began long before the United States existed and still goes on. [Separate into two sentences.]
2. Slavery has existed in Mauritania for centuries it continues today. [Join with a comma and a coordinating conjunction.]
3. Members of Mauritania's ruling group are called the Beydanes, they are an Arab Berber tribe also known as the White Moors. [Recast as one independent clause.]
4. Another group in Mauritania is known as the Haratin or the Black Moors, they are native West Africans. [Separate into two sentences.]
5. In modern-day Mauritania many of the Haratin are still slaves, they serve the Beydanes. [Join with a semicolon.]

EXERCISE 36.2 Revise the following paragraph, eliminating comma splices by using a period or a semicolon. Then revise the paragraph again, this time using any of these three methods:

> Separate independent clauses into sentences of their own.
>
> Recast two or more clauses as one independent clause.
>
> Recast one independent clause as a dependent clause.

Comment on the two revisions. What differences in rhythm do you detect? Which version do you prefer, and why?

My sister Julie is planning a spring wedding, obviously she is very excited. At first, she hoped for a simple affair, in fact, she wanted to elope with her fiancé, Mike. My mother was not happy about that, neither was Mike's mother. Julie agreed to a small party, however, it soon began to grow and grow. Julie decided to invite all her college roommates, also Mike wanted his boss and her husband to attend. The intimate restaurant she first chose could not hold all the guests, now she had to find a new venue. They finally decided on a small ceremony in the backyard for family members only, then a gigantic party afterward for family, friends, and co-workers.

37 Sentence Fragments

Sentence fragments are often used to make writing sound conversational, as in this Facebook status update:

> Realizing that there are no edible bagels in this part of Oregon. Sigh.

Or they often create a special effect, as in this familiar advertisement: "Got milk?" As these examples show, fragments—groups of words that are punctuated as sentences but are not sentences—often appear in intentionally informal writing and in public writing that aims to attract attention or give a phrase special emphasis. But think carefully before using fragments for special effect in academic or professional writing, where some readers might regard them as errors.

EXERCISE 37.1 Choose an advertisement that contains intentional fragments from a newspaper, magazine, or website. Rewrite the advertisement to eliminate all sentence fragments. Be prepared to explain how your version and the original differ in impact and why you think the copywriters for the ad chose to use fragments rather than complete sentences.

37a Revising phrase fragments

A **phrase** is a group of words that lacks a **subject**, a **verb**, or both. When a phrase is punctuated like a sentence, it becomes a fragment. To revise a phrase fragment, attach it to an independent clause, or make it a separate sentence.

▸ **CNN is broadcasting the debates~~.~~ ~~With~~ with discussions afterward.**

With discussions afterward is a prepositional phrase, not a sentence. The editing combines the phrase with an independent clause.

LaunchPad Solo
macmillan learning

Clarity: Fragments > LearningCurve and Exercises

- **The town's growth is controlled by zoning laws/, ~~A~~ a strict set of regulations for builders and corporations.**

  A strict set of regulations for builders and corporations is a phrase renaming *zoning laws*. The editing attaches the fragment to the sentence containing that noun.

- **Kamika stayed out of school for three months after Linda was born. ~~To~~ She did so to recuperate and to take care of her baby.**

  The revision—adding a subject (*she*) and a verb (*did*)—turns the fragment into a separate sentence.

Fragments beginning with transitions. If you introduce an example or explanation with a transitional word or phrase like *also*, *for example*, *such as*, or *that*, be certain you write a sentence, not a fragment.

- **Joan Didion has written on many subjects/, ~~Such~~ such as the Hoover Dam and migraine headaches.**

  The second word group is a phrase, not a sentence. The editing combines it with an independent clause.

37b Revising compound-predicate fragments

A fragment occurs when one part of a compound **predicate** lacks a subject but is punctuated as a separate sentence. Such a fragment usually begins with *and*, *but*, or *or*. You can revise it by attaching it to the independent clause that contains the rest of the predicate.

- **They sold their house/ ~~And~~ and moved into an apartment.**

37c Revising clause fragments

A **dependent clause** contains both a subject and a verb, but it cannot stand alone as a sentence; it depends on an independent clause to complete its meaning. A dependent clause usually begins with a **subordinating conjunction**, such as *after*, *because*, *before*, *if*, *since*, *that*, *though*, *unless*, *until*, *when*, *where*, *while*, *who*, or *which*. You can usually combine dependent-clause fragments with a nearby independent clause.

- **When I decided to switch to part-time work/, I gave up a lot of my earning potential.**

If you cannot smoothly attach a clause to a nearby independent clause, try deleting the opening subordinating word and turning the dependent clause into a sentence.

- **Most injuries in automobile accidents occur in two ways. ~~When~~ An ~~an~~ occupant either is hurt by something inside the car or is thrown from the car.**

EXERCISE 37.2 Revise each of the following fragments, either by combining fragments with independent clauses or by rewriting them as separate sentences. Example:

> Zoe looked close to tears. Standing with her head bowed.
>
> Standing with her head bowed, Zoe looked close to tears.
>
> **or**
>
> Zoe looked close to tears. She was standing with her head bowed.

1. Autumn is a season of lavish bounty and stunning natural beauty. A season of giving thanks.
2. September is the perfect time to run outdoors. Avoiding the need to wait for a treadmill at a crowded gym.
3. To carve pumpkins and see scary movies. What better month than October?
4. We decided to go camping one weekend in October. Pitching tents and setting up camp.
5. I can't tell if he is skipping the Halloween party because he is genuinely ill. Or if he just doesn't have an idea for a costume.

EXERCISE 37.3 Underline every fragment you find in the following paragraph. Then revise the paragraph. You may combine or rearrange sentences as long as you retain the original content.

To study abroad or not. That is a major decision for many college students. Some will consider domestic programs at universities across the country. Traditionally, approaching their junior year. Opportunities for study in major cities and in small villages. Programs to satisfy every interest and major. There's a lot to think about. Applications, courses, airfare, accommodations, and visas. Those who accept the challenge are generally rewarded. With a once-in-a-lifetime opportunity. Students who travel to foreign destinations can thoroughly immerse themselves in the culture, language, traditions, and foods of their host country. And end up with new friends, an enhanced résumé, and a sense of self-reliance. Why not check with your college today? To see what kinds of foreign and domestic study programs you might apply to.

Punctuation/ Mechanics

38 Commas 346

39 Semicolons 357

40 End Punctuation 360

41 Apostrophes 362

42 Quotation Marks 365

43 Other Punctuation 370

44 Capital Letters 377

45 Abbreviations and Numbers 380

46 Italics 384

47 Hyphens 386

38 Commas

It's hard to go through a day without encountering directions of some kind, and commas often play a crucial role in how you interpret instructions. See how important the comma is in the following directions for making hot cereal:

Add Cream of Wheat slowly, stirring constantly.

That sentence tells the cook to *add the cereal slowly.* If the comma came before the word *slowly*, however, the cook might add all of the cereal at once and *stir slowly*.

38a Setting off introductory elements

In general, use a comma after any word, **phrase**, or **clause** that precedes the **subject** of the sentence.

- **However, health care costs keep rising.**
- **Wearing new tap shoes, Audrey prepared for the recital.**
- **To win the game, players need both skill and luck.**
- **Fingers on the keyboard, Maya waited for the test to begin.**
- **While her friends watched, Lila practiced her gymnastics routine.**

Some writers omit the comma after a short introductory element that does not seem to require a pause after it. However, you will never be wrong if you use a comma.

EXERCISE 38.1 In the following sentences, add any commas that are needed after the introductory element. Example:

Before pasteurization, the natural pathogens in milk often caused disease.

LaunchPad Solo
macmillan learning

Punctuation: Commas > LearningCurve and Exercises

1. Named after its inventor pasteurization is the process of heating liquids in order to destroy viruses and harmful bacteria.
2. Unlike sterilization pasteurization does not destroy all the pathogens in a food.
3. Instead pasteurization tries to reduce the number of all living organisms so they cannot cause illness.
4. While there are many methods of pasteurization the most commonly used is called HTST (for High Temperature/Short Time).
5. Although there are many foods and beverages that are pasteurized we generally think of the process in relation to dairy products.

38b Separating clauses in compound sentences

A comma usually precedes a **coordinating conjunction** (*and*, *but*, *or*, *nor*, *for*, *so*, or *yet*) that joins two **independent clauses** in a compound sentence.

- **The climbers must reach the summit today, or they will have to turn back.**

With very short clauses, you can sometimes omit the comma (*She saw her chance and she took it*). But always use the comma if there is a chance the sentence will be misread without it.

- **I opened the heavy junk drawer, and the cabinet door jammed.**

Use a semicolon rather than a comma when the clauses are long and complex or contain their own commas.

- **When these early migrations took place, the ice was still confined to the lands in the far north; but eight hundred thousand years ago, when man was already established in the temperate latitudes, the ice moved southward until it covered large parts of Europe and Asia.** —Robert Jastrow, *Until the Sun Dies*

EXERCISE 38.2 Use a comma and a coordinating conjunction (*and, but, or, for, nor, so,* or *yet*) to combine each of the following pairs of sentences into one sentence. Delete or rearrange words if necessary. Example:

> **There is a lot of talk these days about computer viruses~~.~~, yet many ~~Many~~ people do not know what they really are.**

1. Computer viruses are software programs. They are created to spread from one computer to another.
2. A biological virus cannot replicate itself. A virus must inject its DNA into a cell to reproduce.
3. Similarly, a computer virus must hitch on to some other computer program. Then it can launch itself.
4. These viruses can be totally destructive or basically benign. When people think of computer viruses, they generally think of the former.
5. Most viruses spread easily via attachments. People should never open an email attachment unless they know the sender.

 Checklist

Editing for Commas

Research for this book shows that five of the most common errors in college writing involve commas.

- Check that a comma separates an introductory word, phrase, or clause from the main part of the sentence. (38a)
- Look at every sentence that contains a coordinating conjunction (*and*, *but*, *for*, *nor*, *or*, *so*, or *yet*). If the groups of words before and after this conjunction both function as complete sentences, use a comma before the conjunction. (38b)
- Look at each adjective clause beginning with *which*, *who*, *whom*, *whose*, *when*, or *where* and at each phrase and appositive. If the rest of the sentence would have a different meaning without the clause, phrase, or appositive, do not set off the element with commas. (38c)
- Make sure that adjective clauses beginning with *that* are not set off with commas. Do not use commas between subjects and verbs, verbs and objects or complements, or prepositions and objects; to separate parts of compound constructions other than compound sentences; to set off restrictive clauses; or before the first or after the last item in a series. (38i)
- Do not use a comma alone to separate your sentences. (See Chapter 36.)

38c Setting off nonrestrictive elements

Nonrestrictive elements are word groups that do not limit, or restrict, the meaning of the noun or pronoun they modify. Setting nonrestrictive elements off with commas shows your readers that the information is not essential to the meaning of the sentence. **Restrictive elements**, on the other hand, *are* essential to meaning and should *not* be set off with commas. The same sentence may mean different things with and without the commas:

- ▶ **The bus drivers rejecting the management offer remained on strike.**
- ▶ **The bus drivers, rejecting the management offer, remained on strike.**

The first sentence says that only *some* bus drivers, the ones rejecting the offer, remained on strike. The second says that *all* the drivers did.

Since the decision to include or omit commas influences how readers will interpret your sentence, you should think especially carefully about what you mean and use commas (or omit them) accordingly.

RESTRICTIVE — Drivers *who have been convicted of drunken driving* should lose their licenses.

In the preceding sentence, the clause *who have been convicted of drunken driving* is essential because it explains that only drivers who have been convicted of drunken driving should lose their licenses. Therefore, it is *not* set off with commas.

NONRESTRICTIVE — The two drivers involved in the accident, *who have been convicted of drunken driving*, should lose their licenses.

In this sentence, however, the clause *who have been convicted of drunken driving* is not essential to the meaning because it does not limit what it modifies, *The two drivers involved in the accident*, but merely provides additional information about these drivers. Therefore, the clause *is* set off with commas.

To decide whether an element is restrictive or nonrestrictive, mentally delete the element, and see if the deletion changes the meaning of the rest of the sentence. If the deletion *does* change the meaning, you should probably not set the element off with commas. If it *does not* change the meaning, the element probably requires commas.

Adjective and adverb clauses. An adjective clause that begins with *that* is always restrictive; do not set it off with commas. An adjective clause beginning with *which* may be either restrictive or nonrestrictive; however, some writers prefer to use *which* only for nonrestrictive clauses, which they set off with commas.

RESTRICTIVE CLAUSES

- **The claim *that men like seriously to battle one another to some sort of finish* is a myth.**

  —John McMurtry, "Kill 'Em! Crush 'Em! Eat 'Em Raw!"

  The adjective clause is necessary to the meaning because it explains which claim is a myth; therefore, the clause is not set off with commas.

- **The man/ who rescued Jana's puppy/ won her eternal gratitude.**

  The adjective clause is necessary to the meaning because it identifies the man, so it takes no commas.

NONRESTRICTIVE CLAUSES

- **I borrowed books from the rental library of Shakespeare and Company, *which was the library and bookstore of Sylvia Beach at 12 rue de l'Odeon.***

  —Ernest Hemingway, *A Moveable Feast*

  The adjective clause is not necessary to the meaning of the independent clause and therefore is set off with a comma.

An adverb clause that follows a main clause does *not* usually require a comma to set it off unless the adverb clause expresses contrast.

- **The park became a popular gathering place, although nearby residents complained about the noise.**

  The adverb clause expresses contrast, so it is set off with a comma.

Phrases. Participial **phrases** may be restrictive or nonrestrictive. Prepositional phrases are usually restrictive, but sometimes they are not essential to the meaning of a sentence and thus are set off with commas.

NONRESTRICTIVE PHRASES

▸ **The NBA star's little daughter, refusing to be ignored, interrupted the interview.**

Using commas around the participial phrase (*refusing to be ignored*) makes it nonrestrictive.

Appositives. An **appositive** is a **noun** or noun phrase that renames a nearby noun. When an appositive is not essential to identify what it renames, it is set off with commas.

NONRESTRICTIVE APPOSITIVES

▸ **Savion Glover, the award-winning dancer, taps like poetry in motion.**

Savion Glover's name identifies him; the appositive *the award-winning dancer* provides extra information.

RESTRICTIVE APPOSITIVES

▸ **Mozart's opera/ *The Marriage of Figaro*/ was considered revolutionary.**

The phrase is restrictive because Mozart wrote more than one opera. Therefore, it is *not* set off with commas.

EXERCISE 38.3 First, underline the restrictive or nonrestrictive elements in the following sentences. Then, use commas to set off the nonrestrictive elements in any of the sentences that contain such elements. Example:

> ***A Tale of Two Cities*, one of Charles Dickens's most famous works, was first published in 1859.**

1. Everyone who runs in the race will get a T-shirt and a small backpack.
2. Mammals that have pouches to protect their young are known as marsupials.
3. Wasabi a root that is related to horseradish originated in Japan.
4. Plagiarism does occur on college campuses even though it is dishonest and illegal.
5. The game will go into overtime if neither team scores within the next two minutes.

38d Separating items in a series

- **He has plundered our seas, ravaged our coasts, burnt our towns, and destroyed the lives of our people.**

  —Declaration of Independence

You may see a series with no comma after the next-to-last item, particularly in newspaper writing. Occasionally, however, omitting the comma can cause confusion.

- **All the cafeteria's vegetables—broccoli, green beans, peas, and carrots—were cooked to a gray mush.**

  Without the comma after *peas*, you wouldn't know if there were three choices (the third being a *mixture* of peas and carrots) or four.

Coordinate adjectives—two or more adjectives that relate equally to the noun they modify—should be separated by commas.

- **The long, twisting, muddy road led to a shack in the woods.**

In a sentence like *The cracked bathroom mirror reflected his face*, however, *cracked* and *bathroom* are not coordinate because *bathroom mirror* is the equivalent of a single word, which is modified by *cracked*. Hence they are *not* separated by commas.

You can usually determine whether adjectives are coordinate by inserting *and* between them. If the sentence makes sense with the *and* added, the adjectives are coordinate and should be separated by commas.

- **They are sincere *and* talented *and* inquisitive researchers.**

  The sentence makes sense with the *ands*, so the adjectives should be separated by commas: *They are sincere, talented, inquisitive researchers.*

- **Byron carried an elegant ~~and~~ pocket watch.**

  The sentence does not make sense with *and*, so the adjectives *elegant* and *pocket* should not be separated by commas: *Byron carried an elegant pocket watch.*

See 39b for separating items in a series with semicolons.

EXERCISE 38.4 In the following sentences, add any commas that are needed to set off words, phrases, or clauses in a series. Example:

The waiter brought water, menus, and an attitude.

1. I am very excited to see Alcatraz visit Chinatown and tour Napa Valley.
2. The moon circles the earth the earth revolves around the sun and the sun is just one star in the galaxy.
3. The ball sailed over the fence across the road and through the Wilsons' window.
4. Lin-Manuel Miranda says the only shows he saw as a kid were *Les Miz Cats and Phantom.*
5. They found employment in truck driving farming and mining.

38e Setting off parenthetical and transitional expressions

Parenthetical expressions add comments or information. Because they often interrupt the flow of a sentence, they are usually set off with commas.

- ▸ Some studies have shown that chocolate, of all things, helps prevent tooth decay.

Transitions (such as *as a result*), **conjunctive adverbs** (such as *however*), and other expressions used to connect parts of sentences are usually set off with commas.

- ▸ Ozone is a by-product of dry cleaning, for example.

38f Setting off contrasting elements, interjections, direct address, and tag questions

- ▸ I asked you, *not your brother,* to sweep the porch.
- ▸ *Holy cow,* did you see that?
- ▸ Remember, *sir,* that you are under oath.
- ▸ The governor did not veto the bill, *did she?*

EXERCISE 38.5 Revise each of the following sentences, using commas to set off parenthetical and transitional expressions, contrasting elements, interjections, words used in direct address, and tag questions. Example:

Passengers, thank you for your attention.

1. Ouch that tetanus shot really hurt!
2. Doctor Ross you are over an hour late for our appointment.
3. Consider furthermore the impact of environmental destruction on future generations.
4. The West in fact has become solidly Republican in presidential elections.
5. Last year I am sorry to say six elms had to be destroyed.

38g Setting off parts of dates and addresses

Dates. Use a comma between the day of the week and the month, between the day of the month and the year, and between the year and the rest of the sentence, if any.

- **On Wednesday, November 26, 2008, gunmen arrived in Mumbai by boat.**

Do not use commas with dates in inverted order or with dates consisting of only the month and the year.

- **Kerry dated the letter 5 August 2016.**
- **Thousands of Germans swarmed over the wall in November 1989.**

Addresses and place names. Use a comma after each part of an address or a place name, including the state if there is no ZIP code. Do not precede a ZIP code with a comma.

- **Forward my mail to the Department of English, The Ohio State University, Columbus, Ohio 43210.**
- **Portland, Oregon, is much larger than Portland, Maine.**

38h Setting off quotations

Commas set off a quotation from words used to introduce or identify the source of the quotation. A comma following a quotation goes *inside* the closing quotation mark.

- **A German proverb warns, "Go to law for a sheep, and lose your cow."**
- **"All I know about grammar," said Joan Didion, "is its infinite power."**

Do not use a comma following a question mark or an exclamation point.

- **"Out, damned spot!/" cries Lady Macbeth.**

Do not use a comma to introduce a quotation with *that* or when you do not quote a speaker's exact words.

- **The writer of Ecclesiastes concludes that/ "all is vanity."**
- **Patrick Henry declared/ that he wanted either liberty or death.**

EXERCISE 38.6 Revise each of the following sentences, using commas appropriately with dates, addresses and place-names, titles, numbers, and quotations. Example:

The store's original location was 2373 Broadway, New York City.

1. "Education is not the filling of a pail, but the lighting of a fire" said William Butler Yeats.
2. The White House address is 1600 Pennsylvania Avenue Washington DC.
3. On July 21 1969 Neil Armstrong became the first person to walk on the moon.
4. "Neat people are lazier and meaner than sloppy people" according to Suzanne Britt.
5. Ithaca New York has a population of about 30000.

38i Avoiding unnecessary commas

Excessive use of commas can spoil an otherwise fine sentence.

Around restrictive elements. Do not use commas to set off restrictive elements—elements that limit, or define, the meaning of the words they modify or refer to (38c).

- I don't let my children watch movies/ that are violent.
- The actor/ Denzel Washington/ might win the award.

Between subjects and verbs, verbs and objects or complements, and prepositions and objects. Do not use a comma between a subject and its **verb**, a verb and its **object** or complement, or a **preposition** and its object.

- Watching movies late at night/ allows me to relax.
- Parents must decide/ what time their children should go to bed.
- The winner of/ the prize for community service stepped forward.

In compound constructions. In compound constructions other than compound sentences, do not use a comma before or after a coordinating conjunction that joins the two parts (38b).

- Improved health care/ and more free trade were two of the administration's goals.

  The *and* joins parts of a compound subject, which should not be separated by a comma.

- Mark Twain trained as a printer/ and worked as a steamboat pilot.

  The *and* joins parts of a compound predicate, which should not be separated by a comma.

In a series. Do not use a comma before the first or after the last item in a series.

- The auction included/ furniture, paintings, and china.
- The swimmer took slow, elegant, powerful/ strokes.

EXERCISE 38.7 Revise each of the following sentences, deleting unnecessary commas. If a sentence contains no unnecessary commas, write *Correct*. Example:

> **Insomniacs are people/ who have a hard time sleeping soundly.**

1. Contrary to popular belief, insomnia is not simply a matter, of being unable to sleep well at night.
2. Insomniacs do indeed wake up at night, but, studies have demonstrated that they also have trouble napping during the day.
3. Why can't insomniacs sleep soundly at night, or nap when they are tired?
4. In many cases, insomniacs suffer, from anxiety.
5. Doctors and sleep researchers, have long considered anxiety to be a common result of getting too little sleep.

39 Semicolons

The following public-service announcement, posted in New York City subway cars, reminded commuters what to do with a used newspaper at the end of the ride:

> Please put it in a trash can; that's good news for everyone.

The semicolon in the subway announcement separates two clauses that could have been written as separate sentences. Semicolons, which create a pause stronger than that of a comma but not as strong as the full pause of a period, show close connections between related ideas.

39a Linking independent clauses

Although a comma and a **coordinating conjunction** often join **independent clauses** (38b), semicolons provide writers with more subtle ways of signaling closely related clauses. The clause following

Punctuation: Semicolons > LearningCurve and Exercises

a semicolon often restates an idea expressed in the first clause; it sometimes expands on or presents a contrast to the first.

- **Immigration acts were passed; newcomers had to prove, besides moral correctness and financial solvency, their ability to read.**
  —Mary Gordon, "More Than Just a Shrine"

  The semicolon gives the sentence an abrupt rhythm that suits the topic: laws that imposed strict requirements.

If two independent clauses joined by a coordinating conjunction contain commas, you may use a semicolon instead of a comma before the conjunction to make the sentence easier to read.

- **Every year, whether the Republican or the Democratic party is in office, more and more power drains away from the individual to feed vast reservoirs in far-off places; and we have less and less say about the shape of events which shape our future.** —William F. Buckley Jr., "Why Don't We Complain?"

A semicolon should link independent clauses joined by a **conjunctive adverb** such as *however* or *therefore* or a **transition** such as *as a result* or *for example.*

- **The circus comes as close to being the world in microcosm as anything I know; in a way, it puts all the rest of show business in the shade.** —E. B. White, "The Ring of Time"

EXERCISE 39.1 Combine each of the following pairs of sentences into one sentence by using a semicolon. Example:

I decided to start my diet this week~~.~~; ~~Not~~ not surprisingly, a package just arrived from my mother with brownies, cookies, and three different flavors of popcorn.

1. This sofa is much too big. It will never fit inside my Prius.
2. The business could no longer afford to pay its bills or its employees. Therefore, the owners filed for bankruptcy.
3. German shepherds are known for their intelligence. They are also known for their protective behavior.

4. Once students live off-campus, most begin cooking their own meals. Nevertheless, some choose to maintain their school dining plans.
5. Natalia ran a marathon in four hours and two minutes. Unfortunately, this time did not qualify her for the Boston Marathon.

39b Separating items in a series containing other punctuation

Ordinarily, commas separate items in a series (38d). But when the items themselves contain commas or other punctuation, semicolons make the sentence clearer.

- **Anthropology encompasses archaeology, the study of ancient civilizations through artifacts,; linguistics, the study of the structure and development of language,; and cultural anthropology, the study of language, customs, and behavior.**

39c Avoiding misused semicolons

Use a comma, not a semicolon, to separate an independent clause from a **dependent clause** or **phrase**.

- **The police found fingerprints;, which they used to identify the thief.**
- **The new system would encourage students to register for courses online;, thus streamlining registration.**

Use a colon, not a semicolon, to introduce a series or list.

- **The reunion tour includes the following bands;: Urban Waste, Murphy's Law, Rapid Deployment, and Ism.**

EXERCISE 39.2 Revise each of the following sentences to correct the misuse of semicolons. If the semicolon in a sentence is appropriate as written, write *Correct.* Example:

The new system would encourage high school students to take more academic courses;, thus strengthening college preparation.

1. To make the tacos, I need to buy; ground beef, beans, and tortillas.
2. For four glorious but underpaid weeks; I'll be working in Yosemite this summer.
3. Luis enjoys commuting to work on the train; although it can get crowded at rush hour.
4. Some gardeners want; low-maintenance plants, limited grass to mow, and low water usage.
5. Alicia slept through most of her art history lectures; as a result, she failed the course.

40 End Punctuation

Periods, question marks, and exclamation points often appear in advertising to create special effects:

Just do it.

Got milk?

Ask our experts today!

End punctuation tells us how to read each sentence—as a matter-of-fact statement, a question for the reader, or an enthusiastic exclamation.

40a Using periods

Use a period to close sentences that make statements or give mild commands.

- **All books are either dreams or swords.** —Amy Lowell
- **Don't use a fancy word if a simpler word will do.**
  —George Orwell, "Politics and the English Language"

A period also closes indirect questions, which report rather than ask questions.

- **I asked how old the child was.**

In American English, periods are used with most abbreviations. However, more and more abbreviations are currently appearing without periods.

Mr.	MD	BCE *or* B.C.E.
Ms.	PhD	AD *or* A.D.
Sen.	Jr.	PM *or* p.m.

Some abbreviations rarely if ever appear with periods. These include the postal abbreviations of state names, such as *FL* and *TN*, and most groups of initials (*GE*, *CIA*, *AIDS*, *YMCA*, *UNICEF*). If you are not sure whether an abbreviation should include periods, check a dictionary or follow the style guidelines you are using for a research paper. (For more about abbreviations, see Chapter 45.)

Do not use an additional period when a sentence ends with an abbreviation that has its own period.

- **The social worker referred me to John Pintz Jr./**

40b Using question marks

Use question marks to close sentences that ask direct questions.

- **How is the human mind like a computer, and how is it different?**

—Kathleen Stassen Berger and Ross A. Thompson, *The Developing Person through Childhood and Adolescence*

Question marks do not close indirect questions, which report rather than ask questions.

- **She asked whether I opposed his nomination?.**

40c Using exclamation points

Use an exclamation point to show surprise or strong emotion. Use these marks sparingly because they can distract your readers or suggest that you are exaggerating.

- **In those few moments of geologic time will be the story of all that has happened since we became a nation. And what a story it will be!**

—James Rettie, "But a Watch in the Night"

EXERCISE 40.1 Revise each of the following items, inserting end punctuation in the appropriate places and eliminating any inappropriate punctuation. If a sentence is correct as written, write *Correct*. Example:

> **Over the centuries, some of history's most interesting characters have been women!.**

1. In China, the brief reign of Empress Wu from 690 to 705 CE saw some changes that benefited women.
2. "Which Harry Potter book did you like best," Georgia asked Harriet?
3. Do you remember who said, "Be the change you want to see in the world?"
4. The child cried, "Ouch" as her mother pulled off the bandage!
5. Stop, thief.

40d Using end punctuation in informal writing

In informal writing, especially on social media, writers today are more likely to omit end punctuation entirely. Research also shows that ellipses (. . .), or "dots," are on the rise; they can be used to signal a trailing off of a thought, to raise questions about what is being left out, to leave open the possibility of further communication, or simply to indicate that the writer doesn't want or need to finish the sentence. Exclamation marks can convey an excited or a chatty tone, so they are used more frequently in informal writing, though they get old pretty quickly—and advertisers call them the "kiss of death." And some writers have argued that using a period at the end of a text or tweet rather than no punctuation at all can suggest that the writer is irritated or angry. The meaning of end punctuation is changing in informal contexts, so pay attention to how others communicate, and use what you learn in your own social writing.

41 Apostrophes

The little apostrophe can make a big difference in meaning. The following sign at a neighborhood swimming pool, for instance, says something different from what the writer probably intended:

Punctuation: Apostrophes > LearningCurve

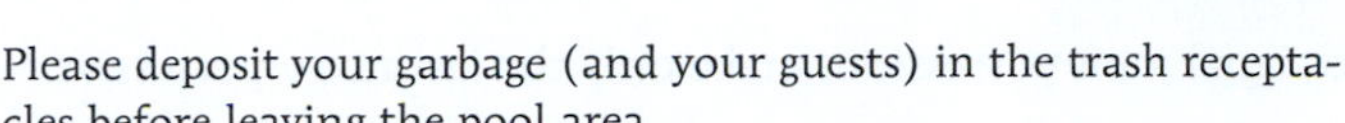
Please deposit your garbage (and your guests) in the trash receptacles before leaving the pool area.

The sign indicates that the guests, not their garbage, should be deposited in trash receptacles. Adding a single apostrophe would offer a more neighborly statement: *Please deposit your garbage (and your guests') in the trash receptacles before leaving the pool area.*

41a Signaling possessive case

The possessive case denotes ownership or possession. Add an apostrophe and *-s* to form the possessive of most singular **nouns**, including those that end in *-s*, and of **indefinite pronouns** (31d). The possessive forms of personal **pronouns** do not take apostrophes: *yours, his, hers, its, ours, theirs.*

- The bus's fumes overpowered her.
- George Lucas's movies have been wildly popular.
- Anyone's guess is as good as mine.

Plural nouns. To form the possessive case of plural nouns not ending in *-s*, add an apostrophe and *-s*. For plural nouns ending in *-s*, add only the apostrophe.

- The men's department sells business attire.
- The clowns' costumes were bright green and orange.

Compound nouns. For compound nouns, make the last word in the group possessive.

- Both her daughters-in-law's birthdays fall in July.

Two or more nouns. To signal individual possession by two or more owners, make each noun possessive.

- Great differences exist between Jerry Bruckheimer's and Ridley Scott's films.

  Bruckheimer and Scott produce different films.

To signal joint possession, make only the last noun possessive.

- **Wallace and Gromit's creator is Nick Park.**
  Wallace and Gromit have the same creator.

EXERCISE 41.1 Complete each of the following sentences by inserting *'s* or an apostrophe alone to form the possessive case of the italicized words. Example:

> **Many Internet scare stories are nothing but old *wives'* tales.**

1. Internet rumors circulate widely because of *people* good intentions.
2. The *Internet* power to inform is great, but so is its power to play tricks on unsuspecting people.
3. A *hoax* creators count on *recipients* kind hearts and concern for the well-being of their families and friends.
4. *Consumers* fears fuel some of the Internet medical scares.
5. Have you heard the one about how *deodorants* ingredients supposedly clog your pores and cause cancer?

41b Signaling contractions

Contractions are two-word combinations formed by leaving out certain letters, which are replaced by an apostrophe (*it is, it has/it's; will not/won't*).

Contractions are common in conversation and informal writing. Academic and professional work, however, often calls for greater formality.

Distinguishing *its* and *it's*. *Its* is a possessive **pronoun**—the possessive form of *it*. *It's* is a contraction for *it is* or *it has*.

- **This disease is unusual; its symptoms vary from person to person.**
- **It's a difficult disease to diagnose.**

EXERCISE 41.2 Revise each of the following sentences so that it uses contractions. Remove any misused apostrophes. Example:

> I'll
> **~~I will~~ bring some meatballs to the potluck dinner.**

1. Genevieve was not even three years old when she moved here from Germany, so she does not have a German accent.
2. You will see plenty of advertisements on television for alcoholic beverages, but you will not see any for tobacco products.
3. Whose dog keeps scratching it's ears?
4. It has been almost ten years, but I cannot forget how I felt on the night we received the terrible news.
5. Let us go to the later movie, after he has had a chance to finish his homework.

41c Understanding apostrophes and plural forms

Many style guides now advise against using apostrophes for plurals.

▸ **The gymnasts need marks of 8s and 9s in order to qualify for the finals.**

Other guidelines call for an apostrophe and *-s* to form the plural of numbers, letters, and words referred to as terms.

▸ **The five Shakespeare's in the essay were spelled five different ways.**

Check your instructor's preference.

42 Quotation Marks

"Hilarious!" "A great family movie!" "A must see!" Quotation marks are a key component of statements like these from movie ads; they make the praise more believable by indicating that it comes from people other than the movie promoter. Quotation marks identify a speaker's exact words or the titles of short works.

42a Signaling direct quotation

▸ **The crowd chanted "Celtics, Celtics" as they waited for the game to begin.**

Punctuation: Quotation Marks > LearningCurve

▸ **Jasmine smiled and said, ^“Son, this is one incident that I will never forget.^”**

Use quotation marks to enclose the words of each speaker within running dialogue. Mark each shift in speaker with a new paragraph.

> “I want no proof of their affection,” said Elinor; “but of their engagement I do.”
>
> “I am perfectly satisfied of both.”
>
> “Yet not a syllable has been said to you on the subject, by either of them.” —Jane Austen, *Sense and Sensibility*

Single quotation marks. Single quotation marks enclose a quotation within a quotation. Open and close the quoted passage with double quotation marks, and change any quotation marks that appear *within* the quotation to single quotation marks.

▸ **Baldwin says, ^“The title ^‘The Uses of the Blues^’ does not refer to music; I don’t know anything about music.^”**

Long quotations. To quote a passage that is more than four typed lines, set the quotation off by starting it on a new line and indenting it one-half inch from the left margin. This format, known as block quotation, does not require quotation marks.

In “Suspended,” Joy Harjo tells of her first awareness of jazz as a child:

> My rite of passage into the world of humanity occurred then, via jazz. The music made a startling bridge between the familiar and strange lands, an appropriate vehicle, for . . . we were there when jazz was born. I recognized it . . . as a way to speak beyond the confines of ordinary language. (84)

This block quotation, including the ellipsis dots and the page number in parentheses at the end, follows the style of the Modern Language Association, or MLA (see Chapter 15). The American Psychological Association, or APA, has different guidelines for setting off block quotations (see Chapter 16).

Poetry. When quoting poetry, if the quotation is brief (fewer than four lines), include it within your text. Separate the lines of the poem with slashes, each preceded and followed by a space, in order to tell the reader where one line of the poem ends and the next begins.

> In one of his best-known poems, Robert Frost remarks, "Two roads diverged in a yellow wood, and I— / I took the one less traveled by / And that has made all the difference."

To quote more than three lines of poetry, indent the block one-half inch from the left margin. Do not use quotation marks. Take care to follow the spacing, capitalization, punctuation, and other features of the original poem.

> The duke in Robert Browning's poem "My Last Duchess" is clearly a jealous, vain person, whose arrogance is illustrated through this statement:
>
> She thanked men—good! but thanked
> Somehow—I know not how—as if she ranked
> My gift of a nine-hundred-years-old name
> With anybody's gift. (lines 31–34)

EXERCISE 42.1 In the following sentences, add quotation marks each time someone else's exact words are being used. Some sentences may not require quotation marks; mark correct sentences *Correct*. Example:

> **"Your phone's ringing!" yelled Phil from the end of the hall.**

1. My mother told us we had to get in the car immediately or she wouldn't drive us.
2. It's not fair, she told him. You always win.
3. Call me Ishmael is the first sentence of Herman Melville's novel *Moby Dick*.
4. I could not believe the condition of my hometown, he wrote.
5. Keep your opinions to yourselves, Dad muttered as he served the lumpy oatmeal.

42b Identifying titles of short works and definitions

Use quotation marks to enclose the titles of short poems, short stories, articles, essays, songs, sections of books, and episodes of television and radio programs. Quotation marks also enclose definitions.

- **The essay "The Art of Stephen Curry" analyzes some reasons for the success of the Warriors' star.**
- **In social science, the term *sample size* means "the number of individuals being studied in a research project."**

—Kathleen Stassen Berger and Ross A. Thompson,
The Developing Person through Childhood and Adolescence

EXERCISE 42.2 Revise each of the following sentences by using quotation marks appropriately to signal both titles and definitions. Example:

One of the best short stories we read last semester was "The Story of an Hour" by Kate Chopin.

1. The term *emoji*, which means a small digital image used to express an emotion, comes from Japanese.
2. The Red Wheelbarrow is often considered to be William Carlos Williams's most important poem.
3. The Rolling Stones song Time Is on My Side was first recorded by Irma Thomas.
4. My favorite episode of *Glee* is Wheels, especially since the cast performed the song Defying Gravity from *Wicked*.
5. The *New York Times* article Dealing with Student Debt helps college graduates understand the best way to handle their student loans.

42c Using quotation marks with other punctuation

Periods and commas go *inside* closing quotation marks.

- **"Don't compromise yourself," said Janis Joplin. "You are all you've got."**

Colons, semicolons, and footnote numbers go *outside* closing quotation marks.

- I felt one emotion after finishing “Eveline”: sorrow.
- Tragedy is defined by Aristotle as “an imitation of an action that is serious and of a certain magnitude.”[1]

Question marks, exclamation points, and dashes go *inside* if they are part of the quoted material, *outside* if they are not.

PART OF THE QUOTATION

- The cashier asked, “Would you like a receipt?”

NOT PART OF THE QUOTATION

- What is the theme of “The Birth-Mark”?

42d Avoiding misused quotation marks

Do not use quotation marks for indirect quotations—those that do not use someone’s exact words.

- Mother smiled and said that ~~“~~she was sure she would never forget the incident.~~”~~

Do not use quotation marks merely to add emphasis to particular words or phrases.

- The hikers were startled by the appearance of a ~~“~~gigantic~~”~~ grizzly bear.

Do not use quotation marks around slang or colloquial language; they create the impression that you are apologizing for using those

For Multilingual Writers

Quoting in American English

Remember that the way you mark quotations in American English (“ ”) may not be the same as in other languages. In French, for example, quotations are marked with *guillemets* (« »), while in German, quotations take split-level marks („ “). American English and British English offer opposite conventions for double and single quotation marks. If you are writing for an American audience, follow the U.S. conventions for quotation marks.

words. If you have a good reason to use slang or a colloquial term, use it without quotation marks.

▶ **After our twenty-mile hike, we were completely exhausted and ready to "turn in."**

EXERCISE 42.3 Revise each of the following sentences, using quotation marks appropriately.

1. Should America the Beautiful replace The Star-Spangled Banner as the national anthem?
2. In the chapter called The Last to See Them Alive, Truman Capote shows the utterly ordinary life of the Kansas family.
3. Several popular films have used Abba hits such as Dancing Queen and Take a Chance on Me.
4. After working a double shift, we were completely "exhausted."
5. My dictionary defines isolation as the quality or state of being alone.

43 Other Punctuation

Parentheses, brackets, dashes, colons, slashes, and ellipses are everywhere. Every URL includes colons and slashes, many sites use brackets or parentheses to identify updates and embedded media, and dashes and ellipses are increasingly common in writing that expresses conversational informality.

You can also use these punctuation marks for more formal purposes: to signal relationships among parts of sentences, to create particular rhythms, and to help readers follow your thoughts.

43a Using parentheses

Use parentheses to enclose material that is of minor or secondary importance in a sentence—material that supplements, clarifies, comments on, or illustrates what precedes or follows it.

Punctuation: Other Punctuation Marks > LearningCurve

> **Inventors and men of genius have almost always been regarded as fools at the beginning (and very often at the end) of their careers.**
> —Fyodor Dostoyevsky

> ***Hamilton* (the musical by Lin-Manuel Miranda) won eleven Tony Awards in 2016.**

Parentheses are also used to enclose textual citations and numbers or letters in a list.

> **Freud and his followers have had a most significant impact on the ways abnormal functioning is understood and treated (Joseph, 1991).**
> —Ronald J. Comer, *Abnormal Psychology*

The in-text citation in this sentence shows the style of the American Psychological Association (APA).

> **Five distinct styles can be distinguished: (1) Old New England, (2) Deep South, (3) Middle American, (4) Wild West, and (5) Far West or Californian.**
> —Alison Lurie, *The Language of Clothes*

With other punctuation. A period may be placed either inside or outside a closing parenthesis, depending on whether the parenthetical text is part of a larger sentence. A comma, if needed, is always placed *outside* a closing parenthesis (and never before an opening one).

> **Gene Tunney's single defeat in an eleven-year career was to a flamboyant and dangerous fighter named Harry Greb ("The Human Windmill"), who seems to have been, judging from boxing literature, the dirtiest fighter in history.**
> —Joyce Carol Oates, *On Boxing*

43b Using brackets

Use brackets to enclose any parenthetical elements in material that is itself within parentheses. Brackets should also be used to enclose any explanatory words or comments you are inserting into a quotation.

> **Eventually, the investigation had to examine the major agencies (including the National Security Agency [NSA]) that were conducting covert operations.**

▶ **Massing notes that "on average, it [Fox News] attracts more than eight million people daily."**

The bracketed words clarify the meaning of *it* in the original quotation.

In the quotation in the following sentence, the artist Gauguin's name is misspelled. The bracketed word *sic*, which means "so," tells readers that the person being quoted—not the writer who has picked up the quotation—made the mistake.

▶ **One admirer wrote, "She was the most striking woman I'd ever seen—a sort of wonderful combination of Mia Farrow and one of Gaugin's [*sic*] Polynesian nymphs."**

EXERCISE 43.1 Revise the sentences below, using parentheses and brackets correctly. Change any other punctuation as needed.

1. The words *media elite* have been said so often usually by people who are themselves elite members of the media that the phrase has taken on a life of its own.
2. Are the media really elite, and are they really liberal, as talk-show regulars (Ann Coulter, for example argue)?
3. Media critic Eric Alterman has coined the term "so-called liberal media" [SCLM] because he believes that the media have been intimidated by criticism.
4. An article in the *Journal of Communication* discussing the outcome of recent U.S. elections explained that "claiming the media are liberally biased perhaps has become a core rhetorical strategy" used by conservatives, qtd. in Alterman 14.
5. Some progressive groups (including Fairness and Accuracy in Reporting (FAIR)) keep track of media coverage of political issues.

43c Using dashes

Use dashes to insert a comment or to highlight material in a sentence.

▶ **The pleasures of reading itself—who doesn't remember?—were like those of Christmas cake, a sweet devouring.**

—Eudora Welty, "A Sweet Devouring"

A single dash can be used to emphasize material at the end of a sentence, to mark a sudden change in tone, to indicate hesitation in speech, or to introduce a summary or an explanation.

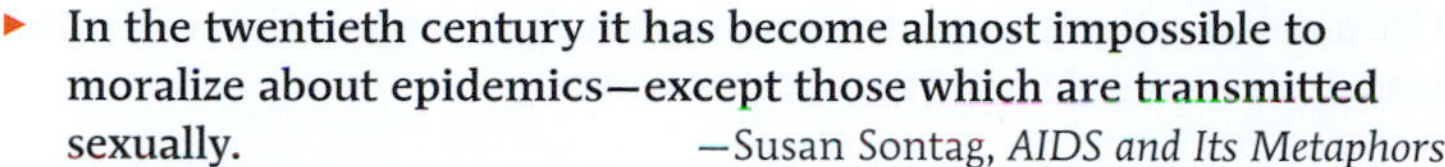

▸ **In the twentieth century it has become almost impossible to moralize about epidemics—except those which are transmitted sexually.**
—Susan Sontag, *AIDS and Its Metaphors*

▸ **In walking, the average adult person employs a motor mechanism that weighs about eighty pounds—sixty pounds of muscle and twenty pounds of bone.**
—Edwin Way Teale

Dashes give more emphasis than parentheses to the material they enclose or set off. Many word-processing programs automatically convert two typed hyphens with no spaces before or after into a solid dash.

EXERCISE 43.2 Revise the following sentences so that dashes are used correctly. Example:

In some states—California, for example—banks are no longer allowed to charge ATM users an additional fee for withdrawing money.

1. Many consumers accept that they have to pay additional fees for services like bank machines if they don't want to pay, they don't have to use the service.
2. Nevertheless—extra charges seem to be added to more and more services all the time.
3. Some of the charges are ridiculous why should hotels charge guests a fee for making a toll-free telephone call?
4. The hidden costs of service fees are irritating people feel that their bank accounts are being nibbled to death.
5. But some of the fees consumers are asked to pay—are more than simply irritating.

43d Using colons

Use a colon to introduce an explanation, an example, an appositive, a series, a list, or a quotation.

▸ **At the baby's one-month birthday party, Ah Po gave him the Four Valuable Things: ink, inkslab, paper, and brush.**
—Maxine Hong Kingston, *China Men*

Use a colon rather than a comma to introduce a quotation when the lead-in is a complete sentence on its own.

- **In his presentation, Tristan Harris made a stark claim: "Never before in history have the decisions of a handful of designers (mostly men, white, living in San Francisco, aged 25–30) working at three companies had so much impact on how millions of people around the world spend their attention."**

Colons are also used after salutations in letters; with numbers indicating hours, minutes, and seconds; with ratios; with biblical chapters and verses; with titles and subtitles; and in bibliographic entries in some styles.

- **Dear Dr. Goswami:**
- **4:59 PM**
- **a ratio of 5:1**
- **Ecclesiastes 3:1**
- ***Hillbilly Elegy: A Memoir of a Family and Culture in Crisis***
- **Boston, MA: Bedford/St. Martin's**

Misused colons. Do not put a colon between a **verb** and its **object** or complement (unless the object is a quotation), between a **preposition** and its object, or after such expressions as *such as*, *especially*, and *including*.

- **Some natural fibers are: cotton, wool, silk, and linen.**
- **In poetry, additional power may come from devices such as: simile, metaphor, and alliteration.**

EXERCISE 43.3 Insert a colon in each of the following sentences that needs one. Remove any misused colons. Example:

I like most seafood except: salmon, oysters, and clams.

1. The reading at their wedding Mass was from 1 Corinthians 13, 4–7.
2. The emcee looked out at the crowd and dared us to make more noise "I can't hear you!"
3. All we could do was watch as the other boats reeled in fish after fish, bass, pike, trout, and perch.

4. Rose has trophies for several different sports, including: basketball, lacrosse, softball, and soccer.
5. My roommate's annoying habits include: forgetting to lock the door, leaving dirty dishes in the sink, and playing loud video games late at night.

43e Using slashes

Use a slash to separate alternatives.

▶ **Then there was Daryl, the cabdriver/bartender.**

—John L'Heureux, *The Handmaid of Desire*

Use a slash, preceded and followed by a space, to divide lines of poetry quoted within running text.

▶ **The speaker of Sonnet 130 says of his mistress, "I love to hear her speak, yet well I know / That music hath a far more pleasing sound."**

Slashes also separate parts of fractions and Internet addresses: 1/3, https://nytimes.com.

43f Using ellipses

An ellipsis is three equally spaced dots that indicate that something has been omitted from a quoted passage. Just as you should carefully use quotation marks around any material that you are quoting directly from a source, so you should carefully use an ellipsis to indicate that you have left out part of a quotation that otherwise appears to be a complete sentence. Ellipses have been used in the following example to indicate two omissions—one in the middle of the first sentence and one at the end of the second sentence.

ORIGINAL TEXT

▶ **The quasi-official division of the population into three economic classes called high-, middle-, and low-income groups rather misses the point, because as a class indicator the amount of money is not as important as the source.**

—Paul Fussell, "Notes on Class"

WITH ELLIPSES

▸ **As Paul Fussell argues, "The quasi-official division of the population into three economic classes . . . rather misses the point. . . ."**

When you omit the last part of a quoted sentence, add a period before the ellipsis—for a total of four dots. Be sure a complete sentence comes before the four dots. If your shortened quotation ends with a source citation (such as a page number, a name, or a title), place the documentation source in parentheses after the three ellipsis points and the closing quotation mark but before the period.

▸ **Packer argues, "The Administration is right to reconsider its strategy . . ." (34).**

You can also use an ellipsis to indicate a pause or a hesitation in speech in the same way that you can use a dash for that purpose. (For more uses of ellipses in informal writing, see 40d.)

▸ **Then the voice, husky and familiar, came to wash over us—"The winnah, and still heavyweight champeen of the world . . . Joe Louis."** —Maya Angelou, *I Know Why the Caged Bird Sings*

You are probably used to seeing ellipses everywhere on social media. Author Clay Shirkey thinks the "ellipsis explosion" results from people trying to emulate speaking, with ellipses used to indicate a pause in the way that "ah" or "uh" does in speech. But overuse can get out of hand and lead to sloppy writing. When you use ellipses, make sure you use them to good effect.

EXERCISE 43.4 Read the following passage. Then assume that the underlined portions have been left out in a reprinting of the passage. Indicate how you would use ellipses to indicate those deletions. Example:

Saving money is difficult ~~for young people in entry-level positions~~ . . . but it is important.

Should young people who are just getting started in their careers think about saving for retirement? Those who begin to save in their twenties are making a wise financial decision. They are putting away money that can earn compound interest for decades. Even if they save only a hundred dollars a month, and even if they stop saving when they hit age thirty-five, the total forty years later will be impressive. On the other hand, people who wait until they are fifty to begin saving will have far less money put aside at the age of sixty-five.

44 Capital Letters

Capital letters are a key signal in everyday life. Look around any store to see their importance: you can shop for Levi's or *any* blue jeans, for Pepsi or *any* cola, for Kleenex or *any* tissue. In each of these instances, the capital letter indicates the name of a particular brand.

44a Capitalizing the first word of a sentence

With very few exceptions, capitalize the first word of a sentence. If you are quoting a full sentence, capitalize its first word.

▸ **Kennedy said, "Let us never negotiate out of fear."**

Capitalization of a nonquoted sentence following a colon is optional.

▸ **Gould cites the work of Darwin: The [*or* the] theory of natural selection incorporates the principle of evolutionary ties among all animals.**

Capitalize a sentence within parentheses unless the parenthetical sentence is inserted into another sentence.

▸ **Gould cites the work of Darwin. (Other researchers cite more recent evolutionary theorists.)**

▸ **Gould cites the work of Darwin (see p. 150).**

When citing poetry, follow the capitalization of the original poem. Though most poets capitalize the first word of each line in a poem, some do not.

▸ **Morning sun heats up the young beech tree**
leaves and almost lights them into fireflies

—June Jordan, "Aftermath"

Mechanics: Capital Letters > LearningCurve

44b Capitalizing proper nouns and proper adjectives

Capitalize proper **nouns** (those naming specific persons, places, and things) and most **adjectives** formed from proper nouns. All other nouns are common nouns and are not capitalized unless they are used as part of a proper noun: *a street*, but *Elm Street*.

Capitalized nouns and adjectives include personal names; nations, nationalities, and languages; months, days of the week, and holidays (but not seasons of the year); geographical names; structures and monuments; ships, trains, aircraft, and spacecraft; organizations, businesses, and government institutions; academic institutions and courses; historical events and eras; and religions, with their deities, followers, and sacred writings. For trade names, follow the capitalization you see in company advertising or on the product itself.

PROPER	COMMON
Alfred Hitchcock, Hitchcockian	a director
Brazil, Brazilian	a nation, a language
Pacific Ocean	an ocean
Challenger	a spacecraft
Library of Congress	a federal agency
Political Science 102	a political science course
the Qur'an	a holy book
Catholicism	a religion
Cheerios, iPhone	cereal, a smartphone
Halloween	a holiday in the fall

44c Capitalizing titles before proper names

When used alone or following a proper name, most titles are not capitalized. One common exception is the word *president*, which many writers capitalize whenever it refers to the President of the United States.

Professor Gordon Chang	my history professor
Dr. Teresa Ramirez	Teresa Ramirez, our doctor

 For Multilingual Writers

Learning English Capitalization

Capitalization systems vary considerably. Arabic, Chinese, Hebrew, and Hindi, for example, do not use capital letters at all. English may be the only language to capitalize the first-person singular pronoun (*I*), but Dutch and German capitalize some forms of the second-person pronoun (*you*)—and German also capitalizes all nouns.

44d Capitalizing titles of works

Capitalize most words in titles of books, articles, speeches, stories, essays, plays, poems, documents, films, paintings, and musical compositions. Do not capitalize articles (*a*, *an*, *the*), **prepositions**, **conjunctions**, and the *to* in an **infinitive** unless they are the first or last words in a title or subtitle.

Walt Whitman: A Life	Declaration of Independence
"As Time Goes By"	*Hamilton*
"Lemonade"	*The Living Dead*

44e Revising unnecessary capitalization

Capitalize compass directions only if the word designates a specific geographical region.

- ▶ John Muir headed west, motivated by the desire to explore.
- ▶ Water rights are an increasingly contentious issue in the West.

Capitalize family relationships only if the word is used as part of a name or as a substitute for the name.

- ▶ When she was a child, my mother shared a room with my aunt.
- ▶ I could always tell when Mother was annoyed with Aunt Rose.

EXERCISE 44.1 Capitalize words as needed in each of the following sentences. Example:

T S E T W L F F
t. s. eliot, who wrote *the waste land*, was an editor at faber and faber.

1. oscar isaac, who plays poe dameron in the *star wars* franchise, was born in guatemala.
2. the battle of lexington and concord was fought in april 1775.
3. i will cite the novels of vladimir nabokov, in particular *pnin* and *lolita.*
4. i wondered if my new levi's were faded enough.
5. We drove east over the hudson river on the tappan zee bridge.

45 Abbreviations and Numbers

Anytime you look up an address, you see an abundance of abbreviations and numbers, as in the following listing from a Google map:

Tarrytown Music Hall   13 Main St   Tarrytown, NY

Abbreviations and numbers allow writers to present detailed information in a small amount of space.

45a Using abbreviations

Certain titles are normally abbreviated.

Ms. Lisa Ede	Henry Louis Gates Jr.
Mr. Mark Otuteye	Cheryl Gold, MD

Religious, academic, and government titles should be spelled out in academic writing but can be abbreviated in other writing when they appear before a full name.

Rev. Fleming Rutledge	Reverend Rutledge
Prof. Jaime Mejía	Professor Mejía
Sen. Kamala Harris	Senator Harris

Business, government, and science terms. As long as you can be sure your readers will understand them, use common abbreviations such as *PBS*, *NASA*, and *DNA*. If an abbreviation may be unfamiliar, spell out the full term the first time you use it, and give the abbreviation in parentheses; after that, you can use the abbreviation by itself. Use abbreviations such as *Co.*, *Inc.*, *Corp.*, and *&* only if they are part of a company's official name.

- ▶ **The Comprehensive Test Ban (CTB) Treaty was first proposed in the 1950s. For those nations signing it, the CTB would bring to a halt all nuclear weapons testing.**
- ▶ **Sears, Roebuck & Co. was the only large ~~corp.~~ corporation in town.**

With numbers. The following abbreviations are acceptable with specific years and times.

399 BCE ("before the Common Era") *or* 399 BC ("before Christ")
49 CE ("Common Era") *or* AD 49 (*anno Domini*, Latin for "year of our Lord")
11:15 AM (*or* a.m.)
9:00 PM (*or* p.m.)

Symbols such as % and $ are acceptable with figures (*$11*) in academic writing, but not with words (*eleven dollars*). Units of measurement can be abbreviated in charts and graphs (*4 in.*) but not in the body of a paper (*four inches*).

In notes and source citations. Some Latin abbreviations required in notes and in source citations are not appropriate in the body of a paper.

cf.	compare (*confer*)
e.g.	for example (*exempli gratia*)
et al.	and others (*et alii/et aliae*)
etc.	and so forth (*et cetera*)
i.e.	that is (*id est*)
N.B.	note well (*nota bene*)

In addition, except in notes and source citations, do not abbreviate such terms as *chapter*, *page*, and *volume* or the names of months, states, cities, or countries. Two exceptions are *Washington, D.C.*, and *U.S.* The latter abbreviation is acceptable as an **adjective** but not as a **noun**: *U.S. borders* but *in the United States.*

EXERCISE 45.1 Revise each of the following sentences to eliminate any abbreviations that would be inappropriate in academic writing. If a sentence is correct, write *Correct.* Example:

> international
> **The ~~intl.~~ sport of belt sander racing began in a hardware store.**

1. Nielson Hardware in Point Roberts, WA, was the site of the world's first belt sander race in 1989.
2. The power tools are placed on a thirty-ft. track and plugged in; the sander to reach the end first wins.
3. Today, the International Belt Sander Drag Race Association (IBSDRA) sponsors tours of winning sanders, an international championship, and a website that sells IBSDRA T-shirts.
4. An average race lasts two seconds, but the world champion modified sander raced the track in 1.52 secs.
5. The fastest sanders run on very coarse sandpaper—a no. sixteen grit is an excellent choice if it's available.

45b Using numbers

If you can write out a number in one or two words, do so. Use figures for longer numbers.

> thirty-eight
> ▸ **Her screams were ignored by ~~38~~ people.**

> 216
> ▸ **A baseball is held together by ~~two hundred sixteen~~ red stitches.**

If one of several numbers *of the same kind* in the same sentence requires a figure, you should use figures for all the numbers in that sentence.

> $100
> ▸ **An audio system can range in cost from ~~one hundred dollars~~ to $2,599.**

When a sentence begins with a number, either spell out the number or rewrite the sentence.

Taxpayers spent sixteen million dollars for
▸ 119 years of CIA labor. ~~cost taxpayers sixteen million dollars.~~

In general, use figures for the following:

ADDRESSES	23 Main Street; 175 Fifth Avenue
DATES	May 13, 2004; 30 August 2007; 4 BCE; the 1860s
DECIMALS AND FRACTIONS	65.34; 8½
EXACT AMOUNTS OF MONEY	$7,348; $1.46 trillion; $2.50; thirty-five (*or* 35) cents
PERCENTAGES	77 percent (*or* 77%)
SCORES AND STATISTICS	an 8–3 Red Sox victory; an average age of 22
TIME OF DAY	6:00 AM (*or* a.m.)

EXERCISE 45.2 Revise the numbers in the following sentences as necessary for correctness and consistency. If a sentence is correct, write *Correct*. Example:

> There are 365 ~~three hundred sixty-five~~ days in a year, except for leap years, which have 366 ~~three hundred sixty-six~~ days.

1. *The Simpsons* has been on the air for more than 28 seasons, making it the longest-running prime-time series ever in American television.
2. After 4 years of college, I expect to graduate on June ten, 2019.
3. The hotel is located at three-zero-one Dauphin Street, New Orleans, Louisiana.
4. The last time she checked, Kira had 3,457 friends on Facebook; I have only eighty-two, and I like it that way!
5. 248 new members joined the public radio station during this year's pledge drive, compared with just 92 new members last year.

46 Italics

The slanted type known as *italics* is more than just a pretty typeface. Indeed, italics give words special meaning or emphasis. In the sentence "Many people read *People* on the subway every day," the italics (and the capital letter) tell us that *People* is a publication. You may use your computer to produce italic type; if not, underline words that you would otherwise italicize.

46a Italicizing titles

In general, use italics for titles and subtitles of long works; use quotation marks for shorter works (42b).

BOOKS	*Fun Home: A Family Tragicomic*
CHOREOGRAPHIC WORKS	Agnes de Mille's *Rodeo*
FILMS AND VIDEOS	*Black Panther*
LONG MUSICAL WORKS	*The Magic Flute*
LONG POEMS	*Bhagavad Gita*
MAGAZINES AND JOURNALS	*Ebony;* the *New England Journal of Medicine*
NEWSPAPERS	the Cleveland *Plain Dealer*
PAINTINGS AND SCULPTURE	Georgia O'Keeffe's *Black Iris*
PAMPHLETS	Thomas Paine's *Common Sense*
PLAYS	*Two Trains Running*
RADIO SERIES	*All Things Considered*
ALBUM-LENGTH RECORDINGS	Kendrick Lamar's *Damn*
SOFTWARE	*Quicken*
TELEVISION SERIES	*GLOW*

Do not italicize titles of sacred books, such as the Bible and the Qur'an; public documents, such as the Constitution and the Magna Carta; or your own papers.

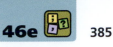

46b Italicizing words, letters, and numbers used as terms

- On the back of LeBron James's jersey was the famous *23*.
- One characteristic of some New York speech is the absence of postvocalic *r*—for example, pronouncing the word *four* as "fouh."

46c Italicizing non-English words

Italicize words from other languages unless they have become part of English—like the French "bourgeois" or the Italian "pasta," for example. If a word is in an English dictionary, it does not need italics.

- At last one of the phantom sleighs gliding along the street would come to a stop, and with gawky haste Mr. Burness in his fox-furred *shapka* would make for our door.

—Vladimir Nabokov, *Speak, Memory*

46d Italicizing names of aircraft, ships, and trains

Spirit of St. Louis Amtrak's *Silver Star* U.S.S. *Iowa*

46e Using italics for emphasis

Italics can help create emphasis in writing, but use them sparingly for this purpose. It is usually better to create emphasis with sentence structure and word choice.

- Great literature and a class of literate readers are nothing new in India. What is new is the emergence of a gifted generation of Indian writers *working in English*. —Salman Rushdie

Mechanics: Italics > LearningCurve

EXERCISE 46.1 In each of the following sentences, underline any words that should be italicized, and circle any italicized words that should not be. If a title requires quotation marks instead of italicization, add them. Example:

> **The *United States* still abounds with regional speech – for example, many people in the Appalachians still use local words such as crick and holler.**

1. *Regionalism*, a nineteenth-century literary movement, focused on the language and customs of people in areas of the country not yet affected by industrialization.
2. Regional writers produced some American classics, such as Mark Twain's Huckleberry Finn and James Fenimore Cooper's Last of the Mohicans.
3. Twain, not an admirer of Cooper's work, wrote a scathing essay about his predecessor called *The Literary Offenses of James Fenimore Cooper*.
4. Some of the most prolific regional writers were women like Kate Chopin, who wrote her first collection of short stories, Bayou Folk, to help support her family.
5. The stories in *Bayou Folk*, such as the famous *Désirée's Baby*, focus on the natives of rural Louisiana.

47 Hyphens

Hyphens are undoubtedly confusing to many people—hyphen problems are now one of the twenty most common surface errors in student writing (see p. 36). The confusion is understandable. Over time, the conventions for hyphen use in a given word can change (*tomorrow* was once spelled *to-morrow*). New words, even compounds such as *firewall*, generally don't use hyphens, but controversy continues to rage over whether to hyphenate *email* (or is it *e-mail*?). And some words are hyphenated when they serve one kind of purpose in a sentence and not when they serve another.

Checklist

Editing for Hyphens

- Double-check compound words to be sure they are properly closed up, separated, or hyphenated. If in doubt, consult a dictionary. (47a)
- Check all terms that have prefixes or suffixes to see whether you need hyphens. (47b)
- Do not hyphenate two-word verbs or word groups that serve as subject complements. (47c)

47a Using hyphens with compound words

Compound nouns. Some are one word (*rowboat*), some are separate words (*hard drive*), and some require hyphens (*sister-in-law*). You should consult a dictionary to be sure.

Compound adjectives. Hyphenate most compound **adjectives** that precede a noun, but not those that follow a noun.

a *well-liked* boss	My boss is *well liked.*
a *six-foot* plank	The plank is *six feet long.*

In general, the reason for hyphenating compound adjectives is to make meaning clear.

- **Designers often use potted plants as living-room dividers.**

  Without the hyphen, *living* may seem to modify *room dividers.*

Never hyphenate an *-ly* adverb and an adjective.

- **They used a widely-distributed mailing list.**

Fractions and compound numbers. Use a hyphen to write out fractions and to spell out compound numbers from twenty-one to ninety-nine.

one-seventh fifty-four thousand

47b Using hyphens with prefixes and suffixes

The majority of words containing prefixes or suffixes are written without hyphens, such as *antiwar* or *Romanesque*. Following are some exceptions:

BEFORE CAPITALIZED BASE WORDS	un-American, non-Catholic
WITH FIGURES	pre-1960, post-1945
WITH CERTAIN PREFIXES AND SUFFIXES	all-state, ex-partner, self-possessed, quasi-legislative, mayor-elect, fifty-odd
WITH COMPOUND BASE WORDS	pre-high school, post-cold war
FOR CLARITY OR EASE OF READING	re-sign, anti-inflation, troll-like

Re-sign means "sign again"; the hyphen distinguishes it from *resign*, which means "quit." In *anti-inflation* and *troll-like*, the hyphens separate confusing clusters of vowels and consonants.

47c Avoiding unnecessary hyphens

Unnecessary hyphens are at least as common a problem as omitted ones. Do not hyphenate the parts of a two-word verb such as *depend on*, *turn off*, or *tune out* (35b).

- **Each player must pick~~-~~up a medical form before volleyball tryouts.**

  The words *pick up* act as a verb and should not be hyphenated.

However, be careful to check that two words do indeed function as a verb in the sentence; if they function as an adjective, a hyphen may be needed.

- **Let's sign up for the early class.**

  The verb *sign up* should not have a hyphen.

- **Where is the sign-up sheet?**

  The adjective *sign-up*, which modifies the noun *sheet*, needs a hyphen.

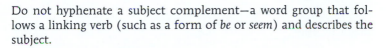

Do not hyphenate a subject complement—a word group that follows a linking verb (such as a form of *be* or *seem*) and describes the subject.

- **Audrey is almost fourteen-years-old.**

EXERCISE 47.1 Insert hyphens as needed. A dictionary will help you with some of these items. If an item does not require a hyphen, write *Correct*. Example:

full-bodied wine

1. a thirty nine year old woman
2. my ex mother in law
3. singer songwriter Leslie Feist
4. devil may care attitude
5. widely known poet

Glossary of Usage

Conventions of usage might be called the "good manners" of discourse. And just as manners vary from culture to culture and time to time, so do conventions of usage. Matters of usage, like other language choices you must make, depend on what your purpose is and on what is appropriate for a particular audience at a particular time.

a, an Use *a* with a word that begins with a consonant (*a book*), a consonant sound such as "y" or "w" (*a euphoric moment, a one-sided match*), or a sounded *h* (*a hemisphere*). Use *an* with a word that begins with a vowel (*an umbrella*), a vowel sound (*an X-ray*), or a silent *h* (*an honor*).

accept, except The verb *accept* means "receive" or "agree to." *Except* is usually a preposition that means "aside from" or "excluding." *All the plaintiffs except Mr. Kim decided to accept the settlement.*

advice, advise The noun *advice* means "opinion" or "suggestion"; the verb *advise* means "offer advice." *Doctors advise everyone not to smoke, but many people ignore the advice.*

affect, effect As a verb, *affect* means "influence" or "move the emotions of"; as a noun, it means "emotions" or "feelings." *Effect* is a noun meaning "result"; less commonly, it is a verb meaning "bring about." *The storm affected a large area. Its effects included widespread power failures. The drug effected a major change in the patient's affect.*

aggravate The formal meaning is "make worse." *Having another mouth to feed aggravated their poverty*. In academic and professional writing, avoid using *aggravate* to mean "irritate" or "annoy."

all ready, already *All ready* means "fully prepared." *Already* means "previously." *We were all ready for Lucy's party when we learned that she had already left.*

all right, alright Avoid the spelling *alright*.

all together, altogether *All together* means "all in a group" or "gathered in one place." *Altogether* means "completely" or "everything considered." *When the board members were all together, their mutual distrust was altogether obvious.*

allude, elude *Allude* means "refer indirectly." *Elude* means "avoid" or "escape from." *The candidate did not even allude to her opponent. The suspect eluded the police for several days.*

allusion, illusion An *allusion* is an indirect reference. An *illusion* is a false or misleading appearance. *The speaker's allusion to the Bible created an illusion of piety.*

a lot Avoid the spelling *alot*.

already See *all ready, already*.

alright See *all right, alright*.

altogether See *all together, altogether*.

among, between In referring to two things or people, use *between*. In referring to three or more, use *among*. *The relationship between the twins is different from that among the other three children.*

amount, number Use *amount* with quantities you cannot count; use *number* for quantities you can count. *A small number of volunteers cleared a large amount of brush.*

an See *a, an*.

and/or Avoid this term except in business or legal writing. Instead of *fat and/or protein*, write *fat, protein, or both*.

any body, anybody, any one, anyone *Anybody* and *anyone* are pronouns meaning "any person." *Anyone* [or *anybody*] *would enjoy this film. Any body* is an adjective modifying a noun. *Any body of water has its own ecology. Any one* is two adjectives or a pronoun modified by an adjective. *Customers could buy only two sale items at any one time. The winner could choose any one of the prizes.*

anyplace In academic and professional discourse, use *anywhere* instead.

anyway, anyways In writing, use *anyway*, not *anyways*.

apt, liable, likely *Likely to* means "probably will," and *apt to* means "inclines or tends to." In many instances, they are interchangeable. *Liable* often carries a more negative sense and is also a legal term meaning "obligated" or "responsible."

as, as if, like In academic and professional writing, use *as* or *as if* instead of *like* to introduce a clause. *The dog howled as if* [not *like*] *it were in pain. She did as* [not *like*] *I suggested.*

assure, ensure, insure *Assure* means "convince" or "promise"; its direct object is usually a person or persons. *She assured voters she would not raise taxes. Ensure* and *insure* both mean "make certain," but *insure* usually refers specifically to protection against financial loss. *When the city rationed water to ensure that the supply would last, the Browns could no longer afford to insure their car-wash business.*

as to Do not use *as to* as a substitute for *about. Karen was unsure about* [not *as to*] *Bruce's intentions.*

at, where See *where.*

awhile, a while Always use *a while* after a preposition such as *for*, *in*, or *after. We drove awhile and then stopped for a while.*

bad, badly Use *bad* after a linking verb such as *be*, *feel*, or *seem.* Use *badly* to modify an action verb, an adjective, or another verb. *The hostess felt bad because the dinner was badly prepared.*

bare, bear Use *bare* to mean "uncovered" and *bear* to refer to the animal or to mean "carry" or "endure": *The walls were bare. The emptiness was hard to bear.*

being as, being that In academic or professional writing, use *because* or *since* instead of these expressions. *Because* [not *being as*] *Romeo killed Tybalt, he was banished to Padua.*

beside, besides *Beside* is a preposition meaning "next to." *Besides* can be a preposition meaning "other than" or an adverb meaning "in addition." *No one besides Francesca would sit beside him.*

between See *among, between.*

brake, break *Brake* means "to stop" and also refers to a stopping mechanism: *Check the brakes. Break* means "fracture" or an interruption: *The coffee break was too short.*

breath, breathe *Breath* is a noun; *breathe*, a verb. "*Breathe*," *said the nurse, so June took a deep breath.*

bring, take Use *bring* when an object is moved from a farther to a nearer place; use *take* when the opposite is true. *Take the box to the post office; bring back my mail.*

can, may *Can* refers to ability and *may* to possibility or permission. *Since I can ski the slalom well, I may win the race.*

can't hardly *Hardly* has a negative meaning; therefore, *can't hardly* is a double negative. This expression is commonly used in some varieties of English but is not used in academic English. *Tim can* [not *can't*] *hardly wait.*

censor, censure *Censor* means "remove that which is considered offensive." *Censure* means "formally reprimand." *The newspaper censored stories that offended advertisers. The legislature censured the official for misconduct.*

compare to, compare with *Compare to* means "regard as similar." *Jamie compared the loss to a kick in the head. Compare with* means "examine to find differences or similarities." *Compare Tim Burton's films with David Lynch's.*

complement, compliment *Complement* means "go well with." *Compliment* means "praise." *Guests complimented her on how her earrings complemented her gown.*

comprise, compose *Comprise* means "contain." *Compose* means "make up." *The class comprises twenty students. Twenty students compose the class.*

conscience, conscious *Conscience* means "a sense of right and wrong." *Conscious* means "awake" or "aware." *Lisa was conscious of a guilty conscience.*

consequently, subsequently *Consequently* means "as a result"; *subsequently* means "then." *He quit, and subsequently his wife lost her job; consequently, they had to sell their house.*

continual, continuous *Continual* means "repeated at regular or frequent intervals." *Continuous* means "continuing or connected without a break." *The damage done by continuous erosion was increased by the continual storms.*

could of *Have*, not *of*, should follow *could, would, should*, or *might*. *We could have* [not *of*] *invited them.*

criteria, criterion *Criterion* means "standard of judgment" or "necessary qualification." *Criteria* is the plural form. *Image is the wrong criterion for choosing a president.*

data *Data* is the plural form of the Latin word *datum*, meaning "fact." Although *data* is used informally as either singular or plural, in academic or professional writing, treat *data* as plural. *These data indicate that fewer people are smoking.*

different from, different than *Different from* is generally preferred in academic and professional writing, although both of these phrases are widely used. *Her lab results were no different from* [not *than*] *his.*

discreet, discrete *Discreet* means "tactful" or "prudent." *Discrete* means "separate" or "distinct." *The leader's discreet efforts kept all the discrete factions unified.*

disinterested, uninterested *Disinterested* means "unbiased." *Uninterested* means "indifferent." *Finding disinterested jurors was difficult. She was uninterested in the verdict.*

distinct, distinctive *Distinct* means "separate" or "well defined." *Distinctive* means "characteristic." *Germany includes many distinct regions, each with a distinctive accent.*

doesn't, don't *Doesn't* is the contraction for *does not*. Use it with *he*, *she*, *it*, and singular nouns. *Don't* stands for *do not*; use it with *I*, *you*, *we*, *they*, and plural nouns.

each other, one another Use *each other* in sentences involving two subjects and *one another* in sentences involving more than two.

effect See *affect, effect.*

elicit, illicit The verb *elicit* means "draw out." The adjective *illicit* means "illegal." *The police elicited from the criminal the names of others involved in illicit activities.*

elude See *allude, elude.*

emigrate from, immigrate to *Emigrate from* means "move away from one's country." *Immigrate to* means "move to another country." *We emigrated from Norway in 1999. We immigrated to the United States.*

ensure See *assure, ensure, insure.*

enthused, enthusiastic Use *enthusiastic* rather than *enthused* in academic and professional writing.

equally as good Replace this redundant phrase with *equally good* or *as good*.

every day, everyday *Everyday* is an adjective meaning "ordinary." *Every day* is an adjective and a noun, meaning "each day." *I wore everyday clothes almost every day.*

every one, everyone *Everyone* is a pronoun. *Every one* is an adjective and a pronoun, referring to each member of a group. *Because he began after everyone else, David could not finish every one of the problems.*

except See *accept, except.*

explicit, implicit *Explicit* means "directly or openly expressed." *Implicit* means "indirectly expressed or implied." *The explicit message of the ad urged consumers to buy the product, while the implicit message promised popularity if they did so.*

farther, further *Farther* refers to physical distance. *How much farther is it to Munich? Further* refers to time or degree. *I want to avoid further delays.*

fewer, less Use *fewer* with nouns that can be counted. Use *less* with general amounts that you cannot count. *The world needs fewer bombs and less hostility.*

firstly, secondly, etc. *First, second,* etc., are more common in U.S. English.

flaunt, flout *Flaunt* means to "show off." *Flout* means to "mock" or "scorn." *The drug dealers flouted authority by flaunting their wealth.*

former, latter *Former* refers to the first and *latter* to the second of two things previously mentioned. *Kathy and Anna are athletes; the former plays tennis, and the latter runs.*

further See *farther, further.*

good, well *Good* is an adjective and should not be used as a substitute for the adverb *well. Gabriel is a good host who cooks well.*

hanged, hung *Hanged* refers to executions; *hung* is used for all other meanings.

hardly See *can't hardly.*

herself, himself, myself, yourself Do not use these reflexive pronouns as subjects or as objects unless they are necessary. *Jane and I* [not *myself*] *agree. They invited John and me* [not *myself*].

he/she, his/her Better solutions for avoiding sexist language are to eliminate pronouns entirely or to make the subject plural. Instead of writing *Everyone should carry his/her driver's license,* try *Drivers should carry their licenses* or *People should carry their driver's licenses.*

himself See *herself, himself, myself, yourself.*

hopefully *Hopefully* is often used informally to mean "it is hoped," but its formal meaning is "with hope." *Sam watched the roulette wheel hopefully* [not *Hopefully, Sam will win*].

hung See *hanged, hung.*

illicit See *elicit, illicit.*

illusion See *allusion, illusion.*

immigrate to See *emigrate from, immigrate to.*

implicit See *explicit, implicit.*

imply, infer To *imply* is to suggest indirectly. To *infer* is to guess or conclude on the basis of indirect suggestion. *The note implied they were planning a small wedding; we inferred we would not be invited.*

inside of, outside of Use *inside* and *outside* instead. *The class regularly met outside* [not *outside of*] *the building.*

insure See *assure, ensure, insure.*

irregardless, regardless *Irregardless* is a double negative. Use *regardless.*

is when, is where These vague expressions are often incorrectly used in definitions. *Schizophrenia is a psychotic condition in which* [not *is when* or *is where*] *a person withdraws from reality.*

its, it's *Its* is the possessive form of *it*. *It's* is a contraction for *it is* or *it has*. *It's important to observe the rat before it eats its meal.*

kind, sort, type These singular nouns should be modified with *this* or *that*, not *these* or *those*, and followed by other singular nouns, not plural nouns. *Wear this kind of dress* [not *those kind of dresses*].

know, no Use *know* to mean "understand." *No* is the opposite of *yes*.

later, latter *Later* means "after some time." *Latter* refers to the second of two items named. *Juan and Chad won all their early matches, but the latter was injured later in the season.*

latter See *former, latter* and *later, latter.*

lay, lie *Lay* means "place" or "put." Its main forms are *lay, laid, laid*. It generally has a direct object, specifying what has been placed. *She laid her books on the desk. Lie* means "recline" or "be positioned" and does not take a direct object. Its main forms are *lie, lay, lain. She lay awake until two.*

leave, let *Leave* means "go away." *Let* means "allow." *Leave alone* and *let alone* are interchangeable. *Let me leave now, and leave* [or let] *me alone from now on!*

lend, loan In academic and professional writing, do not use *loan* as a verb; use *lend* instead. *Please lend me your pen so that I may fill out this application for a loan.*

less See *fewer, less.*

let See *leave, let.*

liable See *apt, liable, likely.*

lie See *lay, lie.*

like See *as, as if, like.*

likely See *apt, liable, likely.*

literally *Literally* means "actually" or "exactly as stated." Use it to stress the truth of a statement that might otherwise be understood as figurative. Do not use *literally* as an intensifier in a figurative statement. *Mirna was literally at the edge of her seat* may be accurate, but *Mirna is so hungry that she could literally eat a horse* is not.

loan See *lend, loan.*

loose, lose *Lose* is a verb meaning "misplace." *Loose* is an adjective that means "not securely attached." *Sew on that loose button before you lose it.*

lots, lots of Avoid these informal expressions meaning "much" or "many" in academic or professional discourse.

may See *can, may.*

may be, maybe *May be* is a verb phrase. *Maybe* is an adverb that means "perhaps." *He may be the head of the organization, but maybe someone else would handle a crisis better.*

might of See *could of.*

moral, morale A *moral* is a succinct lesson. *The moral of the story is that generosity is rewarded. Morale* means "spirit" or "mood." *Office morale was low.*

myself See *herself, himself, myself, yourself.*

no See *know, no.*

nor, or Use *either* with *or* and *neither* with *nor.*

number See *amount, number.*

off, of Use *off* without *of. The spaghetti slipped off* [not *off of*] *the plate.*

OK, O.K., okay All are acceptable spellings, but avoid the term in academic and professional discourse.

one another See *each other, one another.*

or See *nor, or.*

outside of See *inside of, outside of.*

passed, past Use *passed* to mean "went by" or "received a passing grade": *The marching band passed the reviewing stand.* Use *past* to refer to a time before the present: *Historians study the past.*

per In formal writing, use the Latin *per* only in standard technical phrases such as *miles per hour*. Otherwise, find English equivalents. *As mentioned in* [not *As per*] *the latest report, the country's average daily food consumption is only 2,000 calories.*

percent, percentage Use *percent* with a specific number; use *percentage* with an adjective such as *large* or *small. Last year, 80 percent of the members were female. A large percentage of the members are women.*

plus *Plus* means "in addition to." *Your salary plus mine will cover our expenses.* In academic writing, do not use *plus* to mean "besides" or "moreover." *That dress does not fit me. Besides* [not *Plus*], *it is the wrong color.*

precede, proceed *Precede* means "come before"; *proceed* means "go forward." *Despite the storm that preceded the ceremony, the wedding proceeded on schedule.*

principal, principle When used as a noun, *principal* refers to a head official or an amount of money; when used as an adjective, it means "most significant." *Principle* means "fundamental law or belief." *Albert went to the principal and defended himself with the principle of free speech.*

proceed See *precede, proceed.*

quotation, quote *Quote* is a verb, and *quotation* is a noun. *He quoted the president, and the quotation* [not *quote*] *was preserved in history books.*

raise, rise *Raise* means "lift" or "move upward." (Referring to children, it means "bring up.") It takes a direct object; someone raises something. *The guests raised their glasses to toast. Rise* means "go upward." It does not take a direct object; something rises by itself. *She saw the steam rise from the pan.*

rarely ever Use *rarely* by itself, or use *hardly ever. When we were poor, we rarely went to the movies.*

real, really *Real* is an adjective, and *really* is an adverb. Do not substitute *real* for *really*. In academic and professional writing, do not use *real* or *really* to mean "very." *The old man walked very* [not *real* or *really*] *slowly.*

reason is because Use either *the reason is that* or *because*—not both. *The reason the copier stopped is that* [not *is because*] *the paper jammed.*

reason why Avoid this expression in formal writing. *The reason* [not *reason why*] *this book is short is market demand.*

regardless See *irregardless, regardless.*

respectfully, respectively *Respectfully* means "with respect." *Respectively* means "in the order given." *Karen and David are, respectively, a juggler and an acrobat. The children treated their grandparents respectfully.*

rise See *raise, rise.*

set, sit *Set* usually means "put" or "place" and takes a direct object. *Sit* refers to taking a seat and does not take an object. *Set your cup on the table, and sit down.*

should of See *could of.*

since Be careful not to use *since* ambiguously. In *Since I broke my leg, I've stayed home*, the word *since* might be understood to mean either "because" or "ever since."

sit See *set, sit.*

so In academic and professional writing, avoid using *so* alone to mean "very." Instead, follow *so* with *that* to show how the intensified condition leads to a result. *Aaron was so tired that he fell asleep at the wheel.*

someplace Use *somewhere* instead in academic and professional writing.

some time, sometime, sometimes *Some time* refers to a length of time. *Please leave me some time to dress. Sometime* means "at some indefinite later time." *Sometime I will take you to London. Sometimes* means "occasionally." *Sometimes I eat sushi.*

sort See *kind, sort, type.*

stationary, stationery *Stationary* means "standing still"; *stationery* means "writing paper." *When the bus was stationary, Pat took out stationery and wrote a note.*

subsequently See *consequently, subsequently.*

supposed to, used to Be careful to include the final *-d* in these expressions. *He is supposed to attend.*

sure, surely Avoid using *sure* as an intensifier. Instead, use *certainly. I was certainly glad to see you.*

take See *bring, take.*

than, then Use *than* in comparative statements. *The cat was bigger than the dog.* Use *then* when referring to a sequence of events. *I won, and then I cried.*

that, which A clause beginning with *that* singles out the item being described. *The book that is on the table is a good one* specifies the book on the table as opposed to some other book. A clause beginning with *which* may or may not single out the item, although some writers use *which* clauses only to add more information about an item being described. *The book, which is on the table, is a good one* contains a *which* clause between the commas. The clause simply adds extra, nonessential information about the book; it does not specify which book.

then See *than, then.*

they, them The pronouns *they* and *them* have traditionally been used to refer to plural antecedents. However, when the gender of a singular antecedent is not known or is nonspecific, *they* or *them* is increasingly seen as an acceptable and appropriate choice over singular pronouns such as *him* or *her*: *Someone left their jacket on the bus.*

thorough, threw, through *Thorough* means "complete": *After a thorough inspection, the restaurant reopened. Threw* is the past tense of *throw*, and *through* means "in one side and out the other": *He threw the ball through a window.*

to, too, two *To* generally shows direction. *Too* means "also." *Two* is the number. *We, too, are going to the meeting in two hours.* Avoid using *to* after *where*. *Where are you flying* [not *flying to*]?

two See *to, too, two*.

type See *kind, sort, type*.

uninterested See *disinterested, uninterested*.

unique Some people argue that unique means "one and only" and object to usage that suggests it means merely "unusual." In formal writing, avoid constructions such as *quite unique*.

used to See *supposed to, used to*.

very Avoid using *very* to intensify a weak adjective or adverb; instead, replace the adjective or adverb with a stronger, more precise, or more colorful word. Instead of *very nice*, for example, use *kind, warm, sensitive, endearing*, or *friendly*.

way, ways When referring to distance, use *way*. *Graduation was a long way* [not *ways*] *off*.

well See *good, well*.

where In formal writing, use *where* alone, not with words such as *at* and *to*. *Where are you going* [not *going to*]?

which See *that, which*.

who, whom In formal writing, use *who* if the word is the subject of the clause and *whom* if the word is the object of the clause. *Monica, who smokes incessantly, is my godmother*. (*Who* is the subject of the clause; the verb is *smokes*.) *Monica, whom I saw last winter, lives in Tucson*. (*Whom* is the object of the verb *saw*.) Because *whom* can seem excessively formal, some writers rephrase sentences to avoid it.

who's, whose *Who's* is a contraction for *who is* or *who has*. *Who's on the patio? Whose* is a possessive form. *Whose sculpture is in the garden? Whose is on the patio?*

would of See *could of*.

your, you're *Your* shows possession. *Bring your sleeping bag along. You're* is the contraction for *you are*. *You're in the wrong sleeping bag*.

yourself See *herself, himself, myself, yourself*.

Index

with Glossary of Terms

Words in **blue** are followed by a definition. **Boldface** terms in definitions are themselves defined elsewhere in this index.

A

a, an, 307, 309, 391
abbreviations, 361
abilities and disabilities, 253–54
"about" page, evaluating, 100
abstract
- APA style, 177, 195, 202
- CSE style, 234, 239
- evaluating, 102
- MLA style, 162

academic writing
- authority in, 2–3
- claim, 3
- directness and clarity, 3–4
- expectations for, 2–4, 67–69
- genres of, 67–73
- reflection, 40–41
- rhetorical analysis, 50–53
- "standard" English for, 255
- thesis, 3
- *See also* writing projects

accept, except, 391
accessibility of presentations, 253–54
acknowledgments of sources, 116–17

active voice, 286 The form of a **verb** when the **subject** performs the action: *Lata* <u>*sang*</u> *the chorus.*
- for conciseness, 282
- and passive voice, 282, 301–2
- shifts to passive voice, 286

AD, CE, 381
addresses and place names, commas for, 354

adjective, 36 A word that modifies, quantifies, identifies, or describes a **noun** or words acting as a noun.
- absolute concepts, 321
- capitalization, 32, 139, 141, 146, 177, 184, 186, 189, 195, 220, 225, 236, 377–80
- clause, commas with, 350
- comparatives and superlatives, 320–21
- compound, 36, 387
- coordinate, 352
- hyphens with, 36, 387
- after linking verb, 389
- proper, 32, 378

adverb, 317 A word that qualifies, modifies, limits, or defines a **verb**, an **adjective**, another adverb, or a **clause**, frequently answering the question *where? when? how? why? to what extent?* or *under what conditions?*
- absolute concepts, 321

adverb *(continued)*
clause, commas with, 350
comparatives and superlatives, 321
hyphens with, 387
after linking verbs, 319
adverbial particle, 337
advice, advise, 391
a few, many, 308
affect, effect, 391
aggravate, 391

agreement, 311 The correspondence between a **pronoun** and its **antecedent** in **person**, number, and gender (*Mr. Fox and his sister*) or between a **verb** and its **subject** in person and number (*She and Moe are friends*).

pronoun-antecedent, 326, 331–34
subject-verb, 311–16
varieties of English and forms of *be,* 317
alignment, in design, 17
a little, much, 307
all. See indefinite pronoun
all ready, already, 391
all right, alright, 391
all together, altogether, 391
allude, elude, 392
allusion, illusion, 392
a lot, 392
already, all ready, 391
alright, all right, 391
altogether, all together, 391
AM, a.m., 381
Amazon reviews, 39
Americans with Disabilities Act, 253
among, between, 392
amount, number, 392
an, a, the, 379
analogies, 59, 264
analysis, 6–7, 48. *See also* critical thinking and reading; evaluating sources; synthesis
and, 275
and/or, 392
annotated bibliography, 111–12. *See also* working bibliography
annotating, 47, 106

antecedent, 315, 326 The **noun** or noun **phrase** that a **pronoun** replaces.

agreement with pronouns, 326–33
agreement with verbs, 315
any. See indefinite pronoun
any body, anybody, any one, anyone, 392
anyplace, 392
anyway, anyways, 392

APA style, 174–209 The citation style guidelines issued by the American Psychological Association.

abstracts, 177
citing books, 186–89
citing digital sources, 190
citing other sources, 198–200
citing sources without models, 190
combining parts of models, 185
content notes, 175–76
database sources, 175
in-text citations, 178–82
list of examples, 178
parts of, 175
long quotations, 177

manuscript format, 176–77
parts of citations, 175
past tense in reports, 289
references
formatting, 184
list of examples, 181, 183
models for, 185–200
sample student writing, 200–209
signal phrases in, 178–80, 184
source maps
articles from databases, 194, 196
articles from print periodicals, 190
books, 187
tables or figures, 182
understanding, 174
verb tense in, 178
apostrophes, 362–65
appeals, in argument
emotional, 54
ethical, 54
logical, 54
Toulmin argument, 54–55

appositive, 351 A **noun** or noun **phrase** that adds identifying information to a preceding noun or noun phrase: *Zimbardo, an innovative researcher, designed the experiment.*

colons with, 373
commas with, 351
apt, liable, likely, 392
arguable statements, 56

argument, 53–66 A **text** that makes and supports a **claim**.

alternative, 57, 60
appeals, 54–55, 57–59
audience, considering, 7–8
elements of, 54–55
organizing, 59–60
sample student essay, 60–66
statements, examples of, 56
thesis or claim, 54–55
Toulmin argument, 54–55
articles (*a, an, the*), 379
articles from databases
citing
APA style, 194
Chicago style, 222
MLA style, 150
searching for, 93–94
articles in periodicals
capitalizing titles, 379
citing
APA style, 189–91
Chicago style, 219–24
CSE style, 239–40
MLA style, 146–48
evaluating, 102–3
popular and scholarly, 91–92
titles, styles for, 367–68
as, as if, like, 392
assignments. *See* writing projects
assumptions
about abilities and disabilities, 253–54
for arguments, 54–55, 57
audience and, 89, 246
cultural, 246
examining, 249–54
about gender and pronoun preferences, 250–52
about race and ethnicity, 252–53
in texts, 47, 49
assure, ensure, insure, 393
as to, 393
at, where, 393

attitude. *See* stance
audience
  analyzing, 7–8, 246–48
  appeals to, 54, 55, 56–59
  informal versus formal writing, 4–6, 248, 258–61
  sharing and reflecting with, 39–41
  stance and tone for, 8
  varieties of English language, 255–57
audio. *See* visuals and media
author credentials, 91, 98, 100
authority
  in academic writing, 2–3
  audience expectations, 247–48
  in sources, 91, 95, 98, 99, 113
  See also credibility
author listings
  APA style, 184–86
  Chicago style, 216–17
  CSE style, 237–44
  MLA style, 139–41
auxiliary verb, 293–96. *See also* helping verb
awhile, a while, 393

B

bad, badly, 319, 393
bar and line graphs, 20
bare, bear, 393
base form, 290–92 The form of a **verb** listed in a dictionary (*go*).
  conditional sentences, 304–5
  forming auxiliary verbs, 295
  with *may,* 293
BC, BCE, 381
been as auxiliary verb, 293–94
being as, being that, 393
between, 393
be verbs
  agreement with subjects, 291
  as irregular verbs, 290–91, 311
  and passive voice, 277–79, 294
  progressive tense, 294–95, 299
  in varieties of English, 296
  wordiness and, 281
bias, scrutinizing, 98
bibliographies
  annotated, 111–12
  APA style, 182–200
  Chicago style, 213–14, 215–30
  as library resources, 94
  MLA style, 128–29
  research project, 94
block quotations. *See* quotations, long
Blogger, 39
blogs or discussion groups, citing
  APA style, 197
  Chicago style, 227
  MLA style, 156
bookmarking online, 95
books
  capitalizing titles, 378, 379
  citing
    APA style, 186–89
    Chicago style, 216–19
    CSE style, 237–39
    MLA style, 141–46
  italics for titles, 384
both . . . and, 284. *See also* correlative conjunctions
brackets
  punctuation, 371–72
  for quotations, 114
  for *sic,* 372

brainstorming, 10
brake, break, 393
breath, breathe, 393
bring, take, 393
business terms, abbreviations, 381
but, 275. *See also* coordinating conjunctions

C

can, may, 393
can't hardly, 394
capital letters, 377–80
cartoons, 21

case, 326–28 The form of a **noun** or **pronoun** that reflects its grammatical role: *He ate* (subjective). *His food was cold* (possessive). *I saw him* (objective).

catalogs, library, 92–93
CE, AD, 381
censor, censure, 394
cf., compare (*confer*), 381
charts, 19, 22, 83. *See also* visuals and media
checklists
  analyzing texts, 48–49
  citing digital sources
    APA style, 192
    MLA style, 151
  citing sources without models
    APA style, 192
    Chicago style, 215
    MLA style, 139
  class blogs, wikis, and forums, 45
  common errors (Top Twenty), 28
  drafting, 13–14
  editing
    for commas, 348
    for hyphens, 387
    pronouns, 329
    subject-verb agreement, 313
    verbs, 293
  formatting references, 184
  paragraphs, strong, 16
  presentations, 84
  reference models, combining parts of, 185
  search techniques, 93
  subject-verb agreement, 292
  U.S. academic style, 3
  visuals and media, 22
  writing inventory, 23
chemistry lab report, 75–77

***Chicago* style, 210–33** Citation guidelines based on *The Chicago Manual of Style.*

  citations, in-text, 212–13
  citing sources without models, 215
  long quotations in, 212
  manuscript format, 211–24
  notes and bibliographic entries
    formatting, 215–18
    list of examples, 214–15
    models for, 215–30
  sample student writing, excerpts from, 230–34
  signal phrases, 213
  source maps
    articles from databases, 222
    works from websites, 226
  understanding, 210
  verb tense in, 114
  visuals, labeling, 212

claim, 3–4, 54 An arguable statement.

clarity in academic writing, 3–4

clause, 29 A group of words containing a **subject** and a **predicate**. An **independent clause** can stand alone as a **sentence**, while a **dependent clause** must be attached.

in comma splices, 338
commas with, 339
dangling modifier, 324–25
fixing fused sentences, 338–40
if clause, 303
joined with a dash, 340
that clause, 303
truths or scientific facts, 300

clichés, 264
close reading of poems, 72–75
clustering, 11
code meshing, 256

coherence, 15 Also called "flow," the quality that makes a **text** seem unified.

collaboration among student writers, 9–10
collective nouns
agreement with antecedents, 331
agreement with verbs, 313–14
colloquial language, 256, 369–70
colon, 373–74
capitalization with, 377
with a list or series, 359, 373
with quotation marks, 368–69
color
in design, 17, 18
in storyboarding, 13
commas
with adjective clauses, 350
with adverb clauses, 350
with appositives, 351
in compound sentences, 33–34
with contrasting elements, 353
with coordinating conjunctions, 32
with dates and addresses, 354
in direct address, 353
editing for, 348
with independent clauses, 347
with interjections, 353
with introductory elements, 29, 346
with items in a series, 32, 352
with nonrestrictive elements, 33, 349–51
with parenthetical and transitional expressions, 353
with quotation marks, 31, 355
with restrictive elements, 32, 349–51
splices, 34–35, 338
with tag questions, 353
unnecessary, 31–32, 356

comma splice, 34–35, 338–39 An error in formal writing resulting from joining two **independent clauses** with only a comma.

comment, as part of thesis statement, 11
common errors. *See* Top Twenty
common ground, building, 249–54
common knowledge, 117
communication, 249–54
community, or sense of place, 256–57

comparative, 320–21 The *-er* or *more* form of an **adjective** or **adverb** used to compare two things (*happier, more quickly*).

comparatives versus superlatives, 320–21
compare to, compare with, 394
comparisons, complete, 274
complement, compliment, 394
complements. *See* object complements; subject complements
complete sentences, 272–74
compliment, complement, 394
compose, comprise, 394
compound adjectives, 387
compound antecedents, 331
compound base words, hyphens with, 388
compound nouns, 387
compound numbers, 387
compound predicates, 343
compound sentences, 347
compound structures
  avoiding unneeded commas, 388–89
  commas with, 347
  consistency in, 274
  and pronouns, 328
compound subjects, 312–13
compound words, 265, 387
comprise, compose, 394

conciseness, 279–80 Using the fewest possible words to make a point effectively.

  in emails, 6
  in headings, 78
  in sentences, 279–80
  in summarizing, 48
conclusions
  of arguments, 60
  of presentations, 82
  of research projects, 120
conditional sentences, 304–5

conjunction, 32 A word or words joining **words, phrases,** or **clauses**. *See* **coordinating conjunctions**; **correlative conjunctions**; **subordinating conjunction**.

conjunctive adverb, 339 A word (such as *consequently, moreover,* or *nevertheless*) that modifies an **independent clause** following another independent clause. A conjunctive adverb generally follows a semicolon and is followed by a comma: *Thoreau lived simply at Walden; however, he regularly joined his aunt for tea in Concord.*

  commas with, 339
  to fix fused sentences, 339
connotation, 261
conscience, conscious, 394
consequently, subsequently, 394
consistency, in sentences, 272–66
content notes (APA) style, 175–76
context
  cultural, 48
  in research, 46, 89
  for public writing, 67, 78–81
  See also rhetorical situation
continual, continuous, 394
contractions, 364
contrast, in design, 17
conventions of writing. *See* genre; "standard" English
convince, arguing to, 55
coordinate adjectives, 352

coordinating conjunctions, 32, 275 The words *and, but, for, nor, or, so,* and *yet,* which give the same emphasis to both the elements they join: *Restaurants are expensive, so I cook.*

commas with, 339
to fix fused sentences, 339
to link clauses, 339, 347, 357
no commas with, 32, 319
semicolons with, 339, 358
yet, 275, 339
coordination and subordination, 275–79
copyrighted materials, 112, 116

correlative conjunctions, 284 Paired **conjunctions** (*both . . . and, either . . . or, neither . . . nor, not only . . . but also*) used to connect equivalent elements.

parallelism, 284
could of, would of, should of, might of, 394

count noun, 306 A **noun** referring to something that can be directly counted: *women, trees.* Contrast with **noncount noun**.

court cases, in MLA style, 163
credibility, 257
criteria, criterion, 394
critical thinking and reading, 46–50

CSE style, 234–44 The citation style guidelines issued by the Council of Science Editors.

in-text citations, 235–36
manuscript format, 234–35
references
formatting, 236
list of examples, 237
models for, 237–42
sample student writing, 242–44
cultures, communication across, 246–48
currency, of source, 102

D

-d, -ed endings, 290
dangling modifiers, 324–25
dashes
with clauses, 372–73
with quotation marks, 369
data, 394
databases and indexes, as library resources, 93–94
dates and addresses
commas in, 354
numbers in, 383
deadlines, for collaborating, 10
definitions and quotation marks, 367–68
denotation, 261

dependent clause, 271, 273 Sometimes called a "subordinate clause," a word group that contains a **subject** and a **predicate** but can't stand alone as a **sentence** because it begins with either a **subordinating conjunction** (*because, although*) or a **relative pronoun** (*that, which*).

fixing clause fragments, 343–44
fixing comma splices, 340
in sentence openings, 271
subjunctive mood and, 302
with *who, whom*, 327–28

design decisions, 17–22. *See also* formatting; visuals and media
details, in paragraphs, 15
determiners, 307–8
diagrams, 20
dialects, regional, 255
diction. *See* word choice
different from, different than, 395
digital and nonprint sources, citing
  APA style, 191–200
  Chicago style, 219–24
  CSE style, 240–41
  MLA style, 149–57
digital object identifier (DOI), 193, 220
direct address, 353
direct discourse, 287
direct questions, 361
direct quotations, 365–67
directness and clarity, 3–4
disciplinary style, analyzing, 68
disciplines, writing in, 67–69
discovery. *See* exploring a topic
discreet, discrete, 395
disinterested, uninterested, 395
disruptive modifiers, 323–24
distinct, distinctive, 395
diversity of audience, 8
documentation
  APA style, 174–209
  Chicago style, 210–33
  complete, 30
  CSE style, 234–44
  MLA style, 124–73
  plagiarism, avoiding, 117–19
  rhetorical situation and, 105
  visuals and media, 4
  writing in the genres, 69
doesn't, don't, 395
DOI (digital object identifier)
  APA style, 193
  Chicago style, 220, 221
  MLA style, 125
dots. *See* ellipses
double comparatives and superlatives, 321
doublespeak, 259–60
drafting, 10–16
  checklist for, 14
  research project, 119–20
  working theses, 11–12

E

each. See determiners; indefinite pronoun
each other, one another, 395
-ed, -d endings, 290
editing, 23–26
  and proofreading, 25–26, 120
  Top Twenty (common errors), 28–36
effect, affect, 395
e.g. (for example), 381
either . . . or, 284. *See also* correlative conjunctions
Elbow, Peter, 44
electronic sources. *See* digital and nonprint sources
elicit, illicit, 395
ellipses
  in APA references, 185
  indicating omission in quote, 107, 115, 375–76
  informal writing, 362
  in MLA references, 170, 339–40
  in quotations, 107, 114–15

elliptical constructions, 328
elude, allude, 395
emails or messages
  citing in MLA style, 157
  formality of, 6
emigrate from, immigrate to, 395
emotional appeals, 59, 60
emphasis
  dashes for, 373
  double comparatives and superlatives, 321
  italics for, 385
  sentence structure for, 342
empty words, eliminating, 280
EndNote software, 106
end punctuation, 360–62
English language, varieties of, 254–57, 317
ensure, assure, insure, 395
enthused, enthusiastic, 395
equally as good, 395
-er, -est ending, 320–21
errors, common. *See* Top Twenty
-es, -s ending, 311–13
essays. *See* sample student writing
et al. (and others), 381
etc., 381
ethical appeals, 54
euphemisms, 259–60
evaluating sources, 97–112
  annotated bibliography, 112
  guidelines for, 98–99
  keeping track, 105–6
  reading and analyzing, 104
  source maps, 102–3
  synthesizing, 104–5
every day, everyday, 395
every one, everyone, 396
evidence, 54–55 Support for an argument's **claim**.
  in academic writing, 4
  analysis of, 48
  in argument, 49, 54–55, 57, 59
  audience and, 8
  in the disciplines, 69
  essential, for summarizing, 48
  firsthand and secondhand, 54
  gathering and researching, 12–13, 57, 105
  in paragraphs, 15
  persuasive, 247–48
  planning and drafting, 13–14
  Toulmin argument, 54–55
  uses of, 68–69
  See also sources
except, accept, 396
exclamation points, 361
explanatory notes, in MLA style, 128–29
expletives, 281–82
explicit, implicit, 396
exploring a topic, 10–11

F

Facebook, 39, 41
fact-checking, 48–49, 97–98
FactCheck.org, 97
facts, and use of gerunds, 296, 298
farther, further, 396
faulty predication, 273
fewer, less, 396
field research, 95–97
figures. *See* visuals and media
firstly, secondly, 396

first person (*I, we, us*), 286, 311
flaunt, flout, 396
fonts, 18, 26
footnotes
  in APA style, 175
  in *Chicago* style, 211, 212
for, 275. *See also* coordinating conjunctions
foreign words, italics for, 385
formality
  in academic writing, 4–5
  and word choice, 258
  in writing process, 248
formatting
  in APA style, 176–77
  in *Chicago* style, 211–24
  in CSE style, 234
  IMRAD organization, 70
  MLA style, 129–30
  for writing projects, 9, 17–19
former, latter, 396

fragments, 36, 248, 342–44 A group of words that is not a complete **sentence** but is punctuated as one. Usually a fragment lacks a **subject**, a **verb**, or both, or it is a **dependent clause**.

freewriting, 10, 44
further, farther, 396

fused (run-on) sentence, 34, 338–40 A **sentence** in which two **independent clauses** are run together without a **conjunction** or punctuation between them (*My dog barked he woke me up*).

future perfect, 299
future perfect progressive, 299
future progressive, 299

future tense, 299–300 The **tense** of a **verb** that indicates an action or condition has not yet happened: *They <u>will arrive</u> next week*.

G

gathering evidence, 12–13, 57, 105

gender-neutral pronouns, 251 Alternatives to gendered third-person **pronouns**. For example, *they* is a gender-neutral pronoun that refers to plural **antecedents** and can also be used as an alternative to *he/she* in third-person singular. Pronouns like *ve/ver/vis, ze/hir/hirs,* or *ze/zir/zirs* are also used in transgender and intersex communities.

  sexist language, 250–51, 332
general versus specific language, 263

genre A form of communication used for a particular purpose and incorporating certain conventional features. Some common examples include lab reports, researched essays, brochures, invitations, etc.

  in academic disciplines, 67–72
  and audience, 5, 9
  headings in, standard, 18–19
  in public writing, 71–72
  sample student writing, 73–75

gerund, 296 A verbal form that ends in *-ing* and functions as a **noun**: *<u>Sleeping</u> is a bore.*

  versus infinitives, 296–98
  pronouns and possessive case, 326–27

good, well, 319, 396
Google Drive, 10
Google searches, 94, 95
government sources, 94, 95, 100
government terms, abbreviations for, 380–81

H

handouts, for presentations, 82
hanged, hung, 396
hardly, 396
have as auxiliary verb, 293–94
headings
  in APA style, 177
  in *Chicago* style, 212
  in CSE style, 234
  formatting, 17–19
  in MLA style, 130
  organization (IMRAD), 70
  parallelism in, 283
helping verb, 293–95 A **verb** such as a form of *be, do,* or *have* or a **modal** combined with a main verb.
herself, himself, myself, yourself, 396
he/she, his, her, 396
high-stakes writing, 44
himself, herself, myself, yourself, 396
historical sources, 90–92
homonyms, overlooked by spell checkers, 265
hopefully, 397
hung, hanged, 396
hyphens, 386–89
hypothesis, 89–90

I

I, me, my, 326–27
ideas, main, 276–79
i.e. (that is), 381
if clauses, 303
illicit, elicit, 397
illusion, 397
illustrations, 20–21
immigrate to. See emigrate from, immigrate to
imperative mood, 302
implicit, 397
imply, infer, 397
in, on, 336
in contrast, 271
indefinite articles, 309
indefinite pronoun, 314–15 A word such as *each, everyone,* or *nobody* that does not refer to a specific person or thing.
  agreement with antecedents, 332
  agreement with verbs, 314–15
  possessive case, 363
  you, it, and *they,* 333
indenting
  in APA format, 175, 184
  in *Chicago* notes and bibliography, 212–13
  in CSE list of references, 236
  long quotations
    in APA style, 177
    in *Chicago* style, 212
    in MLA style, 130
  in MLA format, 129
  in MLA works cited, 137
independent clause, 273 A word group containing a **subject** and a **predicate** that can stand alone as a **sentence**.

commas used with, 339
fused sentences and, 338–40
semicolons used with, 339
in sentence structure, confusing, 272–73
indexes, for research, 93–94
indirect discourse, 287
indirect questions, 360, 361
infer, imply, 393

infinitive, 278 *To* plus the **base form** of a **verb** (*to go, to run, to hit*), which can serve as a **noun**, an **adverb**, or an **adjective**: *One option is* *to leave* (noun). *We stopped* *to rest* (adverb). *He needs time* *to adjust* (adjective).

versus gerunds, 296–97
split, 323
informal writing
ellipses with, 362
end punctuation, 362
letter writing, 258
social media and, 4–5
in writing process 248
-ing words, 290, 294–95, 297
inside of, outside of, 397
Instagram, 39
instructor comments, 10, 23
insure, assure, ensure 393
intentions and infinitives, 296–97

interjection, 353 An exclamation of surprise or other strong emotion: *Ouch!*

Internet sources, credible, 94–95
interviews
citing in MLA style, 156
in field research, 95–96
in-text citations
in APA style, 175, 177–83
in *Chicago* bibliography and notes, 212–15
in CSE style, 235–36, 238
in MLA style, 127, 130–36
parentheses for, 130–31, 371
reasons for, 124
signal phrases, 130–31
intransitive verbs, 298
introductions
in arguments, 59, 82
to chemistry reports, 75–76
in IMRAD organization, 70
planning and drafting, 13
in presentations, 82
introductory elements, commas with, 346
invitational argument, 55
irregardless, regardless, 397

irregular verb, 290–92 A **verb** that does not form the **past tense** and past **participle** by adding *-ed* or *-d* to the **base form**.

is, are, was, were, been (*be* verbs), 281
is when, is where, 397
it, this, that, and *which,* vague use of, 333
it, you, they, 333
italics, 384–86
items in a series
colons preceding, 359, 373
commas with, 352, 356
parallelism and, 283
semicolons with, 359
its, it's, 397

J

jargon, 259
journals. *See* articles in periodicals
just as . . . so, 284. *See also* correlative conjunctions

K

key words and phrases
  annotating, 47
  brainstorming, 10
  for paragraph coherence, 15
  in presentations, 83
  repetition of, 16, 17
  in specialized vocabularies, 67–68
keyword searches, 93, 94
kind, sort, type, 397
know, no, 397

L

labels, for figures. *See* visuals and media, labeling
lab report, 75–77
language
  avoiding stereotypes, 249
  building common ground, 249–52
  gender and pronoun preferences, 250–52
  See also word choice
later, latter, 397
Latin terms, abbreviations for, 381
latter, former, 397
lay, lie, 298, 397
leave, let, 398
lend, loan, 398
length of sentences, 270
less, fewer, 398
let, leave, 398
letters
  informal and formal, 258
  in portfolio, 40, 41
  See also newsletter, sample
liable, apt, likely, 392
librarians, reference, 92–94
library research, 91–94
lie, lay, 298, 397
like, as, as if, as though, 292
likely, liable, apt, 392
limiting modifier, 322
line graphs, 20
line spacing. *See* spacing
linking verb, 315 A **verb** that suggests a state of being, not an action.
  and adjectives, 319
links to audio and visual sources, 21
listening
  analytically, 46–50
  beginnings and endings of talks, 82
  and collaboration, 9–10
  and reading purposefully, 53
list of references. *See* APA style; CSE style
list of works cited. *See* MLA style, works cited
literally, 398
literary present tense, 300
literature review, 75, 242–44
little, much, 307
loan, lend, 398

logical appeals, 54, 58
long quotations. *See* quotations, long
loose, lose, 398
lots, lots of, 398
low-stakes writing, 44–45
-ly adverbs, 318, 387

M

magazines. *See* articles in periodicals
main clause. *See* independent clause
main ideas, distinguishing, 110, 119, 276–79. *See also* thesis
main verbs, 293–94
manuscript format. *See* formatting
many, a (few), 307
maps, 20
margins, 17, 18. *See also* formatting
margins and spacing
  in APA style, 176–77
  in *Chicago* style, 212
  in CSE style, 234
  in MLA style, 129
may as modal verb, 293–94
may, can, 393
me, my, I, 326–27
meaning, clarifying, 246–47
measurement, units of, 381
metaphors, 59, 264
might of. See could of
misinformation, 88
misplaced modifiers, 322
missing words, 32
mixed metaphors, 264
mixed sentence structure, 272–73 A common writing problem in which a **sentence** begins with one grammatical pattern and switches to another (also called "faulty structure").

MLA style, 124–73 The citation style guidelines issued by the Modern Language Association.
  author listings, 139–40
  books, 141–46
  citations, in-text, 139
  context of sources, 124–29
  digital written-word sources, 149–57
  elements of citations, 125–27
  explanatory notes, 128–29
  in-text citations, 130–36
  list of examples, 131
  manuscript format, 129–30
  other sources, 161–63
  parts of citations, 127–28
  print periodicals, 146–48
  sample student writing, 73–75, 163–73
  source maps
    articles from databases, 150
    articles in print periodicals, 147
    books, 142
    works from websites, 155
  sources, context of, 124–29
  understanding, 124
  visual, audio, media, and live sources, 157–61
  works cited
    formatting, 138
    list of examples, 137–38
    models for, 141–63

modal, 293–94 A kind of **helping verb** that has only one form and shows possibility, necessity, or obligation: *can, could, may, might, must, shall, should, will, would, ought to.*

plus base form of verb, 294
in verb phrase, 294

Modern Language Association (MLA). *See* MLA style

modifier, 280, 318 A word, **phrase**, or **clause** that acts as an **adjective** or an **adverb**, qualifying the meaning of another word, phrase, or clause.

absolute concepts, 321
dangling, 324–25
disruptive, 323–24
limiting, 322
misplaced, 322–23
placement of, 322–25
and split infinitives, 323
squinting, 323

mood, 302–3 The form of a **verb** that indicates the writer's attitude toward the idea expressed. The indicative mood states fact or opinion (*I am happy*); the imperative gives commands (*Keep calm*); and the subjunctive refers to a condition that does not exist (*If I were rich . . .*).

moral, morale, 398
more. See indefinite pronoun
most. See indefinite pronoun
much. See indefinite pronoun
much, a (little), 307
multilingual writers
adjectives with plural nouns, 318
capitalization, 379
English, global varieties, 256
fancy language, 260
plagiarism, 118
quoting, 369
sentence length, 339
sources, identifying, 110
thesis, review by peers, 120
thesis, stating a, 11
usage, checking with search engines, 297

multimedia presentations, 85–86. *See also* presentations
my, me, I, 326–27
myself, yourself, himself, herself, 396

N

name-year format, CSE style, 235, 236
N.B. (note well), 381
n.d. (no date), in APA style, 181
necessary words, 284
neither . . . nor, 312. *See also* correlative conjunctions
nevertheless, 271
newsletter, sample, 81
newspapers. *See* articles in periodicals
no, know, 397

noncount noun, 306 A **noun** referring to a collection of things or to an idea that cannot be directly counted: *sand, rain, violence.* Contrast with **count noun**.

none. See indefinite pronoun
non-English words, 385

nonprint sources. *See* digital and nonprint sources

nonrestrictive element, 33
A word, **phrase**, or **clause** that provides more information about, but does not change, the essential meaning of a **sentence**. Nonrestrictive elements are set off from the rest of the sentence with commas: *My instructor, who is perceptive, liked my introduction.*

appositives, 351

nor, or, 275, 398

not . . . but, 284. *See also* correlative conjunctions

notes
- abbreviations in, 381–82
- *Chicago* style, 212–13, 215–30
- MLA style, 128–29
- *See also* footnotes

note-taking, 97–106
- annotated bibliography, 111
- paraphrasing, 108–10
- quoting, 107
- sample annotated bibliography, 111–13
- sources, keeping track of, 105–6
- summarizing, 110
- synthesizing sources, 104–5

not only . . . but also, 284. *See also* correlative conjunctions

noun, 31, 32, 34, 285–86 A word that names a person, place, thing, or idea.
- and adjectives, 308, 318
- antecedents for pronouns, 326
- appositives, commas with, 351
- articles, using with nouns, 309–10
- collective-noun as antecedent, 306
- count and noncount, 306
- determiners, common, 307–8
- parallelism, 282–83
- possessive, 363–64
- proper, 378–79
- sexist language, 250–51

noun phrases, 305–11

number, amount, 392

number (singular or plural)
- apostrophes and plural forms, 363
- determiners, 307–8
- pronoun-antecedent agreement, 331–32
- subject-verb agreement, 313–14

numbers
- abbreviations and, 381
- colons with, 374
- figures for, 382–83
- fractions and compound, 387
- hyphens with, 387
- notes and source citations, 371
- plural of, 365
- spelling out, 382
- as terms, 385

O

object, 32, 326–28 A **noun** or **pronoun** receiving the action of a **verb** (*We mixed paints*) or following a **preposition** (*on the road*).
- avoid colons, 374
- avoid commas, 356
- of preposition, 335
- transitive verbs, 298–99, 337

object complements, 32
objective case, 326–27
observation, in field research, 96–97
off, of, 399
OK, O.K., okay, 399
one another, each other, 395
online sources. *See* digital and nonprint sources
opinion, personal. *See* stance
opinion surveys, 96–97
opposing points of view, 57, 60
or. See coordinating conjunctions
or, nor, 275, 398
oral presentation. *See* presentations
organization
  of arguments, 59–60
  of paragraph, 15
  planning and drafting, 13–14
  storyboard for, 13
  and thesis, 4
  of writing project, 13
outlines, 13–14, 83, 119, 121
outside of, inside of, 399

P

page numbers
  in APA style, 177
  in *Chicago* style, 212
  in CSE style, 234
  in MLA style, 129
paragraphs, 14–16
parallelism
  with conjunctions and prepositions, 284
  ideas, paired, 283–84
  for paragraph coherence, 15
  for sentence structure, 33
  in series or list, 283
paraphrasing
  integrating, 115
  of other authors, 108–10, 115
  plagiarism in, 109
  present tense in, 300
parentheses, 370–71
parenthetical citations. *See* in-text citations
parenthetical expressions, 353
participial phrases, 350
participle, 290–92 A word formed from the **base form** of a **verb**. The present participle always ends in *-ing* (*going*). The past participle ends in *-ed* (*ruined*) unless the verb is **irregular**. A participle can function as an **adjective** (*the singing frog, a ruined shirt*) or form part of a **verb phrase** (*You have ruined my shirt*).
particles, adverbial, 337
parts of speech, 289–344 The eight grammatical categories describing how words function in a **sentence** (**adjectives, adverbs, conjunctions, interjections, nouns, prepositions, pronouns, verbs**).
passed, past, 399
passive voice, 294–95, 302 The form of a **verb** when the **subject** is being acted on, not acting: *The batter was hit by a pitch.*
  versus active voice, 301–2
  and forms of *be*, 293–94
  shifts in voice, 285–88
  wordiness of, 281
past participles, 290–95, 298

past perfect, 299
past perfect progressive, 299
past progressive, 299

past tense, 290–92, 311 The **tense** of a **verb** that indicates an action or condition has already happened: *They arrived yesterday*.

auxiliary verbs, forming, 295
subject-verb agreement, 311
transitive and intransitive verbs, 298
using simple tenses, 299–301

per, 399
percent, percentage, 399

perfect progressive, 299–300 The **perfect tense** of a **verb** showing an ongoing action completed at some point in the past, present, or future, with the main verb in the *-ing* form: *The workers had been striking for a month before the settlement. He has been complaining for days. The construction will have been continuing for a year in May.*

perfect tense, 294–95, 299–300 The **tense** of a **verb** showing a completed action in the past, present, or future: *They had hoped to see the parade but got stuck in traffic. I have never understood this equation. By then, the governor will have vetoed the bill.*

APA style for research reports, 301

periodicals. *See* articles in periodicals
periods
with abbreviations, 361
with ellipses, 376
end punctuation, 360
informal writing, 362
with parentheses, 371
with quotation marks, 368
with source citations, 376
permission to reprint, 116

person, 286, 311 The point of view of a **subject**. The first person refers to itself (*I*); the second person addresses *you*; the third person refers to someone else (*they*).

pronoun-antecedent agreement, 331
pronoun preferences, 251
shifts in, 286
subject-verb agreement, 311

personal opinion. *See* stance
personal pronouns
in compound and elliptical structures, 328
as direct object, 337
possessive, 363
who, whom, 327–28
persuasive writing. *See* argument
photographs, 21. *See also* visuals and media
phrasal verbs, 337

phrase, 29, 273 A group of words that lacks a **subject**, a **verb**, or both.

appositives, 351
commas with, 29, 346–47, 349–51
coordination and subordination, 275–79, 339, 357
dangling modifier, 324–25
introductory elements, 29, 346–47

phrase (*continued*)
noun, 305–8, 351
parallelism, 282–84
prepositional, 334–38
in sentence openings, 271
and sentence structure, 273
signal, 114
wordy, replacing, 281–82
pie charts, 20
place names
abbreviated, 361
commas with, 354
plagiarism
avoiding, 117–19
documentation, to avoid, 30
paraphrase, unacceptable, 108–9
unintentional, 48, 64–65, 70–71, 107, 118
planning
and drafting, 13–14
for presentations, 83–85
for research, 90
plays
capitalization for titles, 379
citing in MLA style, 134
italics for titles, 379
plurals
apostrophes, 365
collective nouns, 35, 313–14
compound subjects, 312–13
count nouns, 306
determiners with, 307–8
gender and pronoun preferences, 250–51
nouns, possessive case, 363
pronoun-antecedent agreement, 35, 331
shifts in point of view, 286
"singular *they*," 331
subject-verb agreement, 313–15
words with plural form that are singular, 331
plus, 399
PM, *p.m.*, 381
podcasts, citing
APA style, 200
Chicago style, 228
CSE style, 241
MLA style, 160
poetry
capital letters, use of, 377, 379
cited, in MLA style, 152
italics for titles, 367, 384
quoting and quotation marks, 366–67
slashes used with, 375
spacing, 367
titles of, 366–67
point of view, shifts in, 286
PolitiFact, 97
popular sources, 91–92
portfolios, 40

possessive form, 34 The form of a **noun** or **pronoun** that shows possession. Personal pronouns in the possessive case don't use apostrophes (*ours*, *hers*), but possessive nouns and indefinite pronouns do (*Harold's*, *everyone's*).

apostrophes for, 363
compound nouns, 363
its and *it's*, 364
nouns and phrases, 363–64
plural nouns, 363
pronouns, 326, 327, 363
postal abbreviations, 361

poster, 78. *See also* visuals and media
practicing a presentation, 82
precede, proceed, 399

predicate, 33, 300 The **verb** and related words in a **clause** or **sentence**. The predicate expresses what the **subject** does, experiences, or is. The simple predicate is the verb or **verb phrase**: *We have been living in the Atlanta area.* The complete predicate includes the simple predicate and its **modifiers**, **objects**, and complements: *We have been living in the Atlanta area.*

compound, 343
and subjects, matching, 273
truths and facts, and present tense, 300

prefixes, hyphens with, 388

preposition, 29, 32, 298 A word or word group that indicates the relationship of a **noun** or **pronoun** to another part of the **sentence**: *From the top of the ladder, we looked over the rooftops.*

for clarity, 284
commas, unneeded, 31, 325
gerunds following, 298
idiomatic use of, 29
phrases, 334–37
relating to space and time, 336
words, omitted, 32

prepositional phrases, 334–36
presentations
accessibility of, tips for, 253
citing, in APA style, 199
creating, 82–86
sample excerpts, 85–86
signpost language, 82–83

present participles, 290–92, 295, 298
present perfect progressive tense, 299

present perfect tense, 299–300 The **tense** of a **verb** that indicates an action or a condition has been completed before the present: *The team has worked together well.*

present progressive, 299

present tense, 299–301 The **tense** of a **verb** that indicates a general truth or a current action or condition: *Things fall apart. We live off campus.*

agreement with noun, 311
with *if*, 305

previewing, 46

primary source, 90 A research source that provides firsthand knowledge of raw information.

principal, principle, 399
proceed, precede, 399

progressive, 277–78, 281–82 The *-ing* form of a **verb** showing a continuing action in the past, present, or future: *He was snoring during the lecture. The economy is improving. Business schools will be competing for this student.*

projects. *See* writing projects

pronoun, 30–31, 34, 35, 326–34 A word used in place of a **noun**.

and adjectives, 318
agreement with antecedents, 315, 326, 331–33

pronoun (*continued*)
agreement with verbs, 314
and compound structures, 328
gerunds and possessive case of, 327
indefinite, 314–15, 332
possessive, 326
relative, 315
sexist, 331
"singular *they,*" 331
subject complements, 327
pronouns, gender of, and preferences, 251–52
proofreading, 6, 120, 266
proper names with titles, 378
proper nouns and adjectives, 378
proximity, in design, 17
public speaking. *See* presentations
publisher or sponsor, evaluating, 98, 100, 102
punctuation
apostrophes, 362–64
brackets, 371–72
colons, 373–74
commas, 29, 31–34, 346–56
dashes, 369, 373
ellipses, 375–76
exclamation points, 361
parentheses, 370–71
periods, 360–61
question marks, 361
quotation marks, 365–69
semicolons, 275, 357–59
slashes, 375
purpose for writing, 5–6
analysis of, 46
in annotation, 47
in field research, 96
in listening and reading, 53
for presentations, 82
for public writing, 72, 79, 81, 82
for research projects, 89, 91

Q

qtd. in, MLA style, 135
qualifiers, in arguments, 3, 54
question and hypothesis, 89–90
question marks, 355, 361, 369
questionnaire, 96–97
questions
commas with, 353
direct, 95–96
exploring topics, 10–11
indirect, 360
in introduction of paper, 119
opinion surveys, 96–97
research and working hypothesis, 89–90
sources, reading and analyzing, 104
tag, 353
quickwrites, 44
quotation, quote, 399
quotation marks
capital letters, use of, 377
commas with, 31, 355
definitions, 368
misused, avoiding, 369
with other punctuation, 368
poetry, 366–67
quotations, long, 130, 366
for short works, 31
single, 366
titles of works, 368
quotations
block, 366
brackets in, 114, 372

capitalization in, 377
citations, MLA style, 132
colons before, 374
commas with, 355
direct, 105, 114, 287, 365
ellipses with, 107, 375–76
indirect, 287
integrating, 35, 113–15
long
APA style, 177, 179
Chicago style, 212
MLA style, 130, 366
missing words, avoiding, 32
note-taking and, 100–102, 106–7
past tense, in APA style, 289
plagiarism, avoiding, 117–19
of poetry, 366–67
present tense in, 300
"selective," avoiding, 113
sic (so), use of, 372
signal phrases for, 114, 365
synthesizing, 104–5
titles of works, 367–68

R

race and ethnicity, 252–53
raise, rise, 298, 400
rarely ever, 400
readers. *See* audience
reading and analyzing sources, 104
reading critically, 46–50, 89–90, 104
reading responses, 45
real, really, 400
reasoning, 68
reason is because, 400
reason why, 400
redundant words, 280
references, list of. *See* APA style; CSE style
reference works, 90, 92
reflecting, 40–41
RefWorks software, 106
regardless, irregardless, 397
regular and irregular verb forms, 290–92

regular verb, 290 A **verb** that forms the **past tense** and past **participle** by adding *-d* or *-ed* to the **base form** (*care, cared, cared; look, looked, looked*).

relative pronouns, 315
repetition, in design, 17
research (research projects)
acknowledgments, 116–17
articles, evaluating, 102–3
audience, 89
bibliography, annotated, 111–12
challenges to, 88
citing sources, 116–17
APA style, 174–209
Chicago style, 210–33
CSE style, 234–44
MLA style, 124–73
drafting, 119–20
editing and proofreading, 120
evaluating sources, 97–104
fact-checking, 48–49, 97–98
field research, 95–97
integrating sources, 112–19
integrating visuals and media, 116
note-taking, 105–12
outline, 121

research (*continued*)
paraphrases and summaries, integrating, 115
paraphrasing, 108–10
plagiarism, avoiding, 117–19
process, beginning, 89–90
purpose for, 89, 91
question and hypothesis, 89–90
quotations, integrating, 113–15
quoting, 107, 113
reviewing and revising, 120
sources, 89, 90–97, 100–103
sources, keeping track of, 105–6
summarizing, 110
synthesizing sources, 104–5
topic, exploring, 10–11, 89–90
websites, evaluating, 100–101
working title and introduction, 119
writing, 119–21
respectfully, respectively, 400

restrictive element, 32, 349–51
A word, **phrase**, or **clause** that changes the essential meaning of a **sentence**. A restrictive element is not set off from the rest of the sentence with commas or other punctuation: *The tree that I hit was an oak.*

reviewing and revising, 120
Rheingold, Howard, 97
rhetorical analysis, 50–53

rhetorical situation, 2 The whole context for a piece of writing, including the person communicating, the topic and the person's attitude toward it, and the intended audience.

rise, raise, 298, 400
Rogerian argument, 55
running heads (APA style), 176
run-on sentences, 338–41

S

-s, -es ending, 311–13
sample student writing
annotated bibliography, 111–12
argument essay, 61–66
causal analysis essay, 200–209
chemistry lab report, 75–77
close reading of poetry, 72–75
literature review, excerpt, 242–44
newsletter, 81
outline of a research project, 121
paragraph, 16
presentation, excerpts from, 85–86
psychology literature review, 75
research-based argument, 164–73
research-based history essay, excerpts, 230–32
research projects
in APA style, 201–9
in *Chicago* style, 231–33
in CSE style, 243–44
in MLA style, 164–73
rhetorical analysis, 50–53
web comic, 80
web page, 79
scholarly sources, 91–92
sciences, writing in
abbreviations for, 381

passive voice for, 302
verb tense for, 114, 178, 301
See also research (research projects)
script for presentations, 83
search techniques, 93

secondary source, 90–91 A research source that reports information from research done by others.

second person, 286
semicolons, 275
avoiding misuse of, 359
independent clauses, 357–58
items in a series, 359

sentence, 29, 269–88 A group of words containing a **subject** and a **predicate** and expressing a complete thought. *See also* sentence structure; Top Twenty (common errors)

capitalization, 377
comparisons, complete, 274
compound structures, 274, 356
conciseness, 279–81
conditional sentences, 304–5
consistency, 272–76
contrasting elements and commas, 353
coordination and subordination, 275–78
direct and indirect discourse, 287
elliptical construction, 328
fused, and comma splices, 34, 338–42
ideas, relation of equal, 275–76
interjections, 353
length, 270
openings, 270–71
parallelism, 282–84
point of view, shifts in, 286
revising shifts, 285–88
structure, confusing, 272–73
structure, simplifying, 281–82
tense, shifts in, 285
voice, shifts in, 286
sentence fragments. *See* fragments
sentence structure
revising, 272–73
simplifying, 281–82
varying, 270–71
series of items, commas in, 352
set, sit, 298, 400
sexist pronouns, 332
sharing with audiences, 39
shifts
code meshing, 256
in discourse, 287
between general and specific ideas, 15
in point of view, 286
in style, and plagiarism, 119
in varieties of English, 254–57
in verb tense, 33, 285–86
in voice, 286
short works and quotation marks, 367–68
should of. See could of
sic (so), 372
signal phrases, 114, 130–33, 139, 178–84, 213
signpost language, 82–83
similes, metaphors, and analogies, 59, 264

simple tenses, 299–300 Past (*It happened*), present (*Things fall apart*), or future (*You will succeed*) forms of **verbs**.

since, 400

single quotation marks, 366
singular nouns, 306, 307–9, 311–12
"singular *they,*" 331
sit, set, 298, 400
skimming, 46
slang and colloquial language, 258, 369–70
slashes, 367, 375
slides, 83
Snopes.com, 97
so, 275, 400
social media
  citing
    APA style, 197
    Chicago style, 227–28
    MLA style, 156–57
  informal versus formal writing, 4–6
  sharing with audiences, 39
  unreliability, 88
software for presentations, 83
some, enough, 307
someplace, 400
some time, sometime, sometimes, 401
sort, type, kind, 397
source maps
  APA style
    articles from databases, 194
    articles from print periodicals, 190
    books, 187
    works from websites, 196
  Chicago style
    articles from databases, 222
    works from websites, 226
  evaluating articles, 102–3
  evaluating web sources, 100–101
  MLA style
    articles from databases, 150
    articles from print periodicals, 147
    books, 142
    works from websites, 155
sources
  acknowledging, 116–17
  annotating, 47
  browsing, 11
  choosing, 89–95
  citing and documenting
    APA style, 174–209
    Chicago style, 210–33
    CSE style, 234–44
    MLA style, 124–73
  ethical use of, 113
  evaluating, 98–103
  field research, 95–97
  integrating, 112–19
  library, 92–94
  list of, preparing, 120
  note-taking and, 105–6
  online, 93–94, 95–96, 97, 106
  quoting, paraphrasing, and summarizing, 113–15
  reading and analyzing, 104
  synthesizing, 104–5
spacing, 17, 18. *See also* formatting
specific versus general language, 263
spelling, 29, 31, 266
split infinitives, 323–24
squinting modifiers, 323–24
stance
  considering, 8, 68
  evaluating, of source, 99
  research project, 89, 120
"standard" English, 255

state names and abbreviations, 361, 382
stationary, stationery, 401
stereotypes, avoiding, 249
structure. *See* organization; sentence structure
student writing. *See* sample student writing

subject, 273 The **noun** or **pronoun** and related words that indicate who or what a **sentence** is about. The simple subject is the noun or pronoun: *The timid gray mouse ran away.* The complete subject is the simple subject and its **modifiers**: *The timid gray mouse ran away. See also* topic

- active and passive voice, 301–2
- matching with predicates, 273
- -verb agreement, 311–16

subject complements, 36, 315, 326, 327
subjective case, 326–28
subject-verb agreement
- with *be* verbs, 311
- with collective nouns, 313–14
- with compound subjects, 312–13
- with indefinite pronouns, 314–15
- with linking verbs, 315
- with relative pronouns, 315
- with subjects ending in *-s*, 316
- with subjects that follow the verb, 316
- with titles of works, 316
- with *who, which,* and *that,* 315
- with words between subject and verb, 312
- with words used as words, 316

subjunctive mood, 302–4 The form of a **verb** used to express a wish, a suggestion, a request or requirement, or a condition that does not exist: *If I were president, I would change things.*

subordinate clause. *See* dependent clause

subordinating conjunction, 340, 343 A word or **phrase** such as *although, because,* or *even though* that introduces a **dependent clause**: *Think carefully before you answer.*

- excessive use of, 278
- linking clauses, 340
- list of common conjunctions, 277
- and sentence fragments, 343
- sentence openings, 270–71

subsequently, consequently, 394
suffixes, hyphens with, 388
summarizing texts, 48, 110
- present tense in, 300
- research process, 110
- *See also* quotations; paraphrasing

summary, 48 A brief retelling of the main points of a **text**.

- critical reading, 48
- integrating, 68, 69, 115
- note-taking and, 110
- present tense for, 300

Sunlight Foundation, 97

superlative, 309 The *-est* or *most* form of an **adjective** or **adverb** used to compare three or more items (*happiest, most quickly*).

supposed to, used to, 401
sure, surely, 401

surveys, 96–97

synthesis, 104–5 Grouping ideas and information together in such a way that the relationship among them is clear.

T

tables, 20. *See also* visuals and media
tag questions, and commas for, 353
take, bring, 393
technical language. *See* jargon

tense, 33, 285, 290 The form of a **verb** that indicates the time when an action takes place—past, present, or future. Each tense has **simple** (*I enjoy*), **perfect** (*I have enjoyed*), **progressive** (*I am enjoying*), and **perfect progressive** (*I have been enjoying*) forms.

simple tenses, 299–300

text Traditionally, words on paper, but now anything that conveys a message.

genres, 8, 67–72
reading critically, 46–50
rhetorical situation and, 2

than, then, 401
that, this, it, and *which,* vague use of, 333
that, who, which, and verb agreement, 315
the, a, an, 379
then, than, 401
there is, there are expletive constructions, 281
these, those, 308

thesis, 3–4 A statement that indicates the main idea or **claim** of a piece of writing. Thesis statements should include a topic—the subject matter—and a comment that makes an important point about the topic.

or claim, in arguments, 54–55, 57
research process, 89
working, 11–12

they, them, 401
they, you, it, 333
third person, 286, 311
this, that, it, and *which,* vague use of, 333
this, these, that, those, 307
thorough, threw, through, 401
those, these, 308
thought pieces, 44–45
time for writing, 9
titles
abbreviating, 380
in APA style, 176
capital letters for, 378–79
in *Chicago* style, 211
in CSE style, 234
evaluating, 102
italics for, 384
in MLA style, 129
of poems, 366–67
quotation marks for, 367–68
subject-verb agreement, 316
to, too, two, 402
tone in writing, 8
topic, 10–11
choosing, 7
research process, 89
strategies for exploring, 10–11
in working thesis, 11

topic sentence, 3, 15
Top Twenty (common errors), 27–38
apostrophes, unnecessary or missing, 34
capitalization, unnecessary or missing, 32
commas, missing after introductory element, 29
commas, missing in compound sentence, 33–34
commas, missing with nonrestrictive elements, 33
commas, unnecessary, 31–32
comma splices, 34–35
documentation, incomplete or missing, 30
hyphens, unnecessary or missing, 36
pronoun-antecedent agreement, 35
pronoun reference, vague, 30
quotation marks, error with, 31
quotations, poorly integrated, 35
sentence structure, confusing, 32–33
sentences, fused (run-on), 34
spelling errors, 31
verb tense, shifts, 33
words, missing, 32
words, wrong, 28–29
Toulmin argument, 54–55

transition, 15, 339 A word or **phrase** that signals a progression from one **sentence** or part of a sentence to another.

commas with, 271
fused sentences, 339
semicolons with, 339
sentence fragments, 343
sentence openings, 271
sentence openings, 270–71
transitional expressions, 343
truths or scientific facts, and present tense, 300
tweets, citing in MLA style, 157
Twitter, 39
two, to, too, 402
two-word verbs, used idiomatically, 336–37
type, kind, sort, 397
typos and spell checkers, 266

U

understand, arguing to, 55
uninterested, disinterested, 395
unique, 402
U.S. academic style, 3
used to, supposed to, 401

V

varieties of English, 255–58
code meshing, 256
forms of *be*, 317
"standard," 255

verb, 32, 285 A word or **phrase**, essential to a **sentence**, that expresses the action of a sentence or **clause**. Verbs change form to show **tense**, number, **voice**, and **mood**.

agreement with subject, 311–17
and auxiliary verbs, 293–95

verb (*continued*)
- conditional sentences, 304–5
- mood of, 302–3
- parallelism, 282–85
- regular and irregular forms, 290–92
- sequencing of tenses, 301
- -*s* form of verbs, 311–12
- split infinitives, 323–24
- strong, 281
- tenses, using, 285, 290–92
- two-word, used idiomatically, 336–37
- verb phrases, 290–305
- voice, active and passive, 286, 301–2

verb phrase, 293 A main verb and one or more **helping verbs**, acting as a single verb.

very, 402

ve/ver/vis, 251

visuals and media
- in APA style, 177
- audience, 116
- bar and line graphs, 20
- cartoons, 21
- in *Chicago* style, 212
- diagrams, 20
- emotional appeals, 59
- ethical use of, 22
- integrating, 116
- labeling, 22, 70
- links to audio or video material, 21
- logical appeal, 54
- maps, 20
- in MLA style, 130
- photos or illustrations, 21
- pie charts, 20
- presentations, 82–85
- research process, 116
- tables and figures, CSE style, 234

voice, 282 The form of a **verb** that indicates whether the **subject** is acting or being acted on. In the **active voice**, the subject performs the action: *Parker played the saxophone.* In the **passive voice**, the subject receives the action: *The saxophone was played by Parker.*
- active and passive, 282, 286
- -recognition technologies, 254
- shifts in, 286

W

warrant, 54 An assumption, sometimes unstated, that connects an argument's **claim** to the reasons for making the claim.

way, ways, 402

we and *us,* 328

web comic, 80

web page for fundraising, 79

websites
- citing in MLA style, 153–55
- evaluating, 98–99
- fact-checking, 48–49, 97–98
- MLA style (source map), 142, 150

web sources, evaluating, 100–101

well, 312. *See also good, well*

what, whose, which, 307

whether . . . or, 284. *See also* correlative conjunctions

which, that, this, and *it,* vague use of, 333
which, whose, what, 307
who, which, and *that* and subject-verb agreement, 315
who, whom, 327–28, 402
whose, which, what, 307
who's, whose, 402
win, arguing to, 55
word choice
  for abilities and disabilities, 253–54
  clichés, 264
  code meshing, 256
  denotation and connotation, 261
  doublespeak, 259–60
  euphemisms, 259–60
  examining assumptions, 249
  figurative language, 263–64
  gender-neutral terms, 250–51
  general and specific language, 263
  jargon, 259
  metaphors, similes, and analogies, 59, 264
  mixed metaphors, 264
  pompous language, 259–60
  for race and ethnicity, 252–53
  sexist, 250
  signpost, for presentations, 82–83
  slang and colloquial language, 258
  spell checkers, 265–67
  "standard" English, 255
  See also language
word pictures, 10
wordy phrases, replacing, 280
working bibliography, 106–7, 111–12, 117, 120
working thesis, three characteristics of, 12
working title and introduction, 119
works cited. *See* MLA style
world audiences, expectations of, 248
would of. See could of
writing process
  analyzing the rhetorical situation, 2–10
  audience, 247–48
  choosing a topic, 10
  developing a working thesis, 11–12
  developing paragraphs, 14–16
  editing and proofreading, 25–26
  evidence and research, 12–13
  exploring a topic, 10–11
  formal versus informal style, 248
  genres and disciplines, 67–72
  organization, across cultures, 248
  planning and drafting, 13–14
  reviewing, 24
  revising, 24
  varying sentences, 270–71
writing projects
  analyzing assignments for, 6–7
  arguments, 53–60
  collaborative, 9–10
  in the disciplines, 67–69
  genres and, 67–70
  presentations, 82–86
  public writing, 71–72
  reflection, 40–41

writing projects (*continued*)
  See also academic writing; research (research projects)
writing to learn, 44
writing to make something happen in the world, 67–72. *See also* public writing
wrong words, 28–29

Y

yet, 275. *See also* coordinating conjunctions
you, indefinite use of, 333
you, it, they, 333
your, you're, 402
yourself, myself, himself, herself, 396
YouTube, 39

Z

ze/hir/hirs, 251
ze/zir/zirs, 251

Revision Symbols

Numbers in bold refer to sections of this book.

abbr	abbreviation **45a**
ad	adjective/adverb **32**
agr	agreement **31, 34b**
awk	awkward
cap	capitalization **44**
case	case **34a**
cliché	cliché **22d**
com	incomplete comparison **24d**
concl	weak conclusion
cs	comma splice **36**
def	define
dm	dangling modifier **33c**
doc	documentation **15–18**
emph	emphasis unclear
ex	example needed
frag	sentence fragment **37**
fs	fused sentence **36**
hyph	hyphen **47**
inc	incomplete construction **24**
it	italics **46**
jarg	jargon **22a**
lc	lowercase **44**
lv	language variety **21**
mix	mixed construction **24, 28**
mm	misplaced modifier **33a**
ms	manuscript format **15c, 16b, 17b, 18a**
no ,	no comma **38i**
num	number **45b**
¶	paragraph
//	faulty parallelism **27**
para	paraphrase **13b**
pass	inappropriate passive **28b, 29f**
ref	unclear pronoun reference **34c**
run-on	run-on (fused) sentence **36**
sexist	sexist language **20b, 34b**
shift	shift **28**
slang	slang **22a**
sp	spelling **22e**
sum	summarize **13b**
trans	transition
verb	verb form **29**
vs	verb sequence **29e**
vt	verb tense **29e**
wc	word choice **22**
wrdy	wordy **26**
wv	weak verb **26d**
ww	wrong word **22e**
. ? !	period, question mark, exclamation point **40a–c**
,	comma **38**
;	semicolon **39**
’	apostrophe **41**
“ ”	quotation marks **42**
( ) [ ] —	parentheses, brackets, dash **43a–c**
: / . . .	colon, slash, ellipses **43d–f**
^	insert
∼	transpose
⁀	close up
X	delete

For Multilingual Writers

Look for the "Multilingual" icon to find advice of special interest to international students and others whose home language is not English.

- Understanding expectations for academic writing **1a**
- Adapting genre structures **9c**
- Meeting audience expectations **19c**
- Building verb phrases **29b**
- Using infinitives and gerunds **29c**
- Using conditional sentences appropriately **29h**
- Understanding count and noncount nouns **30a**
- Using determiners **30b**
- Using articles **30c**
- Choosing the right preposition **35a**
- Using two-word verbs idiomatically **35b**

Boxed Tips for Multilingual Writers

Stating a Thesis **11**

Identifying Sources **110**

Thinking about Plagiarism as a Cultural Concept **118**

Asking Experienced Writers to Review a Thesis **120**

Recognizing Global Varieties of English **256**

Avoiding Fancy Language **260**

Checking Usage with Search Engines **297**

Using Adjectives with Plural Nouns **318**

Judging Sentence Length **339**

Quoting in American English **369**

Learning English Capitalization **379**

Contents

QUICK START MENU i

How This Book Can Help You v

WRITING PROCESSES

1 A Writer's Choices 2
- a Expectations for academic writing
- b Informal and formal writing
- c Email and other "in-between" writing
- d Assignment and purpose
- e Topic
- f Audiences
- g Stance and tone
- h Time, genre, medium, and format
- i Collaboration

2 Exploring, Planning, and Drafting 10
- a Exploring a topic
- b Developing a working thesis
- c Gathering credible evidence
- d Planning and drafting
- e Developing paragraphs

3 Making Design Decisions 17
- a Design principles
- b Appropriate formats
- c Visuals and media
- d Ethical use of visuals and media

4 Reviewing, Revising, and Editing 23
- a Reviewing
- b Revising
- c Editing and proofreading

Top Twenty Tips for Editing Your Writing 27

5 Sharing and Reflecting on Your Writing 39
- a Sharing with audiences
- b Creating a portfolio
- c Reflecting on your own work
- d STUDENT WRITING: REFLECTION

CONTEXTS FOR WRITING, READING, AND SPEAKING

6 Learning from Low-Stakes Writing 44
- a The value of low-stakes writing
- b Types of low-stakes assignments

7 Reading and Listening Analytically, Critically, and Respectfully 46
- a Previewing
- b Annotating
- c Summarizing
- d Analyzing
- e STUDENT WRITING: RHETORICAL ANALYSIS

8 Arguing Ethically and Persuasively 53
- a Listening purposefully and openly
- b Identifying basic appeals
- c Analyzing the elements of an argument
- d Arguing purposefully
- e Making an argument
- f Organizing an argument
- g STUDENT WRITING: ARGUMENT ESSAY

9 Writing in a Variety of Disciplines and Genres 67
- a Expectations of academic disciplines
- b Understanding and using genres
- c Adapting genre structures
- d Choosing genres for public writing
- e STUDENT WRITING: SAMPLES IN A VARIETY OF DISCIPLINES AND GENRES

10 Creating Presentations 82
- a Task, purpose, and audience
- b Memorable introduction and conclusion
- c Structure and signpost language
- d Script
- e Visuals
- f Practice
- g Delivery
- h STUDENT WRITING: PRESENTATION EXCERPTS

RESEARCH

11 Conducting Research 88
- a Understanding challenges to research
- b Beginning the research process
- c Choosing among types of sources
- d Using library resources
- e Finding credible Internet sources
- f Doing field research

12 Evaluating Sources and Taking Notes 97
- a Checking facts
- b Evaluating potential sources
- c Reading and analyzing sources
- d Synthesizing sources
- e Keeping track of sources
- f Quoting, paraphrasing, and summarizing
- g Creating an annotated bibliography
- h STUDENT WRITING: ANNOTATED BIBLIOGRAPHY ENTRIES

13 Integrating Sources and Avoiding Plagiarism 112
- a Using sources ethically
- b Integrating source material